IMAGES OF
SALVATION
IN THE NEW
TESTAMENT

BRENDA B. COLIJN

IVP Academic

An imprint of InterVarsity Press
Downers Grove, Illinois

InterVarsity Press
P.O. Box 1400, Downers Grove, IL 60515-1426
World Wide Web: www.ivpress.com
E-mail: email@ivpress.com

InterVarsity Press® is the book-publishing division of InterVarsity Christian Fellowship/USA®, a movement of
students and faculty active on campus at hundreds of universities, colleges and schools of nursing in the United States
of America, and a member movement of the International Fellowship of Evangelical Students. For information
about local and regional activities, write Public Relations Dept., InterVarsity Christian Fellowship/USA, 6400
Schroeder Rd., P.O. Box 7895, Madison, WI 53707-7895, or visit the IVCF website at <www.intervarsity.org>.

Design: Cindy Kiple
Images: Parable of The Lost Coin by Fetti or Feti Domenico/Gemaeldegalerie Alte Meister at Dresden,
Germany/©Staatliche Kunstsammlungen Dresden/The Bridgeman Art Library

ISBN 978-0-8308-3872-1

Printed in Canada ∞

Library of Congress Cataloging-in-Publication Data

Colijn, Brenda B., 1952-
  Images of salvation in the New Testament / Brenda B. Colijn.
    p. cm.
  Includes bibliographical references and index.
  ISBN 978-0-8308-3872-1 (pbk.: alk. paper)
  1. Salvation—Christianity—Biblical teaching. 2. Bible
N.T.—Criticism, interpretation, etc. I. Title.
  BS2545.S25C65 2010
  234—dc22

                                                                          2010019868

P 25 24 23 22 21 20 19 18 17 16 15 14 13 12 11 10 9 8 7 6 5 4 3 2 1

Y 31 30 29 28 27 26 25 24 23 22 21 20 19 18 17 16 15 14 13 12 11 10

To my students

CONTENTS

ACKNOWLEDGMENTS

I AM BLESSED TO WORK in a professional environment that is both challenging and nurturing. This book would not have been possible without the support of the faculty and administration of Ashland Theological Seminary, who granted me the study leave that enabled me to lay the foundation for the project. I am also grateful for the many constructive and encouraging conversations on salvation and life that I have had with my colleagues over the years. Some of the ideas in these pages (especially on discipleship, *sōtēria* and being in Christ) originated in articles I wrote for the *Ashland Theological Journal*. Those topics have been reworked for this volume. The material on pilgrimage and worship in Hebrews is a revision of my article "Let Us Approach: Soteriology in the Epistle to the Hebrews," published in the *Journal of the Evangelical Theological Society* 39 (December 1996): 571-86, used with permission.

Both my writing and my well-being have benefited from the patient direction of my editor at InterVarsity Press, Jim Hoover. The content and form of the project are much improved because of his constructive criticism, as well as that of the reviewers who read my first draft. Any remaining deficiencies in the final version are, of course, my own.

I am also blessed with wonderful family and friends. Throughout the project, I have appreciated the understanding and forbearance of my husband Henk, who supported me in many practical ways and managed not to ask too often about how the book was going. Particular thanks are due to Jaunita Eichman, Rich Hagopian and Ryan McLaughlin for reading my manuscript and offering suggestions, as well as to Patti Barone for preparing the subject and author indexes. Finally, I am grateful for the stimulation and motivation afforded by my interactions with my students—past, present and future—to whom this book is dedicated.

ABBREVIATIONS

ABD   David Noel Freedman et al., eds. *The Anchor Bible Dictionary.* 6 vols. New York: Doubleday, 1992.

BAGD   Walter Bauer, William F. Arndt, F. Wilbur Gingrich and Frederick W. Danker. *A Greek-English Lexicon of the New Testament and Other Early Christian Literature.* 2nd ed. Chicago: University of Chicago Press, 1979.

BDB   Francis Brown, Edward Robinson, S. R. Driver, Charles A. Briggs and Wilhelm Gesenius. *The New Brown, Driver, Briggs, Gesenius Hebrew and English Lexicon.* Peabody, Mass.: Hendrickson, 1979.

DBI   Leland Ryken, James C. Wilhoit and Tremper Longman III, eds. *Dictionary of Biblical Imagery.* Downers Grove, Ill.: InterVarsity Press, 1998.

DJG   Joel B. Green, Scot McKnight and I. Howard Marshall, eds. *Dictionary of Jesus and the Gospels.* Downers Grove, Ill.: InterVarsity Press, 1992.

DPL   Gerald F. Hawthorne, Ralph P. Martin and Daniel G. Reid, eds. *Dictionary of Paul and His Letters.* Downers Grove, Ill.: InterVarsity Press, 1993.

DTIB   Kevin J. Vanhoozer, ed. *Dictionary for Theological Interpretation of the Bible.* Grand Rapids: Baker, 2005.

IDB   Buttrick, George Arthur, ed. *The Interpreter's Dictionary of the Bible.* 4 vols. Nashville: Abingdon, 1962.

ISBE   Geoffrey W. Bromiley, ed. *The International Standard Bible Encyclopedia*. 4 vols. Rev. ed. Grand Rapids: Eerdmans, 1979-1988.

NIDNTT   Colin Brown, ed. *The New International Dictionary of New Testament Theology*. 4 vols. Grand Rapids: Zondervan, 1986.

TDNT   Gerhard Kittel and Gerhard Friedrich, eds. *Theological Dictionary of the New Testament*. Translated by Geoffrey W. Bromiley. 10 vols. Grand Rapids: Eerdmans, 1965-1976.

INTRODUCTION

A BANK BRANCH IN A GROCERY STORE near my home was promoting its home equity loans. For just $211 a month, the sign announced, you could obtain "education," "vacation," "restoration"—or even (in large letters) "salvation." That sign struck me as a peculiarly American innovation: Pelagianism on the installment plan. Given the price, however, perhaps it was just cheap grace.

While it is understandable that secular society recasts salvation in a way that serves its own interests, it is unfortunate that the church sometimes does the same. Dietrich Bonhoeffer recognized this when he charged that the church promoted "cheap grace."[1] Reviewing church history, John Driver has argued that "the church has constantly been tempted to interpret the [New Testament] from the perspective of its own level of conduct. The church has often toned down the obvious meaning of primitive Christian testimony because it could no longer imagine it possible to take the gospel with such seriousness."[2]

So how do we avoid distorting the gospel and short-changing salvation? We must keep returning to the source, to the New Testament vision of what God has done in Christ and how we can participate in it. Like Nathaniel, we must respond to Philip's invitation to "come and see" (Jn 1:46). The most fundamental question then becomes "What does salvation in the New Testament look like?"

The New Testament does not develop a systematic doctrine of salva-

---

[1]"Cheap grace means the justification of sin without the justification of the sinner." Dietrich Bonhoeffer, *The Cost of Discipleship* (London: SCM Press, 2004), p. 3.

[2]John Driver, *Images of the Church in Mission* (Scottdale, Penn.: Herald, 1997), p. 22.

tion. Instead, it presents us with a variety of pictures taken from different perspectives. From one angle, the human predicament is rebellion against God. Salvation looks like living under God's universal reign. From another angle, the human predicament is bondage to both internal and external forces. Salvation looks like freedom from those forces. From yet a third angle, the human predicament looks like alienation from God, from other people, from creation and even from one's own best self. Salvation looks like the restoration of those relationships.

This variety reflects the diversity of New Testament writers and their concerns, as well as the diversity of their audiences and their needs. It also results from the missional orientation of the New Testament—the need to proclaim the gospel in different terms to reach different contexts. For example, while the Gospel writers talk about the kingdom of God in the Jewish context of Jesus' ministry, Paul uses the metaphor of citizenship to make similar points to his Greco-Roman audience in Philippi. Furthermore, the variety of images attests to the complexity of both the human problem and its solution. No single picture is adequate to express the whole.

This reliance on images is typical of the Bible: "The Bible is much more a book of images and motifs than of abstractions and propositions. . . . The Bible is a book that *images* the truth as well as stating it."[3] As Rowan Williams observes, "It is significant that imagery has played so great a part in the development of soteriology. All theories of salvation are heavily marked by particular metaphors, and—as in the NT itself—Christian worship has always employed a wide range of such metaphors."[4] If we want to know how the New Testament writers understood salvation, we must engage with the images they used to depict it.

WHAT IS AN IMAGE?

An *image* is any expression of sensory experience, whether visual, auditory or otherwise. Like any verbal expression, an image is "literal" when it follows well-established conventions of language; it is "figurative" when it

---

[3]*DBI*, p. xiii.
[4]Rowan D. Williams, "Soteriology," in *The Encyclopedia of Christianity*, 5 vols., ed. Erwin Fahlbusch et al., trans. G. W. Bromiley (Grand Rapids: Eerdmans, 1999-2008), 5:123.

uses language in new and unusual ways.[5] The *imagery* of a literary work consists of its figurative language, especially its comparative language, considered as a whole.[6]

Figures of comparison are among the most common types of figurative language. Similes create explicit comparisons using "like" or "as" ("as a deer longs for flowing streams"; "like sheep without a shepherd"). Metaphors create implicit comparisons ("I am the bread of life"; "beware of the yeast of the Pharisees"). An analogy is a more complex comparison which points out correspondences between one thing or concept and another, often in order to argue for further similarities between them ("The kingdom of heaven may be compared to someone who sowed good seed in his field . . ." Mt 13:24).

Theologians have long recognized that all theological language is analogical. We talk about God in terms of more mundane things, because we assume that some similarity exists between the Creator and the creation—especially between God and human beings, who are made in God's image. Human beings themselves are analogies (however flawed) of the divine. In the words of Abraham Heschel, humans are *theomorphic*.[7] Thus it is appropriate to use images drawn from human life to express truth about God.

Jesus himself did much of his teaching about the kingdom of God in similes, metaphors and analogies: the kingdom of God is like a mustard seed, a wedding banquet, an expensive pearl, a king who gave a great banquet. Likewise, much of the New Testament teaching about salvation is presented in images drawn from the everyday life of the writers and their audiences: covenant, kingdom, birth, rescue, redemption, priesthood, contest. We recognize that these images are metaphorical. When we read that we were bought with a price, we do not imagine Jesus going to the heavenly cash box and drawing out enough bills to cover his purchase. When we say that we must be reborn, we do not, with Nicodemus, ask how we can re-enter our mothers' wombs.

---

[5]Anthony Thiselton, "Semantics and New Testament Interpretation," in *New Testament Interpretation: Essays on Principles and Methods*, ed. I. Howard Marshall (Grand Rapids: Eerdmans, 1977), p. 94.

[6]G. B. Caird, *The Language and Imagery of the Bible* (Grand Rapids: Eerdmans, 1997), p. 149.

[7]Heschel suggests that we should think about divine/human analogies from the other direction. For example, instead of thinking of God's concern for justice as an anthropomorphism, we should think of human concern for justice as a theomorphism. Abraham Heschel, *The Prophets* (New York: HarperCollins, 2001), p. 349.

Identifying language about salvation as metaphorical does not diminish its truthfulness: "Literal and metaphorical are terms which describe types of language, and the type of language we use has very little to do with the truth or falsity of what we say and with the existence or nonexistence of the things we refer to."[8] People can lie or fantasize in literal language, just as they can tell the truth in figurative language. For example, the statement "Jesus was a Gentile" is literal but false; the statement "Jesus lives in the believer" is metaphorical but true.

Biblical metaphors express truth. In some cases, metaphors can express truth more effectively than non-metaphorical language, especially when the subject involves realities that cannot be fully captured in ordinary speech. The only way we can grasp the ineffable is by comparing it to more concrete things in our experience. But all metaphors, as comparisons, are limited. They resemble their subjects in some ways and differ from them in others. Problems arise when we push metaphors beyond their intended boundaries and expect them to cover everything about their subjects.

Similar problems occur when we take these images too literally. Different branches of the church have tended to specialize in certain images—such as justification or the new birth—and present them as if they expressed *what really happens* in salvation, while other images are *mere metaphors*. On the contrary, *all of these images are metaphors*, and *all of these images express what really happens*. To be more precise, each image is a picture of salvation as seen from one perspective, posing and answering one set of questions. When seen together, they balance and qualify one another. We need all of them in order to gain a comprehensive understanding of salvation.

The subjects of the following chapters would be classified as metaphors or analogies. Salvation is compared to more mundane realities in the lives of the New Testament authors and their audiences for the purpose of conveying spiritual truth. However, I will often use the more general term *image* to describe these constructs for four reasons. First, previous studies of theological themes in the New Testament provide good precedent for this use.[9] Second, the term "image" lacks the negative connotations that

---

[8]Caird, *Language and Imagery*, p. 131.
[9]Paul Minear's *Images of the Church in the New Testament* (Philadelphia: Westminster Press, 1977) was a seminal work in this area. See also John Driver, *Images of the Church in Mission*

sometimes accompany the word "metaphor," such as when the truthfulness of an expression is called into question by describing it as "merely" metaphorical. Third, "image" suggests a degree of indeterminacy. These images are not fully developed theological models that specify all relevant details and set clear boundaries.[10] They suggest rather than define, and some of them overlap with one another. Finally, the term "image" reminds us of the pictorial quality of these analogies. They invite us to envision a scene that captures the meaning of salvation. Some of these pictures have higher resolution than others. Each of them is a snapshot, in the sense that each one captures an aspect of salvation as seen from a particular perspective. All of them together create a three-dimensional view.

WHY DO WE USE IMAGES?

Images are fundamental to human thought and speech. "Our ordinary conceptual system, in terms of which we both think and act, is fundamentally metaphorical."[11] Most, if not all, language is metaphorical at base. Much of what we regard as literal language actually consists of dead metaphors—figurative expressions that have become so commonplace that we are no longer struck by them. We take for granted that a bank has branches, that a department has a head, and that large buildings can have wings. Dead metaphors are victims of their own success—that is, they capture their subject so well that they become the standard way of referring to that subject, so that we come to think of them as literal. Their insights are no longer fresh and surprising but taken for granted.[12] However, new metaphors are being coined all the time, because people are constantly finding

---

(Scottdale, Penn.: Herald, 1997) and *Understanding the Atonement for the Mission of the Church* (Scottdale, Penn.: Herald, 1986).

[10]Sallie McFague describes a model as "a sustained and systematic metaphor." *Metaphorical Theology: Models of God in Religious Language* (Minneapolis: Fortress, 1982), p. 67. In contrast to models, biblical images are not systematic, although some are more sustained than others. Even the cultic imagery of Hebrews, as elaborate as it is, is more metaphor than model, because it blends together the pictures of Jesus as high priest, Jesus as perfect sacrifice, Jesus as forerunner into the sanctuary, etc. For examples of theological models, see Avery Dulles, *Models of Revelation* (Maryknoll, N.Y.: Orbis, 1992); and *Models of the Church*, expanded ed. (New York: Doubleday, 1987).

[11]George Lakoff and Mark Johnson, *Metaphors We Live By* (Chicago: University of Chicago Press, 1980), p. 3.

[12]Colin Gunton, "*Christus Victor* Revisited: A Study in Metaphor and the Transformation of Meaning," *The Journal of Theological Studies* 36, no. 1 (1985): 133.

new ways to make sense of their experience.[13]

Figurative language plays a critical role in both cognition and creativity. In metaphor, a term is transferred from its usual referent to another one for the purpose of illuminating the new referent.[14] This transfer helps us to understand new things by comparing them to things we already know: "Rationality consists just in the continuous adaptation of our language to our continually expanding world, and metaphor is one of the chief means by which this is accomplished."[15] Because metaphor is so important in structuring our experience, it plays a large role in defining what we think of as real.[16] For example, someone who thinks that "love is war" may experience romantic relationships differently from someone who thinks that "love is a game." Politicians and advertisers constantly urge us to accept their metaphors and thereby allow them to define our reality in ways advantageous to them.

Thus metaphors not only define the world, they can also redefine it. According to Paul Ricoeur, metaphors open our minds to new possibilities, new ways of seeing the world: "Metaphor is the rhetorical process by which discourse unleashes the power that certain fictions have to redescribe reality."[17] If we allow a new metaphor to become part of our conceptual system, it can create a new reality for us by shaping our perceptions and guiding our future actions. Our further experiences will then reinforce the interpretive power of the metaphor. "In this sense metaphors can be self-fulfilling prophecies."[18] New ways of seeing can lead to new ways of living.

No wonder, then, that metaphors play such an important role in the New Testament writers' descriptions of the new thing that God has done in Jesus. They are asking their audiences to entertain new ideas and to see cherished beliefs from a new perspective. As Paul declares, "From now on,

---

[13]Lakoff and Johnson, *Metaphors We Live By*, p. 139.

[14]Caird, *Language and Imagery*, p. 66.

[15]Mary B. Hesse, "The Explanatory Function of Metaphor," appendix to *Models and Analogies in Science* (Notre Dame, Ind.: University of Notre Dame Press, 1966), p. 259; cited in Paul Ricoeur, *The Rule of Metaphor: Multi-Disciplinary Studies of the Creation of Meaning in Language*, trans. Robert Czerny with Kathleen McLaughlin and John Costello (Buffalo: University of Toronto Press, 1977), p. 243. Lakoff and Johnson refer to metaphor as "imaginative rationality." *Metaphors We Live By*, p. 235.

[16]Lakoff and Johnson, *Metaphors We Live By*, p. 146.

[17]Ricoeur, *Rule of Metaphor*, p. 7.

[18]Lakoff and Johnson, *Metaphors We Live By*, pp. 145, 156.

therefore, we regard no one from a human point of view; even though we once knew Christ from a human point of view, we know him no longer in that way" (2 Cor 5:16). The Christ event has changed reality, so new metaphors are needed to redescribe it.

Paul and others use metaphors (such as the language of sacrifice) to reframe the meaning of the cross. As G. B. Caird observes, "Literally, the death of Christ was no sacrifice, but a criminal execution, regarded by the one side as a political necessity and by the other as a miscarriage of justice. But because Christ himself chose to regard his death as a sacrifice, and by his words at the Last Supper taught his disciples so to do, he transformed its tragedy into something he could offer to God to be used in the service of his purpose."[19] What appeared to be defeat is re-envisioned as victory.

This reenvisioning can work both ways. An effective metaphor can change our perception of both the thing described and the term used to describe it. Speaking of the cross as a victory transforms our perceptions not only of Jesus' death but also of the idea of victory itself. In this view, real victory is not military conquest, but the kind of thing that happens when Jesus goes to the cross. Christians who accept the cross as the definition of victory would then have to say that Constantine misconstrued the cross when he interpreted it as an omen of his military success.[20]

Why are images so useful for this task of re-envisioning? First, figurative language is more vivid and arresting than literal language. It captures the attention and the imagination, and by doing so, takes root in the memory. Second, images make abstract ideas easier to understand by expressing them in concrete terms. In their concreteness, figurative expressions are often more concise than literal expressions, because they capture the essence of their subject without the need for long explanations. For example, it is more laborious to refer to "someone who is putting on a false display of friendship in order to gain your trust so that he can harm you later" than to refer to "a wolf in sheep's clothing." Figurative language is especially useful for describing realities (such as metaphysical concepts) that elude or exceed the capacity of ordinary speech.

Third, images have an important role in forming and sustaining identity. "In them the imagination of the community is reflected and

---

[19]Caird, *Language and Imagery*, p. 157.
[20]Gunton, "*Christus Victor* Revisited," pp. 143-44.

nourished."[21] Metaphors of salvation are particularly significant in this regard: "To know ourselves to be liberated, forgiven, redeemed, reconciled, justified, and adopted into the family of God is an essential foundation for adequately perceiving and soundly basing our identity."[22] Central metaphors drawn from salvation history both expressed and shaped the early church's understanding of what God had done in Christ.[23] They continue to maintain the identity of the believing community.

Finally, images are "powerful vehicles for carrying a vision." Biblical images are often grounded in particular experiences in salvation history, such as the exodus event. "When authentic experience fades, the images tend to lose their meaning and become abstract."[24] They no longer have the power to fire the imagination of God's people. Moreover, metaphors can become distorted over time. For example, Jesus' saying about the impossibility of a camel passing through the eye of a needle (Mk 10:25-27) emphasizes that riches can keep people from salvation. By the eleventh century, however, some commentators were identifying "the eye of a needle" as a gate in Jerusalem through which camels could pass with difficulty—on their knees! While this reinterpretation created a clever sermon illustration (and perhaps soothed the conscience of a wealthy church), there is no evidence that such a gate ever existed.[25] When these distortions occur, a fresh examination of the biblical images can revitalize the church's vision and call it back to its proper mission. Returning to the biblical text allows Scripture again to be "useful for teaching, for reproof, for correction, and for training in righteousness" (2 Tim 3:16).

IMAGES OF SALVATION

Just as figurative language is a complex topic, so is salvation. The term "salvation" itself (the technical term is *soteriology*) can be defined in different ways. For example, many theologians, such as William Placher, define soteriology as the work of Christ (the atonement). By contrast, Millard

[21]Minear, *Images of the Church*, p. 17.
[22]John Driver, *Understanding the Atonement*, p. 18.
[23]For a study of how Old Testament images shaped the telling of the Jesus story, see Willard M. Swartley, *Israel's Scripture Traditions and the Synoptic Gospels: Story Shaping Story* (Peabody, Mass.: Hendrickson, 1994).
[24]Driver, *Images of the Church in Mission*, p. 16. See also Caird, *Language and Imagery*, p. 152.
[25]Gordon D. Fee and Douglas Stuart, *How to Read the Bible for All Its Worth*, 2nd ed. (Grand Rapids: Zondervan, 1993), p. 21. The comment on conscience is my own.

Erickson states, "Salvation is the application of the work of Christ to the lives of humans."[26] Broadly understood, soteriology or salvation includes both of these dimensions. As the answer to the human predicament, salvation involves both the divine provision of salvation in Christ and human appropriation of that salvation.[27] Joseph Fitzmyer refers to these two dimensions as "objective redemption" and "subjective redemption."[28] This study will explore salvation in the broad sense. The discussion of each image will address both divine and human actors, although greater attention will be given to the reception of salvation than to the atonement.[29]

Theology always develops in particular contexts. Protestant understandings of salvation were born in the theological struggles of the Reformation and have been influenced by later developments such as the Enlightenment, Protestant Scholasticism, Pietism, Revivalism and the fundamentalist/modernist controversy. The multiplication of denominational traditions has led to the need to define and defend denominational distinctives over against the distinctives of other traditions. Western Christians have also been influenced by the individualism, compartmentalization and consumerism of Western culture.

All of these influences have led Christians to conceive of salvation in particular ways, shaped by the controversies of the past and the cultures of the present. While these conceptions of salvation have preserved valuable insights, they also have significant limitations. For example, the stress on "faith alone" has made it difficult for many Protestants to provide a theological foundation for ethics. Furthermore, Western individualism and consumerism push the church toward a distorted view of salvation that caters to self-interest and makes Christians blind to much personal and social sin.

These limitations surface in our language about salvation, such as when

---

[26]William C. Placher, *Essentials of Christian Theology* (Louisville: Westminster John Knox, 2003), p. 188; Millard J. Erickson, *Christian Theology*, 2nd ed. (Grand Rapids: Baker, 1998), p. 902.

[27]For an instance of the broader definition, see "Soteriology," in Stanley J. Grenz, David Guretzki and Cherith Fee Nordling, *Pocket Dictionary of Theological Terms* (Downers Grove, Ill.: InterVarsity Press, 1999), p. 108.

[28]Joseph A. Fitzmyer, "Reconciliation in Pauline Theology," in *To Advance the Gospel: New Testament Studies* (New York: Crossroad, 1981), p. 163.

[29]For images of the atonement, see Driver, *Understanding the Atonement*. As the title suggests, Driver's work focuses on the provision of salvation rather than on the reception of it.

we use "salvation" to mean "conversion," as in "Are you saved?" Other expressions such as "inviting Jesus into your life" and "asking Jesus to be your personal savior" seem to imply that Jesus exists to meet our needs. The chief motivation for this study is my conviction that the church's language about salvation is inadequate for expressing biblical teaching or for reaching contemporary people.

The church faces a number of challenges today. Modernist assumptions, with which Western Christians are familiar, are being challenged by postmodernism. As Paul Minear observed nearly fifty years ago, modernism gives priority to rational, scientific discourse, while "other forms of speech (parables, riddles, pictures, images, allegories) circulate only under a heavy discount."[30] However, the emergence of postmodernism has led people to rediscover the value of the image. A recovery of biblical images may give Christians the language they need to address this new context.

As many have observed, the center of gravity of Christianity is shifting from Europe and America to the Two-Thirds World. Questions and answers about salvation are growing out of new contexts and are representing new voices: women, African Americans and indigenous theologies of Africa, Asia and Latin America. The church must also confront the issues raised by the presence of other world religions. New conversations are urgently needed on a variety of fronts. In its diversity, the religious scene of the present day is coming more and more to resemble the world of the first century church.

In order to engage in the necessary conversations, the church will need the full spectrum of resources that the New Testament provides. A fresh examination of the biblical data on salvation will correct and enrich our present understandings. It can revitalize both our theology and our practice, as well as providing resources for dialogue.

In both the theology and the life of the church, the formative power of images is often overlooked. Images shape the way we think and feel about ourselves and about God. They also shape our expectations. "The images we use reflect what we are; they also largely determine what we will become."[31] Our images of salvation will encourage us in complacency or challenge us to seek the fullness of life in Christ. We will live up to—or

---

[30]Minear, *Images of the Church*, p. 21.
[31]Driver, *Understanding the Atonement*, p. 12.

down to—whatever picture we have of salvation. If we want to be faithful to Scripture and relevant to contemporary cultures, we must make sure that picture is as rich and three-dimensional as possible.

THIS BOOK

With this framework in mind, let's return to one of our opening questions: what does salvation look like? This book attempts to answer that question. As we will see, salvation looks like

- a committed relationship with God and God's people (chap. 2, Inheritance in the New Covenant).

- citizenship in a new country where everyone follows Jesus (chap. 3, Citizens of the Kingdom, Disciples of the King).

- sharing in the life of God (chap. 4, The Life of the Age to Come).

- a fresh start for human beings and creation itself (chap. 5, I Am About to Do a New Thing).

- being rescued from danger in order to be safe and whole (chap. 6, Deliverance Belongs to the Lord).

- liberation from captivity or bondage (chap. 7, My Chains Fell Off, My Heart Was Free).

- restoration of broken relationships and a broken world (chap. 8, No Longer Strangers).

- vindication as members of the true people of God (chap. 9, Justification by Faith[fulness]).

- being chosen by God for service and blessing (chap. 10, Election in Christ for the Sake of the World).

- an intimate spiritual union with Christ and other believers (chap. 11, Transformation by Participation).

- a special vocation to be God's priestly people (chap. 12, A People Holy to the Lord).

- a pilgrimage or struggle that requires endurance (chap. 13, Call to Endurance).

Chapter one describes the method of the study. Subsequent chapters, while following a thematic approach, take on a roughly canonical shape. Chapter two focuses on an image that expresses the New Testament writers' sense of transition between old and new covenants (expressed in the Christian division between Old and New Testaments). Chapters three and four explore themes in the Gospels. Chapters five through eight focus on themes common to the Gospels and Paul. Chapters nine and ten address two central images of salvation in Paul: justification and election. Chapters eleven and twelve take up images common to Paul and the General Epistles. Finally, chapter thirteen examines a cluster of images in Hebrews and Revelation. Each chapter concludes with a list of suggestions for further reading that includes both introductory and more advanced material, as well as some that focuses on practical application.

This study is intended for seminary students, pastors and educated laypeople. It engages with scholarship to enrich the discussion, but it does not provide a comprehensive survey of the literature. At the same time, I hope that the insights reached through this study will be of some benefit to ongoing academic conversations on these topics. The recent reawakening of interest in the theological interpretation of Scripture may make this study particularly timely.

Although I will attempt to interpret the New Testament on its own terms, no interpreter is without a context. It seems appropriate to identify mine. I am a white female seminary professor, an ordained minister in the Brethren Church of Ashland, Ohio, and a theologian in the Anabaptist/Brethren tradition working in an evangelical setting. These experiences and commitments no doubt have influenced my reading of Scripture. On the other hand, I adopted the Anabaptist/Brethren tradition as an adult because I believed that it best fit the understandings I had already reached through my study of Scripture. The interaction between one's preunderstandings and the text form the well-known hermeneutical circle (or spiral). My understanding of salvation has been deepened and enriched though my study of the New Testament images. I hope that the reader, whatever his or her preunderstandings, will have the same experience.

FOR FURTHER READING

Caird, G. B. *The Language and Imagery of the Bible*. Grand Rapids: Eerdmans, 1997.

Driver, John. *Images of the Church in Mission*. Scottdale, Penn.: Herald, 1997.

———. *Understanding the Atonement for the Mission of the Church*. Scottdale, Penn.: Herald, 1986.

Gunton, Colin. "*Christus Victor* Revisited: A Study in Metaphor and the Transformation of Meaning." *The Journal of Theological Studies* 36, no. 1 (1985): 129-45.

Lakoff, George and Mark Johnson. *Metaphors We Live By*. Chicago: University of Chicago Press, 2003.

McFague, Sallie. *Metaphorical Theology: Models of God in Religious Language*. Minneapolis: Fortress, 1982.

Minear, Paul. *Images of the Church in the New Testament*. Philadelphia: Westminster Press, 1977.

Ricoeur, Paul. *The Rule of Metaphor: The Creation of Meaning in Language*. Translated by Robert Czerny with Kathleen McLaughlin and John Costello. 3rd ed. New York: Routledge, 2003.

Thiselton, Anthony. "Semantics and New Testament Interpretation." In *New Testament Interpretation: Essays on Principles and Methods*. Edited by I. Howard Marshall, pp. 75-104. Grand Rapids: Eerdmans, 1977.

Wright, Christopher J. H. *Salvation Belongs to Our God: Celebrating the Bible's Central Story*. Christian Doctrine in Global Perspective. Edited by David Smith. Downers Grove, Ill.: InterVarsity Press, 2007.

I

ON METHOD

ONE DAY IN MY CLASS on biblical hermeneutics, I asked a student to read a particular passage aloud. Afterward, not recognizing the translation, I asked him, "What Bible are you using?" With a blank look, he offered tentatively, "The Holy Bible?"

Some segments of the church no doubt feel that biblical scholars and theologians devote themselves to complicating the obvious. I certainly could have been clearer in my question to my student. Be this as it may, the scholarly debates of the last hundred years have ensured that anyone who claims to address both Bible and theology in the same book must explain what she thinks she is doing. Hence this chapter on method.

This study lies at the intersection of three fields of inquiry: New Testament theology, literary criticism and theological hermeneutics (or the theological interpretation of Scripture). None of these fields is monolithic, and all of them are contested. Nevertheless, all three contribute useful lenses through which to view the images of salvation.

NEW TESTAMENT THEOLOGY

Writing in 1993, Donald Hagner declared that the discipline of New Testament theology existed in a state of "methodological confusion."[1] The situation has not improved since then. A survey of the debates about the purpose and method (and even the possibility) of New Testament theology

---

[1]Donald A. Hagner, "Biblical Theology in the Last Twenty Years," in George Eldon Ladd, *A Theology of the New Testament*, ed. Donald A. Hagner, rev. ed. (Grand Rapids: Eerdmans, 1994), p. 15.

is beyond the scope of this chapter.[2] Instead, I will simply describe my own understanding of the term and discuss what that discipline contributes to this study.

The term "biblical theology" can be used in two senses—in a specific sense, referring to the theology contained in the Bible, and in a more general sense, referring to any theology that claims to be based on the Bible.[3] Many Christians, especially those in conservative circles, conflate these two senses. In my New Testament theology course, for example, I have found that my students, most of whom are evangelicals, have a difficult time distinguishing between biblical theology and systematic or doctrinal theology. They assume that the church's doctrines can be found fully formed on the surface of the biblical text; thus doing theology just requires citing chapter and verse. This is not actually the case, as anyone can attest who has tried to moderate discussions between advocates for competing interpretations that all claim to be biblical.

In the taxonomy of biblical disciplines, biblical theology (consisting of Old Testament theology and New Testament theology) falls between exegesis and theology. It synthesizes the results of biblical exegesis and makes them available to those wishing to study the development of doctrine, as well as those attempting to draw on both biblical and historical theology in order to construct doctrinal or systematic theology. As an intermediate discipline between biblical studies and theology, biblical theology falls into the no-man's-land between disciplines that are strictly separated in the academy. This is one reason it has sometimes been a battleground for competing interests.

This book is an exercise in New Testament theology in the more specific sense. It assumes that the appropriate source of *New Testament* theology is the collection of books that compose what the church has called the New Testament (as opposed to noncanonical materials, although those materials may illuminate the canonical books). Similarly, the appropriate content of New Testament *theology* is the theological thought of the New Testament writers (as opposed to the religion of the first Christians, re-

---

[2]For such a survey, see Gerhard F. Hasel, *New Testament Theology: Issues in the Current Debate* (Grand Rapids: Eerdmans, 1984); and Dan O. Via, *What Is New Testament Theology?* Guides to Biblical Scholarship: New Testament Series (Minneapolis: Fortress Press, 2002).
[3]Hasel, *New Testament Theology*, p. 16.

constructed from biblical and extrabiblical sources).[4] The teaching of Jesus should play a foundational role in New Testament theology, although we must take into consideration the dual nature of the Gospels as records of Jesus' ministry as well as theological documents written from a later perspective.

As New Testament theology, this study explores how the New Testament documents depict salvation, rather than developing a comprehensive doctrine of salvation. It focuses on biblical concepts rather than concepts drawn from systematic theology. For example, the process of salvation from conversion to final perfection is often described in systematic theology with the terms justification, sanctification and glorification. In the New Testament, however, these terms are not distinguished in this way. Justification is an eschatological reality impinging upon the present in believers' relationship with Christ. Sanctification, for the believer, is both a past-tense event and a future to pursue. Even glorification does not refer solely to the end of the salvation process but also to the progressive transformation that leads to this goal.

As New Testament theology, this study is descriptive rather than prescriptive, historical rather than contemporary (with an exception I will mention in a moment). It focuses on the theological concepts of the New Testament writers in their original contexts, so that we can hear them in their own voice and encounter them on their own terms. I am using the word "historical" not in the sense of "reconstructing the historical origins of the theological ideas behind the biblical texts"[5] but in the sense of attempting to understand the texts, as they stand, in their historical and cultural contexts. In the words of Krister Stendahl's classic essay, I will focus more on "what it meant" than on "what it means."[6]

Constructing theology that has contemporary relevance is not the proper task of biblical theology; however, if its proper task is done well, its findings will be relevant to the present day. The New Testament documents make extensive theological claims. These claims, passed down

---

[4]These points may seem obvious to most Christians, but they bear mentioning here because some scholars have advocated approaches to New Testament theology that depreciate the canon and rule theology out of bounds. See the discussions in Hasel and Via cited above.

[5]Daniel J. Treier, *Introducing Theological Interpretation of Scripture: Recovering a Christian Practice* (Grand Rapids: Baker, 2008), p. 108.

[6]Krister Stendahl, "Biblical Theology, Contemporary," in *IDB*, 1:418-32.

through the history of the church, still remain the foundation of Christian faith and practice.

Biblical theology in the specific sense is the most important source of validation and renewal for biblical theology in the general sense. It serves as a safeguard against proof-texting, which is the constant temptation of theologians who claim that their theology is consistent with the teaching of the Bible.[7] The descriptive task of biblical theology is indispensable— *not* because we should divorce the Bible from theology, but because *only in this way* can we be confident that our theology is biblical in any meaningful sense. For these reasons, I will focus on the meaning of the images of salvation in their original context, although I will conclude each chapter with some reflections on contemporary application.

LITERARY CRITICISM

The study of images has its origin in literary criticism, where it has been a staple for centuries. Literary criticism has contributed numerous approaches to the interpretation of the New Testament. These approaches have illuminated the text in fresh ways, especially in the case of genres such as narrative and poetry that were not well served by traditional biblical criticism.[8] While the Bible is *more* than literature, it is not *less*. Analyzing its literary features is a necessary part of interpretation.

Literary criticism tends to deal with the text as it stands, rather than with the text's prehistory or the historical development of the ideas behind the text. Unlike the historical-critical method, which often attributes differences in style to differences in authorship, literary approaches treat a

---

[7]Daniel Treier calls biblical theology "a historically oriented critical check upon the proof-texting inclinations of theologians that will nevertheless retain Scripture as the ground for making doctrinal claims" (*Introducing Theological Interpretation*, p. 24).

[8]Dan O. Via has acknowledged the usefulness of literary criticism in discerning the content and structure of the biblical text (*New Testament Theology*, p. 127). For an introduction to the literary criticism of the Bible, see Tremper Longman III, *Literary Approaches to Biblical Interpretation*, Foundations of Contemporary Interpretation, ed. Moisés Silva (Grand Rapids: Zondervan, 1987); and Leland Ryken and Tremper Longman III, *A Complete Literary Guide to the Bible* (Grand Rapids: Zondervan, 1993). For surveys of literary studies of the Bible, see Mark Minor, *Literary-Critical Approaches to the Bible: An Annotated Bibliography* (West Cornwall, Conn.: Locust Hill Press, 1992); Mark Minor, *Literary-Critical Approaches to the Bible: A Bibliographical Supplement* (West Cornwall, Conn.: Locust Hill Press, 1996); and Duane F. Watson and Alan J. Hauser, *Rhetorical Criticism of the Bible: A Comprehensive Bibliography with Notes on History and Method* (New York: E. J. Brill, 1994).

text as a literary whole, unless closer examination suggests otherwise. Literary features of a text are assumed to be intentional strategies adopted by the writer for a rhetorical purpose. Whether consciously chosen or not, literary features such as structure, characterization, parallelism and figurative language have rhetorical effects and can be analyzed accordingly.

Some literary critics approach the rhetorical situation from the reader's side, arguing that readers actually create the meaning of texts. Because of my presuppositions about the nature of Scripture, however, I do not follow this approach. This study assumes a communication model in which the biblical authors intend to communicate a message to their original audiences and employ a number of literary techniques to do so. While readers certainly bring their own perspectives to bear on texts, including the Bible, the most fruitful approach to biblical texts is not creativity but receptivity.

Literary criticism brings to New Testament study a concern for intertextuality. Although the most important determiner of the meaning of a text is its immediate context, texts can still be illuminated by bringing them into conversation with other texts. This is especially true for the Bible, in which earlier books influenced later books, and which as a whole has become the canon of sacred Scripture. Thus some literary approaches can resemble canonical and theological interpretation.[9]

In keeping with a literary approach, this study examines the New Testament documents as we have them, in most cases setting aside issues of composition. I will refer to books by their traditional authorial designations for ease of reference. I will further assume that the disputed Pauline Epistles (the Pastorals, Colossians, Ephesians and 2 Thessalonians), even if not authored by Paul, are still consistent with his thought.

As an exercise in literary criticism, this study engages in close reading of biblical images of salvation in their literary contexts. It does not attempt to be an exhaustive survey of New Testament imagery or of New Testament teaching on salvation. Two considerations have governed the choice of images: importance and breadth of coverage. On the one hand, I have tried to address the most important salvation images

---

[9]D. A. Carson argues that biblical theology must be "committed to intertextual study." "Current Issues in Biblical Theology: A New Testament Perspective," *Bulletin for Biblical Research* 5 (1995): 30.

used by the New Testament writers.[10] On the other hand, I have tried to represent the variety of images appearing in the Gospels, Acts, the Epistles and Revelation rather than restricting the study to the more familiar Pauline concepts.

While respecting the diverse authorship of the New Testament as well as the varied contexts in which these images occur, I will explore intertextual connections in order to synthesize the meaning of these images for different authors and for the New Testament as a whole. For example, the book of Hebrews makes explicit the cultic background of sanctification, which is less obvious in Paul's letters. Similarly, the kingdom of God in the Synoptics and Paul's metaphor of citizenship illuminate one another. Taken together, they reinforce the absolute allegiance demanded by the gospel, as well as the sense of belonging that it makes possible.

THEOLOGICAL HERMENEUTICS

Theological hermeneutics, or the theological interpretation of Scripture, is a developing movement that rejects the academic divide between biblical studies and theology. Its proponents argue for the propriety of interpreting the Bible from a position of faith in order to address theological concerns. Advocates are not united in their methods or in their evaluation of biblical theology. For some, theological interpretation and biblical theology (properly understood) are synonyms. For others, biblical theology is too academy-focused and too tainted by the pretended objectivity of the historical-critical method. They believe that a new discipline is needed.[11]

In any case, the theological interpretation of Scripture is not a particular method but a set of presuppositions and a particular goal: "to communicate the theological messages in the text on the assumption that they have something (Christian) to say to the present. It teaches Christians how

---

[10]By "important," I have in mind both the significance of the image in the thought of the New Testament writer and its significance in the history of theology.

[11]Kevin J. Vanhoozer, "Introduction: What Is Theological Interpretation of the Bible?" in *DTIB*, pp. 22-23. For a survey of this developing field, see Treier, *Introducing Theological Interpretation*. For one example of what this might look like in practice, see the work of "The Scripture Project" presented in Ellen F. Davis and Richard B. Hays, *The Art of Reading Scripture* (Grand Rapids: Eerdmans, 2003). The term "theological hermeneutics" is used, e.g., by Joel B. Green, "Scripture and Theology: Uniting the Two So Long Divided," in *Between Two Horizons: Spanning New Testament Studies & Systematic Theology*, ed. Joel B. Green and Max Turner (Grand Rapids: Eerdmans, 2000), p. 37.

to read their scriptures and invites others to look at the Bible this way. It is a kind of practical or applied hermeneutics."[12] As this statement implies, theological interpretation is carried out within the church and aims to serve the church rather than the academy.

Theological hermeneutics approaches the Bible as Christian Scripture, emphasizing the "ultimate coherence" of Old and New Testaments and focusing on theological concerns.[13] It thus respects the canon and expects the whole of Scripture to illuminate the parts. Some interpreters read Scripture in light of tradition (embodied, for example, in the creeds). Because Scripture is the medium of divine revelation, it should be read not simply for information but in order to know God.[14]

In this view, the Bible is neither a collection of texts for us to master nor a reflection of our own presuppositions. It is both "subject" and "other," in that it has the power to address us with demands for change.[15] It is performative discourse that intends to shape our lives: "As Scripture, the Bible is present as an alternative framework within which to construe our lives, and so challenges those who would be Christian by calling for a creative transformation of the patterns by which we make sense of our lives, and by which we interact with and within the world."[16] In other words, it calls its readers and hearers to conversion. We will return to this point at the conclusion of this chapter.

I share many of the presuppositions associated with the theological interpretation of Scripture. For example, I agree that the outcome of interpretations is determined not only by the method used, but also by the presuppositions with which the method is used. Even the historical examination of biblical texts can produce quite different results depending

---

[12]Robert Morgan, "New Testament Theology," in *Biblical Theology: Problems and Perspectives*, ed. Steven J. Kraftchick, Charles D. Myers Jr. and Ben C. Ollenburger (Nashville: Abingdon, 1995), p. 106.

[13]Francis Watson, *Text and Truth: Redefining Biblical Theology* (Grand Rapids: Eerdmans, 1997), pp. 6, 8. Watson proposes a biblical theology that integrates text (biblical studies) and truth (theology). He argues that the separation of these two disciplines has resulted in the distortion of both. The biblical scholar reads texts apart from their truth claims, and the theologian talks about truth in the abstract, rather than in its concrete textual expression (pp. 4, 27).

[14]Treier, *Introducing Theological Interpretation*, pp. 201-3; Joel B. Green, *Seized by Truth: Reading the Bible as Scripture* (Nashville: Abingdon, 2007), p. 11.

[15]Green, *Seized by Truth*, pp. 156-57.

[16]Ibid., 25. The concept of performative discourse comes from speech-act theory. For an introduction to this field, see Richard S. Briggs, "Speech-Act Theory," in *DTIB*, pp. 763-66.

on the interpreters' preunderstandings about the nature of history and the possibility of God's involvement in it.

Advocates of postmodern and ideological perspectives have argued persuasively that all interpretations are conditioned by the interpreter's personal experiences and social location. All human beings are embedded in various contexts that influence their perceptions and judgments. There is no neutral place to stand from which to construct completely objective interpretations. For this reason, theological constructs must be provisional and open to correction. Although not included in the traditional list of theological virtues (faith, hope and love), honesty and humility remain important qualities for theologians.

I have described my own social location in the Introduction. My epistemological perspective is consistent with "critical realism" as defined by N. T. Wright: it qualifies as "realism" because of its belief that reality exists independent of the observer, but it is "critical" because it contends that human beings, as observers, are finite and flawed.[17] Thus "objective" reality exists, but our knowledge of that reality is neither immediate nor objective. As a consequence, we can know reality, even divine reality, but we cannot know that reality comprehensively or perfectly—at least not in this life.

Besides critical realism, I bring to the task of interpretation a number of theological presuppositions. For instance, I believe that the New Testament is a record of, a witness to, and a reflection on God's self-disclosure in Jesus of Nazareth, the Messiah of Israel and the Son of God. Despite the diversity of the New Testament documents, they demonstrate a common commitment to an overarching narrative (or "metanarrative") of God's covenant faithfulness revealed through the Old Testament and climaxing in the life, death and resurrection of Jesus Christ. Despite their differences, the New Testament writers see themselves as practitioners of the same faith, even members of the same family. Jan van der Watt uses a helpful architectural metaphor to express a similar idea: "It is not as if one is transported from one unrelated world to the next when reading the dif-

---

[17]N. T. Wright, *The New Testament and the People of God* (Minneapolis: Fortress, 1992), pp. 32-35. Wright contrasts critical realism with positivism (or naïve realism) and phenomenalism. See also Ben F. Meyer, *Critical Realism and the New Testament*, Princeton Theological Monograph Series (Allison Park, Penn.: Pickwick Publications, 1989); and *Reality and Illusion in New Testament Scholarship: A Primer in Critical Realist Hermeneutics* (Collegeville, Minn.: Liturgical Press, 1994).

ferent New Testament documents. One realizes that one is in different rooms, when you move from Mark to Luke, or from Matthew to John or to Paul, but you cannot escape the impression that you are in the same house. The architecture remains the same."[18]

I approach the Bible with theological interests, from a position of faith. I believe that because the New Testament documents make theological claims, theological concerns belong to the task of interpretation from the outset. The best perspective from which to examine these claims is a perspective within the community of faith, for whom the documents were written. Since the New Testament is foundational for the faith and life of the church, New Testament theology remains relevant for the church today. Having an accurate understanding of the theology of the New Testament is indispensable for anyone who regards the Bible as authoritative.

One of the most significant issues that arises when we interpret the Bible theologically is the role of tradition. Catholics straightforwardly assert that the Bible should be read through the lens of tradition.[19] Protestants in general and evangelicals in particular are reluctant to acknowledge their reliance on tradition, citing the slogan *sola scriptura*, itself a legacy of Protestant tradition.[20] When used as a slogan, *sola scriptura* oversimplifies the issue of authority and fails to acknowledge the deep intellectual and emotional attachment that Protestants have to their own traditions. This is true even for those groups who insist most strongly that their theology is "biblical." (Witness the heated rhetoric in some quarters over the "New Perspective" on Paul.)[21]

Any reexamination of New Testament texts runs the risk of challenging accepted interpretations. For those who believe in the authority of Scrip-

---

[18]Jan G. van der Watt, "Soteriology of the New Testament," in *Salvation in the New Testament: Perspectives on Soteriology*, ed. Jan G. van der Watt, Supplements to Novum Testamentum, ed. M. M. Mitchell and D. P. Moessner (Boston: E. J. Brill, 2005), p. 506.

[19]Paul VI, Dogmatic Constitution on Divine Revelation, *Dei Verbum* (18 November 1965), 8-9.

[20]Evangelicals seem to be developing a greater interest in the Great Tradition in recent years, as demonstrated by the Ancient Christian Commentary on Scripture (InterVarsity Press) and other projects that engage with the church fathers. For a programmatic essay on the relationship of evangelical theology to tradition, see Alister E. McGrath, "Engaging the Great Tradition: Evangelical Theology and the Role of Tradition," in *Evangelical Futures: A Conversation on Theological Method*, ed. John G. Stackhouse Jr. (Grand Rapids: Baker Books, 2000), pp. 139-58.

[21]See chapter nine for a discussion of the New Perspective.

ture, however, this is a risk well worth taking. If *sola scriptura* means anything, it means that Scripture has primacy over tradition—even Protestant
tradition.

As an Anabaptist, I believe that tradition should be viewed in terms of
community rather than authority. Tradition enlarges our hermeneutical
community by bringing us into conversation with other believers across
time. While we should respect and learn from our elders in the faith, we
need not be afraid of asking questions of them and even disagreeing with
them. They are located in their own contexts just as we are in ours. We can
learn from their mistakes as well as from their wisdom—just as, someday,
our successors will learn from ours. Tradition can broaden our perspective.
It is most valuable, however, when it provides a window through which to
see the text, rather than a wall that restricts our view.

One of the purposes of this exploration of biblical images of salvation is
to enable us to evaluate our own traditions. Some chapters will retrieve
images that have been neglected; others will attempt to recover the biblical
sense of images that have been frequently appropriated (or misappropri-
ated) by the church. All Christians, from the scholar consciously working
within the Great Tradition to the student pondering the authority of the
notes in his study Bible, have the responsibility to go back to the source
and find out what the foundational texts say.

INTERPRETING IMAGES

Interpreting metaphors would seem to be easy. As figures of comparison,
metaphors have two parts: the subject of the comparison (often called the
tenor) and the thing with which the subject is compared (often called the
vehicle).[22] We can think of the vehicle as "carrying" meaning that will be
"delivered" to the tenor. When Jesus calls Herod a fox (Lk 13:32), "Herod"
is the tenor, and "fox" is the vehicle. Jesus uses the connotations of "fox" to
suggest something about Herod. To interpret a metaphor, we should presumably identify the vehicle and then transfer appropriate characteristics
of the vehicle to the tenor. Put another way, instead of focusing on the image, we focus on the concept expressed by the image.[23] In the case of

---

[22]The terms "tenor" and "vehicle" were coined by I. A. Richards in *The Philosophy of Rhetoric*
(1936).
[23]Van der Watt, "Soteriology," p. 521.

Herod, we interpret Jesus' statement to mean that Herod is a sly or crafty person. Broadly speaking, the images of salvation in this book are vehicles that communicate something about their tenor, salvation.

However, for several reasons, metaphors are not always easy to interpret. First, we may not be familiar with the vehicle. If we had never heard of foxes, we would have no idea what Jesus was suggesting about Herod. Moreover, the connotations of vehicles can change. When I use this example in class, my students start smiling, because they immediately think of the use of "fox" in modern American slang to mean a sexy person, usually a woman. They realize, however, that this connotation would not have been in Jesus' mind! To understand the vehicle, we must pay careful attention to the historical and literary context in which it is used.

Second, we may not be sure of the ground of the comparison. What qualities of the vehicle should we transfer to the tenor? When Jesus called Herod a fox, he obviously did not mean that Herod had four feet or a bushy tail. Sometimes the ground of a comparison is specified: Jesus had compassion on the crowds "because they were *harassed and helpless*, like sheep without a shepherd" (Mt 9:36, italics mine). When the ground is not specified, however, metaphors have a degree of indeterminacy.[24] Instances of a metaphor elsewhere, especially by the same author, may illuminate its meaning, but the best guide for interpretation is the immediate context of the particular instance. A given author can use the same metaphor in different ways. For example, Paul uses the image of the temple of the Holy Spirit in reference to the church in 1 Corinthians 3:16-17 but in reference to the body of the individual Christian in 1 Corinthians 6:19-20.

Third, since vehicles do not resemble their tenors in all possible ways, it is important to know when to *stop* interpreting. In the parable of the unjust judge, for example, the point is perseverance in prayer (Lk 18:1-8). We are not to identify God with the unjust judge and conclude that God does not have our best interests at heart. Similarly, when New Testament writers call salvation our inheritance, they do not mean that we will receive it when our heavenly Father dies! With this in mind, when we consider Jesus' statement that he came to give his life as a ransom (Mk 10:45), are we to

---

[24]G. B. Caird contrasts metaphor with code, such as Morse code, in which each sign always has a single, precise meaning. *The Language and Imagery of the Bible* (Grand Rapids: Eerdmans, 1997), p. 148.

inquire into the hypothetical recipient of the ransom, or is that beyond the scope of the metaphor?[25]

Fourth, some scholars have argued that it is inappropriate to "translate" metaphors at all. They insist that rational analysis deprives metaphors of the communicative power they possess *as metaphors*.[26] I will address this issue in the final section of this chapter.

The final challenge of interpreting metaphors of salvation occurs at the level of synthesis. We may be tempted to pick and choose among the biblical images because some of them may seem clearer than others or may fit more neatly into a rational system. Theological traditions naturally prefer some images to others because they seem to reinforce the distinctives of those traditions. However, this selectivity has impoverished the church's understanding of salvation. It has also deprived us of examples of contextualizing that could serve as models for our task of communicating the gospel in our own settings.

The chapters that follow will take an inductive approach, moving from the individual instances of an image toward a synthesis of the meaning of that image. This approach should allow us to appreciate the diversity of the New Testament witnesses. Placing each image in its historical and literary contexts will both clarify its meaning and suggest points of connection for contemporary application.

Despite their diversity, these images assume a shared narrative of salvation history that builds through the Old Testament and climaxes in Christ. This story of redemption is refracted through the Christ event like light through a prism. Each image expresses an aspect of redemption as seen through Christ. We need the whole spectrum in order to fully see the light. Put another way, the images are "building blocks" of the "master story" of redemption. If we want to understand that story, we have to put the blocks together. Thus once we have understood each image on its own, we should attempt to see the images in light of one another and in the

---

[25]Colin Gunton declares that "only the literal-minded" would ask such a question. Colin Gunton, "*Christus Victor* Revisited: A Study in Metaphor and the Transformation of Meaning," *The Journal of Theological Studies* 36, no. 1 (1985): 134.

[26]For example, see Anthony Thiselton, "Semantics and New Testament Interpretation," in *New Testament Interpretation: Essays on Principles and Methods*, ed. I. Howard Marshall (Grand Rapids: Eerdmans, 1977), p. 95. Thiselton believes that it is a mistake to press metaphors for a greater degree of specificity than the New Testament texts express. The writers may have intended the images to be open-ended (p. 94).

context of the whole picture.[27] In the final chapter, I will reflect on what we can say on the basis of an examination of all the images.

This study focuses on images and concepts rather than on words. As James Barr has pointed out, theological content is communicated not by single words but by larger syntactical units, such as the sentence or the speech.[28] This is why I have grouped together different expressions that describe similar concepts. It is also why I have chosen to investigate all of these images rather than simply analyzing the words that are translated as "save" and "salvation."[29] Nevertheless, since ideas are expressed in words, some discussion of the meaning of words will be necessary. This is especially important in the case of biblical words that have become technical terms in the history of theology.

WHAT IT MEANT AND WHAT IT MEANS

While different readers of a biblical text might agree on "what it meant" to the New Testament writer, they are less likely to agree on "what it means" (or should mean) to people today. The primacy of historical investigation in modern biblical studies has meant that modern interpreters carefully distinguish between historical meaning and contemporary relevance. To move from one to the other requires carefully defined steps: "Many today imagine that the movement from Bible to theology is a three-stage process, from exegesis to (descriptive) biblical theology to (prescriptive) systematic theology. At more popular levels, the same hermeneutic is prescribed in three steps: observation, interpretation, application."[30]

---

[27]For the "building blocks" metaphor, see van der Watt, "Soteriology," p. 519, 521. Concerning images of the atonement, John Driver states, "The value of any one of these images depends on allowing it to remain in relationship to all of the rest." *Understanding the Atonement for the Mission of the Church* (Scottdale, Penn.: Herald, 1986), p. 19.

[28]James Barr, *The Semantics of Biblical Language* (Philadelphia: Trinity Press International, 1961), p. 263.

[29]The English "save" and "salvation" are usually translations of the Greek *sōzō* and *sōtēria*. These terms are discussed in chapter six.

[30]Green, "Scripture and Theology," p. 33. Scott J. Hafemann divides biblical theology itself into a "threefold project" consisting of description ("mapping out the content of the biblical witness"), analysis of development within the canon, and synthesis ("striving to describe in even greater scope a pan-biblical theology"). "Biblical Theology: Retrospect and Prospect," in *Biblical Theology: Retrospect and Prospect*, ed. Scott J. Hafemann (Downers Grove, Ill.: InterVarsity Press, 2002), pp. 19-20. In his recent New Testament Theology, I. Howard Marshall states that his method involves description, analysis, development and attempted synthesis. He leaves application to the theologians. I. Howard Marshall, *New Testament Theology: Many*

This logical approach is appealing, and its influence is visible in this book. It is not without problems, however. First, it underestimates the difficulty of describing even "what it meant" accurately, given that interpreters are as contextually located as the texts they examine. Second, it neglects the role of the Holy Spirit, who will "guide [Jesus' disciples] into all the truth" (Jn 16:13). Third, this is not the most common way in which Scripture influences the present. The majority of Scripture consists of narrative and poetry. Its most pervasive influence is not informational but formational. This is especially true of its images. Finally, how do we apply metaphors? What kind of authority do they have?

In response to the first difficulty, we must become as self-aware as possible, both with the help of our own communities of faith and with the help of those who disagree with us. While we cannot eliminate our biases, we can compensate for them. The experience of those who have changed because of their reading of Scripture demonstrates that the hermeneutical circle need not be a vicious one.

In response to the second difficulty, we can make room for the Holy Spirit in our interpretation. In Anabaptist traditions, the Spirit is understood to work in conjunction with the written word to testify to Christ. While the Spirit's help is no substitute for research, a prayerful reliance on the Spirit is perfectly compatible with such research. If our ultimate goal is not simply knowledge but wisdom, the best way to reach that goal is through reliance on the One who "searches everything, even the depths of God" (1 Cor 2:10).

The third difficulty leads us to consider the formative power of images. As noted in the introduction, metaphors have the power of fiction to "redescribe" reality.[31] Like stories, metaphors create a world in which we are invited to participate. We are shaped not just by our thoughts about them but by our experience of them. They can influence our ideas and emotions even without our conscious awareness. In this way, they have the power either to reinforce or to subvert our view of ourselves and the world.[32] In order to fully appropriate biblical images, we must learn to

---

Witnesses, One Gospel (Downers Grove, Ill.: InterVarsity Press, 2004), p. 47.

[31]Paul Ricoeur, *The Rule of Metaphor: Multi-Disciplinary Studies of the Creation of Meaning in Language,* trans. Robert Czerny with Kathleen McLaughlin and John Costello (Buffalo: University of Toronto Press, 1977), p. 7.

[32]Caird, *Language and Imagery,* p. 153; Wright, *People of God,* p. 40.

inhabit the story they create and then perform it.[33]

As Jesus points out to his disciples in the parable of the soils (Mk 4:1-20), receptivity is key. Only those who are receptive to Jesus' teaching will be able to understand his parables. "Do you not understand this parable?" he asks them. "Then how will you understand all the parables?" (Mk 4:13). In order to comprehend these metaphors of transformation, we need to be open to being changed. Only then can the metaphors achieve their performative aim. Jesus' description of the good soil as both receptive and productive (Mk 4:20) underscores the connection between perception and action—or between faith and practice. Images of salvation call for an "epistemology of obedience."[34] Only by *living* them will we fully understand them (see Jn 7:17).

To properly interpret these images thus requires a "hermeneutic of consent."[35] While a hermeneutic of suspicion has its uses—especially as a challenge to traditional interpretations—faith documents can best be understood from the perspective of faith. Actually, as Richard Hays advises, biblical interpreters need a hermeneutic of both trust and suspicion—trust in the God behind the text, which prompts us to open ourselves to the text and be formed by it, and suspicion of ourselves and our institutions, who often have vested interests in particular interpretations. Interpreting Scripture is "a matter of faithful struggle to hear and discern." As interpreters, we are responsible for handling the Bible "in a way that opens up its message and both models and fosters trust in God."[36]

Samuel Taylor Coleridge described something like a hermeneutics of consent when he declared that readers of poetry must engage in "that will-

---

[33]Joel B. Green uses the phrase "inhabit Scripture's own story" in "Scripture and Theology," p. 42. On performing Scripture, see Nicholas Lash, "Performing the Scriptures," in *Theology on the Way to Emmaus* (London: SCM Press, 1986), pp. 37-46. Scot McKnight discusses performing the gospel in *Embracing Grace: A Gospel for All of Us* (Brewster, Mass.: Paraclete, 2005), pp. 10-11.

[34]The term is from John Driver, *Understanding the Atonement for the Mission of the Church* (Scottdale, Penn.: Herald, 1986), p. 36.

[35]The term was coined by Peter Stuhlmacher. See his *Historical Criticism and Theological Interpretation: Toward a Hermeneutics of Consent*, trans. Roy A. Harrisville (Philadelphia: Fortress, 1977). Stuhlmacher outlines his own convictions about method in *How to Do Biblical Theology*, Princeton Theological Monograph Series, ed. Dikran Y. Hadidian (Allison Park, Penn.: Pickwick Publications, 1995).

[36]Richard B. Hays, "Salvation by Trust? Reading the Bible Faithfully," *The Christian Century*, February 26, 1997, pp. 221-22.

ing suspension of disbelief for the moment, which constitutes poetic faith."[37] The suspension of disbelief evoked by poetry explains why images can be transformational. Biblical images invite us to entertain a way of looking at the world that places Christ at the center. If we respond to their invitation, they will form in us a faith that is more than momentary, and more than poetic.

The final difficulty, the question of how to apply metaphors, elicits responses that reveal the interpreter's presuppositions about language and about the Bible. Sallie McFague argues that recognizing the metaphorical nature of biblical language means recognizing the "relative and pluralistic" nature of the Bible. She says that we must move beyond biblical metaphors in order to avoid "the idolatry of religious language" that results from taking the metaphors as correct and literal expressions of truth. If we are wedded to these images, we will be unable to speak meaningfully to our contemporary context.[38]

I agree that we must find fresh ways to express the gospel in our contemporary contexts. We must do more than simply restate the biblical images. But I believe that it is possible to recognize the authority of biblical metaphors without falling into "idolatrous" literalism. To do this, I would suggest that we regard these images as *controlling metaphors*. The controlling metaphor of a poem directs the development of the poem and gives coherence to the whole. In a similar way, the New Testament metaphors of salvation should direct the development of our theology and of our lives. The fresh images we create must be consistent with what the biblical images reveal. Our efforts to paint pictures for our contemporaries will be more faithful and effective if we have first captured the biblical vision—or better, if it has captured us.

I am not suggesting that we select a single controlling metaphor from among these images, or that we should regard some of them as more normative than others, but that we regard them *together* as controlling metaphors. A complex of controlling metaphors may not resolve all possible questions we may have. In the final analysis, however, interpreting New Testament images of salvation requires more than rational study. It re-

---

[37]Samuel Taylor Coleridge, *Biographia Literaria* (New York: Dutton, 1971), p. 169.
[38]Sallie McFague, *Metaphorical Theology: Models of God in Religious Language* (Minneapolis: Fortress, 1982), pp. 4, 22-23.

quires trust, humility and the guidance of the Holy Spirit. It calls for "shifts in what we value, and how we perceive—that is, transformations at the level of our dispositions and commitments."[39] In short, what we need is what Paul Minear calls a "conversion of the communal imagination."[40] While this study will not bring us to perfection, I hope it will contribute to such a conversion.

FOR FURTHER READING

Barr, James. *The Semantics of Biblical Language.* Philadelphia: Trinity Press International, 1961.

Carson, D. A. "Current Issues in Biblical Theology: A New Testament Perspective." *Bulletin for Biblical Research* 5 (1995): 17-41.

Green, Joel B., and Max Turner. *Between Two Horizons: Spanning New Testament Studies & Systematic Theology.* Grand Rapids: Eerdmans, 2000.

Hafemann, Scott J., ed. *Biblical Theology: Retrospect and Prospect.* Downers Grove, Ill.: InterVarsity Press, 2002.

Hasel, Gerhard. *New Testament Theology: Basic Issues in the Current Debate.* Grand Rapids: Eerdmans, 1978.

Hultgren, Arland J. "Salvation: Its Forms and Dynamics in the New Testament." *Dialog* 45, no. 3 (Fall 2006): 215-22.

Lash, Nicholas. "Performing the Scriptures." In *Theology on the Way to Emmaus*, pp. 37-46. London: SCM Press, 1986.

Stendahl, Krister. "Biblical Theology, Contemporary." In *IDB*, 1:418-32.

Treier, Daniel J. *Introducing Theological Interpretation of Scripture: Recovering a Christian Practice.* Grand Rapids: Baker, 2008.

van der Watt, Jan G., ed. *Salvation in the New Testament: Perspectives on Soteriology.* Supplements to Novum Testamentum. Edited by M. M. Mitchell and D. P. Moessner. Boston: Brill, 2005.

Via, Dan O. *What Is New Testament Theology?* Minneapolis: Fortress, 2002.

---

[39]Green, "Scripture and Theology," p. 36.

[40]Minear, *Images of the Church*, p. 17. Like Minear, Green calls for a "full-blown conversion" (*Seized by Truth*, p. 43).

2

INHERITANCE IN
THE NEW COVENANT

PERCY BYSSHE SHELLEY, ENGLISH POET and skeptic, reflecting
on the idea of Jesus Christ as God's Son and heir, commented ironically
that "the reversion of an estate with an immortal incumbent would be
worth little."[1] No doubt he would have found it even more amusing that
believers will share Jesus' inheritance with him. Shelley's observation reminds us of the limits of a metaphor.

The image of inheritance is used in both Old and New Testaments to
express the blessings received by those who share in a covenant relationship with God. In fact, our terms *Old Testament* and *New Testament* are
derived from New Testament writers' images of the old and new covenants.
These writers interact very specifically with Old Testament passages and
themes in light of the coming of Christ. Some scholars have argued that
covenant is the central concept of the theology of the Old Testament.[2]
Whether central or not, the image of covenant creates significant continuity between the understandings of salvation in Old and New Testaments.[3]

---

[1]Percy Bysshe Shelley, "On the Devil and Devils," in *Shelley's Prose, or, The Trumpet of a Prophecy*,
ed. David Lee Clark (Albuquerque: University of New Mexico Press, 1954), p. 267.
[2]See Walther Eichrodt, *Theology of the Old Testament*, Old Testament Library (Philadelphia:
Westminster Press, 1961). Most scholars would say that covenant is not broad enough to provide a conceptual unity to the entire Old Testament, although it is an important theme. For a
survey of scholarship on covenant, see Ernest W. Nicholson, *God and His People: Covenant and
Theology in the Old Testament* (Oxford: Clarendon, 1986).
[3]Walter Brueggemann traces the theme of covenant through Old and New Testaments in *The
Bible Makes Sense*, rev. ed. (Cincinnati: St. Anthony Messenger Press, 2003). My discussion
of the New Covenant will not engage with covenant theology per se or address the disputes

It also offers a perspective on salvation that could speak powerfully to our own times.

COVENANTS IN THE OLD TESTAMENT

The word translated as "covenant" is *bĕrît* in Hebrew. *Bĕrît* occurs 286 times in the Old Testament. It means a formal pact or agreement between two or more parties. A *bĕrît* can be made between two individuals, such as Laban and Jacob (Gen 31:44) or David and Jonathan (1 Sam 18:3). The term is also used to describe the alliance established by marriage (Mal 2:14). More broadly, it can refer to a treaty or alliance between nations, such as Judah and Aram (1 Kings 15:19). It can even function as a constitution that sets the terms between a king and his subjects (2 Kings 11:17).[4] The concept of covenant seems to have arisen as an extension of kinship, which was the structure of society among ancient peoples. Covenants developed as a formalized way of uniting different clans or incorporating outsiders into existing kinship groups.[5]

In many ways a covenant is similar to a contract. It is an agreement between two parties to enter into a relationship that will be governed by the benefits and obligations stipulated in the agreement. There are usually penalties for breaking the agreement. However, God's covenants are in some ways unlike a typical contract. For example, while contracts are usually between equal parties who come together for mutual benefit, God takes the initiative to establish covenants for the benefit of human beings. Because of the inequality of the parties involved, the recipients of God's covenants cannot negotiate terms; they can choose only to be faithful or unfaithful to them. While contracts are usually for a limited time, God's covenants are usually open-ended. Elmer Martens argues that a contract is "thing-oriented," is established in order to gain benefits, and depends on performance, while a covenant is "person-oriented," is established out of a desire for relationship, and depends on loyalty.[6]

---

between Reformed theology and dispensationalism; it will simply examine covenant as an image of salvation.

[4]See "בְּרִית," in *BDB*, pp. 136-37.

[5]Steven L. McKenzie, *Covenant*, Understanding Biblical Themes (St. Louis, Mo.: Chalice, 2000), pp. 11-12.

[6]Elmer A. Martens, *God's Design: A Focus on Old Testament Theology*, 3rd ed. (N. Richland Hills, Tex.: BIBAL Press, 1998), p. 82.

God's covenants, especially the Mosaic covenant, resemble a suzerain/ vassal covenant—a common agreement in the Ancient Near East between an overlord and a vassal state. In these agreements, the more powerful party would initiate a pact with a lesser party, promising the vassal protection and other benefits in exchange for the vassal's allegiance and obedience. Scholars have observed that the book of Deuteronomy takes the form of such a covenant. The only element missing from the form in Deuteronomy is the traditional call upon the gods to witness and enforce the agreement. The God of Israel needs no other gods to ratify his covenants. The heavens and the earth are witnesses to the covenant, but they will not enforce it (Deut 4:25-26).

All covenants have a basic stipulation that governs the specific obligations of the agreement.[7] Ancient suzerain/vassal covenants would often express this stipulation in terms of love. The vassal was required to love the overlord rather than other lords and to express this love as "loyalty, service, and obedience."[8] The demand for exclusive allegiance, expressed in terms of love, also occurs in the Shema: "Hear, O Israel: The LORD is our God, the LORD alone. You shall love the LORD your God with all your heart, and with all your soul, and with all your might" (Deut 6:4-5). The love of God mentioned here is "a love defined by and pledged in the covenant—a covenantal love."[9] This language of love and loyalty reveals the roots of covenant in the kinship structure of ancient Semitic society. Covenant is "an extension of familial relationship."[10]

At the heart of God's covenants is the relationship expressed by what scholars have called the covenant formula: "I will be your God, and you will be my people" (Gen 17:7-8; Ex 6:7; Jer 31:33). According to Walter Brueggemann, this promise declares "an intimate connection to and solidarity with Israel that is to be expressed as presence."[11] While the specifics of individual covenants may differ, Martens sees a fourfold pattern to God's covenant promises: "This plan is one to bring deliverance, to sum-

---

[7]Ibid., p. 77.

[8]William L. Moran, "The Ancient Near Eastern Background of the Love of God in Deuteronomy," *Catholic Biblical Quarterly* 25 (1963): 82.

[9]Ibid., p. 78.

[10]Scott Hahn, "Covenant in the Old and New Testaments: Some Current Research (1994-2004)," *Currents in Biblical Research* 3, no. 2 (2005): 265.

[11]Walter Brueggemann, *Theology of the Old Testament: Testimony, Dispute, Advocacy* (Minneapolis: Fortress, 1997), p. 171.

mon a people who will be peculiarly his own, to offer himself for them to know and to give to them land in fulfillment of his promise." Thus God's purposes in establishing his covenants can be summed up as "deliverance, community, knowledge of God, and abundant life."[12]

For God's covenant partners, love and obedience go hand in hand:

> Yahweh is the one who loves Israel, who loves what was not-yet-Israel, and who by the full commitment of Yahweh's self causes Israel to be. . . . The initiatory act of love, rescue, and designation is made by a sovereign who in this act of love does not cease to be sovereign. Therefore this relationship, marked by awe and gratitude for its inexplicable generosity, brings with it the expectations and requirements of the sovereign who initiates it. . . . [Israel's life with Yahweh] entails a full relationship of self-giving and self-regarding in which embrace of commandment (in obedience) and embrace of love (in trust) are of a piece.[13]

God's powerful and creative love both expects and makes possible a response of love from his covenant partners. On God's part, covenant faithfulness entails protection, provision and rescue. On Israel's part, it entails the development of "covenant virtues" such as love, obedience, faithfulness and exclusive worship of God.[14]

Grasping this concept of covenant is critical for understanding the role of law in the Old Testament. The law is given to Israel as an expression of the covenant relationship between Israel and God. It is founded on God's grace, shown in his deliverance of Israel from Egypt: "I am the LORD your God, who brought you out of the land of Egypt, out of the house of slavery; you shall have no other gods before me" (Ex 20:2). The law is not an abstract legal code or a set of requirements for gaining God's favor. It has meaning only in the context of Israel's covenant relationship with God. It forms and informs Israel as God's people in their relationship with God, one another and other nations.

The concept of covenant has significant implications for salvation. First, it shows that God desires authentic relationships with human beings. God is a covenant maker and covenant keeper.[15] God seeks out cov-

---

[12]Martens, *God's Design*, p. ix.
[13]Brueggemann, *Theology of the Old Testament*, pp. 414-15, 417, 419.
[14]McKenzie, *Covenant*, p. 140.
[15]Brueggemann, *Bible Makes Sense*, p. 54.

enant partners, makes himself available to them, and allows himself to be affected by them, just as they are affected by him.[16] When Israel turns away from God, the prophets express God's reaction in the language of personal betrayal: "The LORD said to me again, 'Go, love a woman who has a lover and is an adulteress, just as the LORD loves the people of Israel, though they turn to other gods and love raisin cakes'" (Hos 3:1).

Second, although based on God's gracious initiative, God's covenants require human response in order to be viable. "Covenant is not only imposed, but also accepted. It calls with both the stern voice of duty and the tender accents of the lover, with both stick (curse, death) and carrot (blessing, life) in hand."[17] Once accepted, the covenant must be faithfully kept. Covenant is a reciprocal relationship, even though the responsibilities of the two parties are not identical.[18] The obligations of the covenant do not establish the relationship but guide how it is lived out.

Third, because God's covenants are almost always corporate, they emphasize the importance of group solidarity. Even God's covenant with Abraham applies to Abraham's descendants as well. This corporate solidarity was the norm in both Old and New Testament cultures. Unlike modern Western cultures, which view people primarily as individuals, these cultures viewed people primarily as members of a family or tribe and only secondarily as individuals. Persons were deeply embedded in their social contexts, and they believed that true personhood consisted of being dependent on others, especially those in authority. Unlike moderns who assume that the true self lies in the "inner depths" of an individual, they assumed that the true self was revealed in external characteristics and actions.[19] Each person was regarded as a representative of the groups to which he or she belonged. The actions of each person reflected on the group, whose interests and honor took priority over those of the individual. Corporate identity superseded individual identity. Furthermore, the leader of a group, representing the group, could take action that would bind all of

---

[16]Ibid., p. 410.

[17]Jon D. Levenson, *Sinai and Zion: An Entry into the Jewish Bible* (Minneapolis: Winston, 1985), p. 81. Levenson is discussing the covenant renewal ceremony.

[18]Hahn, "Covenant," p. 285.

[19]Robert A. Di Vito, "Old Testament Anthropology and the Construction of Personal Identity," *Catholic Biblical Quarterly* 61 (1999): 221, 224-25, 233.

its members.[20] Such corporate solidarity is evident in the sin and judgment of Achan (Josh 7:1-26), as well as in the household conversions and baptisms in the book of Acts (Acts 10:24-48; 16:15, 34).

Finally, because a covenant is a relationship, the issue of loyalty is more basic than the specific stipulations. For this reason, it can be difficult to tell when the covenant has been irretrievably broken.[21] God frequently goes beyond his covenant obligations in order to reestablish the relationship with his covenant partners. Through Jeremiah, God proclaims to Israel, "I have loved you with an everlasting love; therefore I have continued my faithfulness to you" (Jer 31:3). Even as Israel goes into exile for their disobedience, God promises to restore them to the land (Jer 32:26-44). He even promises them a new covenant that will empower them to be more faithful to him.

COVENANTS IN THE NEW TESTAMENT

In the New Testament, covenant is expressed by the term *diathēkē*, which has much the same meaning as *bĕrît*. All instances of *diathēkē* in the New Testament refer to one of God's covenants with human beings mentioned in the Old Testament. Because *diathēkē* (unlike *bĕrît*) can also mean a will or testament, New Testament authors sometimes engage in wordplay that involves both senses.[22] For example, the writer of Hebrews interprets the new covenant as Jesus' last will and testament (Heb 9:16-17). This wordplay is facilitated by the language of inheritance, which is common to both concepts. Both testaments and covenants require a death—the death of the testator in one case, and the death of the covenant sacrifice in the

---

[20]Bruce J. Malina, *The New Testament World: Insights from Cultural Anthropology*, rev. ed. (Louisville: Westminster John Knox, 1993), pp. 45-47, 66-67. See also David deSilva, *Honor, Patronage, Kinship & Purity: Unlocking New Testament Culture* (Downers Grove, Ill.: InterVarsity Press, 2000), p. 158.

[21]Martens, *God's Design*, p. 81.

[22]See "διαθήκη," in *BAGD*, p. 183. The authors note that *diathēkē* is an appropriate translation of *bĕrît* in that God's agreements are not contracts between equals but expressions of the initiator's will, as would be the case in a testament. Although *bĕrît* is not used for a will, the idea of inheritance is certainly present in the Old Testament. For example, God gives the land to Israel as an inheritance (Deut 32:9). Numerous laws spell out how the inheritance of the various tribes must be handled. The Levites receive the priesthood as their inheritance (Josh 18:7) and the tithe as their portion (Num 18:24). God himself chooses the people as his inheritance (Ps 33:12; cf. Ex 34:9). The Psalmist often declares that God is his portion (Ps 16:5; 73:26; 119:57).

other. The sense of *diathēkē* as testament is the basis of the division of the Christian Bible into Old Testament and New Testament—that is, the bodies of writing associated with the old covenant and the new covenant.

Although the word for covenant occurs less frequently in the New Testament than in the Old, the concept is everywhere in the background, shaping the writers' understanding of God's relationship with believers. It is not defined because it is assumed.[23] It is the framework for the ideas of justification and election (see chaps. 9 and 10).[24] It comes to the fore in the language of inheritance, in the theme of promise and fulfillment, and in the covenant formula, "I will be their God, and they shall be my people" (2 Cor 6:16; Heb 8:10; cf. Rev 21:3, 7). Because of the foundational place of covenant in the thinking of the New Testament writers, it will be important to keep this idea in mind as we examine other images of salvation.[25]

Several Old Testament covenants are important for understanding salvation in the New Testament: God's covenant with Abraham (Gen 17:1-22), God's covenant with Moses and Israel (Ex 34:27), God's covenant with David (2 Sam 7:8-16; 23:5), and the new covenant prophesied by Jeremiah (Jer 31:31-34). New Testament writers use all of these to explain the significance of what God has done in Jesus. The Davidic covenant plays an important role in defining the identity of Jesus, the Messianic Son of David. The Mosaic covenant forms the backdrop for Jesus' ministry in the Gospels and is discussed extensively in Hebrews. The Abrahamic covenant is important for Paul, because it enables him to resolve the central theological problem of his ministry—the issue of the relationship of Jews and Gentiles in the plan of God.

The new covenant prophesied by Jeremiah is especially significant:

> The days are surely coming, says the LORD, when I will make a new covenant with the house of Israel and the house of Judah. It will not be like the covenant that I made with their ancestors when I took them by the hand to

---

[23]John Bright, *The Authority of the Old Testament* (Grand Rapids: Baker, 1967), pp. 204-5.

[24]On justification and righteousness as covenant terms, see Stanley E. Porter, "The Concept of Covenant in Paul," in *The Concept of the Covenant in the Second Temple Period*, ed. Stanley E. Porter and Jacqueline C. R. de Roo (Leiden: Brill, 2003), pp. 282-83.

[25]Besides the Jewish concept of covenant, the New Testament writers could draw on the similar Greco-Roman concept of patron/client relations to express the reciprocal relationship of blessing and obligation involved in salvation. See chapters 3 and 4 of deSilva's *Honor, Patronage, Kinship and Purity.*

bring them out of the land of Egypt—a covenant that they broke, though I was their husband, says the LORD. But this is the covenant that I will make with the house of Israel after those days, says the LORD: I will put my law within them, and I will write it on their hearts; and I will be their God, and they shall be my people. No longer shall they teach one another, or say to each other, "Know the LORD," for they shall all know me, from the least of them to the greatest, says the LORD; for I will forgive their iniquity, and remember their sin no more. (Jer 31:31-34)

The new covenant would be the solution to the covenant-breaking of God's people. God would forgive their sins and engage with them more intimately, embedding his expectations in their hearts instead of in an external code. God's people would not have to be taught to know him, because that knowledge would be built into them, so to speak. As transformed people, they would be able, at last, to be God's faithful covenant partners.

A similar passage in Ezekiel looks forward to the renewal of covenant after exile:

I will sprinkle clean water upon you, and you shall be clean from all your uncleannesses, and from all your idols I will cleanse you. A new heart I will give you, and a new spirit I will put within you; and I will remove from your body the heart of stone and give you a heart of flesh. I will put my spirit within you, and make you follow my statutes and be careful to observe my ordinances. Then you shall live in the land that I gave to your ancestors; and you shall be my people, and I will be your God. (Ezek 36:25-28)

Like Jeremiah, Ezekiel envisions a time when God will transform the hearts of his people, enabling them to keep God's commands and enjoy the blessings of the covenant. A new spirit within them will empower this transformation. Both Jeremiah and Ezekiel seem to anticipate a new era in which God's people will be able to keep God's covenant more faithfully because of their more internal motivation and their more immediate access to God. In this respect, the new covenant could be regarded as a *renewed* covenant rather than an entirely new one.[26]

The New Testament presents the new covenant in terms of both continuity and contrast. The idea of covenant itself is in continuity with the Old

---

[26]Werner E. Lemke, "Jeremiah 31:31-34," *Interpretation* 37 (1983): 186.

Testament. Furthermore, the new covenant is explicitly connected to the prophecy in Jeremiah 31, as well as to the Abrahamic covenant, with its character of promise. The contrast emerges when the new covenant is compared with the Mosaic covenant, which is viewed as coming to an end.[27] Both Paul and the author of Hebrews refer to the Mosaic covenant and the new covenant as *two* covenants, suggesting that the latter is not simply the renewal of the former.[28] The "newness" of the new covenant consists in the permanent forgiveness of sins; the writing of God's law on the people's hearts; and the universal, more intimate knowledge of God. The New Testament writers assert that sins have been forgiven in Christ, and the other two promises have been fulfilled in the outpouring of the Holy Spirit.

The New Testament writers believe that Jesus has established the new covenant. The Synoptic Gospels show Jesus at the Last Supper claiming this directly: "This is my blood of the covenant, which is poured out for many" (Mk 14:24). The parallel account in Matthew 26:28 makes the allusion clearer by adding "for the forgiveness of sins." Luke and Paul make it explicit: "This cup that is poured out for you is the new covenant in my blood" (Lk 22:20; cf. 1 Cor 11:25).

Jesus sees his death as a sacrifice that will put into effect a new relationship between God and human beings. His blood will purify the people of God by granting them forgiveness of sins and will "consecrate them to their new relationship with God."[29] All of the eschatological blessings that God had promised to his people will be mediated by Christ.[30] By reinterpreting the Passover celebration, Jesus implies that the covenant he will inaugurate will resemble but surpass the covenant of Sinai. "That is, just as the Passover meal commemorated deliverance from bondage and the establishing of Israel as a kingdom which was covenantally related to Yah-

---

[27]I. Howard Marshall, "Some Observations on the Covenant in the New Testament," in *Jesus the Saviour: Studies in New Testament Theology* (Downers Grove, Ill.: InterVarsity Press, 1990), p. 282, 285. See also William J. Dumbrell, *Covenant and Creation: A Theology of Old Testament Covenants* (Nashville: Nelson, 1984), p. 199.

[28]Susanne Lehne, *The New Covenant in Hebrews*, Journal for the Study of the New Testament Supplement Series, ed. David Hill (Sheffield, U.K.: JSOT Press, 1990), pp. 76-77.

[29]Leon Morris, *The Apostolic Preaching of the Cross*, 3rd ed. (Grand Rapids: Eerdmans, 1965), p. 105.

[30]Roy A. Harrisville, *The Concept of Newness in the New Testament* (Minneapolis: Augsburg, 1950), p. 47.

weh, so the words and actions of Jesus at the Last Supper portray deliverance from bondage and the establishing of a kingdom covenantally related to God."[31]

Old Testament covenants were often accompanied by a blood sacrifice and celebrated by a common meal (Ex 24:3-11). This combination explains why Jesus connects his body and blood to the bread and the cup to be consumed by his followers. When his followers observe this meal in the future, they will be celebrating—and committing themselves to—the new covenant that Jesus' death has brought about. Their repeated observance of the Lord's Supper will help God's people remember their responsibilities under the new covenant, just as the festivals and the regular reading of the law did under the old (see 1 Cor 11:25). The illness and death of some believers in Corinth suggest that the new covenant may contain curses for covenant breaking, as did the old.[32]

Jesus is the fulfillment of all the promises of God under the old covenant (2 Cor 1:20). He inaugurates God's kingdom on earth. In fact, it might be said that the kingdom of God is the form that the new covenant takes.[33] Jesus also forgives sins, as the new covenant promised (Mk 2:5-11). His resurrection marks the beginning of the age of fulfillment (Acts 13:32-33). He pours out the Holy Spirit upon his disciples at Pentecost, also in fulfillment of God's promise (Joel 2:28-32; Acts 2:16-21). His disciples declare that forgiveness of sins and the Holy Spirit are now available to everyone who responds to the gospel invitation (Acts 2:38-39).

Paul identifies himself as a minister of the new covenant (*kainē diathēkē*): "Our competence is from God, who has made us competent to be ministers of a new covenant, not of letter but of spirit; for the letter kills, but the Spirit gives life" (2 Cor 3:5-6). He contrasts this new covenant with the old covenant (*palaia diathēkē*)—that is, the Mosaic covenant: "Indeed, to this very day, when [the Jews] hear the reading of the old covenant, that same veil is still there, since only in Christ is it set aside. Indeed, to this very day whenever Moses is read, a veil lies over their minds; but when one turns to the Lord, the veil is removed" (2 Cor 3:14-16). For

---

[31]John J. Hughes, "Hebrews IX 15ff. and Galatians III 15ff.: A Study in Covenant Practice and Procedure," *Novum Testamentum* 21, no. 1 (January 1979): 54.

[32]J. Guhrt, "Covenant, Guarantee, Mediator," in *NIDNTT* 1:369-70.

[33]Ibid., 1:369. He argues that the "underlying thought" of covenant has been "taken over" in the New Testament by the concept of the kingdom of God.

Paul, Jesus is the key to understanding both old and new covenants, because he is promised in the old and present in the new. He is the mediator of the new covenant, as Moses was of the old (Gal 3:19; 1 Tim 2:5). Because of Christ, Gentiles can share in the covenant (Eph 2:12; 3:6).

The inheritance of believers under the new covenant is variously described as God's kingdom (Mt 25:34; 1 Cor 15:50; Jas 2:5); salvation (Heb 1:14); and eternal life (Mt 19:29; Mk 10:17; Tit 1:2; 1 Jn 2:25). The land promised to God's people under the old covenant is universalized to include the whole world.[34] Jesus declares that the meek will inherit the earth (gē, which can be translated "earth" or "land"; Mt 5:5). Similarly, Paul asserts that Abraham was promised the world (kosmos; Rom 4:13). Given that the kingdom of God will extend throughout creation, believers' inheritance in the kingdom has a similar effect of universalizing the land promise.

In the patriarchal culture of the first century, it is notable that both women and slaves are specifically said to share in the inheritance (Col 3:24; 1 Pet 3:7). In the latter passage, Peter uses women's status as heirs to counsel their husbands to be considerate toward them. Paul declares that all of God's people now have inheritance rights: "There is no longer Jew or Greek, there is no longer slave or free, there is no longer male and female; for all of you are one in Christ Jesus. And if you belong to Christ, then you are Abraham's offspring, heirs according to the promise" (Gal 3:28-29). The notion of being an heir embodies the eschatological tension between "already" and "not yet": someone who becomes an heir already has a new status in the present but does not yet possess the inheritance.[35] The experience of women and slaves since the first century has borne out this tension.

Luke and Paul emphasize the coming of the Holy Spirit as the fulfillment of the promise of God (Lk 24:49; Acts 1:4; 2:33). The Spirit seals believers as belonging to God (Eph 1:13), fulfilling the new covenant promise to write God's law on his people's hearts. The indwelling Spirit enables God's people to know God intimately as "Abba" and empowers believers to live the obedient lives the law commanded but could not pro-

---

[34]Thomas Edward McComiskey, *The Covenants of Promise* (Grand Rapids: Baker, 1985), pp. 199-209.

[35]Victor Paul Furnish, *Theology and Ethics in Paul* (Nashville: Abingdon, 1968), pp. 127-28. See chapter three for a fuller discussion of "already" and "not yet."

duce (Rom 8:3-4, 14-16). "The whole of life under the new covenant is now lived in and by the Spirit, including worship, one's relationship to God, and everyday life itself. . . . The gift of the Spirit [is] the new covenant *replacement* of Torah and the new covenant *fulfillment* of Torah's righteous requirement."[36] But believers' experience of the Spirit now is just the "downpayment" (*arrabōn*) on the full inheritance to come (Eph 1:14). The presence and activity of the Spirit create the "newness" of the new covenant; the Spirit both anticipates the consummation and propels God's people toward that goal.[37]

COVENANTS IN PAUL

Although the word *diathēkē* is rare in Paul's writings, the concept of covenant is important in his thinking. When Paul does use the word *diathēkē*, scholars debate whether he intends it to mean covenant or testament. The answer has implications for such theological issues as covenant theology, law and gospel, faith and works, and the relationship between Israel and the church.[38] These debates are too technical for our discussion, although some of the issues will be clarified as we examine Paul's arguments. For our purposes, the idea of covenant is more important than the term *diathēkē*. As apostle to the Gentiles, Paul takes up the topic of covenant in order to explain how his gospel can embrace both Jews and Gentiles.

The idea of covenant receives an extended treatment in Galatians and Romans. In Galatians 3–4, Paul refers to it in order to refute the Judaizers, who are demanding that Gentile Christians observe the Jewish law in order to be complete. Both here and in Romans, Paul is doing a delicate balancing act, trying to affirm the goodness and divine origin of the Mosaic covenant while asserting that Gentile Christians should not be bound by it. He manages this by arguing that the new covenant, which is open to Gentiles as well as Jews, is the fulfillment of the Abrahamic covenant, which predates the covenant of Sinai. He is drawing on the culture's preference for antiquity as having greater authority. While Paul does not mention the new covenant specifically, his reference to the promise of the Holy

---

[36]Gordon D. Fee, *Paul, the Spirit, and the People of God* (Peabody, Mass.: Hendrickson, 1996), pp. 98, 101.

[37]Harrisville, *Newness in the New Testament*, pp. 60-61.

[38]For an overview of the discussion, see Hahn, "Covenant," pp. 263-92.

Spirit (Gal 3:14) suggests that he has it in mind.

Paul contrasts God's covenants with Abraham and Israel, noting that the first was expressed as promise and the second was expressed as law. The Abrahamic covenant promised blessing to Abraham's "seed" (offspring; Gal 3:16), but also, through Abraham, to the nations (Gal 3:8). Because this covenant was a promise that must be accepted by faith, those who have faith are the true descendants of Abraham (Gal 3:6-7). Thus believing Gentiles, like believing Jews, are among Abraham's offspring. Through their disobedience, the heirs of the old covenant brought the covenant curses on themselves (Gal 3:10). But Christ intervened, "becoming a curse for us" (Gal 3:13). He suffered as a covenant breaker in solidarity with unfaithful Israelites and godless Gentiles, so that both might receive the blessing of the promised Spirit.[39] The Abrahamic covenant, having been ratified, cannot be changed or annulled (Gal 3:15).[40] It is unaffected by the stipulations of the law, which came later (Gal 3:17).

With the covenant of promise in place, the only remaining question is the identity of the heir(s). Here Paul argues that the promise was made not to Abraham's "seeds" (that is, multiple descendants) but only to a single "seed," who is Christ (Gal 3:16). Thus Jesus Christ, not Israel, is the heir to the promise. The purpose of the law was to keep order until the heir should arrive (Gal 3:23-25). Now that the heir has come, anyone who is united with him will share in the inheritance: "And if you belong to Christ, then you are Abraham's offspring, heirs according to the promise" (Gal 3:29).

In Galatians 4, Paul uses the language of inheritance to urge the Galatians not to turn back to the Mosaic law, a disciplinarian who is no longer needed now that Christ has come. When they were minors (before Christ), they were essentially the same as slaves under the command of their guard-

---

[39]James D. G. Dunn, *Theology of Paul the Apostle* (Grand Rapids: Eerdmans, 1998), p. 227.

[40]John J. Hughes, in an extensive investigation of *diathēkē* in biblical and extrabiblical Greek, concludes that it should be translated "covenant" in Galatians 3:15ff and Hebrews 9:15ff. He notes, for example, that wills of the time could indeed be changed, even after they were ratified, while covenants could not ("Hebrews ix 15ff," pp. 69-70). However, Paul may be engaging in wordplay here, drawing upon the example of human wills to illuminate God's covenants. See James D. G. Dunn, "Did Paul Have a Covenant Theology?" in *The Concept of the Covenant in the Second Temple Period*, ed. Stanley E. Porter and Jacqueline C. R. de Roo (Leiden: Brill, 2003), p. 291. The use of *diathēkē* in Hebrews 9:16-17 seems to be an example of such wordplay.

ians, including the law. But now that Christ has come, they have been adopted by God as heirs and no longer need those guardians (Gal 4:1-7).

In the rest of chapter 4, Paul allegorizes the story of Hagar and Sarah to contrast the old and new covenants. In a daring rhetorical strategy, Paul associates his opponents with Hagar rather than with Sarah, placing them outside the covenant that they claim to be defending. Hagar is the slave woman, representing the old covenant and Mount Sinai. Sarah is the free woman, representing the new covenant and the heavenly Jerusalem. Hagar's child was born according to the flesh, while Sarah's child was born according to the promise. Hagar also represents "the present Jerusalem" or the nation of Israel, who are still in slavery to the law. Sarah, not Hagar, is the mother of Christians, who are children of the promise. Believers in Christ, not the biological descendants of Abraham, will receive the inheritance. Therefore they should stand firm in their freedom and not allow themselves to be enslaved again to the law (Gal 4:21–5:1).

Thus in Galatians, Paul argues that believers in Christ are the true heirs of God's covenant promises, because they are co-heirs with Christ, the promised seed of Abraham. The new covenant, based on God's covenant with Abraham, is sharply distinguished from the Mosaic covenant, which is portrayed in negative terms. For Paul, then, the new covenant is not a renewal of the Mosaic covenant but the fulfillment of all of God's promises to Abraham.

In Romans, although he uses Abraham in a similar way, Paul depicts the relationship between old and new covenants differently because of his different purpose. Paul's concern in Romans is to set out his gospel as apostle to the Gentiles—in other words, to legitimize the Gentile mission. To do this, he must explain how God can be faithful to his covenant with Israel and at the same time admit Gentiles to the people of God without requiring them to keep the law. Some of his arguments are similar to those in Galatians, although they give a greater emphasis to unity and continuity. Instead of picturing a stark contrast between old and new covenants, Paul puts the accent on inclusiveness. Believing Jews and Gentiles have a common source in Abraham, their spiritual ancestor. In Christ, they now form a single organism, rooted in God's Old Testament people and joined together by faith (Rom 11:16-24).

Again Paul goes behind the Mosaic covenant to ground the Gentile mission in the covenant with Abraham. In Romans 4, he argues that the promise of the Abrahamic covenant was not based on law but on faith. Therefore those of faith, whether Jew or Gentile, must be the heirs (Rom 4:13-14). After all, God promised that Abraham would be the father of many nations, not just one (Rom 4:16-17). Just as Abraham's faith in God qualified him to participate in the covenant, the faith of Christians in that same God ("[we] who believe in him who raised Jesus our Lord from the dead") qualifies them to participate, as well (Rom 4:23-24).

Paul gives the promises to Abraham a new covenant reinterpretation, however. In Genesis 12:1-3, Abraham is promised descendents, land and blessing. The promise of many descendants, as we have seen, is broadened and spiritualized to include all those who share Abraham's faith in the God who promised. The promise of land is broadened to include the whole world (Rom 4:13). The promise of blessing is reinterpreted as forgiveness of sins: "So also David speaks of the blessedness of those to whom God reckons righteousness apart from works: 'Blessed are those whose iniquities are forgiven, and whose sins are covered; blessed is the one against whom the Lord will not reckon sin'" (Rom 4:6-8).

Thus Paul insists in both Galatians and Romans that the new covenant is superior to the old (Mosaic) covenant. It is not a new invention but the fulfillment of God's promises to Abraham. Because the inheritance has always been based on God's promise, those who trust in God's promise are the true heirs. Inheritance under the new covenant therefore belongs to both Jews and Gentiles who have faith in Christ, who brings the fulfillment of God's promises.

COVENANTS IN HEBREWS

The language of covenant, promise and inheritance saturates the book of Hebrews. The author has an urgent need to distinguish between old and new covenants because his audience is thinking of returning to the old one. His presentation is less nuanced than Paul's. He is attempting rhetorically to burn the bridges to the old covenant so that his audience will no longer be tempted to cross them. To do this, he sets forth two main arguments. First, the new covenant—in which the audience participates— is superior to the old: "Jesus has now obtained a more excellent ministry, and to that degree he is the mediator of a better covenant, which has been enacted through better promises" (Heb 8:6). Second, the audience cannot return to the old covenant even if they want to, because the old covenant is no longer in force: "In speaking of 'a new covenant,' he has made the first one obsolete. And what is obsolete and growing old will soon disappear" (Heb 8:13).

The author strongly contrasts the new covenant and the Mosaic covenant. He quotes Jeremiah's new covenant prophecy twice (Heb 8:8-12; 10:16-17). He argues that the existence of the new covenant prophecy proves that God "finds fault" with the old covenant—or, more specifically, with his faithless covenant partners (Heb 8:8). The author never says that the old covenant, with its legal stipulations for dealing with sin, did not work. But he argues that it was partial and temporary, merely a type of the full redemption to come: "Since the law has only a shadow of the good things to come and not the true form of these realities, it can never, by the same sacrifices that are continually offered year after year, make perfect those who approach" (Heb 10:1). Ironically, because they had to be repeated over and over, the sacrifices reminded the worshipers that they were still bound to sin (Heb 10:3).

The author identifies two problems with the old covenant: it dealt only with external impurity, and it was just a temporary solution. The new covenant is superior on both counts. First, the blood of Christ has power to cleanse the conscience: "For if the blood of goats and bulls, with the sprinkling of the ashes of a heifer, sanctifies those who have been defiled so that their flesh is purified, how much more will the blood of Christ, who through the eternal Spirit offered himself without blemish to God, purify our conscience from dead works to worship the living God!" (Heb 9:13-14). Thus the new covenant, unlike the old, can transform the worshiper. Second, the sacrifice of Christ deals with sin permanently: "[Christ] has appeared once for all at the end of the age to remove sin by the sacrifice of himself. . . . For by a single offering he has perfected for all time those who are sanctified" (Heb 9:26; 10:14). Jesus has obtained "eternal redemption" (Heb 9:12).

Both covenants are inaugurated with a blood sacrifice, and both depend upon the work of the high priest. The superiority of the new covenant is due to the superiority of Jesus, who is both the sacrifice and the high priest. Jesus is the mediator (*mesitēs*) or guarantor (*engyos*) of the new covenant (Heb 7:22; 9:15). Jesus' sinlessness makes him both the perfect high priest and the perfect sacrifice (Heb 7:26-28; 9:14). His death redeemed believers from their sins under the old covenant and inaugurated the new (Heb 9:15). He offered the blood of his sacrifice (his own blood) in the heavenly sanctuary itself, not in an earthly temple (Heb 9:11-12, 24-26). His everlasting life means that he can intercede for believers forever, providing them eternal redemption (Heb 7:23-25). The risen and ascended Lord remains in the presence of God, opening the way for believers to follow (Heb 6:19-20).

The author's use of cultic language—drawn not from Jeremiah 31 but from other parts of the Old Testament—allows him to claim for the new covenant both continuity and superiority: "(1) By creatively reinterpreting the category of *covenant* from a cultic perspective the author is able to depict the Christ event in *continuity* with and as the perfect fulfillment of the cultic heritage of Israel. (2) By stressing the elements of *newness* and drawing a *contrast* to the former system, he succeeds in presenting Christ as the permanent, definitive, *superior* replacement of that same heritage."[41]

Like Paul, the author connects Christians with the Abrahamic covenant rather than the Mosaic covenant. God promised to bless Abraham and give him many descendants (Heb 6:12-14). By implication, Christians are "heirs of the promise" (Heb 6:17). The author is well aware that land was also part of God's promise to Abraham (Heb 11:8-9), but he translates the promise of entering the land into the promise of entering God's rest. He derives this idea from his reading of Psalm 95, in which God says of the exodus generation, "In my anger I swore, 'They will not enter my rest'" (Heb 3:11; quoting Ps 95:11). Because this promise of rest has never been fulfilled, the author declares, "So then, a sabbath rest still remains for the people of God" (Heb 4:9). This rest is the believer's eschatological inheritance.

Receiving the promised inheritance depends partly upon the believers' perseverance.[42] The author gives numerous examples of heroes of the faith who persevered because they believed in God's promise, even if they did not receive the promise in their lifetimes (Heb 6:15; 11). He exhorts his audience to show the same perseverance, because "he who

---

[41]Lehne, *New Covenant in Hebrews*, pp. 15, 119.
[42]See chapter thirteen for a full discussion of the theme of perseverance in Hebrews.

has promised is faithful" (Heb 10:23, cf. Heb 6:12; 10:36). Esau serves as a negative example of someone who sought the inheritance too late (Heb 12:17). The warning passages in chapters 6 and 10 underscore the danger of turning back.

The new covenant is the final covenant. It is an eternal covenant that provides an eternal inheritance (Heb 9:15; 13:20). The finality of the new covenant means that anyone who violates it by persisting in sin will have no further recourse. There is no other redemption: "Anyone who has violated the law of Moses dies without mercy 'on the testimony of two or three witnesses.' How much worse punishment do you think will be deserved by those who have spurned the Son of God, profaned the blood of the covenant by which they were sanctified, and outraged the Spirit of grace? For we know the one who said, 'Vengeance is mine, I will repay.' And again, 'The Lord will judge his people.' It is a fearful thing to fall into the hands of the living God" (Heb 10:29-31). Anyone who turns away from this covenant will have nothing left.

CONCLUSION

The image of the new covenant tells is a great deal about how the New Testament writers understand salvation. Salvation is a reciprocal relationship with God that involves trust and commitment. It comes as both gift and demand. Although it originates in God's grace and depends upon God's power, it requires a response—and responsibility—from human beings. "In both God's mercy and expectations, it means we are being taken with ultimate seriousness."[43] The heart of the covenant is love. This love is expressed as protection and provision on the part of God and obedience on the part of human beings. As God's covenant partners, believers owe God exclusive loyalty. Although God has demonstrated that his grace goes far beyond what anyone could expect, the new covenant is not a no-fault agreement. For the people of the covenant, faithfulness is not optional.

The new covenant is clearly a corporate image. God has called into existence a *people* to whom he is committed. While people can join the covenant—or leave it—individually, they cannot make separate agreements with God: "There is no solitary covenant with the Lord; it is always

---

[43]Brueggemann, *Bible Makes Sense*, p. 15.

covenant *in a community* of people who have made like commitments and received parallel promises from God."[44] There is only one new covenant. God has declared the terms on which someone can be part of his people. These terms are not subject to negotiation on a case-by-case basis. This corporate solidarity runs counter to the individualism that plays such a significant part in Protestant theology and practice.

This point has significant implications for the church. Some Protestant theologians describe the church as a body constituted by individuals who have covenanted with God and one another.[45] The new covenant would suggest, however, that individuals do not constitute the church by their coming together. God's covenant-creating love has brought the church into being. Individuals can decide whether to accept or reject God's terms—whether to be included in or excluded from God's people—but they do not establish the covenant or the church. Remembering this fact might discourage the notion we sometimes develop that the church belongs to us and exists to meet our needs. The church belongs to God and exists to do God's will.

Furthermore, just as there is only one new covenant, there is only one people of God, composed of both Jews and Gentiles. Recent treatments of covenant have taken pains to repudiate supersessionism—the idea that the church has replaced Israel in God's plan—along with the anti-Semitism to which that view often leads.[46] While this concern is certainly justified, it should not lead us to minimize the differences between the old and new covenants. The new covenant is not simply a renewal of the old, with obedience to the law made easier by the Holy Spirit.[47] Paul insists that believers in Christ are not under law. The author of Hebrews declares that the old covenant is obsolete. The heirs of the Abrahamic covenant are those who believe in Jesus. This means that Christians have no biblical mandate

---

[44]Ibid., p. 75.

[45]Stanley J. Grenz, *Theology for the Community of God* (Grand Rapids: Eerdmans, 2000), pp. 469, 471, 480-81. Grenz states that "the coming together of believers in mutual covenant constitutes the church" (p. 472). He associates this view of the church with Congregationalists and Baptists. While I believe that Grenz is mistaken on this point, he uses the concept of covenant very fruitfully to inform the theme of community around which he organizes his theology.

[46]See, for example, McKenzie, *Covenant.*

[47]For this view, see (for example) C. E. B. Cranfield, "Paul's Teaching on Sanctification," *The Reformed Review* 48, no. 3 (Spring 1995): 223.

to endorse the actions of the modern state of Israel.[48] Our attitude toward conflicts in the Middle East should be governed by our concern for the material and spiritual well-being of everyone involved—with particular familial concern for fellow Christian believers.

Having said that, we must also affirm that the church does not replace Israel. The new covenant is organically related to the old as its fulfillment. The people of God in the new covenant are organically related to the people of God in the old.[49] As Paul spells out in Romans 9–11 and Ephesians 2, the church of Jews and Gentiles is rooted in Israel and dependent upon that heritage for its own existence. Gentiles in particular must not become arrogant toward Israel, for to do so would be to despise God's wisdom and mercy. Paul believes in a future for Israel (Rom 11:11-29)—but not apart from Christ. There is one people of God, one temple of God, built upon the prophets and apostles, whose members stand or fall by their faith in Jesus Christ, the fulfillment of God's covenant promises.

The new covenant is the final covenant, because the work of Christ is finished and complete. God has no backup plan for human redemption. The covenant is both inclusive and exclusive; it offers salvation to the world, both Jews and Gentiles, but only on God's terms. This conviction should influence the way we engage in evangelism, missions, denominational conversations and interfaith dialogue.

The character of promise gives the new covenant a future orientation. Although believers are already heirs with enormous resources, they do not yet possess the inheritance. They must persevere in faithfulness, relying upon the covenant faithfulness of God. However, the hope they have can motivate them to make a difference now. God's promises are "profoundly subversive of the present."[50] They inspire change in light of the future we grasp by faith.

The image of salvation as covenant is sorely needed in a Western cul-

---

[48]John P. Davis, "Who Are the Heirs of the Abrahamic Covenant?" *Evangelical Review of Theology* 29, no. 2 (2005): 149-63.

[49]I do, however, acknowledge what Ben Witherington has pointed out in his blog "Supercessionism [sic], Dispensationalism, and the Present Middle East Crisis—A Christian Stand": the perspective of the author of Hebrews "would inevitably be viewed as supercessionist [sic] by those Jews who had not and did not see Jesus as the completion of God's plans for them or the fulfillment of earlier covenants." (August 5, 2006) <http://benwitherington.blogspot.com/2006/08/supercessionism-dispensationalism-and.html>.

[50]Brueggemann, *Theology of the Old Testament*, p. 173.

ture in which employers, spouses, parents and leaders—sometimes even leaders in the church—do not keep their promises, honor their agreements or maintain their integrity. The church must model a different way to live. "If we are indeed 'in God's image,' then the central task of our life is covenant-making and covenant-keeping."[51] Experiencing covenantal relationships with God and other Christians would go a long way toward healing broken lives. We can more effectively nurture someone else's relationship with God if we can include them in our own.

A covenantal understanding of salvation warns against both complacency and judgmentalism. On the one hand, it means that salvation is not a transaction that is completed at conversion. It requires more commitment and follow-through than coming forward in a worship service or signing a card. On the other hand, it reminds us that salvation is as complex as any relationship—or more so, since this relationship is with the God of the universe. When engaging in discipleship and spiritual formation, the church should beware of formulas, quick fixes and superficial judgments. Covenant means long-term obedience, which we can do more successfully together. To be faithful, we must depend upon the Holy Spirit, God's fulfilled promise, who gives us a foretaste of the glorious inheritance to come.

FOR FURTHER READING

Brueggemann, Walter. *The Bible Makes Sense.* Rev. ed. Cincinnati: St. Anthony Messenger, 2003.

———. *Theology of the Old Testament: Testimony, Dispute, Advocacy.* Minneapolis: Fortress, 1997.

Chennattu, Rekha M. *Johannine Discipleship as a Covenant Relationship.* Peabody, Mass.: Hendrickson, 2006.

Dumbrell, William J. *Covenant and Creation: A Theology of Old Testament Covenants.* Grand Rapids: Baker, 1993.

Eichrodt, Walther. *Theology of the Old Testament.* Old Testament Library. Philadelphia: Westminster Press, 1961.

Hahn, Scott. "Covenant in the Old and New Testaments: Some Current Research (1994-2004)." *Currents in Biblical Research* 3, no. 2 (2005): 263-92.

Harrisville, Roy A. *The Concept of Newness in the New Testament.* Minneapolis: Augsburg, 1960.

---

[51]Brueggemann, *Bible Makes Sense*, p. 4.

Lehne, Susanne. *The New Covenant in Hebrews.* Journal for the Study of the New Testament Supplement Series. Edited by David Hill. Sheffield, U.K.: JSOT Press, 1990.

Lemke, Werner E. "Jeremiah 31:31-34." *Interpretation* 37 (1983): 183-87.

Marshall, I. Howard. "Some Reflections on the Covenant in the New Testament." In *Jesus the Saviour: Studies in New Testament Theology*, pp. 275-89. Downers Grove, Ill.: InterVarsity Press, 1990.

Martens, Elmer A. *God's Design: A Focus on Old Testament Theology.* 3rd ed. N. Richland Hills, Tex.: BIBAL, 1998.

McKenzie, Steven L. *Covenant.* Understanding Biblical Themes. St. Louis, Mo.: Chalice, 2000.

Porter, Stanley E., and Jacqueline C. R. de Roo, eds. *The Concept of the Covenant in the Second Temple Period* (Leiden: Brill, 2003).

Wright, N. T. *The Climax of the Covenant: Christ and the Law in Pauline Theology.* Minneapolis: Fortress, 1992.

———. *The New Testament and the People of God.* Minneapolis: Fortress, 1992, pp. 259-79.

3

CITIZENS OF THE KINGDOM,
DISCIPLES OF THE KING

WHEN HE WAS SEVEN, MY HUSBAND, along with his Dutch parents, became a naturalized citizen of the United States of America. To do this, he was required to renounce all allegiance to any foreign power. He promised to support and defend his new nation and to obey its laws. At the end of the ceremony, he received an American flag. He was disappointed to discover that it had only forty-nine stars, despite Hawaii's recent statehood. Apparently the officials in charge were not very sensitive to symbolism!

When Jesus inaugurated his ministry by announcing the arrival of the kingdom of God (Mk 1:15), he was heralding a change of administration. God was reasserting his rule over creation. No longer would "the ruler of this world" (Jn 12:31) exercise dominion over human beings. Those who welcomed Jesus' announcement expressed through the symbol of baptism their allegiance to this new kingdom and its king.

The kingdom of God is one of the most comprehensive images of salvation in the New Testament. Familiar doctrinal terms like justification and redemption are nearly absent from Matthew, Mark and Luke, and the word "salvation" (*sōtēria*) is uncommon. But the first three Gospels have a great deal to say about what God is doing to restore his creation, expressed in their vision of the kingdom of God. The kingdom is to the Synoptic Gospels what eternal life is to the Fourth Gospel and salvation language is to Paul. The issues of allegiance and commitment raised by this image are as relevant for Christians today as they were then.

WHAT IS THE KINGDOM?

The kingdom of God (*basileia tou theou*) was widely investigated by biblical scholars in the twentieth century.[1] Despite some divergence of opinion, New Testament scholars have reached general consensus on several points: the kingdom of God is the central theme of Jesus' preaching; many of Jesus' kingdom sayings are authentic; the kingdom of God refers to God's reign, rather than to a physical realm; it is both present and future; and it is present in the preaching and ministry of Jesus.[2]

Although it is the standard translation, the word "kingdom" does not capture the nuances of the Greek *basileia*, which can mean both king*dom* and king*ship*. The term refers to the reign or dominion of God, God's rule over creation. The verb form, *basileuō*, is usually translated "reign." The coming of this kingdom is what Jesus taught his disciples to pray for: "Your kingdom come. Your will be done, on earth as it is in heaven" (Mt 6:10). The Lord's Prayer gives us a helpful short definition of the kingdom: the kingdom is the sphere in which God's will is perfectly done. Christians pray for the kingdom to come on earth, so that the whole creation will reflect the character and will of its creator. George Eldon Ladd defines the coming of the kingdom as follows: "It is the action of the sovereign God of heaven by which his reign is restored in power to those areas of his creation which he has permitted in rebellion to move outside the actual acknowledgement of his rule."[3]

Scholars have debated whether the kingdom of God is a spiritual or social reality. However, these two options are not mutually exclusive. If God's will is done on earth, both personal and social realities will be transformed:

> If, in fact, the very heart of God's reign is summed up in the relationship

---

[1]For a survey of scholarship, see George Eldon Ladd, *A Theology of the New Testament*, ed. Donald A. Hagner, rev. ed. (Grand Rapids: Eerdmans, 1993); see also Wendell Willis, *The Kingdom of God in 20th-Century Interpretation* (Peabody, Mass.: Hendrickson, 1987); and Howard A. Snyder, *Models of the Kingdom* (Nashville: Abingdon, 1991).

[2]I. Howard Marshall, "The Hope of a New Age: The Kingdom of God in the New Testament," *Themelios* 11 (1985): 5-15. Snyder sees six pairs of terms that stand in tension with one another in the New Testament picture of the kingdom: present vs. future, individual vs. social, spirit vs. matter, gradual vs. climactic, divine action vs. human action, and the church's relation to the kingdom (*Models of the Kingdom*, pp. 16-17).

[3]George Eldon Ladd, *Crucial Questions About the Kingdom of God* (Grand Rapids: Eerdmans, 1952), p. 83.

between God and people becoming whole, then it is making its entry wherever a person's relationship to God through Jesus becomes new. Its viability is not altered by the fact that corporeal existence and the world in general have not yet become whole. On the other hand, it means that its coming cannot be restricted to the matter of a new relationship to God alone; corporeal existence and history must be included because God is also the Creator. For this reason it must be noted that the coming of the kingdom even now, like a refracted light, manifests its influence upon the existing world order.[4]

Krister Stendahl prefers the term "kingdom of God" to "reign of God" because it is harder to spiritualize: "The kingdom is not just a reign of God in our hearts but the stuff that goes with it. That's important—the total social reality."[5]

In the Old Testament, God is called a king, and his sovereignty over creation is affirmed (see Ps 97:1), but that sovereignty is not everywhere acknowledged. Much of creation is in rebellion against him. In a sense, then, God must *become* king over creation again, as Zechariah 14:9 states: "And the LORD will become king over all the earth; on that day the LORD will be one and his name one." God will act decisively to reassert his authority. He will vindicate the righteous, punish the wicked, put an end to evil, and bring peace to his fractured creation. At the outset of his ministry, Jesus proclaims that God is at work in and through him to do just that: "The time is fulfilled, and the kingdom of God has come near; repent, and believe in the good news" (Mk 1:15). The kingdom of God is the focus of Jesus' ministry.

So the kingdom of God (or kingdom of heaven) is what God is doing through Jesus to reassert his rule over creation.[6] Mark 10:13-31 illustrates several important characteristics of the kingdom. Jesus uses a little child to give the disciples a lesson in humility (Mk 10:13-16), and he interacts with a man about the requirements for entering the kingdom (Mk 10:17-22).

---

[4]Leonhard Goppelt, *Theology of the New Testament*, 2 vols., trans. John Alsup (Grand Rapids: Eerdmans, 1981-1982), 1:71.

[5]Krister Stendahl, "Thy Kingdom Come on Earth," *American Baptist Quarterly* 14, no. 1 (March 1995): 17.

[6]The classical dispensational distinction between the kingdom of God and the kingdom of heaven cannot be supported by the evidence from the Gospels. Matthew sometimes uses "heaven" as a polite circumlocution for the name of God, but he predicates the same things of the kingdom of heaven as of the kingdom of God. See, for example, Matthew 19:23-24, where he uses the two terms interchangeably.

Then he interprets this interaction for his disciples (Mk 10:23-31). The man first asks what he must to inherit eternal life (Mk 10:17). In Mark 10:23-25, Jesus equates this with entering the kingdom of God. The disciples respond, "Then who can be saved?" (Mk 10:26). Thus the kingdom of God represents the same reality as salvation and eternal life.

According to this passage, the kingdom of God is supernatural. It is established by God, in God's time and on God's terms. Human beings cannot enter it without an act of God (Mk 10:27). Although the kingdom involves doing God's will (Mk 10:19-20), it cannot be earned but can only be received (Mk 10:15). It is both a present and future reality, as evidenced by Jesus' use of both present and future tenses when he describes the difficulty of entering it (Mk 10:23-24). It is finally eschatological, since it finds its fulfillment not in this age but in the age to come (Mk 10:30).

The kingdom is clearly a corporate or even a cosmic reality, but it is entered individually. Although Jesus generalizes about the wealthy, he is clearly referring to the individual who had been speaking with him. In Mark 12:34, Jesus tells another man, because of his wise answer, that he is not far from the kingdom of God. Most striking in the Mark 10 passage is Jesus' implicit assertion that entering the kingdom depends upon having a relationship of discipleship with Jesus himself. His ultimate answer to the man's question is "Follow me" (Mk 10:21).

The entire narrative suggests that the kingdom involves an inversion of social values.[7] The rich not only are not favored but actually have more difficulty entering the kingdom. "Many who are first will be last, and the last will be first" (Mk 10:31). In fact, the only way to enter the kingdom is to give up all social power and privilege, to receive it like a child (Mk 10:15). Identifying with the kingdom requires one to give up everything—even to be willing to suffer persecution—but it promises the riches of Christian community in this age and eternal life in the next (Mk 10:21, 28-31).

The kingdom of God dominates the Synoptic Gospels and provides the narrative framework for the pictures of salvation in the rest of the New Testament. While it appears in only two passages in the Gospel of John, both passages are central to the book's view of salvation. In chapter 3, Jesus

---

[7]For an extended treatment of this theme, see Donald B. Kraybill, *The Upside-Down Kingdom* (Scottdale, Penn.: Herald, 2003).

tells Nicodemus that one must be born from above in order to inherit the kingdom of God (Jn 3:3, 5). At his trial in chapter 18, he tells the high priest that his kingdom of not of earthly origin (Jn 18:36).

Although kingdom terminology is not central in Paul's letters, probably because his Gentile audiences are less familiar with it, his references to it demonstrate that it forms his understanding of what God has done and is doing in Christ. Colossians describes salvation as a transfer from the kingdom of darkness to the kingdom of Christ (Col 1:13). Paul's sweeping vision of the consummation in 1 Corinthians 15 describes the exalted Christ advancing the kingdom until he defeats all of his enemies, handing the kingdom over to the Father at last "so that God may be all in all" (1 Cor 15:28). Believers will then receive imperishable bodies that will fit them to live in the imperishable kingdom (1 Cor 15:50-57).

The kingdom also informs Paul's ethics. He uses it to frame his counsel to the Roman Christians on the issue of meat sacrificed to idols, advising them that "the kingdom of God is not food and drink but righteousness and peace and joy in the Holy Spirit" (Rom 14:17). He reminds the fractious Corinthians of his apostolic authority by observing that the kingdom "depends not on talk but on power" (1 Cor 4:20). His vice lists typically declare that people who practice such vices will not inherit the kingdom of God (1 Cor 6:9-10; Gal 5:21; Eph 5:5).

Paul sometimes uses a very similar analogy—that of citizenship—to connect with his Greco-Roman audience. To the Philippians, proud of their status as a Roman colony, he states that their true citizenship is in heaven. They are exiles awaiting the return of their Lord from heaven, who will use his kingly power to transform their bodies to resemble his (Phil 3:20-21). Ephesians declares that because of Christ, Gentile believers are no longer "aliens from the commonwealth of Israel" but are "citizens with the saints" (Eph 2:12, 19).

WHEN IS THE KINGDOM?

Throughout the New Testament, the kingdom of God is regarded as an eschatological reality that can be experienced in part now because of Jesus' life, death, resurrection and exaltation. It will be completed when Jesus returns (Mt 25:31, 34; Lk 17:21). Jesus instructs his disciples to work faithfully and be alert for its coming (Mt 25:1-13). Although they have kingdom work to do, they cannot establish the kingdom. Only the King can do that.

The Old Testament prophets had expected that the kingdom would arrive in a decisive intervention by God they sometimes called the Day of the Lord (Joel 2:28-32; Zeph 1:2-18). God would set creation to rights in a single event, bringing the present age to a close and ushering in the age to come. The New Testament writers reframed this expectation in light of what God had done in Jesus. Some Day-of-the-Lord events had already taken place, such as the pouring out of the Holy Spirit and the resurrection of Jesus as the "first fruits" of the general resurrection (1 Cor 15:20). But sin, evil, injustice and death persisted. Creation was still groaning in its bondage to decay (Rom 8:19-22).

The early Christians concluded that the age to come had broken into the present without destroying the present age. George Eldon Ladd has called their view "fulfillment without consummation."[8] Scholars often refer to this understanding of New Testament eschatology as "already and not yet."[9] Paul's panorama of Christian history in 1 Corinthians 15 tells this reframed story. Christians live "between the times" of Christ's first and second coming, working and waiting for the fulfillment of the kingdom.

The kingdom is established by God the Father through Jesus Christ in the power of the Holy Spirit. It is attributed both to the Father (Mt 26:29) and to the Son (Mt 16:28). The Father's love, which seeks the least and the lost, is the wellspring of the kingdom (Lk 15). Jesus exemplifies this love in his own mission (Lk 19:10). He inaugurates the kingdom through his ministry of preaching, healing, exorcism and reconciliation (Mk 1:15; Lk 4:16-21, 43). The presence and the power of the Holy Spirit, operating through his ministry, is the definitive sign that the kingdom is dawning (Mt 12:28).

To establish the kingdom of God, Jesus must defeat another kingdom and its king. At the start of his ministry, he must resist Satan's temptations (Mt 4:1-11). The devil is his adversary in the work of spreading the kingdom (Mt 13:19, 36-43). This is why exorcisms are such a significant fea-

---

[8]George Eldon Ladd, *The Presence of the Future: The Eschatology of Biblical Realism* (Grand Rapids: Eerdmans, 1974), pp. 114, 148-49. See also N. T. Wright, *Jesus and the Victory of God* (Minneapolis: Fortress, 1996), pp. 215-19 for early Christian rethinking of the kingdom of God.

[9]For example, according to Goppelt, Jesus proclaimed that "the reign of God is already coming in the present, but this present coming is in fact not yet the future one." *Theology of the New Testament*, p. 61.

ture of Jesus' ministry. Through his exorcisms, Jesus demonstrates his authority over demonic forces (Mk 1:28). He sets people free from Satan's power (Mt 12:24-32). Moreover, he grants this same authority to his disciples. When the seventy-two return from their successful mission, Jesus says that he saw Satan fall like lightning out of heaven (Lk 10:18). When the early church confesses "Jesus is Lord," they are testifying that Satan—not to mention Caesar—is not.[10]

The proclamation of the kingdom is the announcement of God's lordship over creation. It is not merely the reign of God in the hearts of believers. Nor is it the offer of a new religious option among many. As N. T. Wright observes, "When the herald makes a royal proclamation, he says 'Nero (or whoever) has become emperor.' He does not say 'If you would like to have an experience of living under an emperor, you might care to try Nero.' The proclamation is an authoritative summons to obedience."[11] Those who hear the proclamation are informed of a new reality to which they must adjust. They cannot opt out of that reality; they can only decide how they will position themselves in relation to it.

ENTERING THE KINGDOM

The kingdom thus depends upon divine initiative; it is God's gracious gift, which he has prepared for his people since the world began (Mt 25:34; Lk 22:29, 32). Perhaps this is why Jesus calls people to himself rather than waiting for students to approach him as first-century rabbis would do (Mk 1:20; 2:17).[12] Although calling in the Synoptics does not have the same theological weight as it has in Paul's writings, this still suggests that people come to the kingdom through divine initiative.[13]

The kingdom extends God's generosity to the undeserving; those who

---

[10]Warren Carter interprets the plot of Matthew's Gospel as "an act of imperial negotiation" that subverts the Roman Empire. "Matthew's Gospel: An Anti-Imperial/Imperial Reading," *Currents in Theology and Mission* 34, no. 6 (December 2007): 424-33. See also the extended discussion in Richard A. Horsley, *Jesus and Empire: The Kingdom of God and the New World Disorder* (Minneapolis: Augsburg Fortress, 2002).

[11]N. T. Wright, *What Saint Paul Really Said* (Grand Rapids: Eerdmans, 1997), p. 45.

[12]Martin Hengel, *The Charismatic Leader and His Followers*, trans. James C. G. Greig, ed. John Riches (Edinburgh: T & T Clark, 1996), pp. 50-51. Hengel states that Jesus is not a rabbi (p. 42). He argues that Jesus' call to discipleship has more in common with God's call to the Old Testament prophets, with its requirement of absolute commitment (p. 71).

[13]See Robert A. Guelich, *Mark 1–8:26*, Word Biblical Commentary (Dallas: Word Books, 1989), p. 157.

think they should be first will be last (Mt 20:1-16). Jesus offers the kingdom to everyone—righteous people and sinners, Jews and Gentiles (Mt 8:11-12; 21:31; Lk 13:29). For this reason, the message of the kingdom is the gospel, or good news (*euangelion*, Mk 1:15). The verb *euangelizō* often occurs in the Septuagint to announce good news about "the inbreaking of God's kingly rule."[14]

The offer of the kingdom requires a response. Despite his authority, Jesus invites rather than coerces people to join him. The parable of the soils (Mk 4:3-9, 13-20) indicates that entrance into the kingdom depends not only on divine initiative but also on human receptivity. The sower spreads the seeds without discrimination; the condition of the soil determines the quality of the crop. People must have "ears to hear" in order to understand Jesus' message (Mk 4:9, 23). Not everyone will respond favorably. Those who do will become "children of the kingdom" (Mt 13:38; cf. Mt 13:43).

To enter the kingdom, people must turn away from sin and trust in Jesus. Jesus calls people to repent in light of God's activity in their midst (Mt 11:20; Lk 5:32; 13:1-5). This repentance is a new orientation called for by the new situation.[15] Jesus urges his disciples to take radical action to remove sin from their lives so that they do not jeopardize their place in the kingdom (Mk 9:24-29). He also calls people to make a commitment of faith. People must believe the gospel message (Mk 1:15), and they must trust in Jesus as the agent of the kingdom (Jn 3:16). Faith plays a critical role in Jesus' healings (Mk 2:5; 10:52). He is unable to do many miracles in Nazareth because of their lack of faith (Mk 6:5-6). However, while Jesus emphasizes the power of faith and criticizes people for their unbelief, he does not teach a mechanical relationship between the level of faith and the magnitude of results. His parable of mustard-seed faith implies that the *quantity* of one's faith is not an issue (Lk 17:5-6). He heals the son of the man who cries out, "I believe, help my unbelief!" (Mk 9:24). His pur-

---

[14]C. E. B. Cranfield, *The Gospel According to Saint Mark*, Cambridge Greek Testament Commentary, ed. C. F. D. Moule (Cambridge: Cambridge University Press, 1959), p. 35. He lists such passages as Isaiah 40:9; 41:27; 52:7; 60:6; 61:1; Nahum 1:15; and Psalms 40:9; 96:2. He believes that Mark sees Jesus' preaching in terms of the messenger of the kingdom of God in Second Isaiah, except that for Mark, Jesus is both the announcer and the content of the message. See also G. Friedrich, "εὐαγγελίζομαι κτλ.," in *TDNT* 2:728.

[15]Ben Wiebe, "Messianic Ethics: Response to the Kingdom of God," *Interpretation* 45, no. 1 (January 1991): 37-38.

pose appears to be relational: he seems to want to know whether or not people are willing to trust him.

The coming of the kingdom provokes a crisis of decision: "Grace and judgment cannot be separated in Jesus' preaching of the kingdom. With his advent, the time of decision has come. Jesus calls his hearers to decide for or against the offer he presents."[16] The gospel message divides people into allies and adversaries, into insiders and outsiders. Jesus declares, "Whoever is not with me is against me, and whoever does not gather with me scatters" (Mt 12:30). Although Jesus calls individuals, responding to the call brings those individuals into a new community.[17] This community becomes a "kingdom colony" that lives by the principles of the kingdom as a witness to the world until the kingdom comes in fullness.[18] Those who reject the kingdom will be subject to judgment (Mt 13:36-43, 47-50). To be finally excluded from the kingdom means to suffer eternally (Mt 25:46).

As we saw in the last chapter, the identity of people in the first-century Mediterranean world was primarily corporate rather than individual. That is, people's identity was defined by the groups (family, tribe or party) to which they belonged. They would form close personal connections with those in their "ingroups" while keeping some distance from those in "outgroups."[19] From this perspective, the message of the kingdom invites people to enter a new community and take on a new identity.[20] The ethics of the kingdom are community ethics.[21]

This new ingroup takes priority over all preexisting groups, such as the biological family. When Jesus' family comes to protect the family honor by restraining his embarrassing behavior, he declares that his true family are those who do the will of God. He leaves his biological family "standing outside," while his disciples form a circle around him (Mk 3:21, 31-35).[22]

[16]Georg Strecker, *Theology of the New Testament*, ed. Friedrich Wilhelm Horn, trans. M. Eugene Boring (Louisville: Westminster John Knox Press, 2000), p. 257.
[17]Michael J. Wilkins, *Following the Master: Discipleship in the Steps of Jesus* (Grand Rapids: Zondervan, 1992), p. 141.
[18]Snyder, *Models of the Kingdom*, p. 153.
[19]Bruce J. Malina, *The New Testament World: Insights from Cultural Anthropology* (Louisville: Westminster John Knox Press, 1993), pp. 45-47, 66-68.
[20]For a study of the kingdom of God from an anthropological perspective, see Bruce J. Malina, *The Social Gospel of Jesus* (Minneapolis: Augsburg Fortress, 2000).
[21]Wiebe, "Messianic Ethics," p. 40.
[22]R. T. France, "Matthew, Mark, and Luke," in Ladd, *Theology*, p. 233.

The new community has flexible boundaries, however. When his disciples want to stop someone from casting out demons because he is not one of them, Jesus tells them, "Whoever is not against us is for us" (Mk 9:38-40). He is willing to allow others to identify with his ingroup even though he has not personally approved them.[23]

This concept helps to explain the "secrets of the kingdom" in the Synoptic Gospels. Jesus tells his disciples that they have been entrusted with the secrets of the kingdom, while others have not. In other words, Jesus speaks directly to his ingroup while using parables to veil his teaching from outsiders (Mk 4:11). This ingroup/outgroup distinction sheds light on the quotation from Isaiah that appears in slightly different form in all three Synoptics:

> The reason I speak to them in parables is that "seeing they do not perceive, and hearing they do not listen, nor do they understand." With them indeed is fulfilled the prophecy of Isaiah that says: "You will indeed listen, but never understand, and you will indeed look, but never perceive. For this people's heart has grown dull, and their ears are hard of hearing, and they have shut their eyes; so that they might not look with their eyes, and listen with their ears, and understand with their heart and turn—and I would heal them." (Mt 13:13-15, quoting Is 6:9-10)

Those who do not respond to the gospel message are hardened in their resistance and cannot understand it. However, Jesus' ingroup is not closed. Those who do respond become part of his circle and can receive his direct teaching. All they have to do to learn the secrets of the kingdom is to ask him (Mk 4:10). The parallels in Mark 4:12 and Luke 8:10 say that Jesus speaks in parables "so that" or "in order that" they might not understand. However, it seems unlikely that Jesus would set out deliberately to mystify his hearers. It seems more likely that the resistance of some of the audience derives from the polarizing effect of the gospel message. The *hina* clause ("so that") can be construed as either a cause-and-effect or a result.

The gift of the kingdom brings with it the demand for discipleship. As Ralph Martin observes regarding Mark 12:28-34, "A theoretical acceptance of truth never suffices; it brings a person only in sight of the king-

---

[23]Jesus recognized a *"category of discipleship outside the circle of those who had formally declared for him."* James D. G. Dunn, *Jesus' Call to Discipleship*, Understanding Jesus Today, ed. Howard Clark Kee (Cambridge: Cambridge University Press, 1992), p. 110 (italics in original).

dom (vs. 34). Personal attachment to Jesus and the demands of discipleship are needed to bring a person, however well-meaning and sincere, into the kingdom."[24] Jesus himself shows what living according to the kingdom is like; this is why disciples are called to follow him.[25] Jesus' invitation to discipleship takes the form of a twofold command: "If any want to become my followers, let them deny themselves and take up their cross and follow me" (Mk 10:34). Self-denial and following Jesus parallel the "repent and believe" of the gospel proclamation. In Mark and Luke, Jesus makes this invitation to the crowd, not just to his disciples, suggesting that he regards self-denial and discipleship as conditions of entrance to the kingdom, not options for particularly dedicated believers.[26]

The word for self-denial (aparneomai) is the same word used for Peter's denial of Christ (Mk 14:30, 31, 72).[27] Jesus is demanding absolute loyalty. His disciples must entrust themselves completely to him. They must give allegiance to Jesus before themselves. They must dedicate themselves completely to his mission, even if it means their death. Jesus urges prospective disciples to count the cost before they decide to follow him (Lk 14:26-32). But he describes the kingdom as a treasure that is worth any sacrifice (Mt 13:44-46).

The positive side of self-denial is following Jesus. The word for following, akoloutheō, can mean merely to accompany someone, but it is used especially to express discipleship to Jesus: "Akolouthein signifies self-commitment in a sense which breaks all other ties."[28] The present tense of "follow" in Mark 8:34 (in contrast to the aorist tenses of "deny themselves" and "take up their cross") suggests that discipleship is a continuous process that grows out of the definitive choice to deny oneself and follow Jesus.[29] Jesus' invitation to follow him is thus both gift and demand. Following him means giving up everything in order to receive the gift of the kingdom. The requirements for discipleship make sense only in light of the

---

[24]Ralph P. Martin, New Testament Foundations: A Guide for Christian Students, vol. 1, The 4 Gospels, rev. ed. (Grand Rapids: Eerdmans, 1975), p. 195.

[25]Dunn, Call to Discipleship, p. 31.

[26]Ernest Best, Disciples and Discipleship: Studies in the Gospel According to Mark (Edinburgh: T & T Clark, 1986), p. 10. The parallel in Matthew 16:24 has Jesus addressing only his disciples.

[27]H.-G. Link and E. Tiedtke, "Deny," in NIDNTT 1:455. Best emphasizes that they are to deny themselves, not deny things to themselves (Disciples, p. 8).

[28]G. Kittel, "ἀκολουθέω κτλ.," in TDNT 1:213, 214.

[29]Cranfield, Mark, p. 282.

new situation created by the in-breaking kingdom of God.[30] The call to discipleship is a call to service in and for the kingdom.[31]

Disciples are called to develop a relationship with Jesus (Mk 3:14); to proclaim the kingdom as he does (Mk 3:15; 6:12-13); to forgive as they have been forgiven (Mt 6:12-15; 18:23-35); and to follow Jesus' model of servant leadership (Mk 10:42-45). They are to seek God's kingdom and pray for its coming in fullness (Mt 6:10, 33). While the kingdom is not to be earned by good works, it must be expressed in a life of obedience (Mt 5:20; 7:21). The ethics of the kingdom can be summed up as love— love of God, love of neighbor, and even love of enemies (Mt 5:43-48; 22:37-40).

Disciples of the kingdom are commissioned to call others to the same radical discipleship (Mt 28:18-20). They are "bearers of the salvation of the Kingdom of God for the world."[32] They are to preach the gospel to all nations (Mk 13:10). This is a great privilege and a heavy responsibility. The gospel message is the key that will lock or unlock the kingdom for those who hear it (Mt 16:19). Just as in Jesus' ministry, this preaching will bring about a crisis of decision for its hearers, resulting either in repentance or judgment (Mt 10:11-15). Through the church's message, people will either be brought into the kingdom or hardened against it.

The Gospels present somewhat different perspectives on the life of discipleship. Mark emphasizes discipleship as service, recognizing the difficulties and failures of disciples and their need for restoration by Christ.[33] Matthew highlights the importance of the community of disciples as salt and light in the world.[34] Luke shows the crucial role of the Holy Spirit in empowering disciples to follow Jesus in a life of prayer, compassion and cross-bearing.[35] John views discipleship as a loving relationship with Jesus

---

[30]Wiebe, "Messianic Ethics," p. 33.

[31]Hengel, *Charismatic Leader*, p. 73.

[32]Seyoon Kim, "Salvation and Suffering according to Jesus," *Evangelical Quarterly* 68, no. 3 (July 1996): 205.

[33]Larry W. Hurtado, "Following Jesus in the Gospel of Mark—and Beyond," in *Patterns of Discipleship in the New Testament*, ed. Richard N. Longenecker (Grand Rapids: Eerdmans, 1996), p. 27.

[34]Terence L. Donaldson, "Guiding Readers—Making Disciples: Discipleship in Matthew's Narrative Strategy," in *Patterns of Discipleship*, ed. Longenecker, p. 48.

[35]Richard N. Longenecker, "Taking Up the Cross Daily: Discipleship in Luke-Acts," in *Patterns of Discipleship*, ed. Longenecker, p. 75.

that expresses itself in action, especially in love for one another.[36]

The word for disciple (*mathētēs*) is not found in the New Testament outside the Gospels and Acts. But the concept of discipleship is carried on in metaphorical uses of "following" and "walking," and especially in the idea of imitation. Imitating Christ originates with Jesus himself, who commands his disciples to imitate the example of humble service he sets by washing their feet (Jn 13:15). New Testament writers urge believers to follow the example of Christ, especially in suffering: "For to this you have been called, because Christ also suffered for you, leaving you an example, so that you should follow in his steps" (1 Peter 2:21; cf. 1 Thess 1:6). The example of Christ becomes the test for authentic Christianity: "Whoever says, 'I abide in him,' ought to walk just as he walked" (1 Jn 2:6). Hebrews and Revelation call Christians to follow Jesus, who as pioneer, forerunner and faithful witness, has blazed the trail for them.[37]

Since disciples cannot literally follow a Jesus who is no longer physically present, they follow their leaders and examples in the faith (1 Thess 2:14; Heb 13:7). Paul invites his congregations to follow his own example (1 Cor 4:16; Phil 3:17; 2 Thess 3:7, 9). He seems to regard this as discipleship at second hand: "Be imitators of me, as I am of Christ" (1 Cor 11:1). The faith can be learned most effectively if new believers have someone to follow who can show them the way.

As Jesus and their leaders show them the way, disciples are to "walk" in that way. The language of walking is common in passages of ethical exhortation (paraenesis). For example, Paul begs the Ephesians "to lead a life [literally, "to walk," *peripatēsai*] worthy of the calling to which [they] have been called" (Eph 4:1). To do this, believers must follow the direction of the Holy Spirit: "If we live by the Spirit, let us also be guided [literally, "walk," *stoichōmen*] by the Spirit" (Gal 5:25; cf. Rom 8:4; Gal 5:16). "The call for the worthy walk is based on God's act of deliverance into the new age within the context of the old. This deliverance, effected through Christ and realized by possession of the Holy Spirit, is experi-

---

[36]Melvyn R. Hillmer, "They Believed in Him: Discipleship in the Johannine Tradition," in *Patterns of Discipleship*, ed. Longenecker, pp. 84, 90-91.

[37]See chapter thirteen for more detailed discussion of the images of following in Hebrews and Revelation. The image of participation in Christ is the subject of chapter eleven.

enced in the context of the community of faith."[38] Disciples are to "walk by the Spirit" (*pneumati peripateite*, Gal 5:16, author's translation) because the Spirit provides the discernment and the power to live according to the values of the kingdom.

VALUES OF THE KINGDOM

If Christians view themselves as citizens of God's kingdom, what values should guide their lives? What does the kingdom look like? First, the reign of God is both inclusive and exclusive: it is open to everyone, but it calls for absolute allegiance to God. It creates an alternative society at odds with other reigns:

> In the Roman imperial world, the "gospel" was the good news of Caesar's having established peace and security for the world. Caesar was the "savior" who had brought "salvation" to the whole world. The peoples of the empire were therefore to have "faith" (*pistis/fides*) in their "lord" the emperor. Moreover, Caesar the lord and savior was to be honored and celebrated by the "assemblies" (*ekklesiai*) of the cities such as Philippi, Corinth, and Ephesus. By applying this key imperial language to Jesus Christ, Paul was making him into the alternative or real emperor of the world, the head of an anti-imperial international alternative society.[39]

Some opponents of the Jesus movement recognized this challenge to existing reigns. Pilate ordered that the title "King of the Jews" be mounted on Jesus' cross (Jn 19:19-22). Jewish leaders in Thessalonica complained to Roman officials that Paul and Silas were teaching that Jesus was another king in opposition to Caesar (Acts 17:7).

Second, the reign of God is life-giving. In the age to come, this will mean eternal life in resurrection bodies (Lk 20:34-36). In this age, it means healing and restoration. Jesus' healing miracles were not only testimonies to his identity as Messiah; they were illustrations of the character of the new era Jesus was inaugurating.[40] They showed what life is really supposed to be like. Wholeness is the normal state of the kingdom of God. To live

---

[38]Joseph O. Holloway III, ΠΕΡΙΠΑΤΕΩ *as a Thematic Marker for Pauline Ethics* (San Francisco: Mellen Research University Press, 1992), p. 224.

[39]Horsley, *Jesus and Empire*, pp. 133-34.

[40]Joel B. Green, *Salvation,* Understanding Biblical Themes (St. Louis, Mo.: Chalice Press, 2003), p. 49. Stendahl comments that it would be offensive to think that Jesus would heal suffering people just to make a point about himself. "Thy Kingdom Come," p. 18.

in light of the kingdom, the church should be in the business of restoring wholeness to broken people, broken families and broken communities.

Third, the reign of God is reconciling. It involves intimate fellowship with God and others, often pictured as a banquet (Lk 14:15-24). Jesus promised his disciples that they would eat and drink at his table in the kingdom (Lk 22:28-30). His faithful servants would share the joy of their master (Mt 25:21, 23). The church should nurture the same communion with God and one another that Jesus began with his practice of table fellowship. We can address God as "Abba" and regard one another as brothers and sisters. As we hold our own feasts, we should distribute the invitations as broadly as Jesus did and not exclude anyone whom God may be calling to the table. As Jesus observed, the preaching of the kingdom may draw in all sorts of fish; we should not try to preselect the catch (Mt 13:47-50).

Fourth, the reign of God is righteous and just. God expects his citizens to live by his standards and reflect his character, which would be impossible except for the kingdom power present in the Holy Spirit (Mt 5:48). He calls the unrighteous in order to make them righteous and calls the faithless in order to equip them to be faithful. This means that the church should strive to nurture all its members to maturity in Christ and should develop a culture of loving accountability. As biblical literacy continues to decrease in Western culture, we will need intentional programs of discipleship that help people not just to know the truths of the faith but to live the life of faith, which is better caught than taught.

God's reign demands justice in all areas of life (Lk 4:16-21). It grants dignity and value to all people, especially those who have been marginalized or oppressed by the world (Mt 5:3-12; 19:14). To adequately represent the kingdom, the church should be concerned about both personal morality and social justice.[41] In our personal and communal lives, we should be models of forgiveness, because we recognize how much we have been forgiven (Mt 18:21-35). Forgiveness is the lifeblood of the kingdom.

Finally, the reign of God is transformational. Regardless of its apparent reach, it is powerful and has a far-reaching effect (Mt 13:31-33). It transforms persons, relationships, social structures, even the creation itself:

---

[41]See Glen H. Stassen and David P. Gushee, *Kingdom Ethics: Following Jesus in Contemporary Context* (Downers Grove, Ill.: InterVarsity Press, 2003).

"The saving power of the Kingdom of God which Jesus has brought manifests itself concretely in the restoration of individual wholeness, social *shalom*, and ecological health, as the people of God live by the Kingdom ethic."[42] Although the kingdom is supernatural, it is not otherworldly. God wants to bring his kingdom here on earth—a renewed earth, with renewed people in resurrection bodies who enjoy eternal fellowship with God and with one another.[43]

CONCLUSION

The kingdom of God is a comprehensive picture of what God is up to in the world. It asserts that God has acted in history and will do so again. In fact, God is the Lord of history.[44] The theme of God's kingdom connects the Old Testament with the New Testament and integrates past, present and future. The kingdom of God tells a big story—the biggest story. In a postmodern world that longs for meaning but is wary of abstract doctrine, the kingdom of God tells the story of God's love for his creation, his saving sovereignty that refuses to give up on wayward human beings. It is a compelling narrative that constructs enough meaning for even postmoderns to live by.

Moreover, the kingdom of God tolerates no separation between orthodoxy and orthopraxy, between faith and life. To identify with the kingdom means to make a difference in the world. Howard Snyder's summary is worth quoting in full:

> *The kingdom comes by the mysterious working of God's sovereign Spirit, but also by human faith and obedience.* As we have seen, the polarity between divine and human action is part of the mystery of the kingdom. The church faces the twin temptations of passivity and self-reliant activism. Scripture, however, teaches that the triune God is the primary actor in the drama of redemption, but that he seeks and expects responsible, faithful human action enabled by the Spirit. Christians are given a life to live, a cross to bear, and a kingdom to work for, but they truly fulfill their calling only as they place their confidence in God's action and allow God's Spirit to work through them.[45]

---

[42]Kim, "Salvation and Suffering," p. 203.

[43]Stanley J. Grenz, *Theology for the Community of God* (1994; reprint, Grand Rapids: Eerdmans, 2000), pp. 644-49.

[44]Ladd, *Presence of the Future*, pp. 331, 333.

[45]Snyder, *Models of the Kingdom*, p. 152.

Only God can bring the kingdom. But as we watch and pray for that day, we can be salt and light in the present world (Mt 5:13-14). We can preach the gospel of the kingdom. We can be agents of change in our societies and responsible stewards of creation. Our witness may require suffering and sacrifice (Mt 8:31-34; 10:32-40).[46] But we look forward to the day when the angel will announce, "The kingdom of the world has become the kingdom of our Lord and of his Messiah, and he will reign forever and ever" (Rev 11:15).

The kingdom of God also reminds us of the radical nature of evil. It cannot be overcome through human progress or self-improvement. It must be eradicated by the action of God.[47] While God has defeated evil through the cross and resurrection, evil is not yet banished from creation. God's reign is opposed by both human and nonhuman forces that have a stake in the present evil age. Suffering and spiritual warfare will continue to be a reality for Christians until the kingdom is consummated.

The kingdom of God provides an important corrective to a me-centered view of salvation. Salvation is certainly concerned with what God is doing in "my" life, in the life of every believer. But it is more than that. It is first of all about what God is doing in history. The kingdom of God shows the inadequacy of expressions such as "inviting Jesus into my life." In actuality, Jesus calls us into his kingdom to be part of his great project of reclaiming the world. He invites us to experience in part the blessings of the kingdom while we work toward its realization. Because the kingdom has been inaugurated by Jesus, we can do real, lasting good in the world. But we must live with the tension of the "already" and the "not yet" until Jesus returns. In a sense, the church is a laboratory experiment. As Krister Stendahl puts it, "Jesus expects us to be the guinea pigs for the kingdom!"[48] The way we live out this experiment before the world will influence whether others think the experiment is worth joining.

Cultivating a kingdom perspective would serve the church well today. A "kingdom consciousness" means, for example, that Christians should think of their calling in terms of kingdom work rather than church work. It means that all areas of life, whether "sacred" or "secular," fall within God's sover-

---

[46]Kim has stated that until the eschaton, the life of Christians "is marked by a dialectic of salvation and suffering." "Salvation and Suffering," p. 206.

[47]Ibid., p. 333.

[48]Stendahl, "Thy Kingdom Come," p. 16.

eignty. Christians can give themselves in confidence to the service of others, in both evangelism and social justice, knowing that God's reign will triumph.[49] A kingdom perspective might help us to recognize our fellow citizens in other denominations so that we can spend more time together in fellowship and mission and less time quarreling with one another. We can engage together in work that advances the kingdom, rather than in maintenance that merely keeps our congregations going.

The kingdom of God takes priority over all other allegiances. Baptism is our initiation into citizenship. Whenever we confess that Jesus is Lord, we pledge allegiance to his kingdom. As citizens of the kingdom, we must resist any version of nationalism or patriotism that conflicts with our primary allegiance.[50] We must reject any cultural pressures to abandon kingdom values.[51] We must live, as Hauerwas and Willimon have said, as "resident aliens."[52] The church, as outpost of the kingdom, must be an alternative society that both critiques the present age and points the way to something better. As Paul says, we are ambassadors for Christ (2 Cor 5:20), messengers of the kingdom until it comes.

FOR FURTHER READING

Beasley-Murray, George R. *Jesus and the Kingdom of God.* Grand Rapids: Eerdmans, 1988.

Best, Ernest. *Disciples and Discipleship: Studies in the Gospel According to Mark.* Edinburgh: T & T Clark, 1986.

Dunn, James D. G. *Jesus' Call to Discipleship.* Cambridge: Cambridge University Press, 1999.

Horsley, Richard A. *Jesus and Empire: The Kingdom of God and the New World Disorder.* Minneapolis: Augsburg Fortress, 2002.

Kraybill, Donald B. *The Upside-Down Kingdom.* Scottdale, Penn.: Herald, 2003.

Ladd, George Eldon. *The Presence of the Future: The Eschatology of Biblical Realism.* Grand Rapids: Eerdmans, 1974.

---

[49]Snyder, *Models of the Kingdom*, pp. 154-55.

[50]Richard Horsley, in *Jesus and Empire*, draws provocative parallels between the first century and the twenty-first.

[51]See Rodney Clapp, *A Peculiar People: The Church as Culture in a Post-Christian Society* (Downers Grove, Ill.: InterVarsity Press, 1996). See also John Howard Yoder, *The Politics of Jesus* (Grand Rapids: Eerdmans, 1972).

[52]Stanley Hauerwas and William H. Willimon, *Resident Aliens: Life in the Christian Colony* (Nashville: Abingdon, 1989).

Longenecker, Richard N., ed. *Patterns of Discipleship in the New Testament*. Mc-Master New Testament Studies Series. Edited by Richard N. Longenecker. Grand Rapids: Eerdmans, 1996.

Marshall, I. Howard. "The Hope of a New Age: The Kingdom of God in the New Testament." *Themelios* 11 (1985): 5-15.

Schnackenburg, Rudolf. *God's Rule and Kingdom*. Translated by J. Murray. London: Nelson, 1963.

Segovia, Fernando F., ed. *Discipleship in the New Testament*. Minneapolis: Fortress, 1985.

Snyder, Howard A. *Models of the Kingdom*. Nashville: Abingdon, 1991.

Stassen, Glen H., and David P. Gushee. *Kingdom Ethics: Following Jesus in Contemporary Context*. Downers Grove, Ill.: InterVarsity Press, 2003.

Wiebe, Ben. "Messianic Ethics: Response to the Kingdom of God." *Interpretation* 45, no. 1 (January 1991): 29-42.

Wilkins, Michael J. *Following the Master: A Biblical Theology of Discipleship*. Grand Rapids: Zondervan, 1992.

Willis, Wendell. *The Kingdom of God in 20th-Century Interpretation*. Peabody, Mass.: Hendrickson, 1987.

Wright, N. T. *Jesus and the Victory of God*. Minneapolis: Fortress, 1996.

Yoder, John Howard. *The Politics of Jesus*. Grand Rapids: Eerdmans, 1972.

4

THE LIFE OF THE
AGE TO COME

Eternal Life

A POPULAR BUMPER STICKER of the 1980s proclaimed, "He who dies with the most toys wins!" It was not long before another bumper sticker appeared with the response, "He who dies with the most toys is still dead!" Materialism, however vigorously pursued, is not a very effective antidote to death. In the face of death, people start asking if mortal life is all there is.

Salvation is God's solution to the human predicament. Different images of salvation describe this predicament in different ways. If the problem is covenant breaking, the solution is the new covenant. If the problem is rebellion against God, the solution is the kingdom of God. The solution to death, which entered the world because of sin (Rom 5:12), is life. But the life God provides is not ordinary life, which is enmeshed in sin and ends in death. It is life of an entirely different kind: abundant life (Jn 10:10) or (more commonly in John) eternal life.

Eternal life is the central image of salvation in the Gospel of John. It has the same prominence in the Johannine literature as the kingdom of God in the Synoptic Gospels and *sōtēria* in Paul. Scholars have not agreed on the meaning of the image of eternal life.[1] As we saw in chapter three,

---

[1]For a brief review of the various approaches, see Marianne Meye Thompson, "Eternal Life in the Gospel of John," *Ex Auditu* 5 (1989): 35-36.

the Synoptics use the ideas of salvation, inheriting the kingdom of God, and receiving eternal life in parallel ways (Mk 10:17-27). The three images are used interchangeably in the Gospel of John as well.[2] "In the teaching of Jesus, as in Jewish writings contemporary with the New Testament, the supreme blessing of the kingdom of God is 'life.' For that reason it is often spoken of as 'eternal life,' since it is life in the eternal kingdom, or as the Jews often put it, the life of the age to come."[3]

Technically, the kingdom of God and eternal life are not synonymous. "'Kingdom of God' is the sovereign action of God for the salvation of humankind, an activity which is destined to embrace the universe; 'life' or 'life eternal' is blessed existence under that saving sovereignty, with all the consequences that ensue from that."[4] Eternal life is a theme throughout the New Testament, but it is especially prominent in the Johannine literature.

MORTAL LIFE AND ETERNAL LIFE

The New Testament uses several words for "life." The word *bios* is used twice in 1 John to mean goods or possessions—in other words, one's "living" or the resources that sustain one's life (1 Jn 2:16; 3:17). The same word is used for the widow's offering in Luke 21:4 and the inheritance claimed by the prodigal son in Luke 15:30. The word does not occur in the Fourth Gospel.

A more common word for life is *psychē*. This is the life principle that human beings share with animals (Rev 8:9; 18:13). It is the natural life that a person may "lay down" by dying for someone else: the good shepherd (Jn 10:11), Jesus (Jn 10:17), Peter (Jn 13:37-38), believers for one another (1 Jn 3:16). While the *psychē* usually ends with physical death, it sometimes expresses a consciousness that continues beyond death, such as the "souls" of the martyrs under the heavenly altar who cry out for justice in Revelation 6:9-10. Similarly, when Jesus says that his "soul" is troubled (Jn 12:27), he seems to be referring to his inner life or consciousness rather than to his physical life. In these cases, *psychē* may refer to what moderns would call the "self."

---

[2]Ibid., p. 38.
[3]G. R. Beasley-Murray, *Gospel of Life: Theology in the Fourth Gospel* (Peabody, Mass.: Hendrickson, 1991), p. 2.
[4]Ibid., p. 3.

According to Jesus, laying down the *psychē* for someone else is the highest expression of love (Jn 15:13). Believers must be willing to give up their mortal lives in order to obtain a greater life: "Those who love their life [*psychē*] lose it, and those who hate their life [*psychē*] in this world will keep it for eternal life [*zōē*]" (Jn 12:25). Parallel versions in Matthew 10:39, Mark 8:35 and Luke 9:24 express the same paradox of losing one's life (*psychē*) to save it, but they do not mention eternal life.

The phrase translated "eternal life" in John 12:25 is *zōē aiōnios*. The word *zōē* almost always refers to this special life that is greater than mortal life. This word occurs frequently in the book of Revelation to describe eschatological realities such as the tree of life (Rev 2:7; 22:2, 14, 19); the book of life (Rev 3:5; 13:8; 17:8; 20:12, 15; 21:27); and the water of life (Rev 7:17; 21:6; 22:1, 17). It is the standard word for life in the Fourth Gospel. The word *zōē* and the phrase *zōē aiōnios* have the same meaning.[5] The word *aiōnios* means eternal. What does it mean for life to be eternal?

Eternality is fundamentally a quality of God. In the New Testament, both the Father and the Spirit are called eternal (Rom 16:26; Heb 9:14). Eternality characterizes the life of God in contrast to transitory mortal human life. For example, believers look forward to a resurrection body, which Paul calls "a building from God, a house not made with hands, eternal in the heavens" (2 Cor 5:1). Paul contrasts this eternal body with the "tent" in which believers presently dwell (2 Cor 5:4). He probably does not mean that the believer's resurrection body has existed forever, but that it partakes of the strength and permanence of the life of God, in contrast to the frail mortal body, which had its origin in the dust of the earth (cf. 1 Cor 15:35-50).

Eternality is also associated with the future in contrast to the present. For example, Paul contrasts his present trials with his future resurrection: "For this slight momentary affliction is preparing us for an eternal weight of glory beyond all measure, because we look not at what can be seen but at what cannot be seen; for what can be seen is temporary, but what cannot be seen is eternal" (2 Cor 4:17-18). "What cannot be seen" refers both to the realm of God and to the future God has prepared for his people. In the consummation, the realm of God and the world of mortals will converge,

---

[5]Thompson, "Eternal Life," p. 38.

as pictured in the book of Revelation when the New Jerusalem comes "down out of heaven from God" (Rev 21:2). At that time, as Paul expresses it, "what is mortal [will] be swallowed up by life" (2 Cor 5:4). The eschatological judgment results in states that are eternal because they are final and everlasting: eternal fire (Mt 18:8; Jude 1:7), eternal glory (2 Tim 2:10; 1 Pet 5:10). At that time believers will enter or inherit the eternal kingdom (2 Pet 1:11).

Eternality expresses a long period of time, but not always in the same way. For example, God's "eternal dominion" (1 Tim 6:16) is presumably coextensive with God's own existence. However, the "eternal sin" of blasphemy against the Holy Spirit (Mk 3:29) would be committed in someone's lifetime but would have permanent consequences: "Whoever blasphemes against the Holy Spirit can never have forgiveness." The parallel in Matthew adds "either in this age or in the age to come" (Mt 12:32). In addition to a reality that begins in the present and is everlasting, "eternal" can refer to a reality that began in ages past and terminates in the present. Paul refers to the mystery of God's saving purpose in Christ that was kept secret "for long ages [*chronois aiōniois*] but is now disclosed" (Rom 16:25-26). It can also refer to an event that took place in eternity past: "This grace was given to us in Christ Jesus before the ages began [*chronōn aiōniōn*]" (2 Tim 1:9).

These findings suggest that eternal life is life of long duration, although they do not establish a definitive time frame. Eternal life is also qualitatively different from mortal human life. It is "the life by which God Himself lives."[6] It has the same qualities of immortality and imperishability that characterize God's life. It is a glorious existence. Eternal life is not otherworldly, however, because it includes the resurrection of the body. Salvation enables human beings to participate in the life of God without ceasing to be embodied human beings.

In the Synoptics and Paul, eternal life is generally regarded as a future experience. The Synoptics talk about eternal life as one of the blessings of the kingdom of God. Someone enters or inherits eternal life—the same language used for the kingdom (Mk 9:43; 10:17). Life is the goal of a difficult journey (Mt 7:14). In Matthew 25:46, eternal life is the reward of the

---

[6]Raymond E. Brown, *The Gospel According to John*, 2 vols., Anchor Bible, ed. William Foxwell Albright and David Noel Freedman (New York: Doubleday, 1966), p. 507.

faithful sheep at the eschatological judgment. In Mark 10:30, Jesus declares that those who have left everything for his sake will receive "a hundredfold now in this age—houses, brothers and sisters, mothers and children, and fields with persecutions—and in the age to come eternal life." Thus in the Synoptic Gospels, eternal life is the life of the age to come. It is associated with the consummation of the kingdom of God.

Paul also describes eternal life as a future possession of believers: "If you sow to your own flesh, you will reap corruption from the flesh; but if you sow to the Spirit, you will reap eternal life from the Spirit. So let us not grow weary in doing what is right, for we will reap at harvest-time, if we do not give up" (Gal 6:8-9). Eternal life is the eschatological goal toward which believers strive. It is something believers must "take hold of" (1 Tim 6:12). However, Paul emphasizes that eternal life is God's gift, not something people can earn: "For the wages of sin is death, but the free gift of God is eternal life in Christ Jesus our Lord" (Rom 6:23). Human beings have earned only death, but God offers them eternal life as a gift in Christ.

ETERNAL LIFE IN THE FOURTH GOSPEL

The Gospel of John has same understanding of eschatology as the Synoptics and Paul, but it weights the balance of "already" and "not yet" more toward the "already." Like the other Gospels, the Fourth Gospel associates eternal life with the general resurrection: "This is indeed the will of my Father, that all who see the Son and believe in him may have eternal life; and I will raise them up on the last day" (Jn 6:40).

Jesus claims that he is the mediator of resurrection life: "I am the resurrection and the life [*zōē*]. Those who believe in me, even though they die, will live [*zēsetai*], and everyone who lives [*zōn*] and believes in me will never die [literally, 'does not die into eternity' (*eis ton aiōna*)]" (Jn 11:25-26). As in John 12:25, the apparent paradox depends on the difference between mortal life and eternal life. Even if believers die physically, they still participate in eternal life, and they will live again bodily in the resurrection (Jn 11:25). The second part of Jesus' statement is a bit harder to understand. At first glance, he seems to be saying that believers will never die (Jn 11:26). However, the life these believers possess is eternal life (*zōē*, not *psychē*). Just as Jesus is thinking of a particular kind of life, he is thinking of a particular kind of death. Those who have eternal life will not experience eternal death—that is, death apart from Christ, separated from the source of life, facing judgment and wrath because of sin.[7] "Whoever disobeys the Son will not see life [$z\bar{o}\bar{e}n$], but must endure God's wrath" (Jn 3:36).

However, the Fourth Gospel differs from the Synoptics and Paul in its emphasis on eternal life as a present possession.[8] For John, eternal life is "the life of the Age to Come given here and now."[9] Jesus declares, "Anyone who hears my word and believes him who sent me has eternal life, and does not come under judgment, but has passed from death to life" (Jn 5:24). Similarly, in his first letter, John declares, "I write these things to you who believe in the name of the Son of God, so that you may know that you have eternal life" (1 Jn 5:13). Those who believe in Christ experience eternal life in the present. They have already passed the eschatological judgment and have received the eschatological blessing. However, John's need to reassure believers of this fact suggests that the present reality of eternal life can be overlooked.

Despite the dualistic language and imagery of the Gospel of John, the emphasis on eternal life as present works against a simple dualism of physical versus spiritual or earthly versus heavenly. Life, whether *psyche* or *$z\bar{o}\bar{e}$*, comes from God and depends upon God. Life of any kind is mediated through Jesus Christ, the eternal Word become flesh.[10] Both present and future life depend on people's response to him:

> Very truly, I tell you, the hour is coming, and is now here, when the dead will hear the voice of the Son of God, and those who hear will live. For just as the Father has life in himself, so he has granted the Son also to have life in himself; and he has given him authority to execute judgment, because he is the

---

[7]Paul S. Minear, "The Promise of Life in the Gospel of John," *Theology Today* 49, no. 4 (January 1993): 490, 492. The term "eternal death" is my own.

[8]This more "realized eschatology" was championed by C. H. Dodd, *The Interpretation of the Fourth Gospel* (Cambridge: Cambridge University Press, 1953). Dodd regards eternal life in John as "timeless in quality" as in Plato, although he acknowledges that the Jewish background of the idea includes a sense of dynamism (p. 150). While John does emphasize eternal life as a present experience, the Gospel does not abandon Jewish eschatology for Platonic idealism. Eternal life is powerful and dynamic, bringing life in the present and culminating in the resurrection of the dead. Dodd interprets apparent references to the second coming as Jesus' continued presence with the disciples through the Holy Spirit. Most interpreters believe that the Fourth Gospel views eschatology as both present and future, although present references predominate.

[9]Brown, *John*, p. 507.

[10]C. F. D. Moule, "The Meaning of 'Life' in the Gospels and Epistles of St. John," *Theology* 78, no. 657 (1975): 122, 124. See also Thompson, "Eternal Life," p. 40.

Son of Man. Do not be astonished at this; for the hour is coming when all who are in their graves will hear his voice and will come out—those who have done good, to the resurrection of life, and those who have done evil, to the resurrection of condemnation. (Jn 5:25-29)

John's understanding of eternal life derives from his view of God as the living God.[11] The Father, as Creator, "has life in himself." He does not depend on anyone else for life and can grant life as he pleases. The Father has shared with the Son the power to give life and has granted the Son authority to pronounce the eschatological judgment (cf. Jn 1:4; 17:2). Because the Son has this authority, those who trust in Christ can begin to experience the eschatological blessing of eternal life now. The time of resurrection is "now here," in the sense that people who are physically alive but "dead" in relation to God can come alive to God through faith in Christ. The time of bodily resurrection is "coming" but has not yet arrived.

Eternal life is the life of creation. "This life is truly archetypal, from the beginning and therefore continuing now and forever." When Jesus says that he is "the life" (Jn 11:25; 14:6), we should think of the Prologue of John's Gospel—and behind that, the first chapter of Genesis, in which God brings creation to life by speaking it into existence.[12] Now the Word through which life began has become flesh (Jn 1:14), bringing life-giving power into the midst of a broken creation.

Like the rest of the New Testament, the Fourth Gospel understands eternal life to be everlasting. Death cannot end it.[13] The life Jesus gives is secure, since he can protect believers against any who would destroy them: "I give them eternal life, and they will never perish. No one will snatch them out of my hand" (Jn 10:28). Jesus describes this life as abundant (Jn 10:10)—not just long but full and flourishing.

Eternal life is the gift of the triune God. Father, Son and Spirit are all said to "make alive" (*zōopoieō*, in Jn 5:21; 6:63). Jesus declares that bringing life is the purpose of his coming (Jn 10:10). But the Son is not alone in his mission. He is sent by the Father and, in turn, sends the Spirit to complete the impartation of life: "The Redeemer . . . mediates the saving sov-

---

[11]Thompson, "Eternal Life," p. 39.
[12]Minear, "Promise of Life," p. 488.
[13]Brown, *John*, p. 507.

ereignty of God through the Spirit of Life."[14] The theme of agency runs throughout the Fourth Gospel. The Father sends or "gives" the Son, who speaks and acts on the Father's behalf (Jn 3:16; 6:38). The Son sends the Spirit to indwell believers, who are also sent by the Son to carry on his ministry (Jn 16:7; 20:21-22).

The Son makes eternal life possible by his teaching and by his work of redemption. His disciples acknowledge that he has "the words of eternal life" (Jn 6:68). He conveys the teaching of his Father, whose commandment is eternal life (Jn 12:50). His authority to give the Holy Spirit demonstrates that he speaks the words of God (Jn 3:34). As the light of the world, Jesus can promise that his followers "will never walk in darkness but will have the light of life" (Jn 8:12). Jesus offers to the world the truth that leads to eternal life.[15] Even more importantly, however, he provides eternal life through the cross and resurrection: "And just as Moses lifted up the serpent in the wilderness, so must the Son of Man be lifted up, that whoever believes in him may have eternal life" (Jn 3:14-15). "Jesus dies precisely because of his mission to give life, yet it is his death that turns out to be the means by which he draws all who believe to eternal life."[16] Jesus' exaltation begins at the cross and continues in the resurrection. His going away leads to the outpouring of the Spirit (Jn 16:7).

While the Son makes life possible, it is the Spirit who births new life. People must be born of the Spirit in order to enter the kingdom of God (Jn 3:5-8). The Spirit is compared to flowing, life-giving water that will satisfy people's deepest thirst. Jesus tells the Samaritan woman, "The water that I will give will become in them a spring of water gushing up to eternal life" (Jn 4:14). The Evangelist later explains that Jesus' offer of living water is a reference to the Spirit, whose coming must wait until Jesus' exaltation

---

[14]Beasley-Murray, *Gospel of Life*, p. 76. In a sense, both the Son and the Spirit mediate eternal life (pp. 12, 60-61).

[15]The strong dualism of this Gospel, as well as its emphasis on correct knowledge, has led some scholars to argue that it is a product of Gnosticism. See Rudolf Bultmann, *Theology of the New Testament*, 2 vols., trans. Kendrick Grobel (New York: Charles Scribner's Sons, 1951-1955), 2:3-14. More recent scholarship has moved away from this view. Raymond Brown believes that the evidence favors a Jewish background. *John*, p. lvi. Both Gospel and Epistles share the dualism characteristic of Jewish apocalypticism, as represented in the Dead Sea Scrolls. While they talk about Jesus as the man from heaven, they attempt to counter a Gnostic or docetic view of Christ by emphasizing the concreteness of his incarnation (Jn 1:14; 20:27; 1 Jn 1:1-3).

[16]John T. Carroll, "Sickness and Healing in the New Testament Gospels," *Interpretation* 49, no. 2 (April 1995): 136.

(Jn 7:37-39). Jesus makes eternal life possible and then gives the Spirit who makes it actual by indwelling the believer. To be indwelt by the Spirit of Life is to be connected to the wellspring of eternal life.

RECEIVING ETERNAL LIFE

To receive eternal life, people must have faith (*pistis*). Cultural anthropologists tell us that *pistis* in the New Testament world had the sense of reliability and loyalty. It could be used in reference to the credibility of statements or the reliability of objects. With persons, it meant fidelity in relationships: "Relative to persons, faith is reliability in interpersonal relations: it thus takes on the value of enduring personal loyalty, of personal faithfulness. The nouns 'faith,' 'belief,' 'fidelity,' 'faithfulness,' as well as the verbs 'to have faith' and 'to believe,' refer to the social glue that binds one person to another. This bond is the social, externally manifested, emotionally rooted behavior of loyalty, commitment, and solidarity."[17] This sense of *pistis* as both credibility and fidelity is borne out in the Gospel of John.

In the Gospel of John, to have faith means, first, that people must believe certain things about Jesus. They must believe that Jesus has been sent by the Father (Jn 17:8, 21) and that Jesus is the Messiah and Son of God (Jn 20:31). They must understand that Jesus is more than a miracle worker. Jesus' miracles—or signs—give evidence of who he is (Jn 14:11), but a faith based solely on signs is superficial and inadequate. The crowds demand that Jesus prove himself by miracles, but Jesus responds that their interest is in the food, not in the meaning of the signs (Jn 6:26, 30, 36). Jesus chides Thomas for needing to have physical evidence: "Blessed are those who have not seen and yet have come to believe" (Jn 20:29). Seeing or hearing is not enough. People must see *and believe* (Jn 6:40) or hear *and believe* (Jn 5:24). Those who believe in Jesus without seeing or hearing him—including John's audience and modern Christians—are more blessed than Thomas.

Second, having faith means obeying the teachings of Jesus. Disciples must keep Jesus' commandments in order to remain in his love (Jn 15:10). The Gospel of John makes clear that faith is not just cognitive assent but

---

[17]Bruce J. Malina, "Faith/Faithfulness," in *Biblical Social Values and Their Meaning: A Handbook*, ed. John J. Pilch and Bruce J. Malina (Peabody, Mass.: Hendrickson, 1993), pp. 67-68.

total commitment.[18] Faith and obedience are closely associated: "Whoever believes in the Son has eternal life; whoever disobeys the Son will not see life, but must endure God's wrath" (Jn 3:36). Faith is contrasted with disobedience rather than with unbelief, suggesting that faith and obedience are aspects of the same response. As already noted, the Greek word *pistis* can mean both faith and faithfulness.[19] "So when Jesus called for faith we can be confident that he had in mind not simply assent to a form of words, or a passive expression of trust, but a reliance on God which would become the basis and motivating center for all conduct and relationships."[20] In the Fourth Gospel, truth is not just something to be believed but something to be practiced. Believers must "do the truth" (Jn 3:21, author's translation).

Finally, faith is a relationship with Jesus. Disciples must believe in Jesus himself (Jn 3:16). They must trust him so much that they are willing to lose everything, even their lives, for his sake. The Fourth Gospel locates both truth and life in Jesus himself: "Jesus said to him, 'I am the way, and the truth, and the life. No one comes to the Father except through me'" (Jn 14:6). Jesus does not merely speak the words of God; he himself *is* the Word of God (Jn 1:1, 14). He does not merely give eternal life; he himself *is* eternal life (1 Jn 1:3; 5:20). Jesus himself embodies both the truth and the life of God. Both revelation and redemption take place in relationship to him: "Manifestly, faith is more than a single act but becomes a continuing relationship. To express this attitude John uses the term *remain* . . . to refer to an active holding on to Jesus and his teaching."[21] One must "have" the Son (not just believe in him) in order to have eternal life, because eternal life is found in him (1 Jn 5:11-12).

ETERNAL LIFE AS ABIDING IN CHRIST

Thus in the Fourth Gospel, eternal life is not transactional but relational. Its essence is a personal knowledge of Jesus and his Father (Jn 17:3). This relationship is effected by the Holy Spirit, who by indwelling believers

---

[18]I. Howard Marshall, *New Testament Theology: Many Witnesses, One Gospel* (Downers Grove, Ill.: InterVarsity Press, 2004), p. 521.

[19]"πίστις," in *BAGD*, pp. 662-64.

[20]James D. G. Dunn, *Jesus' Call to Discipleship*, Understanding Jesus Today, ed. Howard Clark Kee (Cambridge: Cambridge University Press, 1992). Dunn uses the construct "faith-faithfulness" to translate *pistis*.

[21]Marshall, *New Testament Theology*, pp. 521-22.

brings them into union with both the Father and the Son: "You know [the Holy Spirit], because he abides with you, and he will be in you. I will not leave you orphaned; I am coming to you. In a little while the world will no longer see me, but you will see me; because I live, you also will live. On that day you will know that I am in my Father, and you in me, and I in you" (Jn 14:17-20). The mutual indwelling of Father and Son is extended to believers through the Spirit. Thus eternal life not just the gift of God but sharing in the life of God.[22] By God's grace, believers can share the intimate communion that exists between the Father and the Son. "Only those who know God, who live in fellowship with God and in harmony with the purposes of God, have eternal life, not because living in fellowship with God merits eternal life as a reward, but because fellowship with the eternal God is already to have a share in God's own life."[23] This union between Christ and believers is expressed in earthy, organic metaphors— eating and drinking, vine and branches, even consuming the flesh and blood of Jesus himself. Eating bread and drinking water "express the spiritual satisfaction of human desires that comes about through this union with Jesus."[24] Jesus compares his relationship with his followers to the union between a vine and its branches (Jn 15:1-11). He is drawing on the Old Testament imagery of Israel as the vineyard of God (Is 5:1-7). As the true vine, Jesus fulfills the expectations that God had of Israel and thereby serves as the source of life for reconstituted Israel.

The vine-and-branches image is more than a reference to Jesus' historical significance, however. It expresses an intimate union between Jesus and his followers, who dwell or remain in one another (Jn 15:4). Disciples receive life and spiritual nourishment through their union with him. They draw from him the strength they need for fruitful or effective ministry. John insists on both mutual indwelling and the expression of that indwelling in action: "The love of the Father for the Son, returned by Him, establishes a community of life between Father and Son, which exhibits itself in that the Son speaks the Father's word and does His works. . . . The disciples are loved by Christ and return His love in obedience; in doing so, they share His life, which manifests itself in doing His

---

[22]Brown, *John*, p. 506.
[23]Thompson, "Eternal Life," p. 40.
[24]Marshall, *New Testament Theology*, p. 520.

works." Thus eternal life is experienced and expressed as love.[25]

Although they have already been "cleansed" or pruned by Jesus' teaching, believers must maintain an ongoing relationship with him in order to sustain their participation in his life. This theme of abiding shows that eternal life is not a thing one receives but a reality in which one participates. Since eternal life means knowing God, it can be experienced only in the context of a reciprocal relationship. Jesus' instruction to remain in him stresses the need for faithfulness in that relationship.[26] Disciples who fail to remain in him will be "thrown away" like unfruitful branches and eventually destroyed (Jn 15:6). But those who do remain in him will experience fullness of joy (Jn 15:11).

This is a corporate image; there is only one vine, and all those who are connected to the vine are connected to one another.[27] Eternal life is God's gift to the community of believers, "the righteous and faithful people of God."[28] Believers share with one another the life-giving love of Christ: "We know that we have passed from death to life because we love one another. Whoever does not love abides in death" (1 Jn 3:14). Branches who isolate themselves from the life-giving vine will not survive.

Some argue that those who possess eternal life can never lose it, because eternal life by definition is everlasting. But if eternal life is primarily qualitative rather than quantitative, there is no guarantee that it can never be lost: "'Eternal' describes the kind of life one has in Christ and not how long he will possess life."[29] The Gospel of John is full of assurances that believers need not fear that eternal life can be taken away from them. Jesus declares, "My sheep hear my voice. I know them, and they follow me. I give them eternal life, and they will never perish. No one will snatch them out of my hand" (Jn 10:27-28). The Shepherd will always protect the sheep. But the Gospel is also clear that obedience and loyalty are necessary dimensions of what it means to believe in Jesus. Eternal life is not a transaction; it is an ongoing relationship between the life-giving Shepherd and

---

[25]Dodd, *Fourth Gospel*, pp. 195-96, 198, 199.

[26]Thompson, "Eternal Life," p. 41, 46.

[27]Janis Rozentals discusses eternal life as a fulfillment of our relationship with God (pp. 56-60), Christ (pp. 61-63), and other people (pp. 63-69). *The Promise of Eternal Life: Biblical Witness to Christian Hope* (Minneapolis: Augsburg, 1987).

[28]Thompson, "Eternal Life," p. 48.

[29]J. W. Roberts, "Some Observations on the Meaning of 'Eternal Life' in the Gospel of John," *Restoration Quarterly* 7, no. 4 (1963): 193.

the sheep who follow him. To turn one's back on that relationship would mean to turn one's back on eternal life.[30]

The most striking imagery for the union of Christ and believers occurs in the Bread of Life discourse (Jn 6:25-71). Jesus declares that he is "the bread of life" or "the living bread that came down from heaven" (Jn 6:35, 48, 51). He probably means both that he is living and that he gives life. In contrast to the manna God provided in the days of Moses, this bread will satisfy every hunger and thirst and will grant eternal life (Jn 6:35, 49-51). Thus far, the bread image could be understood as a metaphor for Jesus' teaching. However, Jesus goes on to declare that the bread is his flesh, and that people must eat his flesh and drink his blood in order to experience eternal life (Jn 6:51, 54-55). Eating his flesh and drinking his blood results in the mutual indwelling of Jesus and the believer (Jn 6:56). Those who refuse to do this "have no life" in them (Jn 6:53).

Jesus' language here would have been highly offensive in his day and has been controversial ever since. He seems to be advocating cannibalism to people who keep Mosaic dietary laws! Consuming blood was grounds for expulsion from the covenant people (Lev 17:10-14). Many of Jesus' disciples decided that this teaching was too much for them and stopped following him (Jn 6:66). Most scholars have understood it as a reference to the Eucharist, especially since there is no account of the Eucharist in the Fourth Gospel. This sacramental understanding supports the view that worshipers consume the actual body and blood of Jesus in the communion elements in order to receive spiritual life. However, this interpretation assumes a developed Eucharistic theology that is more at home in the church fathers than on the lips of Jesus. Moreover, the idea that an act of worship creates mutual indwelling runs counter to the teaching in the rest of the Gospel that indwelling is effected by the Spirit as people trust Jesus and keep his commandments.

However, there is another possible interpretation of this passage. The Fourth Gospel contains several scenes in which Jesus' audience takes his figurative language literally. For example, the Samaritan woman thought that Jesus was offering her an unending supply of flowing water rather than the "living water" of eternal life (Jn 4:10-15). After speaking to the

---

[30]See also the discussion in Robert Shank, *Life in the Son: A Study of the Doctrine of Perseverance* (Minneapolis: Bethany House, 1989), pp. 40-48.

Samaritan woman, Jesus tells his disciples that he has food that they are unaware of. They say to one another, "Surely no one has brought him something to eat?" He tells them that his "food" is to do the will of his Father (Jn 4:33-34). Later, when Jesus tells his disciples that Lazarus has fallen asleep and they suggest waking him up, he must explain to them that Lazarus has died (Jn 11:11-14).

A similar interplay between literal and figurative may be present in John 6. After Jesus tells the crowd that they need to eat his flesh, he explains privately to his disciples, "It is the spirit that gives life; the flesh is useless. The words that I have spoken to you are spirit and life" (Jn 6:63). If the flesh is useless, it seems unlikely that life could be found in consuming Jesus' flesh. Instead, Jesus seems to be speaking metaphorically about the need to consume his words to have eternal life.[31] Nevertheless, Jesus' literal flesh and blood are also life-giving, in the sense that his vicarious death will offer life to humanity. Like the manna, Jesus himself is God's provision of life for his people. In any case, the way one interprets Jesus' words of institution at the Last Supper in the other Gospels will probably influence how one interprets Jesus' comments here.

Participation in eternal life brings with it ethical obligations. Participating in the life of Christ entails living as he would live: "Whoever says, 'I abide in him,' ought to walk just as he walked" (1 Jn 2:6). As agents of Jesus empowered by the Spirit, believers live out Jesus' "new commandment" to love one another as he has loved them (Jn 13:34-35). They can extend love to others because they have been loved themselves (1 Jn 4:19). Love is both the effect and the evidence of eternal life: "We know that we have passed from death to life because we love one another. Whoever does not love abides in death" (1 Jn 3:14). Their gratitude to Christ and their confidence in eternal life enable them to lay down their lives for others as Jesus did for them (1 Jn 3:16). They have the boldness to intercede for one another, knowing that God will grant life to the sinner at their request—as long as the sin is not mortal (1 Jn 5:14-16). Their love and unity will be signs that testify to Jesus so that the world may come to believe (Jn 13:35; 17:21).

---

[31]See the discussion in David Peterson, *Engaging with God: A Biblical Theology of Worship* (Grand Rapids: Eerdmans, 1992), pp. 127-28.

CONCLUSION

Eternal life is the eschatological gift of God, the life of the kingdom of God in the age to come. It is everlasting life. More importantly, it has the qualities of joy and completeness that characterize the life of God. In fact, it *is* the life of God mediated to human beings by the Son of God and generated in them by the Spirit of God. The qualitative dimension of eternal life explains how it can be both present and future. Those who come to know Jesus begin to experience a life that is shaped and sustained by the love of God in Christ. This life cannot be touched by death, and it will be perfected in the resurrection.

While eternal life is the gift of God, experiencing it requires both faith and obedience. Like the kingdom of God, it is both gift and demand. Eternal life, like mortal life, must be lived. It can be lived only in relationship to God and others. Participating in the life of God energizes believers to love one another and lay down their lives so that others may find life.[32] While eternal life is assured for those who have a relationship with Christ, it is not guaranteed to those who turn away. Believers must remain in Christ to draw on the strength he provides.

Thus, in contrast to much popular theology, eternal life in the New Testament is not concerned with the spirit alone and is not confined to the hereafter. It involves both spirit and body, and it begins now. This means that it has significant implications for life in the present. To live out these implications, the church must both teach and model a theology of embodied life that is lived in loving relationship to God and others, beginning now and extending into eternity. Since this life is found in Christ, we must continue to proclaim his message, teach his commandments and nurture believers' relationship to him. We must encourage one another to remain in Christ.

Eternal life is not world-denying but world-affirming, in that the life of human beings has transcendent value because of its transcendent origin.[33] Freedom from the fear of death releases us to live this life more fully. Awareness of eternal life can transform our perception of everyday life: "We will not think ceaselessly of eternity, but we will see everything in this life in the perspective of eternity." In the light of eternity, both the successes and the sufferings of life have value, because we know that God

---

[32]See chapter eleven for a discussion of participation in Christ in Paul's letters.
[33]Moule, "Meaning of 'Life,'" p. 124.

plans to redeem them: "Only one hope can bring meaning into all the circumstances of life: the hope that God will bring this mortal and imperfect life to its consummation."[34]

We need not fear death if we know Christ. Both our life and our death can be seeds of eternal life if we remain in him.[35] Thus while eternal life teaches us to affirm mortal life, we should not regard mortal life as the greatest blessing or the highest good. We should not assume that it should be preserved at all costs, because Jesus has promised us that our life with him will not end with death. This conviction can guide us as we make difficult end of life decisions for ourselves or our loved ones.

However, as an expression of its witness to eternal life, the church should work for and foster fullness of life for all people now—at all stages of life, from conception to death. "Thus those who experience life now can never will death, in any sort or form, for others. Those who have life must be committed to life for the world, whether through the proclamation of the one who is life, the alleviation of physical pain, or the healing of emotional distress."[36] Christians should be at the forefront of the effort to provide adequate health care for all people. We should apply a consistent ethic of life to all social issues, from abortion and euthanasia to capital punishment and war.[37] We must do more to develop a healthy theology of the body that can counter the death-dealing views of Western society, which fosters both hatred of the body and physical indulgence, whether in food, drugs or sex. In order to address the culture, however, we will have to confess and correct our own contributions to the problem.

Finally, as Christians, we should demonstrate—to one another and to the world—the love that characterizes the life of Christ. We can show that it is possible to live by self-giving rather than by self-seeking. We can model community and communion. For people who feel incomplete and yearn for something more, we can point the way to the One who will fulfill all their longings. We have a message of life to proclaim to a culture of death. We can offer people the life they were meant to have. But we can do this only if we live that life to the fullest ourselves.

---

[34]Rozentals, *Eternal Life*, pp. 106, 109.
[35]Moule, "Meaning of 'Life,'" p. 124.
[36]Thompson, "Eternal Life," p. 51.
[37]See, for example, Joseph Cardinal Bernardin et al., *Consistent Ethic of Life*, ed. Thomas G. Fuechtmann (Kansas City, Mo.: Sheed & Ward, 1988).

FOR FURTHER READING

Beasley-Murray, G. R. *Gospel of Life: Theology in the Fourth Gospel.* Peabody, Mass.: Hendrickson, 1991.

Bernardin, Joseph L., et al. *Consistent Ethic of Life.* Edited by Thomas G. Fuechtmann. Kansas City, Mo.: Sheed & Ward, 1988.

Brown, Raymond E. *The Gospel According to John.* 2 vols. Anchor Bible. Edited by William Foxwell Albright and David Noel Freedman. New York: Doubleday, 1966.

Dodd, C. H. *The Interpretation of the Fourth Gospel.* Cambridge: Cambridge University Press, 1953.

Ladd, George Eldon. *A Theology of the New Testament.* Edited by Donald A. Hagner. Rev. ed. Grand Rapids: Eerdmans, 1994, pp. 290-305.

Minear, Paul S. "The Promise of Life in the Gospel of John." *Theology Today* 49, no. 4 (January 1993): 485-99.

Moule, C. F. D. "The Meaning of 'Life' in the Gospel and Epistles of St. John: A Study in the Story of Lazarus, John 11:1-44." *Theology* 78 (1975): 114-25.

Roberts, J. W. "Some Observations on the Meaning of 'Eternal Life' in the Gospel of John." *Restoration Quarterly* 7, no. 4 (1963): 186-93.

Rozentals, Janis. *The Promise of Eternal Life: Biblical Witness to Christian Hope.* Minneapolis: Augsburg, 1987.

Shank, Robert. *Life in the Son: A Study of the Doctrine of Perseverance.* Minneapolis: Bethany House, 1989.

Thompson, Marianne Meye. "Eternal Life in the Gospel of John." *Ex Auditu* 5 (1989): 35-55.

5

I AM ABOUT TO
DO A NEW THING

Regeneration, New Creation

AMONG THE VARIOUS IMAGES of salvation in the New Testament, the new birth is relatively familiar. In contemporary American culture, especially, the term "born again Christian" has become associated with a particular religious subculture. For some, the new birth expresses the truest picture of what it means to be a Christian. For others, it expresses very little besides a narrow-minded fundamentalism.

From the New Testament perspective, both of these notions are misguided. The new birth, or regeneration, is only one picture of salvation used by the New Testament writers to express the new reality created by the coming of Christ. However, it represents an aspect of that reality so important that one cannot participate in the kingdom of God without it. Furthermore, the regeneration of individuals is only part of the work God is doing to restore the whole creation. Whether our view of the human predicament focuses on personal sin, social dysfunction or environmental disorder, the images of regeneration and new creation speak to our situation.

REGENERATION AND NEWNESS
While only Paul uses the Greek word for "newness" (*kainotēs*), the idea of newness appears throughout the New Testament. It is found explicitly in

all but seven books.[1] In Jesus' life, death and resurrection, God has done the "new thing" predicted by the prophets (Is 43:18-19), inaugurating a new age and a new reality.[2] Jesus' initiation of the kingdom of God is "new wine" that requires new wineskins (Mk 2:22). Jesus challenges people with new teaching (Mk 1:27) and gives his disciples a new commandment of Christlike love (Jn 13:34). This newness will be consummated with the new heavens and new earth, in which the people of God dwell with God in the New Jerusalem, and God declares, "See, I am making all things new" (Rev 21:1-5).

In his classic study of "newness" in the New Testament, Roy Harrisville argues that the words for "new" (*kainos* and *neos*) have both temporal and qualitative dimensions. The "new" is recent in time, but it is also qualitatively different from what has come before.[3] By accentuating the new, the biblical writers are not advocating progress, as if more recent is always better. They are talking about eschatological newness, the arrival in history of the eschatological era. The new is characterized by continuity with the past, contrast with the past, dynamism and finality. It has an energy that transposes life-as-it-has-been into a new key, moving it toward the eschatological goal.[4] Newness is fundamental to the concept of regeneration, which refers to the activity of God in restoring the integrity of a creation that has been marred by sin. This restoration involves such a radical transformation that it can be called a new birth (in the Johannine literature) or a new creation (in Paul's letters).

Especially among conservative Christians, regeneration is typically thought of in individual terms. In the New Testament, however, it also has corporate and cosmic dimensions. In fact, these larger dimensions are the context within which the instances of individual regeneration should be understood. The New Testament writings reflect the Jewish eschatological expectation, based upon the Old Testament prophets, that God would act decisively in the future to set his creation to rights. Mark 9:12 (=Mt

---

[1]Roy A. Harrisville, *The Concept of Newness in the New Testament* (Minneapolis: Augsburg, 1960), p. 107.

[2]J. Behm argues that *kainos* is "the epitome of the wholly different and miraculous thing which is brought by the time of salvation. Hence, 'new' is a leading teleological term in apocalyptic promise." "καινός κτλ.," in *TDNT* 1:447.

[3]Harrisville, *Concept of Newness*, p. 13. He argues, contrary to earlier scholarship, that *kainos* and *neos* are synonyms.

[4]Ibid., pp. 43, 20.

17:11) and Acts 3:21 refer to this expected restoration of all things. This restoration could be conceived of in cosmic terms, as in the Mark and Acts passages, or in corporate (national) terms, as when the disciples ask Jesus if it is time for him to restore the kingdom to Israel (Acts 1:6).

The Greek word for regeneration, *palingenesia,* occurs only twice in the New Testament. The word comes from *palin* (again) and *genesis* (birth or origin).[5] It means a new beginning. In Matthew 19:28, regeneration has a cosmic sense: "Jesus said to them, 'Truly I tell you, at the renewal of all things, when the Son of Man is seated on the throne of his glory, you who have followed me will also sit on twelve thrones, judging the twelve tribes of Israel." The disciples, who have left everything to follow Jesus, will reign with him in the new creation.[6]

By contrast, Titus 3:5 applies the language of regeneration to a present personal reality: "He saved us, not because of any works of righteousness that we had done, but according to his mercy, through the water of rebirth and renewal by the Holy Spirit." Through the Holy Spirit, those who believe in Christ can now experience in part the eschatological renewal promised at the consummation. Like the kingdom of God, regeneration has an already/not yet character. The Spirit's renewal of individual lives is a foretaste of the future cosmic renewal. According to James 1:18, regenerated believers are the "first fruits" of the renewal of creation.

REGENERATION AS NEW BIRTH

The central passage for the image of new birth is John 3, Jesus' encounter with Nicodemus. Nicodemus, a Pharisee, comes to Jesus by night to talk with him. He acknowledges Jesus as a teacher sent from God. In an apparent *non sequitur,* Jesus tells him that no one can see the kingdom of God unless he or she is "born again" or "born from above" (*gennēthē anōthen*).

The meaning of this phrase has been much debated. Similar texts in 1 Peter 1:3, 23 clearly mean "born again" or "born anew," but they use the verb *anagennaō* rather than *gennaō anōthen.* Nicodemus certainly under-

---

[5]J. Guhrt, "Birth etc.," in *NIDNTT* 1:184.
[6]Donald A. Hagner translates *en tē palingenesia* as "in the age of the renewing of the world." He surveys the background of the phrase in both Jewish and Greco-Roman contexts. *Matthew 14–28,* Word Biblical Commentary, ed. Bruce M. Metzger, David A. Hubbard and Glenn W. Barker (Nashville: Nelson, 1995), pp. 563, 565. See also David C. Sim, "The Meaning of Παλιγγενεσία in Matthew 19:28," *Journal for the Study of the New Testament* 50 (1993): 3-12.

stands Jesus to mean "again," because he asks how it is possible to enter one's mother's womb a second time (Jn 3:4). However, irony is common in the Gospel of John. Jesus' hearers often misunderstand his statements, usually by taking literally what he means figuratively (see, for example, the Samaritan woman's misunderstanding of "living water" in Jn 4:11 and the disciples' misunderstanding of Jesus' "food" in Jn 4:32-33).[7] All other instances of *anōthen* in the Fourth Gospel mean "from above" or "from the top" (Jn 3:31; 19:11, 23).[8]

In particular, Jesus' function as the representative and revealer of the Father reflects his identity as the one who comes "from above" (Jn 3:31). In this Gospel, one's origin determines one's identity and character. Jesus is "from above," while his opponents are "from below" (Jn 8:23). Thus, Jesus' response to Nicodemus is perhaps not a non sequitur but the answer to a question that Nicodemus has not voiced: to reach the kingdom of God, one must have the proper origin. Jesus is indeed from God (although perhaps not in the way Nicodemus thinks), and everyone must be from God in order to enter God's kingdom. In any case, what Jesus goes on to emphasize is not a second birth but the divine origin of the birth: it comes from the Holy Spirit (Jn 3:6).[9]

This spiritual birth is essential for anyone who wants to "see" or "enter" the kingdom of God. The necessity of regeneration here seems to parallel the necessity of repentance in the Synoptics; the words for repentance (*metanoeō, metanoia*) do not occur in this Gospel.[10] The Gospel of John mentions the kingdom of God only here (Jn 3:3, 5), although Jesus refers to his own kingdom in Jn 18:36. Given Jesus' identity as the agent of God,

---

[7]Raymond E. Brown agrees that *anōthen* is part of the "technique of misunderstanding" in the Fourth Gospel. This rhetorical technique is used by John to introduce a teaching, as Jesus proceeds to clarify the misunderstanding. *The Gospel According to John*, The Anchor Bible, ed. William F. Albright and David Noel Freedman, 2 vols. (New York: Doubleday, 1966), 1:130.

[8]Linda Belleville has argued that *anōthen* means "again" in John 3:3, 7, in part because there is no word in Aramaic that would allow for the same misunderstanding between "again" and "from above" (assuming that the conversation took place in Aramaic). "'Born of Water and Spirit': John 3:5," *Trinity Journal*, n.s., 1 (1980): 125-41. While the linguistic point is significant, the other instances of *anōthen* in John, coupled with the strong themes of origin and agency, combine to give greater support to "from above."

[9]According to F. Büchsel, the Evangelist "always describes birth in terms of its origin." "ἄνω κτλ.," in *TDNT* 1:378.

[10]William Douglas Chamberlain, "For Deliverance and Freedom: The Biblical Doctrine of Repentance," *Interpretation* 4, no. 3 (July 1950): 274.

it seems likely that the two kingdoms are the same. In the latter passage, Jesus declares that his kingdom "is not from this world." His statement concerns origin and character, not location. He does not mean that his kingdom is otherworldly, existing only in heaven, but that its character reflects its origin. Since his kingdom is not earthly but heavenly in origin, it will not employ the violent tactics of earthly kingdoms.

For the same reason, those who enter the kingdom of God must be compatible with it. Since the kingdom of God has its origin in God, who is spirit and requires spiritual worshipers (Jn 4:24), anyone who wants to participate in it must have the same spiritual character. To participate in earthly kingdoms, one needs only to be born of the flesh; to participate in God's kingdom, one must be born "of the Spirit" or "of God" (Jn 3:6; 1:13). Like begets like: "those who are born from the Spirit become like the Spirit."[11] Divine origin also suggests divine initiative. The new birth comes about by the will of God, not by human will.

Jesus responds to Nicodemus that one must be "born of water and Spirit" to enter the kingdom. Much ink has been spilled over the interpretation of this expression. Linda Belleville has identified six categories of interpretations.[12] By far the most common approach through church history has been to understand the expression as a reference to Christian baptism—despite the fact that this would make the statement an anachronism, and therefore an invention of the evangelist placed on the lips of Jesus.[13] A more helpful approach would be to see the expression in terms of the Fourth Gospel itself and the Old Testament background that a "teacher of Israel" like Nicodemus would be expected to know (Jn 3:10). The choice of interpretation depends in part on whether "water and Spirit" refers to two different events (such as natural and spiritual birth) or to a single complex event (such as conversion or baptism). The grammatical construction in Greek leads the majority of scholars to prefer the second

---

[11]Klyne R. Snodgrass, "That Which is Born from *Pneuma* is *Pneuma*: Rebirth and Spirit in John 3:5-6," *The Covenant Quarterly* 49, no. 1 (February 1991): 20.

[12]Belleville, "Water and Spirit," p. 125.

[13]The fourth-century *Apostolic Constitutions* even modifies the text to read as follows: "Unless a person is baptized of water and Spirit, he shall by no means enter the Kingdom of Heaven." Ruth B. Edwards, "New Birth and the Spirit," *Expository Times* 111, no. 8 (May 2000): 269. Brown argues that the primary meaning of the phrase is eschatological renewal, but he posits a "secondary level of sacramental reference" that would have been understood by Christian readers or hearers (*John*, 1:142).

option.[14] So what kind of birth of both water and Spirit might Nicodemus have been expected to understand?

In the Gospel narrative, water and Spirit are joined in chapter 1, when John the Baptist identifies himself as one who baptizes with water and Jesus as one who baptizes with the Spirit (Jn 1:33). Nicodemus might be familiar with John's preaching, but if Jesus is saying that John's baptism is essential for kingdom membership, no one who came to faith after John's imprisonment could qualify. Metaphorically, Jesus could be suggesting that both repentance (represented by John's baptism) and faith (response to Jesus, the giver of the Spirit) are necessary to enter the kingdom.

A more likely possibility, however, is that Jesus is alluding to the Old Testament. Both water and Spirit are used in the Old Testament to represent the life that comes from God. In prophetic passages such as Isaiah 32:15, Isaiah 44:3 and Zechariah 14:8, they symbolize the cleansing and renewal of Israel.[15] In the most significant of these passages, Ezekiel 36:25-27, God promises to sprinkle water on his people to cleanse them and to put a new spirit (God's own spirit) within them. This new spirit will enable God's people to follow God's commandments and live in covenant relationship with God. God's promise is illustrated in Ezekiel 37 when God's Spirit or breath gives life to the dry bones representing Israel.

As a teacher of Israel, Nicodemus would be familiar with the imagery Jesus is using, even if not with his specific point. Jesus seems to be telling him that the time of eschatological renewal is at hand. God is providing the promised cleansing and new spirit to his people. Thus, John 3:5 should read "of water and spirit"—the new spirit that only the Holy Spirit can produce (Jn 3:6).[16] Without this renewal, no one can participate in the coming kingdom.

In similar language, Titus 3:5 says that God saved believers "through

---

[14]See, for example, D. A. Carson, *The Gospel According to John* (Grand Rapids: Eerdmans, 1991), p. 191; and W. L. Kynes, "New Birth," in *DJG*, p. 575.

[15]This has been pointed out by a number of scholars. See, for example, Brown, *John*, 1:140-41; Carson, *John*, p. 195; Kynes, "New Birth," p. 575. J. L. Nuelsen calls John 3 an exegesis of Ezekiel 37:1-10 ("Regeneration," in *ISBE*, 4:68). The evangelist alludes to a similar passage, Isaiah 55:1-3, when he identifies Jesus' "rivers of living water" as the Holy Spirit in John 7:37-39.

[16]On John 3:5 as a reference to the renewed human spirit rather than to the Holy Spirit, see Belleville, "Water and Spirit," p. 138-40; Brown, *John*, 1:140; Carson, *John*, p. 195; and Kynes, "New Birth," p. 575. Snodgrass argues that the Holy Spirit is meant, and concludes that "water and Spirit" refers not to baptism but to "the life-giving activity of the Spirit." "Born from *Pneuma*," p. 19.

the water of rebirth and renewal by the Holy Spirit." Once again, the interpretive questions are whether this expression refers to one event or two and whether "water" refers to baptism. A reference to baptism would not be anachronistic in Titus. However, the use of *palingenesia* in the washing of regeneration (*loutrou palingenesias*) suggests the same eschatological cleansing that seems to be intended in John 3. While this cleansing came to be symbolized by Christian baptism, that is not the same as interpreting Titus 3:5 as a *reference* to baptism.[17]

Gordon Fee argues that the "washing of regeneration and renewal" refers to the single act of the Holy Spirit in regeneration, which cleanses from sin and brings new life. While the idea of baptism may be "lying very close to the surface," this is a metaphor for regeneration, not a shorthand reference to baptism.[18] Donald Norbie makes a slightly different argument: since the phrases "water of rebirth" and "renewal by the Holy Spirit" are actually parallel genitive phrases—literally, "washing of regeneration" and "renewing of Holy Spirit"—it would make sense to interpret them in the same way. Since the second clearly means "renewing by the Holy Spirit," the first plausibly means "washing by regeneration"—that is, the cleansing that is brought about by the new birth.[19] The NRSV translation obscures this possibility; the NIV's "washing of rebirth" is closer to the Greek in this instance.

The aorist tense of "to be born" (*gennēthē*) in John 3:3 and "saved" (*esōsen*) in Titus 3:5 suggest that the new birth is a punctiliar event. The metaphor of birth itself suggests this. While John 3 gives no hint of when the new birth takes place—except that it must occur before one experiences the kingdom—the Titus passage implies that it is a past event for Christians. In his ministry Jesus inaugurated the time of eschatological renewal, which can be experienced as new birth by those who respond to him in faith. John 3 refers primarily to the former, and Titus 3 to the latter.

---

[17]A. Ringwald argues that regeneration was not synonymous with baptism until the second century. "Birth etc.," in *NIDNTT* 1:180.

[18]Gordon D. Fee, *God's Empowering Presence: The Holy Spirit in the Letters of Paul* (Peabody, Mass.: Hendrickson, 1994), pp. 778-83. The quotation is from p. 781.

[19]Donald L. Norbie, "The Washing of Regeneration," *Evangelical Quarterly* 34 (January-March 1962): 37. Norbie notes the parallel in Ezekiel 36. See also George W. Knight III, *The Pastoral Epistles: A Commentary on the Greek Text*, The New International Greek Testament Commentary, ed. I. Howard Marshall and W. Ward Gasque (Grand Rapids: Eerdmans, 1992), pp. 341-42.

For individuals, then, the new birth takes place at conversion. Like Titus 3:5, John 3:5-6 makes clear that regeneration is the work of the Holy Spirit, which seems to be connected with belief in Jesus and his words (Jn 3:11-12, 16). Both James 1:18 and 1 Peter 1:23-25 attribute new birth to the word of God (the gospel message). Together, these passages suggest that the Holy Spirit works through the preaching of the gospel to bring people to faith and new life. This work of the Spirit can be resisted by human beings but not accomplished or manipulated by them. It must simply be received. The testimony is there for all who are willing to hear it (Jn 3:11-16; cf. Acts 7:51).

Although I have argued against the interpretation of John 3 and Titus 3 in terms of baptismal regeneration, I do not want to diminish the function of baptism as a representation of regeneration. Because of their emphasis on punctiliar conversion and their experience in parachurch groups, evangelicals have tended to downplay the importance of baptism. Eric Gritsch has pointed out the tendency of "born again" groups to ignore baptism in their discussions of conversion.[20] This neglect of baptism reinforces the privatism and individualism characteristic of evangelical soteriology. By contrast, the New Testament views baptism as an indispensable public rite of the believing community through which the new believer identifies with the death and resurrection of Christ (Rom 6:3-4) and with the body of Christ (Eph 4:4-6). The act of baptism brings community discernment, support and sanction to bear on the individual's experience of new birth and new life. Thus while baptism is not the means of regeneration, it is a necessary representation of it to the believer, the faith community and the world.

REGENERATION AND NEW LIFE

Even though a number of scholars think of new birth as a family metaphor, the Gospel of John does not explore the birth metaphor in terms of family except at John 1:13.[21] While the New Testament certainly does

---

[20]Eric W. Gritsch, *Born Againism: Perspectives on a Movement* (Minneapolis: Fortress, 1994), p. 92.

[21]See Paul S. Minear's discussion of the Gospel of John in terms of "two families" in *Christians and the New Creation: Genesis Motifs in the New Testament* (Louisville: Westminster John Knox, 1994), pp. 82-102. The two families are that of Adam and that of Christ. He states, "To be born of the Spirit is to enter into this family's inheritance of life and to be rescued from the

describe believers as being part of a new family (the household of God), the image of regeneration seems rather to focus on the origin of the new birth (from above, of God, of the Spirit) to depict a new beginning for believers. The image is not so much relational as moral—a new beginning for an individual and a creation that has been damaged by sin.[22] The ethical context of Titus 3:5 confirms this understanding.

In 1 John, the new birth is an event that transforms the believer's disposition, attitudes and actions. People who have been reborn believe that Jesus is the Christ; their faith in him enables them to obey his commandments and overcome the world, a major source of temptation (1 Jn 5:1-4). The perfect tense of "have been born" (*gegennētai*) indicates that the regeneration of individuals is a completed action that has ongoing effects.[23] Believers can love one another because they know God, who is love (1 Jn 4:7-8). Most notably, someone who has been born of God no longer is inclined toward sin. In fact, 1 John insists that "those who have been born of God do not sin" (1 Jn 3:9; 5:18). Sinning is no longer compatible with their identity, which finds its origin in God. This strongly dualistic language is typical of the Johannine literature; people belong either to God or to the world, and there can be no compromise between light and darkness. Believers do not sin, because God's "seed" (the word or the Holy Spirit) remains in them to continue the renewal begun at their new birth.[24]

However, 1 John recognizes that regeneration does not eliminate people's fallenness. It states that those who say they "have no sin" are engaging

---

other family's inheritance of wrath" (p. 87). Jan G. van der Watt interprets "being born again into the family of God" in light of the first-century Mediterranean family, in which the child would derive his or her identity from the family group. "Salvation in the Gospel According to John," in *Salvation in the New Testament: Perspectives on Soteriology*, ed. Jan G. van der Watt, Supplements to Novum Testamentum, ed. M. M. Mitchell and D. P. Moessner (Boston: E. J. Brill, 2005), pp. 122-24.

[22]According to Guhrt, "Regeneration includes a basic reorientation of moral life." "Birth etc.," in *NIDNTT* 1:185.

[23]I. Howard Marshall notes that 1 John often uses perfect tense to describe the Christian's present condition. *The Epistles of John*, The New International Commentary on the New Testament, ed. F. F. Bruce (Grand Rapids: Eerdmans, 1978), p. 226 n. 31.

[24]Ibid., p. 186. It is the new birth that creates the Christian's moral character. Marshall expresses the Johannine dualism this way: "John makes his statements in absolute terms: the way in which he can interchange subjects and predicates indicates that there is a one-to-one correspondence between those who are born of God and those who do what is right, love one another, believe in Jesus, overcome the world, and refrain from sin. There are no shades of grey here: it is a case of belonging to the light or the darkness, to God or the devil, to righteousness and love or to sin."

in self-deception, and it advises those who sin to confess their sins to God (1 Jn 1:8-9). The reborn believer still "has sin," in the sense of a fallen nature, but no longer engages in a life of sin. First John is not advocating a life of legalistic perfection but advising discernment toward those who claim to be Christians. People who derive their life from God will live in ways that reflect their origin. This should be both an encouragement and a challenge for those who consider themselves Christians. The new birth makes possible a new way of living, but it also calls believers to cooperate with the word and the Spirit to make that new life an experiential reality.

Thus although the Holy Spirit brings about the new birth, the new birth is not simply a metaphor for receiving the Spirit.[25] The Holy Spirit works a change in the disposition or structure of the self.[26] Believers experience a change in their orientation (toward God rather than toward sin) and the beginning of a personal transformation. They possess new freedom and new possibilities—what Paul calls a new self. They have both a new identity and a new community.[27] Their inner renewal expresses itself in their social relationships as they begin to love others as they have been loved. Renewed persons and communities move the world toward the eschatological renewal of all things.

REGENERATION AS NEW CREATION

The expectation of eschatological renewal is in the background of all of the New Testament documents. Isaiah had prophesied that God will create a new heavens and a new earth in which creation will be at peace and will worship the Lord (Is 65:17-25; 66:22-23). The book of Revelation describes the consummation in which the prophet's vision is fulfilled. The creation is renewed, death and suffering are eliminated, and God dwells with human beings. The New Jerusalem is a place of healing and worship (Rev 21:1-5; 22:1-5). The renewed creation will reflect the righteousness of its creator (2 Pet 3:7-13).

---

[25]Brown argues that the new birth primarily involves the reception of the Holy Spirit (*John*, 1:144); Carson believes that it primarily involves the impartation of a new nature (*John*, pp. 195-97).

[26]Renald Showers, *The New Nature* (Neptune, N.J.: Loizeaux Brothers, 1986), pp. 19, 24, 28, 49; Snodgrass, "Born of *Pneuma*," pp. 21-22.

[27]Gail R. O'Day, "New Birth as a New People: Spirituality and Community in the Fourth Gospel," *Word and World* 8, no. 1 (Winter 1988): 53. She argues that the communal dimension of being born again is often neglected by those who use that term (p. 58, 58 n. 11).

The new creation serves a similar theological function for Paul as the new birth serves for John. Both describe eschatological cosmic realities that can be experienced in part in the present as the Spirit begins the work of renewal in persons and in the church. Both serve to motivate believers to live in light of the new reality in the midst of the unredeemed world. To enable this new life, both challenge believers to draw upon the power of the Holy Spirit, who is bringing the new reality to completion.

The new creation takes place on three levels: cosmic (new heavens and new earth), corporate (new humanity) and individual (new self). Different passages emphasize different levels, but the levels can never be completely separated. For example, Romans 8:19-23 poignantly expresses the eschatological tension experienced both by believers and by creation as a whole as they yearn for the redemption of the material world:

> For the creation waits with eager longing for the revealing of the children of God; for the creation was subjected to futility, not of its own will but by the will of the one who subjected it, in hope that the creation itself will be set free from its bondage to decay and will obtain the freedom of the glory of the children of God. We know that the whole creation has been groaning in labor pains until now; and not only the creation, but we ourselves, who have the first fruits of the Spirit, groan inwardly while we wait for adoption, the redemption of our bodies.[28]

Believers, having experienced new spiritual life, long for new physical life in the resurrection (cf. Rom 8:10-11). The creation, subjected to death and decay because of human sin, longs to be set free along with humanity. It groans in labor pains for a birth that is still a future hope. When the new creation arrives, it will bring glorious life. The Holy Spirit, who has given humans spiritual life, will bring about physical renewal also. In the meantime, the Spirit expresses the inarticulate longings of believers and perhaps also those of the rest of creation (Rom 8:11, 26-27).

Paul also uses new creation language to explain what God has done to

---

[28]Richard Hays argues that the new creation is shorthand for the New Testament perspective on eschatology as already and not yet: "Paul's image of 'new creation' stands . . . as a shorthand signifier for the dialectical eschatology that runs throughout the New Testament." Richard B. Hays, *The Moral Vision of the New Testament: A Contemporary Introduction to New Testament Ethics* (New York: HarperSanFrancisco, 1996), p. 198. Hays uses the concept of the new creation as one of three "focal images" to guide the church's "normative use of the New Testament" for ethical discernment and moral formation (p. 195).

unite Jews and Gentiles in Christ. He depicts this corporate new creation in Ephesians 2:14-16: "For he is our peace; in his flesh he has made both groups into one and has broken down the dividing wall, that is, the hostility between us. He has abolished the law with its commandments and ordinances, that he might create in himself one new humanity in place of the two, thus making peace, and might reconcile both groups to God in one body through the cross, thus putting to death that hostility through it." Christ has overcome the most fundamental division in humanity, that between Jews and Gentiles, and has created a single people who worship him and in whom he dwells (Eph 2:19-22). This reconciled people has access to the Father that is made possible by Christ and made actual by the Spirit (Eph 2:18).[29] A "new creation community" has been brought into existence.[30]

Finally, new creation also describes the act of God in bringing new life to individual believers. For Paul, newness describes the reality of life in Christ. Believers have been identified through baptism with Jesus' death and resurrection, so that they now can "walk in newness of life" (Rom 6:4). They no longer live under the "oldness" (*palaiotēti*) of the law but in the "newness" (*kainotēti*) of the Spirit (Rom 7:6, author's translation). Through the Spirit, believers participate in the new era while living in the midst of the old.[31] As they respond to the gospel message in faith, believers are created anew in Christ for a life of good works (Eph 2:8-10). The works of the Christian depend upon the prior re-creative work of God through the word and the Spirit in giving the believer a new orientation and a new motivation.[32]

---

[29]John Reumann argues that Paul's new creation image has to do with human beings: *"New creation* in the Bible refers to the converted believer, or, in the plural, the redeemed community." Even in the passages that apparently refer to the new creation of the cosmos, "the Bible explicates the new heavens and earth, the new creation as the redeemed community." *Creation and New Creation: The Past, Present, and Future of God's Creative Activity* (Minneapolis: Augsburg, 1973), pp. 100, 101. While I agree that the Bible focuses on human beings, I think Reumann has overstated the case. The new creation is not entirely anthropocentric.

[30]Ken Gnanakan, "The Holy Spirit, Creation and New Creation," *Evangelical Review of Theology* 15, no. 2 (April 1991): 105.

[31]Moyer V. Hubbard traces the extensive role of the Holy Spirit in the new creation. *New Creation in Paul's Letters and Thought*, Society for New Testament Studies Monograph Series, ed. Richard Bauckham (Cambridge: Cambridge University Press, 2002), especially chapters 7-11. Hubbard argues that the new creation in 2 Corinthians 5:17 and Galatians 6:15 "functions as an aspect of Paul's *pneumatology*" (p. 234; italics his).

[32]W. Foerster states, "All God's work of creation is by His Word and Spirit." "κτίζω κτλ.," in *TDNT* 3:1034.

Second Corinthians 5:17 and Galatians 6:15 are central for Paul's understanding of the new creation. In 2 Corinthians 5:17, Paul declares, "So if anyone is in Christ, there is a new creation: everything old has passed away; see, everything has become new!" In Galatians 6:15, he states, "For neither circumcision nor uncircumcision is anything; but a new creation is everything!" Scholars are divided over whether the new creation in these two verses refers to the new era or to the transformation of individuals. The anthropological interpretation has been more common through church history, but the eschatological interpretation has become more common recently.[33]

Eschatological renewal seems to play a significant part in both passages. If Paul were talking about individuals, we would expect him to say in the Corinthians passage that "he (or she) is" a new creation, but the Greek has no pronoun and no verb, making "there is" a new creation more likely.[34] Similarly, in Galatians 6, Paul seems to be using "circumcision" and "uncircumcision" as shorthand for the conditions that formerly defined people as Jew or Gentile. The new creation in Christ has made such distinctions obsolete. The old things are gone, because the new creation is not simply a return to the original Edenic state; it is something *new*.[35]

Cosmic, corporate and individual interpretations need not be mutually exclusive, however. The personal transformation that takes place when someone is "in Christ" *is the evidence that* the eschatological new creation has begun. Because the new era has dawned, believers can become new people. Because the new era has dawned, renewed relationships are possible. God's offer of reconciliation goes out through his people (2 Cor 5:18-20). Because the purpose of the law has been fulfilled, Jew and Gentile can

---

[33]For a survey of the history of interpretation, see Hubbard, *New Creation*, pp. 1-8. While Hubbard opts for an anthropological understanding of 2 Corinthians 5:17 and Galatians 6:15, I would argue that the eschatological is primary.

[34]C. K. Barrett argues that 2 Corinthians 5:17 refers not to a new creature but to a new act of creation analogous to the original act of creation. *A Commentary on the Second Epistle to the Corinthians*, Harper's New Testament Commentaries, ed. Henry Chadwick (Peabody, Mass.: Hendrickson, 1973), p. 173. Similarly, Ralph P. Martin states, "The accent falls on a person . . . entering the new order in Christ." *2 Corinthians*, Word Biblical Commentary, ed. Bruce M. Metzger, David A. Hubbard and Glenn W. Barker (Nashville: Nelson, 1986), p. 152. In the words of H.-H. Esser, "Where a person belongs to Christ, new creation is a fact." "Creation etc.," in *NIDNTT* 1:385.

[35]Richard N. Longenecker, *Galatians*, Word Biblical Commentary, ed. Bruce Metzger et al. (Dallas: Word, 1990), p. 296.

now be united in Christ (Gal 3:23-28). The new creation is making itself felt at every level. As W. D. Davies has observed, being in Christ is a call to obedience and forgiveness. These qualities themselves contribute to the new creation: "Where such obedience and such forgiveness break forth, there the world is being renewed, the new creation is in process."[36]

REGENERATION AND THE NEW SELF

Because believers have been re-created in Christ, Paul says that they have a new identity. In Ephesians 4:22-24, he declares, "You were taught to put away your former way of life, your old self, corrupt and deluded by its lusts, and to be renewed in the spirit of your minds, and to clothe yourselves with the new self, created according to the likeness of God in true right-eousness and holiness." Just as human beings were originally created in the image of God, those who have been re-created will find that divine image restored. This new self (*kainos anthrōpos* or *neos anthrōpos*) is a new identity that expresses itself in a new way of life that reflects God's character.

Although this new identity is a creation of God, it also seems to be something that believers can be taught to implement. They must "put on" or "clothe themselves with" their new selves. As they do so they will take on the characteristics of what they are "putting on."[37] Elsewhere, Paul de-scribes this as putting on Christ (Rom 13:14). Scholars of Paul often use the terms indicative and imperative to describe the relationship between what God has done and what believers must do.[38] Since Christians have a new self (indicative), they must put it on (imperative). In other words, be-cause God has given them new power and new potential, they can (and must) live a new life. The resources are now at their disposal, but they have to use them.

In a similar passage, after commanding the Colossians to "put to death, therefore, whatever in you is earthly," Paul adds, "Do not lie to one an-other, seeing that you have stripped off the old self with its practices and have clothed yourselves with the new self, which is being renewed in

---

[36]W. D. Davies, *The New Creation: University Sermons* (Minneapolis: Fortress, 1971), p. 11.

[37]See "ἐνδύω," definition 2b, in *BAGD*.

[38]See especially Rudolf Bultmann, "The Problem of Ethics in Paul," in *Understanding Paul's Ethics: Twentieth Century Approaches*, ed. Brian S. Rosner, trans. Christoph W. Stenschke (Grand Rapids: Eerdmans, 1995), pp. 195-216.

knowledge according to the image of its creator. In that renewal there is no longer Greek and Jew, circumcised and uncircumcised, barbarian, Scythian, slave and free, but Christ is all and in all" (Col 3:5, 9-11). For believers, spiritual renewal is in process. They have experienced a decisive event during which, so to speak, they have changed clothes—possibly a reference to the practice of baptism in the early church—but now they must choose to wear those new clothes every day.[39] As they do so, they are progressively renewed in the image of God. To follow the metaphor a little further, they must grow into their clothes. The new self, as part of the new era, has clear social implications. Believers are challenged to find their identity in Christ rather than in their ethnicity, circumstances or social status. Christ defines not only who they are as individuals but also the primary social group to which they belong—the church. The new self is not an isolated individual but a self-in-relationship. "There can be no true integration of the self except on the basis of true community."[40]

Both of these passages suggest that the renewal of believers is initiated by an act of God (presumably regeneration, perhaps as represented in baptism), but it requires human cooperation to be completed. It thus has an already/not yet quality. Paul's exhortations to his churches to cooperate with the Spirit suggest that the Holy Spirit's work of re-creation can be resisted (Gal 5:16-17, 25; 6:8; Eph 4:30; 1 Thess 4:8).[41] Although spiritual renewal is in process, physical renewal must wait until the resurrection: "For in this tent we groan, longing to be clothed with our heavenly dwelling" (2 Cor 5:2). But the inner transformation taking place gives assurance that the outer one will come: "So we do not lose heart. Even though our outer nature is wasting away, our inner nature is being renewed day by day" (2 Cor 4:16).

Living out a new identity requires a new perspective. Both Romans 12:1-2 and Ephesians 4:23 emphasize that believers must be renewed in their minds. As Paul says immediately before he mentions the new cre-

---

[39]See the discussion in C. F. D. Moule, "'The New Life' in Colossians 3:1-17," *Review and Expositor* 70, no. 4 (Fall 1973): 489.

[40]Max Warren, "In Christ the New Has Come," *Theology Today* 3, no. 4 (January 1947): 480, 477. Harrisville believes that the new self is actually not the individual but the Christian community (*Concept of Newness*, p. 74). I would say rather that the new self is embedded in a network of social relationships.

[41]See Hubbard, *New Creation*, p. 235.

ation in 2 Corinthians 5:17, believers must no longer see things "from a human point of view" (2 Cor 5:16). People accustomed to thinking of themselves in certain ways must be retrained to see themselves and the world differently. This means that the church has an important role to play in the new creation, even at the individual level.

Thus the new creation of individual believers, or the new self, is not a new component added to the constitution of human beings, nor is it simply a metaphor for receiving the Holy Spirit. It is a change in human identity so radical as to be called a new creation. It is the beginning of the transformation of the believer into the image of Christ, a lifelong process directed by the Holy Spirit that will be completed at the resurrection. The Holy Spirit is both the "earnest" of the eschatological goal and the one who "propels" believers toward that goal.[42]

The new creation is also the beginning of the transformation of all the believer's social relationships. It finds fulfillment in the consummation, when all of creation will be transformed to reflect the image of its creator. To be a new creation is to be free from suffering, death and decay; free from the social divisions that alienate and oppress; and free from the sin that prevents human beings from reflecting the image of their creator to the rest of creation.[43]

CONCLUSION

Regeneration, whether considered as new birth or new creation, pictures God's renewal of his fallen creation by the agency of the Holy Spirit. The goal of regeneration is for renewed individuals, a renewed people and a renewed creation to worship God and reflect God's character. It is essentially eschatological, although its reality should be evident now in the transformed lives of Christians and in the life of the church. For individuals, regeneration is a gracious gift of God at conversion that issues in a lifelong process of renewal.

Regeneration has significant implications for the faith and life of the church. It reminds us that salvation is not a private individual experience without social consequences; regeneration extends from the individual life

---

[42]Harrisville, *Concept of Newness*, p. 61.

[43]According to Michael Parsons, "From Paul's argument, to be a new creation is to be essentially free." "The New Creation," *Expository Times* 99, no. 1 (October 1987): 3.

to the life of all creation. In fact, although regeneration is an *event*, it is not an *experience* at all. Those who regard the new birth as a particular type of religious experience should take note that the New Testament nowhere describes it in this way.[44] Given the importance of regeneration, it is significant that the New Testament never dwells on the event itself. Instead, the writers describe the necessity, the origin and the results of regeneration. Their reticence suggests that we should not insist that the event of the new birth should look or feel a certain way.

Furthermore, focusing our attention on the event may be missing the point entirely. For the Christian, the new birth or new creation *as an event* takes place at conversion. But that event is embedded in a *process* of renewal guided by the Holy Spirit that begins well before conversion and extends at least until the consummation. In a process of progressive renewal, it makes no sense to focus all of our attention on a single point. Regeneration is a means to an end; it is the opening of the door into new life. Concentrating on the initial experience rather than the life that grows from it would be like parents neglecting their baby to pore over pictures of the birth.

Regeneration participates in the eschatological tension of the "already" and the "not yet." That means that if we are Christians, we should be neither naive optimists nor pessimists. Our own experience of the Holy Spirit should encourage us that real change is possible. But our own experience of imperfection should remind us that the ultimate renewal lies in the future. Ignoring the crucial "not yet" dimension of regeneration can too easily result in complacency and triumphalism. This may be a particular temptation for those who have been taught that a particular initial experience guarantees final salvation.

Regeneration reminds us that salvation is a dance consisting of God's gracious initiative and our faithful response. On the one hand, regeneration challenges the belief that human self-improvement or social programs can root out entrenched sin and evil. Only God can do that. On the other hand, it challenges the belief that we have no responsibility beyond believing the gospel. Regeneration must be lived out, and the new birth is a call to join God in the work of restoration. The implications for evangelism,

---

[44]The idea that the new birth is a religious experience that includes the assurance of God's forgiveness derives from Pietism, in particular from August Hermann Francke and those who were influenced by him. It has been transmitted to modern believers by way of revivalism.

social justice and environmental stewardship are clear.

As new persons, members of the new community established by Christ, believers have responsibilities toward the rest of creation. Peter Stuhl-macher points out that we should care for creation "as something which will be freed from death and glorified."[45] Ken Gnanakan argues that as members of the new creation community, believers should recognize their responsibility toward the "creation community," those members of God's creation who have not yet been touched by God's work of renewal. He observes, "The relationship between the new and the old creation brings to light this important connection between the people of God and those people within the creation of God." Christians can make "common cause" with non-Christians to address issues of importance to the wider creation. They should also demonstrate to the world the proper stewardship of the nonhuman creation.[46]

Although in one sense it is a past event for Christians, regeneration is future-oriented. As 1 Peter tells us, God "has given us new birth into a living hope" (1 Pet 1:3). That hope should shape the way we live now. If those of us who have experienced the transforming love of God will re-lease that love into the world, our lives will be a sign of hope for humanity and for all of creation.[47]

FOR FURTHER READING

Beale, Gregory K. "The New Testament and New Creation." In *Biblical Theology: Retrospect and Prospect*. Edited by Scott J. Hafemann, pp. 159-73. Downers Grove, Ill.: InterVarsity Press, 2002.

Belleville, Linda. "'Born of Water and Spirit': John 3:5," *Trinity Journal*, n.s., 1 (1980): 125-41.

Davies, W. D. *The New Creation*. Philadelphia: Fortress, 1971.

Harrisville, Roy A. *The Concept of Newness in the New Testament*. Minneapolis: Augsburg, 1960.

Hays, Richard B. *The Moral Vision of the New Testament: A Contemporary Introduction to New Testament Ethics*. New York: HarperSanFrancisco, 1996.

---

[45]Peter Stuhlmacher, "The Ecological Crisis as a Challenge for Biblical Theology," *Ex Auditu* 3 (1987): 11-12.

[46]Ken Gnanakan, "Creation, New Creation, and Ecological Relationships," in *Emerging Voices in Global Christian Theology*, ed. William A. Dyrness (Grand Rapids: Zondervan, 1994), pp. 147, 148, 149-50.

[47]On regeneration as a sign of hope, see Stuhlmacher, "Ecological Crisis," p. 15.

Hubbard, Moyer V. *New Creation in Paul's Letters and Thought*. Society for New Testament Studies Monograph Series. Edited by Richard Bauckham. Cambridge: Cambridge University Press, 2002.

Minear, Paul S. *Christians and the New Creation: Genesis Motifs in the New Testament*. Louisville: Westminster John Knox, 1994.

O'Day, Gail R. "New Birth as a New People: Spirituality and Community in the Fourth Gospel." *Word and World* 8, no. 1 (Winter 1988): 53-61.

Showers, Renald. *The New Nature*. Neptune, N.J.: Loizeaux Brothers, 1986.

Toon, Peter. *Born Again: A Biblical and Theological Study of Regeneration*. Grand Rapids: Baker, 1986.

van der Watt, Jan G. "Salvation in the Gospel According to John." In *Salvation in the New Testament: Perspectives on Soteriology*. Edited by Jan G. van der Watt, pp. 102-31. Supplements to Novum Testamentum. Edited by M. M. Mitchell and D. P. Moessner. Boston: E. J. Brill, 2005.

6

DELIVERANCE BELONGS
TO THE LORD

Sōtēria as Rescue and Healing

"WHEN WERE YOU SAVED?" In my context, a person who asks this question wants to know the date of another person's conversion experience. If speaker and audience come from similar backgrounds, the answer usually follows promptly. If the audience comes from a different background (or has had different experiences), there may be an awkward interlude while crosscultural communication is established.

Many conservative Christians equate "salvation" narrowly with conversion. More broadly, theologians have used "salvation" as an umbrella term that covers all of what Christ has done for humanity and all the blessings that human beings receive from Christ's work. In this chapter, we will explore a very specific topic—the meaning of the *sōtēria* word group, which is behind most of the instances of "save" and "salvation" in English translations of the Bible. We will discover that *sōtēria* means much more than conversion.

As we proceed, it will be especially important not to import into this Greek term whatever understanding we have of the theological doctrine of salvation. Otherwise, our preconceptions may hinder our ability to hear what the text is saying. For example, if we approach the text with the understanding that salvation is a purely spiritual matter, we are likely to ignore the passages in which Jesus heals someone and tells them that their faith has "saved" them. Rather than deciding on a priori grounds what *sōtēria* must mean, we should discover how the term is used in the New Testament.

As we will see, *sōtēria* is not just about the forgiveness of sins but about safety and well-being. It extends to every dimension of life that was damaged by sin. We should also remember that *sōtēria* is just one image that the New Testament writers use to depict salvation. Like any other image, *sōtēria* emphasizes some aspects of the solution more than others.

TERMS AND CONCEPTS

The most common word translated as "save" in the Old Testament is *yāša*, which means "to be roomy, broad" rather than being "hemmed in, constricted, oppressed." Someone who is trapped or oppressed by someone or something else is rescued through the intervention of a third party. People need to be saved from enemies, from danger, from illness, from injustice and violence, and from death.[1] To be saved is to experience rescue from negative circumstances and restoration to positive circumstances. From the Hebrew word *yāša* comes the name *Yeshua* (Joshua or Jesus). This is why the angel tells Joseph that Mary's baby will be called *Jesus* because he will *save* his people from their sins (Mt 1:21).

The Greek word that most closely corresponds to *yāša* is *sōzō*, which is usually used to translate it in the Septuagint. The words *sōzō* (to save) and *sōtēria* (salvation) have the same sense of deliverance from a threat to one's life. Even when this deliverance takes place through human beings, God is ultimately the one who saves.[2] In general, *sōtēria* means "deliverance" or "preservation."[3] In the Greek world, *sōzō* is used for the preservation of documents, for rescue at sea, for deliverance from illness, for deliverance from fate, and for "security and well being in general."[4] In the Septuagint, it is used for the deliverance and welfare of Israel.[5] In the Greco-Roman context of the first century, the most common context for these terms is medical: *sōtēria* refers to health.[6] In the New Testament, the

---

[1]W. Foerster and G. Fohrer, "σῴζω κτλ.," in *TDNT* 7:973, 976.
[2]Foerster and Fohrer, "σῴζω κτλ.," in *TDNT* 7:971, 975, 989-90; J. Schneider and C. Brown, "Redemption etc.," in *NIDNTT* 3:207.
[3]"σωτηρία" in *BAGD*, p. 801.
[4]R. McL. Wilson, "*Sōtēria*," *Scottish Journal of Theology* 6, no. 4 (1953): 409.
[5]Ibid., 409-10.
[6]Joel B. Green, *Salvation*, Understanding Biblical Themes (St. Louis, Mo.: Chalice, 2003), p. 36.

sense of *sōtēria* is extended to include deliverance from sin.

Both *yāša'* and *sōzō* focus on deliverance from threat rather than wholeness *per se*. The latter is emphasized by the words for peace, *šālôm* in the Old Testament and *eirēnē* in the New.[7] However, the idea of deliverance from a state of distress implies a transfer to a state of safety and well-being. Considering both *yāša'* and *sōzō*, Terence Fretheim summarizes salvation as "deliverance from anything inimical to true life, issuing in well-being and a trustworthy world in which there is space to live." He argues that salvation as expressed by these concepts encompasses realities that are usually considered to be mutually exclusive: eschatological and historical, individual and communal, religious and social/economic/political, spiritual and physical, human and nonhuman, event and process, insider and outsider.[8]

As is true of *yāša'*, *sōtēria* is related to God's covenant relationship with his people. Rescuing his people from danger and oppression is one of God's covenant obligations. Zechariah's song in Luke 1:68-79 prophesies that Jesus will be the source of national deliverance for God's people. God has "remembered his holy covenant" and has sent a deliverer for his people, as he had promised, so that they can be "saved from [their] enemies" (Lk 1:68-69, 71-72).

The national context of the promise that Jesus would save his people from their sins (Mt 1:21) has often been overlooked. To a first-century Israelite, the consequences of Israel's sins were evident in the presence of the occupying foreign power, Rome. Israel's history had been a cycle of faithfulness, apostasy, foreign oppression and deliverance. Thus the promise of deliverance from sin might well create the expectation of deliverance from the oppressor, as had happened many times before.[9]

Although Jesus did not bring the political salvation many were expecting, his salvation does have political implications. The term "savior" (*sōtēr*), while not part of their official titles, was often ascribed to Roman emperors because of the protection they afforded their subjects.[10] But the New Testament picture of *sōtēria* challenges other claims of

---

[7]See chapter eight for a discussion of peace.

[8]Terence E. Fretheim, "Salvation in the Bible vs. Salvation in the Church," *Word and World* 13, no. 4 (1993): 364-65 and *passim*.

[9]See the discussion in N. T. Wright, *Jesus and the Victory of God* (Minneapolis: Fortress, 1996), pp. 268-71.

[10]Wilson, "*Sōtēria*," p. 408.

deliverance and protection, including the imperial one. If Jesus is *sōtēr*, Caesar is not.[11]

THREE TENSES OF SALVATION

In the New Testament, *sōzō* is a word with three tenses: it refers to "a past event, a present experience, and a future hope."[12] *Sōtēria* "embraces *all phases of life in the new age.*"[13]

Surprisingly, for those who think of salvation as a past-tense conversion event, New Testament writers emphasize the future. This emphasis is especially striking in Paul. See figure 1 for a summary. In all of the Pauline letters, we find two aorists and one aorist participle, all of which refer to past events; two perfect participles; one present and two present participles, both referring to present events; and thirteen instances of future tense. In addition, one instance of the infinitive refers to a past event, while three infinitives and four subjunctives refer to general truths concerning salvation, such as God's purposes and expectations. The emphasis on future is less marked in other New Testament books. In particular, the Gospels place much more emphasis than Paul on events in the present context of Jesus' ministry, just as Acts focuses on the ministry of the apostles.[14] For example, imperatives tend to cluster in the Gospels and Acts, where people are being confronted with the demand of the gospel proclamation. Moreover, many instances of aorist, perfect and future tenses refer to events taking place in the course of the Gospel narratives. This summary does not include the

---

[11]Richard A. Horsley has written extensively on the ways in which the Christian proclamation of the gospel was a challenge to Roman imperial authority. As noted in chapter three, Caesar was to be celebrated as the savior who had brought salvation to the world. His subjects were called to have faith in him. See Horsley's *Jesus and Empire: The Kingdom of God and the New World Disorder* (Minneapolis: Augsburg Fortress, 2003), p. 134.

[12]A. M. Hunter, *The Gospel According to Paul* (Philadelphia: Westminster Press, 1966), p. 15. Hunter is speaking of Paul's writings, but his statement (partly because of the Pauline writings) applies to the New Testament as a whole. See also the discussion in Michael (E. M. B.) Green, *The Meaning of Salvation* (1965; reprint, Vancouver, B.C.: Regent College Publishing, 1998), pp. 152-89.

[13]Paul S. Minear, "The Hope of Salvation," *Interpretation* 3, no. 3 (July 1949): 266 (italics in original).

[14]B. H. Throckmorton argues that in Luke/Acts "σώζειν and the two nouns almost never refer to the future, but describe rather a present, historical fact." "Σώζειν, σωτηρία in Luke-Acts," *Studia Evangelica* 6, Papers Presented to the 4th International Congress on New Testament Studies Held at Oxford, 1969 (Berlin: Akademie Verlag, 1973), pp. 515-16.

temporal contexts of the noun forms, such as *sōtēria*. I will discuss some of those instances below.

	Paul	Others	NT
Imperfect	0	1	1
Aorist	2	7	9
Aorist participle	1	1	2
Perfect	0	8	8
Perfect participle	2	0	2
Present	1	2	3
Present participle	2	2	4
Future	13	18	31
Future participle	0	1	1
Infinitive (past events)	1	0	1
Infinitive (present events)	0	8	8
Infinitive (future events)	0	6	6
Imperative	0	9	9
Subjunctive or infinitive (general truths)	7	14	21

Figure 1. Tenses of salvation

Sōtēria IN THE GOSPELS AND ACTS

The *sōtēria* word group is used in all four of the Gospels. It is especially prominent in Luke-Acts and comparatively rare in John. An examination of the Synoptic Gospels shows that *sōtēria* has a broad range of meaning. Sometimes it means rescue from physical danger. When Jesus is sleeping through the storm at sea and his disciples beg him to save them, they are not concerned about the state of their souls but about their imminent death by drowning (Mt 8:25). In this sense, even Jesus himself was not "saved," in that he was not spared from death by crucifixion (Mk 15:30-31; Jn 12:27).

Frequently *sōtēria* concerns physical healing. When the woman with the issue of blood is restored after touching Jesus' cloak, Jesus tells her that her faith has "healed" her (Mt 9:22 NIV) or "made [her] well" (NRSV). The Greek is *sesōken*, the perfect tense of *sōzō*. While the NIV and NRSV are helpful in clarifying the focus of Jesus' power in this instance (restoration of health), they obscure the connection between healing and salvation in the New Testament (a connection not obvious in English). Similarly, when Jesus confronts the scribes and Pharisees over his healing of the man with the withered hand, he asks them whether the Sabbath laws are intended "to save life or to destroy it" (Lk 6:9). In the case of the Gerasene (or Gadarene) demoniac, *sōtēria* means deliverance from demonic possession (Lk 8:36). *Sōtēria* can even extend to raising the dead, as when Jesus restores the life of Jairus's daughter (Lk 8:50).

The Gospel writers interpret these healings as signs of the eschatological rescue and healing of God's people that was promised in the Old Testament. For example, Isaiah declares, "Say to those who are of a fearful heart, 'Be strong, do not fear! Here is your God. He will come with vengeance, with terrible recompense. He will come and save you.' Then the eyes of the blind shall be opened, and the ears of the deaf unstopped; then the lame shall leap like a deer, and the tongue of the speechless sing for joy" (Is 35:4-6). The Gospels show this promise being fulfilled in Jesus' ministry: "Jesus answered them, 'Go and tell John what you hear and see: the blind receive their sight, the lame walk, the lepers are cleansed, the deaf hear, the dead are raised, and the poor have good news brought to them'" (Mt 11:4-5).[15]

Jesus' healings and exorcisms are an indication that the kingdom of God is dawning. Their object is not only the alleviation of suffering but also bringing persons to participate in the reign of God. "The fundamental meaning of Jesus' mighty deeds of healing and exorcism is this: God wills human wholeness—in its physical, psychological, and social dimensions—and in Jesus' ministry God's will is accomplished in concrete terms, for the sovereign rule of heaven is exerting itself."[16] Such human wholeness means more than physical well-being, as Jesus' parable of the empty house in Luke 11:24-26 illustrates. When a demon is driven out and nothing better takes its place, it returns to its former residence with seven demons

---

[15]Donald E. Gowan, "Salvation as Healing," *Ex Auditu* 5 (1989): 2-3.
[16]John T. Carroll, "Sickness and Healing in the New Testament Gospels," *Interpretation* 49, no. 2 (April 1995): 137.

worse than itself. Thus someone who experiences the blessings of the coming kingdom but remains unchanged by the kingdom will be left worse off than before. "Put another way, there is more to the experience of healing than a cure. Healing such as Jesus offers—healing that 'saves' and makes whole—must touch every dimension of one's being and living."[17]

This holistic idea of healing derives from the holistic worldview of the first century. Modern Western ideas of sickness and health are based on a disease model, which views sick people as diseased individuals with physical ailments that must be treated through medical intervention. The healing they need has little to do with salvation. By contrast, first century cultures believed that someone's sickness and health were connected not only with the physical state of that individual but also with that person's relationships, and even with the order or disorder of the cosmos. Treatment for illness should consider its physical, social and spiritual dimensions. Thus healing and salvation could not really be separated.[18]

Jesus' healings illustrate this holistic view. Jesus restores the sick to society as well as to health. His healings enable a leper, a demoniac and a woman who has been bleeding for twelve years to return to the community (Lk 5:12-16; 8:26-39, 43-48). He even heals outsiders, such as a Samaritan and a Gentile soldier's slave (Lk 7:1-10; 17:11-19). "Through faith they leave the domain of sickness and sin and enter the sphere of salvation."[19] Through these acts of *sōtēria*, Jesus is creating the healed and healing community predicted by the prophets. No one will be hindered from participating in that community because of disability: "The salvation Jesus brought to all who responded to him, as he healed them physically, psychologically and spiritually, was the ability to live a rich and full life, as the Old Testament prophets had hoped."[20]

Although the physical dimensions of *sōtēria* are more prominent, this term is also used in the Gospels for deliverance we think of as "spiritual," such as the forgiveness of sins.[21] For example, Jesus tells the sinful woman who anoints him that her sins have been forgiven before he adds that her faith has saved her (Lk 7:50). Similarly, healing and forgiveness of sins

---

[17]Ibid., p. 138.
[18]Green, *Salvation*, pp. 41-42.
[19]Carroll, "Sickness and Healing," p. 134.
[20]Gowan, "Salvation as Healing," p. 11-13 (quotation from page 12).
[21]Throckmorton identifies this as an important emphasis in Luke-Acts. "Σώζειν," p. 518.

are connected in the healing of the paralytic, although he word *sōzō* is not mentioned (Mk 2:1-12). Jesus even sometimes uses healing as a metaphor for forgiveness: "Those who are well have no need of a physician, but those who are sick; I have come to call not the righteous but sinners" (Mk 2:17).[22]

Even the specifically religious dimension of *sōtēria* is communal as well as individual. Jesus' disciples ask him, "Lord, are the ones being saved only a few?" (Lk 13:23, author's translation). Luke Timothy Johnson argues that this question makes most sense if salvation is regarded as inclusion in the people of God. Johnson also points to Acts 5:31, when Peter declares to the council that "God exalted [Jesus] at his right hand as Leader and Savior that he might give repentance to Israel and forgiveness of sins."[23]

Sometimes the scope of *sōzō* is ambiguous. As Jesus describes the coming catastrophes in Mark 13, he tells his disciples that "the one who endures to the end will be saved" (Mk 13:13). The reference seems to be to individuals, but is he speaking of physical or spiritual deliverance?[24] The context, which describes persecution and possible martyrdom, suggests the latter. Nevertheless, physical deliverance (such as from the fall of Jerusalem) is not ruled out.[25] Likewise, when Jesus cleanses the ten lepers, it is only when one of them returns to express his gratitude that Jesus tells him,

---

[22]Gowan, "Salvation as Healing," p. 10.

[23]Luke Timothy Johnson, "The Social Dimension of *Sōtēria* in Luke-Acts and Paul," *Society of Biblical Literature Seminar Papers*, no. 32 (1993): 525, 528. While he makes a strong case for the corporate context of *sōtēria*, he is less persuasive when he attempts to interpret all instances of the healing of individuals as "symbolic" of the healing of Israel. Similarly, while *sōtēria* has a strong corporate context in Romans, I would not agree with him that salvation in Romans is "entirely social" (p. 533). He also attempts to downplay the future orientation of salvation in Paul's writings.

[24]For a similarly ambiguous passage in the Epistles, see 1 Timothy 2:15, "Yet she will be saved through childbearing, provided they continue in faith and love and holiness, with modesty." The obscurity of this verse comes both from the ambiguity of "saved" and the debated referents of "she" and "they." Interpreters generally agree that bearing children is not spiritually salvific for women. Are Christian women kept safe through the birth process? Are women redeemed through the birth of Christ? Is Eve's sin overturned by the childbearing of the faithful Mary? The only point that seems clear is that *sōtēria*, whatever it is in this instance, is conditional upon persevering in faith.

[25]Craig A. Evans believes that eschatological salvation is intended. *Mark 8:27–16:20*, Word Biblical Commentary, ed. Bruce M. Metzger, David A. Hubbard and Glenn W. Barker (Nashville: Thomas Nelson, 2001), p. 313. I. Howard Marshall suggests that the ambiguity of *sōzō* in Mark 13:13 led Luke to alter the wording of the parallel statement in Luke 21:19. *The Gospel of Luke*, New International Greek Testament Commentary, ed. I. Howard Marshall and W. Ward Gasque (Grand Rapids: Eerdmans, 1978), p. 770.

"Your faith has saved you" (Lk 17:16, author's translation). Is Jesus referring to the physical healing or to a more comprehensive salvation? The distinction between cleansing and salvation suggests that the leper's gratitude expressed a faith that went beyond a trust in Jesus as healer.[26]

This ambiguity arises because the New Testament writers do not compartmentalize their lives the way modern Western Christians tend to do. They do not divorce the physical from the spiritual or the individual from the social. The salvation Jesus brings reaches into all the corners of someone's life to heal what is broken. Mark 10:24-26 indicates that *sōtēria* is equivalent to entering the kingdom of God. Thus, like the kingdom, *sōtēria* is an eschatological reality that can be experienced in the present because of Christ. Michael Green summarizes Jesus' teaching on *sōtēria* as follows: "Salvation, then, according to Jesus, concerns the whole man. It is concerned with his past, his present and his future. It is the work of rescue achieved by God through his Messiah. It belongs to the kingly rule of God brought into history by Jesus, the Son of Man. The conditions of its acceptance are repentance and faith; the very idea of merit is excluded by grace. But it demands a radical change of life in those who accept it."[27] Those who enter the kingdom have been rescued from the present evil age to experience the blessings of God's saving reign. Their lives should look different as a result.

The range of meaning of *sōzō* makes possible Jesus' paradoxical saying that those who want to save their lives will lose them, and those who lose their lives for his sake will save them (Mk 8:35). Preserving one's mortal life—if that means rejecting Jesus' call to discipleship—can result in the loss of eternal life. By contrast, those disciples who are willing to give up their physical lives in Jesus' service will receive the eternal life that only he can give.

Looking at *sōtēria* in the Gospels provides an important corrective to a view of salvation that is focused solely on the cross. When Protestants talk about Jesus' provision of salvation, they tend to go immediately to the cross. Popular atonement theories such as penal substitution and moral influence focus only on Jesus' death. Even the most familiar ecumenical creeds, such as the Apostles' and Nicene Creeds, move directly from Jesus'

---

[26]Throckmorton, "Σώζειν," pp. 519-20.
[27]Green, *Meaning of Salvation*, p. 117.

birth to his death, as if his life and ministry were just a way for him to pass the time until Passion Week. The Gospels show us that salvation was the focus of Jesus' entire ministry. His preaching brought the knowledge of salvation to God's people. His actions rescued people from sin, sickness, evil and death in order to make them whole. Seen from this perspective, his death and resurrection were the culmination and ultimate expression of his ministry of deliverance.

Sōtēria AS PAST EVENT IN PAUL

Paul uses *sōzō* more than any other New Testament writer. He assumes the covenantal context of *sōtēria*, although he stresses that through Christ "salvation has come to the Gentiles" (Rom 11:11). Because of Christ, the covenant is open to everyone. *Sōtēria* is now available to everyone who has faith, "to the Jew first and also to the Greek" (Rom 1:16). Although Paul does not emphasize the connection of *sōtēria* with the kingdom of God, he does express confidence that God will save him into the kingdom (2 Tim 4:18). For the most part, Paul's letters focus on the meaning of *sōtēria* in the lives of Christians.

As we will see, the three tenses of *sōzō* in Paul's writings roughly correspond to the theological categories of justification, sanctification and glorification. We must not confuse these three *theological categories* with the *biblical images* of justification, sanctification and glorification, however.[28] These biblical images do not correspond neatly with past, present and future dimensions of salvation.

In Paul's writings, *sōzō* in the past tense refers to the work of Christ or to the application of that work to the lives of believers at conversion. For example, 1 Timothy 1:15 states that Jesus "came into the world to save sinners" (the infinitive *sōsai* with an aorist verb). Similarly, Titus 2:11-14 declares that the grace of God was revealed (aorist passive)[29] "bringing salvation to all." Although "salvation" here is a noun (*sōtērios*), the tense of the verb indicates that the atonement is in view. God's grace was revealed in Jesus' mission to provide atonement for everyone. The Titus passage actu-

---

[28]For further discussion of the biblical images of justification, sanctification and glorification, see chapters nine, twelve and eleven, respectively.

[29]The NRSV translation "has appeared" for the aorist *epephanē* obscures the apparent reference to the Christ event.

ally summarizes the content of all three tenses of *sōzō*: "For the grace of God has appeared, bringing salvation to all, training us to renounce impiety and worldly passions, and in the present age to live lives that are self-controlled, upright and godly, while we wait for the blessed hope and the manifestation of the glory of our great God and Savior, Jesus Christ. He it is who gave himself for us that he might redeem us from all iniquity and purify for himself a people of his own who are zealous for good deeds" (Tit 2:11-14). In the past, God's grace toward all people was revealed in Christ, who gave himself in order to redeem and purify a people for himself. In the present, the redeemed renounce sin, live godly lives and pursue good deeds as they wait for Christ's return. In the future, Christ's glory will be revealed when the present age comes to a close.

The Pastoral Epistles also use *sōzō* in the past tense to refer to conversion. Second Timothy 1:9 exhorts believers to rely on the power of God, "who saved us and called us with a holy calling." The parallel between "saved" and "called" (both aorist participles) suggests that "saved" in this instance refers to conversion rather than atonement. Titus 3:4-7 declares, "But when the goodness and loving kindness of God our Savior appeared, he saved us, not because of any works of righteousness that we had done, but according to his mercy, through the water of rebirth and renewal by the Holy Spirit. This Spirit he poured out on us richly through Jesus Christ our Savior, so that, having been justified by his grace, we might become heirs according to the hope of eternal life." God's goodness and love for humanity were manifested in the coming of Christ, and the *sōtēria* that Christ accomplished was applied to individuals through "the water of rebirth and renewal by the Holy Spirit." For a discussion of the last phrase, see chapter five on the new birth. So believers were "saved" (aorist tense) at conversion. In their past-tense *sōtēria*, they were justified and received the Holy Spirit. They are now heirs of eternal life, although eternal life remains a hope rather than a possession until the eschaton.

Romans 8:24 illustrates the future orientation of *sōtēria* in Paul's letters: "In hope we were saved" (*esōthēmen*, aorist passive). Despite the aorist verb, Paul emphasizes how much of *sōtēria* remains a future hope. Believers have already received the Holy Spirit, who reassures them that they are God's children and assists them in their relationship with God (Rom 8:16, 26-27). They are God's heirs (Rom 8:17). But they have not yet received resurrection, the "redemption of [their] bodies" (Rom 8:23). As they wait in hope, they share in Christ's sufferings and groan along with the rest of creation. They long for the day when they will share in Christ's glory and all of creation will be redeemed (Rom 8:17, 21-25). The Holy Spirit guarantees that those who have experienced *sōtēria* in the present will also experience its completion in their bodily resurrection (Rom 8:11). The present groaning of believers and the rest of creation, facilitated by the Spirit, is not the pain of despair but the pain of childbirth. It points not only to the present incompleteness of salvation but also to its future fulfillment.

The only two instances of *sōzō* in perfect tense in the New Testament occur in verses 5 and 8 of Ephesians 2. Verse 8 is part of a well known description of salvation: "For by grace you have been saved through faith, and this is not your own doing; it is the gift of God—not the result of works, so that no one may boast. For we are what he has made us, created in Christ Jesus for good works, which God prepared beforehand to be our way of life" (Eph 2:8-10). The present perfect participle (*sesōsmenoi*) indicates a completed event with continuing effects. In this case, *sōtēria* has already been provided by God's grace and received by faith. It has issued in a way of life characterized by good works.

Instances of past-tense *sōtēria* emphasize God's gracious action in Christ and assure believers of their present participation in the salvation that God has provided. On the basis of that salvation, believers are urged to godly living in the present. The Holy Spirit is both the evidence of past salvation and the promise of future salvation.

Sōtēria AS PRESENT EXPERIENCE IN PAUL

The present tense of *sōzō* refers sometimes to the general offer of salvation and sometimes to the present experience of believers. For example, both 1 Corinthians 1:18 and 2 Corinthians 2:15 refer to those who are "being saved" (the present participle *sōzomenois*). The preaching of the gospel divides people into two groups: those who respond and are therefore being saved and those who reject the message and are therefore perishing. Use of the present participle stresses the immediacy and urgency of the proclamation. As Paul declares in 2 Corinthians 6:2, "See, now is the acceptable time; see, now is the day of salvation!" In these instances, "being saved" refers to conversion.

In other instances, however, Paul uses present tense to address believers about their present experience. He reminds the Corinthians about the gospel he preached to them, "through which also you are being saved, if you hold firmly to the message that I proclaimed to you—unless you have come to believe in vain" (1 Cor 15:2). The verb is present passive indicative (*sōzesthe*), suggesting that believers are being acted upon in the present. *Sōtēria* in the present tense continues to be the work of God. However, believers have the responsibility to "hold firmly" to what they have received. Paul's exhortation implies that future salvation is conditional upon the believer's faithfulness. Believers who turn away from the gospel will find that their conversion or coming-to-faith (*episteusate*, the aorist tense of *pisteuō*) was in vain.

Similarly, in Philippians 2:12-13, Paul instructs his audience to "work out your own salvation with fear and trembling; for it is God who is at work in you, enabling you both to will and to work for his good pleasure." God's ongoing work in their lives both empowers them and obligates them to demonstrate in their lives the qualities that are pleasing to God. The context makes clear that Paul has in mind such qualities as humility, harmony and self-sacrificing love. Thus believers must cooperate with the divine initiative in the outworking of *sōtēria*. The expression "fear and trembling" suggests that there is no room for complacency. In language similar to that of 1 Corinthians 15:2, Paul tells the Philippians that if they "[hold] fast to the word of life," he can boast in the day of judgment that his ministry was not "in vain" (Phil 2:16).

The present tense of *sōzō* serves to remind believers of their responsibility to spread the gospel, remain faithful to God, and cooperate with God's work in their lives. Believers thus participate in present salvation through their obedience. While salvation is initiated and sustained by God, believers' actions have a significant effect on the outcome.[30] Because present salvation is characterized by interpersonal qualities such as unity and love, working out one's salvation must take place in the context of the community of faith.

---

[30]According to E. P. Sanders, one of the pioneers of the "new perspective" on Paul, obedience does not earn salvation (and thus is not works righteousness), but disobedience can exclude one from salvation. E. P. Sanders, *Paul and Palestinian Judaism* (Philadelphia: Fortress, 1977), p. 518.

Sōtēria AS FUTURE HOPE IN PAUL

The predominant tense of *sōzō* in Paul's letters is future. Paul declares to the Romans, "You know what time it is, how it is now the moment for you to wake from sleep. For salvation is nearer to us now than when we became believers; the night is far gone, the day is near. Let us then lay aside the works of darkness and put on the armor of light" (Rom 13:11-12). *Sōtēria* here is clearly eschatological. In light of the eschaton, with its coming judgment, believers should reject sin and live Christlike lives (Rom 13:14).

Future *sōtēria* primarily involves being delivered from God's wrath at the judgment. Paul tells the Thessalonians that Jesus, who himself was rescued from death, will rescue them from "the wrath that is coming" (1 Thess 1:10). "Their reality has therefore been defined with reference to Jesus who as crucified and risen Lord rescues the faithful."[31] Similarly, in Romans, Paul declares, "But God proves his love for us in that while we were still sinners Christ died for us. Much more surely then, now that we have been justified by his blood, will we be saved [*sōthēsometha*] through him from the wrath of God. For if while we were enemies, we were reconciled to God through the death of his Son, much more surely, having been reconciled, will we be saved [*sōthēsometha*] by his life" (Rom 5:8-10; cf. 1 Thess 5:9). Oddly for Protestants, who tend to equate them, "salvation" and "justification" are differentiated here. On the basis of the death of Christ, believers have been justified and reconciled to God. Because they have experienced such mercy while they were God's enemies, believers can confidently expect to receive God's mercy at the judgment now that they are his friends.

According to Romans 8:10, this future *sōtēria* takes place not through Christ's death, as we might expect, but through his life. It is only because Jesus is alive and reigning as Lord that he can save.[32] Believers need not fear God's wrath at the judgment, because they belong to Christ. The author of Hebrews also claims that Christ's ongoing life has salvific power. According to Hebrews 7:25, Jesus can provide eternal salvation for believers "since he always lives to make intercession for them." As the sinless

---

[31]Jacob W. Elias, "Jesus Who Delivers Us from the Wrath to Come," *Society of Biblical Literature 1992 Seminar Papers*, ed. Eugene H. Lovering Jr. (Atlanta: Scholars Press, 1992), p. 131.

[32]2 Peter often uses "Lord and Savior" as a combined title for Jesus (2 Pet 1:11; 2:20; 3:2, 18).

high priest who lives forever, Jesus is the perfect and final mediator between human beings and God. Despite the emphasis in Hebrews on the "once for all" character of Christ's sacrifice, this image suggests that the salvation of believers is dependent not only on the cross but also on the ongoing relationship with God that Jesus' intercession makes possible.

Believers' good works will be evaluated at the judgment, but those works by themselves will not determine their salvation. In 1 Corinthians 3, Paul admonishes those who build the church to be careful how they build, because the quality of their work will be tested by fire on Judgment Day: "If what has been built on the foundation survives, the builder will receive a reward. If the work is burned up, the builder will suffer loss; the builder will be saved, but only as through fire" (1 Cor 3:14-15). Enduring contributions to the church will be rewarded, but the lack of such contributions is not grounds for condemnation.

Future *sōtēria* is associated with glory: "God chose you as the first fruits for salvation through sanctification by the Spirit and through belief in the truth. For this purpose he called you through our proclamation of the good news, so that you may obtain the glory of our Lord Jesus Christ. So then, brothers and sisters, stand firm and hold fast to the traditions that you were taught by us, either by word of mouth or by our letter" (2 Thess 2:13-15; cf. 2 Tim 2:10). The Thessalonians were chosen for *sōtēria* and were called through Paul's preaching of the gospel.[33] They responded in faith and have been set apart by the Holy Spirit. The glory that is the goal of their *sōtēria* is yet future. As they wait for it, they must hold fast to what they have been taught.

In Philippians 3:20-21, Paul specifically identifies the future glory of *sōtēria* with the resurrection: "Our citizenship is in heaven, and it is from there that we are expecting a Savior, the Lord Jesus Christ. He will transform the body of our humiliation that it may be conformed to the body of his glory, by the power that also enables him to make all things subject to himself." Jesus' future work as *sōtēr* will include the transformation of believers' mortal bodies into glorious resurrection bodies that resemble his.[34]

---

[33]For a discussion of election, see chapter ten.

[34]Oscar Cullman argues that the title *sōtēr* participates in the already/not yet tension of the New Testament. Some passages in Paul suggest that Jesus has completed his function as savior,

The future tense of *sōzō*, like the present, urges believers to faithful action and warns against complacency. Although God's provision of future salvation is assured, believers must persevere in order to enter it. The future tense of *sōzō* offers hope and gives strength to endure present struggles in light of the glory that is to come (1 Thess 5:8). It also underscores the central place of resurrection in Paul's understanding of salvation.

Sōtēria IN 1 PETER

Passages in 1 Peter suggest that *sōtēria* is a process of growth. The tense of *sōzō* is present, but the perspective is forward-looking.[35] In 1 Peter 2:2, believers are instructed, "Like newborn infants, long for the pure, spiritual milk, so that by it you may grow into salvation—if indeed you have tasted that the Lord is good" (1 Pet 2:2-3). *Sōtēria* here clearly is not a completed event in the past but a condition in which (or into which) believers grow. In the present, believers participate in their own *sōtēria* by engaging in activities that contribute to their growth. In the context of the letter, these activities include keeping their focus on Christ and living exemplary lives before the world.

Similarly, in 1 Peter 1:9, believers are told, "You are receiving [present participle] the outcome of your faith, the salvation of your souls." Although the verb suggests that *sōtēria* is a present experience, it is described as the "outcome" or goal (*telos*) of their faith, and the context is eschatological. They await "a salvation ready to be revealed in the last time" (1 Pet 1:5). Until that *sōtēria* comes, they must remain faithful even through persecution. The present participle suggests an organic connection between the coming salvation and the strength that sustains them in their present trials.

First Peter connects present *sōtēria* with baptism. After describing Noah's ark, 1 Peter 3:21 states: "And baptism, which this prefigured, now saves you—not as a removal of dirt from the body, but as an appeal to God for a good conscience, through the resurrection of Jesus Christ." This pas-

---

while others suggest that he will do so at the "end of days." *The Christology of the New Testament*, trans. Shirley C. Guthrie and Charles A. M. Hall (Philadelphia: Westminster Press, 1963), p. 244.

[35]Donald G. Miller sees three tenses of salvation in 1 Peter: new birth, growth in Christlikeness, and the fulfillment of the "living hope" instilled in Christians by their new birth. "Deliverance and Destiny: Salvation in First Peter," *Interpretation* 9, no. 4 (October 1955): 418, 419, 421-22. Miller is using "salvation" as a theological category, not focusing on Peter's use of the *sōtēria* word group.

sage is playing on the meanings of *sōzō* as rescue from danger and forgiveness of sins. Just as Noah and his family were "saved through water" (1 Pet 3:20), Christians are saved through baptism. The water itself (the "removal of dirt from the body") is not salvific, however, any more than it was for Noah and his family. The efficient cause of *sōtēria* is the resurrection of Christ, and the instrumental cause is the good conscience of the believer. The appeal for (or pledge of) a good conscience indicates that the believer's rescue looks forward to a life lived according to the will of God.[36]

Sōtēria AS INVITATION AND RESPONSE

Throughout the New Testament, as in the Old, *sōtēria* is regarded as the work of God. It is provided by the Father, accomplished by the Son, and applied by the Spirit. The Father is the source of *sōtēria*; he sends the Son into the world so that it might be saved (Jn 3:17). Jesus is the mediator of *sōtēria*. He came to seek and save the lost (Lk 19:10), and salvation comes only through him (Acts 4:12). Jesus provides *sōtēria* through his healings, his forgiveness, his death and his life (Rom 5:10). The power of *sōtēria* is the power of his resurrection (1 Pet 3:21; cf. Rom 1:4). The Holy Spirit makes *sōtēria* actual in the lives of believers by setting them apart for God and making them holy so that they can share in the glory of Christ (2 Thess 2:13).

Some instances of the verb *sōzō* are simply in passive voice, with divine activity assumed. New Testament writers apply the title *sōtēr* to both the Father and the Son (Tit 1:3-4), but not to the Spirit. While other images of salvation, such as regeneration, emphasize the role of the Holy Spirit, *sōtēria* emphasizes the roles of the Father and the Son. This image highlights the doctrinal development in the New Testament, as the writers apply to Jesus language that was previously reserved for God but remain reticent about applying such language to the Spirit.

If God is the *sōtēr*, what do we make of passages that talk about human

---

[36]I. Howard Marshall observes that *eperōtēma* can mean either question or pledge (such as a legal pledge in a contract). The sense is either an appeal to God for a good conscience or the pledge to maintain a good conscience in the future. *1 Peter*, IVP New Testament Commentary, ed. Grant R. Osborne (Downers Grove, Ill.: InterVarsity Press, 1991), p. 131. Either case is forward-looking. Marshall also argues that the significance of baptism in this passage is not limited to the event of encountering the water but extends to the whole process of coming to faith (p. 130).

beings saving themselves or others? For example, in his Pentecost sermon, Peter urges his hearers, "Save yourselves from this corrupt generation" (Acts 2:40). Paul declares that he has become all things to all people so that he might save some of them (1 Cor 9:22) and warns believers that they may or may not be able to save their unbelieving spouses (1 Cor 7:16). He urges Timothy, "Pay close attention to yourself and to your teaching; continue in these things, for in doing this you will save both yourself and your hearers" (1 Tim 4:16).

A call to people to save themselves is a call to respond to or welcome the gospel message (Acts 2:41). An exhortation to save others is a call to proclaim the gospel message in word and life. Besides sharing the gospel, believers must live exemplary lives so that they create no obstacles to the acceptance of the gospel (1 Cor 9:12). Those in the church continue to need sound teaching and positive examples so that they will mature in the faith and experience future salvation (1 Tim 4:11-15). Sometimes they need the prayers of other believers to recover from illness (Jas 5:15) or the intervention of other believers to turn from sin (Jas 5:20). While the power of *sōtēria* is always God's (see Rom 1:16), human beings participate in God's rescue mission as willing recipients and active agents.[37] The ministry of believers—in proclamation, rescue and healing—is an extension of the ministry of Jesus.

Both the Gospels and the Epistles describe God's offer of *sōtēria* as universal. God wants everyone to be saved (1 Tim 2:4) and has sent Jesus to be the savior of the world (Jn 4:42; 12:47; 1 Jn 4:14). Jesus died not just for the sins of some—those who have believed—but for the sins of the whole world (1 Jn 2:2). Although God offers *sōtēria* to all, only those who respond can receive its full benefits. God is the *sōtēr* of all people, but especially of those who believe—or are faithful (1 Tim 4:10).[38] Even those who do not believe may experience some of God's *sōtēria*, because God pours out blessings on both the righteous and the unrighteous (Mt 5:45; Lk 6:35).

---

[37]In his structural analysis of *sōtēria*, Johnson identifies Moses, John the Baptist, Jesus, the apostles and Paul as agents of *sōtēria*. "Social Dimension of *Sōtēria*," pp. 529.

[38]Luke Timothy Johnson translates this verse as "We have come to hope in a living God who is the savior of all human beings, above all those who are faithful." *Letters to Paul's Delegates: 1 Timothy, 2 Timothy, Titus*, The New Testament in Context, ed. Howard Clark Kee and J. Andrew Overman (Valley Forge, Penn.: Trinity Press International, 1996), p. 165. The verse is usually understood as expressing the distinction between God's universal offer of salvation and the smaller number who benefit from it.

Although Western Christians typically think of salvation in individual terms, the New Testament gives *sōtēria* a communal context, as we would expect in a more communal culture. *Sōtēria* is offered to whole households (Lk 19:9; Acts 11:14; 16:31). People are not saved in isolation but are saved into the church (Acts 2:47). Paul describes God's working out his plan of salvation through people groups (Jews and Gentiles), declaring finally that "all Israel" will be saved (Rom 11:26). Ultimately, God's *sōtēria* will extend to the healing of creation (Rom 8:19-21).

Romans 10:9-17 describes in practical terms how initial *sōtēria* takes place: the community of believers sends someone to preach the gospel; someone else hears the gospel and believes; he or she calls on the Lord for rescue and publicly confesses Christ as Lord. Such a confession is a pledge of allegiance and promise of obedience. The two conditions of confessing Christ as Lord and believing that God has raised him from the dead are not two separate issues but two aspects of a single issue. The resurrection demonstrates that Jesus has defeated sin and death and is now reigning as Lord. Without the resurrection, Jesus would not be Lord of anything and would have no power to save.

Sōtēria seems to require three dimensions of human response: cognitive, affective and volitional. The cognitive dimension consists of grasping the good news expressed in the Scriptures or in the gospel proclamation (Rom 1:16; 2 Tim 3:15; Jas 1:21). The affective dimension takes place in repentance (Mk 1:15; Acts 2:37-40; 2 Cor 7:10). The volitional dimension is the public identification of the believer with Christ in baptism (Acts 2:37-40; 1 Pet 3:21).[39] All of these are associated with *sōtēria*. The most important human response is faith.

Throughout the New Testament, experiences of *sōtēria* are connected with expressions or demonstrations of faith. In the Gospels, *sōtēria* is the evidence of the in-breaking of God's kingdom in the person and ministry of Jesus. The faith involved may simply be faith in Jesus as God's agent or faith in Jesus' power to heal. In the Epistles, *sōtēria* is the intersection of grace and faith—God's loving intention to rescue and heal initiating a relationship of trust and faithfulness.

The Greek word for faith, *pistis*, can also be translated as faithfulness,

---

[39]For a fuller discussion of baptism, see chapter five on regeneration.

just as the word *apistia* can be translated as unbelief or unfaithfulness.[40] The nuances of the words in any particular instance are determined by the context. However, the New Testament nowhere supports an understanding of saving faith as mere intellectual assent divorced from obedience. Saving faith entails faithfulness. Believers are saved *by* grace *through* faith *for* works (Eph 2:8-10). According to Hebrews, Jesus is "the source of eternal salvation for all who obey him" (Heb 5:9). The "things that belong to salvation" include faithfulness, patience and loving service (Heb 6:9-12). As James points out, the faith necessary for salvation is a faith that expresses itself in works (Jas 2:14-17).

It is quite common to speak of saving faith as the gift of God, generally on the basis of Ephesians 2:8-9: "For by grace you have been saved through faith, and this is not your own doing; it is the gift of God—not the result of works, so that no one may boast." This point is often made by those who want to emphasize God's role in salvation to avoid any appearance of human "works." However, "faith" (*pistis*) in Greek is feminine, while "this" in verse 8 (*touto*) is neuter. Thus *touto* likely refers not to *pistis* but to the entire preceding clause. What is "not your own doing," therefore, is not faith in particular, but God's gracious act of salvation in general.[41]

As *sōtēria* demonstrates, salvation is a gift, but it is not a blank check or a free ride. Passages in the Gospels, Paul and Hebrews describe *sōzō* in the future tense as conditional. Those who persevere to the end will be saved (Mt. 10:22; 24:13; Mk 13:13). The Corinthians are being saved if they hold firmly to the Gospel; otherwise they have believed in vain (1 Cor 15:1-2). If Timothy perseveres in his life and doctrine, he will save both himself and his hearers (1 Tim 4:16). Those who shrink back are destroyed, but those who have faith (or are faithful) are saved (Heb 10:39). Other passages, while not using *sōzō*, make the same point: Romans 11:22; Colossians 1:22-23; Hebrews 3:6, 14; 6:11-12; James 1:12; 1 John 2:24-25; Revelation 2:10; 3:5; 21:7. Salvation is received by faith, and faith entails faithfulness.

Salvation is not a transaction but an ongoing relationship between the

---

[40]Compare the NRSV and NIV translations of Romans 3:3. The context makes clear that Paul is speaking of the unfaithfulness or faithlessness of the Israelites (NRSV), not their "lack of faith" (NIV).

[41]See the discussion in William G. MacDonald, "The Spirit of Grace," in *Grace Unlimited*, ed. Clark H. Pinnock (Minneapolis: Bethany House, 1975), p. 87.

Rescuer and the rescued, between the Healer and the healed. The best way to ensure faithfulness is to nurture that relationship. Final salvation, like initial salvation, is appropriated by grace through faith(fulness) (Eph 2:8-10; 1 Pet 1:5). God, of course, will always be faithful and will graciously provide all of the resources the believer needs in order to persevere. The believer's responsive acts of faithfulness are not a means of earning God's favor but a sign of love given and received. As in a marriage, the countless acts of trust and loyalty, both small and great, nourish the relationship and help it grow. Without such expressions, the relationship withers.

CONCLUSION

The New Testament understanding of *sōtēria* can speak powerfully to people today. While some images of salvation seem alien to modern and postmodern people, the need and hope of healing are familiar to everyone. At the most fundamental level, the image of *sōtēria* reminds us of our desperate need. Fallen human beings are not essentially good and free. We are enmeshed in sin and evil, illness and death, and we are powerless to remedy our predicament. We must call upon the only one powerful enough to rescue and heal us. Calling upon Jesus is not like calling the doctor, however. It is as the Lord that Jesus saves. To be healed, we must commit ourselves completely to him. Our allegiance to him means rejecting competing claims of salvation, whether these are offered by other religions, secular ideologies, political authorities, consumer culture or the entertainment industry.

Salvation has two directions: salvation *from* and salvation *for*. These two directions correspond to the meanings of *sōtēria* as rescue and healing. We are rescued from sin, Satan, illness, death and wrath in order to experience healing that brings life in all its fullness. We are also saved *for a purpose*: good works and holy living. We are not saved from suffering, because suffering is an evidence that the salvation of creation is still incomplete. But we are saved in hope because we know that our destiny is a glory that reflects the glory of Christ.

Salvation is not a one-time event completed at conversion. It involves a growth in relationship and in wholeness that is not optional or secondary but essential to what salvation means. The three tenses of *sōzō* remind us that God is intimately involved in our lives—past, present and future—and we must depend upon God throughout our life in faith. We cannot be complacent, because our salvation is not complete until Christ returns. Yet the work of Christ on our behalf and the presence of the Spirit in our lives give us confidence that we will reach that goal. We can have hope for the rest of creation, as well. So instead of looking backward, we should look forward with anticipation and engage in the work God has called us to do.

The New Testament writers remind us of our responsibility to be agents of God's salvation by proclaiming the good news and extending Christ's ministry. They show us that God is not interested in saving "souls" but in rescuing and restoring whole persons in their social relationships. That should be our emphasis, as well. We cannot save ourselves, let alone anyone else, but we have a great deal to do as participants in the salvation God is bringing about.

Christians should carry on Jesus' ministry of healing, whether the illness be physical, emotional, spiritual or social: "The early church understood its message and ministry, as the Body of Christ on earth, to be to preach the forgiveness of sins, to establish a community of acceptance, and to reach out to care for the alienated in soul and body. All of this they summed up with the words salvation and healing. . . . As Christians we work to carry out God's intention to heal the illness of body and soul, among individuals, and to heal sick relationships and the ills of society."[42] We must share Jesus' compassion for the wounded and disabled, as well as for those struggling with sin. As we work for their healing, we should welcome them into a supportive community of God's people.

Such compassionate community is even more critical when a hoped-for cure does not occur. While we trust in God's power to heal, we should also trust in God's wisdom. We should not try to avoid hard questions about suffering and God's will by blaming the lack of a cure on someone's inadequate faith. We should remain open to the possibility that God may choose to heal people in significant ways even in the absence of a cure.[43] "Faith can make whole even when it does not make well."[44]

Salvation is rescue and healing, room to thrive, safety and well-being. It

---

[42]Gowan, "Salvation as Healing," pp. 12-13, 15.
[43]Ibid., pp. 15-16.
[44]Carroll, "Sickness and Healing," p. 139.

is present whenever people receive forgiveness of sins through Christ, but also whenever people experience deliverance from danger or oppression or physical or emotional healing. All of creation is the sphere of God's saving faithfulness, but in this time "between the times," it should be most apparent in the transformed lives of Christians. Even believers, however, have only a partial experience of salvation in this life. The completion of salvation awaits the age to come, when God's people, fully restored and in resurrection bodies, experience with the rest of creation the blessings of God's saving reign.

FOR FURTHER READING

Caird, G. B. *New Testament Theology*. Completed and edited by L. D. Hurst. Oxford: Clarendon, 1995, pp. 118-35.

Carroll, John T. "Sickness and Healing in the New Testament Gospels." *Interpretation* 49, no. 2 (April 1995): 130-42.

Foerster, W., and G. Fohrer. "σῴζω κτλ." In *TDNT* 7:965-1024.

Fretheim, Terence E. "Salvation in the Bible vs. Salvation in the Church." *Word and World* 13, no. 4 (1993): 363-72.

Gowan, Donald E. "Salvation as Healing." *Ex Auditu* 5 (1989): 1-19.

Green, Michael (E. M. B.). *The Meaning of Salvation*. London: Hodder & Stoughton, 1965. Reprint, Vancouver, B.C.: Regent College Publishing, 1998.

Green, Joel B. *Salvation*. Understanding Biblical Themes. St. Louis, Mo.: Chalice, 2003.

Hull, William E. *The Christian Experience of Salvation*. Layman's Library of Christian Doctrine. Nashville: Broadman, 1987.

Hunter, A. M. *The Gospel According to St. Paul*. Philadelphia: Westminster Press, 1966.

Johnson, Luke Timothy. "The Social Dimension of *Sōtēria* in Luke-Acts and Paul." *Society of Biblical Literature Seminar Papers*, no. 32 (1993): 520-36.

Schneider, J., and C. Brown. "Redemption etc." In *NIDNTT* 3:177-223 (esp. pp. 205-21).

Throckmorton, Burton Hamilton. "*Sōzein, sōtēria* in Luke-Acts." *Studia Evangelica* 6, Papers Presented to the 4th International Congress on New Testament Studies held at Oxford, 1969, pp. 515-26. Berlin: Akademie Verlag, 1973.

Wilson, Robert McL. "*Sōtēria*." *Scottish Journal of Theology* 6, no. 4 (1953): 406-16.

7

MY CHAINS FELL OFF,
MY HEART WAS FREE

Redemption, Ransom, Freedom, Forgiveness

CHARLES WESLEY'S GREAT HYMN "And Can It Be" is regarded by some as the unofficial theme song of Ashland Theological Seminary, the institution where I teach. It contains a stanza that describes the liberating power of the gospel:

> Long my imprisoned spirit lay,
> Fast bound in sin and nature's night;
> Thine eye diffused a quickening ray—
> I woke, the dungeon flamed with light;
> My chains fell off, my heart was free,
> I rose, went forth, and followed Thee.
> Amazing love! How can it be,
> That Thou, my God, shouldst die for me?

In modern Western societies, freedom is a cherished value. Political and social freedoms are fought for and celebrated. Freedom of choice is used as the rationale for everything from consumer products to sexual behavior. In contrast to the modern view of freedom as a right to be preserved, however, the New Testament regards human beings as basically unfree.[1] They are enslaved to sin, self and Satan, and they need to be set free. As Wesley's hymn suggests, true freedom can come only through Christ.

---

[1]J. Blunck, "Freedom," in *NIDNTT* 1:718.

This chapter will explore a cluster of images that picture salvation as freedom from negative powers that bind or enslave. For example, the ransom image shows Jesus giving his life in exchange for the lives of others, while the redemption image depicts him buying people out of slavery. While "redemption" is a specific image of salvation in its own right, it has become an umbrella term for the work of Christ. As we did in the discussion of *sōtēria*, we will have to put aside our more general theological assumptions about redemption while we examine what the New Testament has to say about this image.

Freedom describes the condition of Christians who have been liberated from pagan practices and from the cycle of law-sin-death. This is a special concern of Paul's as he proclaims a gospel that does not depend upon the law. Forgiveness specifically deals with being freed from sin. Christians are called to appreciate the magnitude of the blessing they have received, and then, in their gratitude, to extend a similar forgiveness to others. The language of redemption, ransom and purchase can be found throughout the New Testament. Forgiveness is largely a concern of the Gospels, while freedom occurs in the Pauline and Johannine literature.

TERMS AND CONCEPTS

Redemption in the ancient world meant to set someone free from a situation of bondage, usually by paying a ransom price. This was a familiar concept in dealing with prisoners of war, slaves and condemned prisoners.[2] In the Old Testament, land, houses, servants and the firstborn were redeemed. The concept also applied to levirate marriage and to the blood avenger. God redeems Israel from adversity, from oppressors, from enemies and from exile. The paradigm of God's redemption is the exodus. Redemption usually, but not always, involves payment. The exodus is an example of the latter; God redeems his people with no payment but simply by his power: "I will redeem you with an outstretched arm and with mighty

---

[2]F. Büchsel, "λύω κτλ.," in *TDNT* 4:340, 352. Leon Morris insists that the ransom price is key to the concept of redemption. *The Apostolic Preaching of the Cross*, 3rd ed. (Grand Rapids: Eerdmans, 1965), pp. 12-13. D. Francois Tolmie surveys the scholarship on Paul's language of redemption and concludes that it is best understood in the context of slavery, which was a very complex institution in the first century. "Salvation as Redemption: The Use of 'Redemption' Metaphors in Pauline Literature," in *Salvation in the New Testament: Perspectives on Soteriology*, ed. Jan G. van der Watt. Supplements to Novum Testamentum, ed. M. M. Mitchell and D. P. Moessner (Boston: E. J. Brill, 2005), pp. 247-56.

acts of judgment" (Ex 6:6). In this case, God's effort to set his people free is the cost of their redemption: "Yahweh's action is at cost to Himself."[3] Similarly, God declares to Israel in exile, "You were sold for nothing, and you shall be redeemed without money" (Is 52:3). For Israel, freedom was a gracious gift of God, who delivered them from bondage.[4]

The exodus and the social reality of slavery provide the primary framework for understanding redemption in the New Testament.[5] In the exodus, God liberated the Israelites from their slavery in Egypt. But the purpose of the exodus was not fulfilled until God had entered into covenant with the people at Sinai: "There is no freedom without boundaries. . . . The real act of liberation takes place at Sinai with the giving of the Torah. . . . Only the liberating word of God can set people free and bring them to the promised land and eventually to authentic freedom."[6] Somewhat paradoxically, Israel can become truly free only by serving the Lord who has redeemed them. The kind of freedom represented in the exodus event becomes a "core value" in the Bible: "It is a group freedom without submission to alien peoples yet with limits. The limits are defined by the goal of this group freedom, the service of God."[7]

Manumission—the payment of money to free a slave—was a familiar practice in the first century. In sacral manumission, a slave could pay a redemption price to a temple in order to be freed from his or her current master and symbolically become the slave of the god. The New Testament understanding of redemption parallels this practice, with a few notable exceptions: in Christian redemption, the slave contributes nothing to his or her freedom; God is an active participant rather than a symbolic presence; and the former slave's attachment to the deity is real.[8]

---

[3]Morris, *Apostolic Preaching*, p. 22.

[4]Blunck, "Freedom," in *NIDNTT* 1:716.

[5]For an examination of slavery in the first century, see David J. Williams, *Paul's Metaphors: Their Context and Character* (Peabody, Mass.: Hendrickson, 1999), pp. 111-40; and John Byron, *Slavery Metaphors in Early Judaism and Pauline Christianity: A Traditio-Historical and Exegetical Examination*, Wissenschaftliche Untersuchungen zum Neuen Testament 2.Reihe (Tübingen: Mohr Siebeck, 2003).

[6]Göran Larsson, *Bound for Freedom: The Book of Exodus in Jewish and Christian Traditions* (Peabody, Mass.: Hendrickson, 1999), pp. 2, 127-29.

[7]Bruce J. Malina, "Freedom," in *Biblical Social Values and Their Meaning: A Handbook*, ed. John J. Pilch and Bruce J. Malina (Peabody, Mass.: Hendrickson, 1993), p. 80.

[8]G. S. Shogren, "Redemption," in *ABD*, 5:655. Shogren notes the work of A. Deissmann on the idea of sacral manumission.

The concept of redemption in the New Testament is described with two primary sets of terms: *agorazō* and *exagorazō* (to purchase) and a group of words related to *lyō* (to loose or release). The words *agorazō* and *exagorazō* come from the marketplace. New Testament writers use these terms metaphorically to describe the act of redemption. For instance, Revelation describes the 144,000 as having been purchased or redeemed from among humanity (Rev 14:3-4). Purchasing something implies a purchase price. A price is specifically mentioned in 1 Corinthians 6:20 and 7:23. However, a price is not always part of the concept, as evidenced by the injunctions to "redeem the time" in Ephesians 5:16 and Colossians 4:5 (using *exagorazō*).[9]

More important than any price is the fact that those who have been purchased belong to God. This is the central point of the metaphor as Paul uses it.[10] In the first century, slaves who were bought by a new master would acquire the identity, status and obligations associated with the new household to which they now belonged.[11] They were set free from the old master in order to serve the new one.[12] In a similar way, God's ownership of believers means that they must live in ways that honor their new master: "For you were bought with a price; therefore glorify God in your body" (1 Cor 6:20); "You were bought with a price; do not become slaves of human masters" (1 Cor 7:23). Their bodies are not their own to dispose of as they will; they belong to God. Moreover, since God is their master, they should not let themselves be enslaved to human opinions.[13]

The most significant group of words for redemption are forms of the verb *lyō*, which means to loose or release: *lytron* and *antilytron* (ransom or means of redemption); *lytrōtēs* (redeemer, used only of Moses in Acts 7:35); *lytrōsis* and *apolytrōsis* (redemption); and *lytroomai* (to redeem). The New Testament writers' use of the rare word *apolytrōsis* to express redemption may imply that they want to call attention to a special redemp-

---

[9]Tolmie argues that the idea of price is not carried over to the biblical uses of *lyō* and *apolytrōsis*. "Salvation as Redemption," p. 263. It is more remarkable that even the language of purchase (*exagorazō*) does not always imply price. As I will argue below, however, price is not the same as cost.

[10]Morris, *Apostolic Preaching*, p. 55; Tolmie, "Salvation as Redemption," p. 257.

[11]Tolmie, "Salvation as Redemption," p. 267.

[12]Williams, *Paul's Metaphors*, p. 116.

[13]On the last point, see Leon Morris, "Redemption," in *DPL*, p. 785.

tion that cannot be described by the words in ordinary use.[14] These various words depict the work of Christ as freeing human beings from all inimical powers that enslave them.

New Testament writers describe redemption in other language, as well. For example, the word *eleutheroō* (to set free) can be used in a religious sense to mean redemption. Paul declares that the creation itself is longing for the day when it will share "the glorious freedom of the children of God" (Rom 8:21 NIV). In this passage, Paul envisions the eschatological redemption in which humanity and nature will finally be delivered from all afflictions. As we will see, Paul also has a particular concern with freedom in relation to the law. In the Fourth Gospel, Jesus describes his ministry as liberation: "You will know the truth, and the truth will make you free. . . . So if the Son makes you free, you will be free indeed" (Jn 8:32, 36). In the context, Jesus frees those who have become slaves of sin (Jn 8:34).

REDEMPTION AND RANSOM

Redemption is God's gracious gift, accomplished through Christ. According to Paul, believers are "justified by [God's] grace as a gift, through the redemption that is in Christ Jesus" (Rom 3:24). Several passages specify Christ's blood as the means of redemption: "You know that you were ransomed from the futile ways inherited from your ancestors, not with perishable things like silver or gold, but with the precious blood of Christ, like that of a lamb without defect or blemish" (1 Pet 1:18-19; cf. Acts 20:28; Heb 9:12; Rev 1:5; 5:9). These passages clearly picture Jesus' death as a sacrificial offering. Although God's grace lies behind redemption, most passages picture Jesus as the active agent: "To him who loves us and freed us from our sins by his blood . . ." (Rev 1:5). While Jesus is passive in his suffering, he actively provides redemption through his self-sacrifice.

Jesus' only statement about the meaning of his death outside of the Last Supper accounts is a ransom saying: "For the Son of Man came not to be served but to serve, and to give his life a ransom for many" (Mk 10:45; cf. Mt 20:28). The word used in these two passages is *lytron*, which means a ransom or means of redemption. First Timothy 2:6 states that Jesus "gave

---

[14]Morris, "Redemption," p. 785.

himself a ransom for all," using the word *antily*
sages (the only direct references to ransom), Jesu
tary self-sacrifice to set others free. The prefix *
offered himself *in place of others*, not just on the
place in death so that they might live. According --
Caiaphas the high priest recognized the redemptive possibilities in Jesus'
death: "It is better for you to have one man die for the people than to have
the whole nation destroyed" (Jn 11:50). Caiaphas had political concerns in
mind, but the narrator notes that he spoke more truly than he knew (Jn
11:51-52).

The background of Jesus' ransom saying may be the suffering Servant
of God in Isaiah 53 or the vicarious suffering of the Maccabean martyrs
(4 Mac 6:28-29).[16] Along with other scholars, Peter Stuhlmacher argues
that Mark 10:45 echoes Isaiah 43:3-4:

> For I am the LORD your God,
>   The Holy One of Israel, your Savior.
> I give Egypt as your ransom,
>   Ethiopia and Seba in exchange for you.
> Because you are precious in my sight,
>   And honored, and I love you,
> I give people in return for you,
>   Nations in exchange for your life.

God declares that he will give up other nations to redeem his people
from their captivity and restore their relationship with him. In light of this
passage, the ransom saying in Mark suggests that instead of giving up the
nations for Israel, God gives his Son, who willingly offers up his life for
both Jews and Gentiles to reconcile them to God.[17]

For some interpreters, a ransom requires a price, and a price must be
paid to someone. To whom is Christ's ransom paid? F. Büchsel contends

---

[15]Büchsel, "λύω κτλ.," in *TDNT* 4:342-43. Morris emphasizes the substitutionary character of
the words for redemption. *Apostolic Preaching*, p. 34.

[16]S. Page, "Ransom Saying," in *DJG*, p. 660. He notes also that some scholars attribute the saying to a corporate understanding of the "son of man" in Daniel 7.

[17]Peter Stuhlmacher, "Vicariously Giving His Life for Many, Mark 10:45 (Matt. 20:28)," in
Reconciliation, Law, & Righteousness: Essays in Biblical Theology (Philadelphia: Fortress, 1986),
pp. 23-24. Stuhlmacher notes that "later rabbinic interpretation" locates the fulfillment of
Isaiah 43:3-4 at the final judgment (p. 24).

e ransom is paid to God, who demands the death of Christ: "God ... es him."[18] Some of the church fathers believed that the ransom was paid to Satan. Their fanciful elaboration of the ransom image—involving fishhooks, mousetraps and divine trickery—did much to discredit a theologically important picture of salvation.[19]

However, the New Testament never says that the ransom is paid *to* anyone, or even that it is demanded *by* anyone, just that it is provided by God or Christ. As I. H. Marshall has observed, *cost* and *price* are not the same thing. While a price implies a cost, a cost can exist without the payment of a price.[20] "Cost" refers to whatever has been expended by the redeemer to bring about the redemption; "price" indicates that this cost has been established and required by someone else. As noted earlier, God redeems his people in the exodus by the exercise of his power, not by payment of a price.

The point of redemption in the New Testament is the self-sacrifice of Christ, who gave his life to free humanity. In some passages, Paul describes Christ's self-donation without using the words for ransom or redemption: Jesus "gave himself for our sins," and Jesus "loved me and gave himself for me" (Gal 1:4; 2:20). Paul identifies redemption with the person of Jesus himself: Jesus "became for us wisdom from God, and righteousness and sanctification and redemption" (1 Cor 1:30; cf. Eph 1:7). Redemption, therefore, is found only in relationship to Jesus.[21]

Redemption and ransom thus show the costliness of human salvation.

---

[18]Büchsel, "λύω κτλ.," in *TDNT* 4:344.

[19]See, for example, Gregory of Nyssa, *An Address on Religious Instruction* 22–26, in *Christology of the Later Fathers*, ed. Edward R. Hardy, The Library of Christian Classics, Ichthus Edition (Philadelphia: Westminster Press, 1954), pp. 298-304. The Greek title is *Logos Katēchētikos* and is usually translated *Catechetical Oration* (p. 268). Green and Baker survey the development of ransom and other metaphors in church history. Joel B. Green and Mark D. Baker, *Recovering the Scandal of the Cross: Atonement in New Testament & Contemporary Contexts* (Downers Grove, Ill.: InterVarsity Press, 2000), pp. 116-52.

[20]I. Howard Marshall, "The Development of the Concept of Redemption in the New Testament," in *Reconciliation and Hope: New Testament Essays on Atonement and Eschatology Presented to L. L. Morris on his 60th Birthday*, ed. Robert Banks (Grand Rapids: Eerdmans, 1974), p. 153-54 n. 4. Marshall does not rule out the idea of price, however; he sees the idea of price in some passages (p. 156) and the idea of price or cost in about half of the passages dealing with redemption (pp. 168-69 n. 3). C. F. D. Moule contends that all of the sacrificial imagery associated with the work of Christ can be explained in terms of cost. "Preaching the Atonement," in *Forgiveness and Reconciliation and Other New Testament Themes* (London: SPCK, 1998), p. 21.

[21]Büchsel, "λύω κτλ.," in *TDNT* 4:354.

Jesus set human beings free at the cost of his own life. A modern analogy might be a prisoner exchange or a hostage negotiation in which the negotiator takes the place of the hostages. Speculating about a recipient of the ransom is forcing the metaphor beyond its intended purpose.[22] Furthermore, framing redemption in terms of *price* rather than *cost* has led the church astray into unbiblical attempts to quantify salvation, such as the calculation and transfer of merit in the medieval penitential system and the understanding of the atonement as a commercial transaction. If anything, redemption and ransom emphasize the extravagant grace of God offered through the loving self-giving of Christ.

The New Testament is clear that Christ's redemption is universal in its intention: "God our Savior . . . desires everyone to be saved and to come to the knowledge of the truth. For there is one God; there is also one mediator between God and humankind, Christ Jesus, himself human, who gave himself a ransom for all—this was attested at the right time" (1 Tim 2:3-6). Christ's self-sacrifice was an expression of God's universal salvific will. As the sole mediator between God and humanity, Christ offered himself as a ransom for all humanity. The book of Revelation celebrates the multicultural, multiethnic, multilingual character of the redeemed: "You are worthy to take the scroll and to open its seals, for you were slaughtered and by your blood you ransomed for God saints from every tribe and language and people and nation" (Rev 5:9).

However, only those who believe in Christ experience Christ's redemption: "And you also were included in Christ when you heard the word of truth, the gospel of your salvation. Having believed, you were marked in him with a seal, the promised Holy Spirit, who is a deposit guaranteeing our inheritance until the redemption of those who are God's possession—to the praise of his glory" (Eph 1:13-14 NIV). Ephesians 4:30 states that believers have been marked with the seal of the Holy Spirit "for the day of redemption." As those redeemed by Christ, believers receive the Holy

---

[22]Morris, "Redemption," p. 785. See also Reginald H. Fuller, "Jesus Christ as Savior in the New Testament," *Interpretation* 35, no. 2 (April 1981): 152; G. B. Caird, *The Language and Imagery of the Bible* (Grand Rapids: Eerdmans, 1997), p. 17; and Green and Baker, *Recovering the Scandal of the Cross*, p. 102. James D. G. Dunn argues that the debate over payment arose as a result of theological models developed in church history rather than being called for by Paul's image itself or its biblical background. *The Theology of Paul the Apostle* (Grand Rapids: Eerdmans, 1998), p. 228.

Spirit, who marks them as belonging to Christ.

This seal of ownership is not an unconditional guarantee of final redemption, however. Peter warns his audience about false teachers who "even deny the Master who bought them—bringing swift destruction on themselves" (2 Pet 2:1). These false teachers are apparently apostate believers, because Peter says that they have "left the straight road and have gone astray" like Balaam (2 Pet 2:15). They had "escaped the defilement of the world through the knowledge of our Lord and Savior Jesus Christ" but had then "turn[ed] back from the holy commandment that was passed on to them" (2 Pet 2:20, 21). They promise people freedom but are themselves "slaves of corruption" (2 Pet 2:19). Although these false teachers were "bought" or redeemed by Christ, they have turned away and denied him, to their own destruction.[23]

REDEMPTION FROM WHAT?

From what are people redeemed? Luke shows that first-century Jews expected national redemption from oppression. They wanted Messiah to deliver them from their enemies as God had delivered them in the Old Testament. Both Zachariah and Anna interpret the coming of the Messiah in terms of the redemption of Israel (Lk 1:68; 2:38). After Jesus' death, the disciples he meets on the road to Emmaus tell him that they had been hoping that Jesus would redeem Israel (Lk 24:21). Even after Jesus' resurrection, the disciples ask him if it is time for him to restore the kingdom to Israel (Acts 1:6). Only after Pentecost do the disciples fully recognize that the redemption Jesus brings is not a political deliverance but a spiritual one.[24]

This is not to say that redemption has no social or political consequences, but redemption is not concerned first of all with political or social freedom. In fact, as we will see, the truly free Christian may choose to give up some social freedoms for the benefit of others. A spiritual redemption does not mean an individualistic redemption, however. Jesus "gave himself for us that he might redeem us from all iniquity and purify for himself a people of his own who are zealous for good deeds" (Tit 2:14). This passage

---

[23]1 Peter 2:1 begins the discussion of false teachers in future tense, but by 1 Peter 2:10 the tense has shifted to present.

[24]Blunck argues that *eleutheria* in the New Testament never refers to political freedom. "Freedom," in *NIDNTT* 1:717.

suggests that redemption is corporate as well as individual. Rather than national Israel, the redeemed are now the church, composed of both Jews and Gentiles.

While Jesus did not advocate a program of political revolution, he did teach and model values that challenged the foundations of the society of his time: "Socioeconomic liberation, if it was not his direct aim, is the proper concern of those who accept his radical value-system."[25] Jesus' followers were to be an alternative society in which the leaders did not dominate, the resources were shared, and all persons were equally valued. His table fellowship and healings liberated people from their social marginalization as well as from their sin and disease.

Similarly, while Paul does not condemn the institution of slavery, he does use his influence with Philemon to secure the forgiveness—and possibly the freedom—of Philemon's runaway slave Onesimus. While Paul's advice to slaves in 1 Corinthians 7:21 is ambiguous and contested, the majority of scholars today tend to favor the reading that slaves who have the opportunity to gain their freedom should make use of that opportunity (see NRSV mg.).[26] While he does not preach on economic systems, Paul does advise the Corinthians to make up the financial lack of the Jerusalem church so that their own needs may be met in their turn (2 Cor 8:13-15). He wants to see a "fair balance" (NRSV) or "equality" (NIV) in financial resources among his congregations. The liberation that comes from following Jesus or being "in Christ" does have social and political implications.

In the Gospels and Acts, people are set free from illness, demonic oppression and death. For example, when Jesus heals the woman who had been bent over for eighteen years, he announces that she has been set free from her bondage (Lk 13:12, 16). Likewise, when Jesus heals the deaf man with the speech impediment, the evangelist states that the man's tongue was released from its bonds (Mk 7:35). In his Pentecost sermon, Peter proclaims that Jesus has been freed from death in the resurrection (Acts 2:24). The words used in these passages are *lyō* and *apolyō*.

---

[25]R. T. France, "Liberation in the New Testament," *The Evangelical Quarterly* 58 (1986): 16. See his entire article (pp. 3-23) for a discussion of the language of liberation in the New Testament.

[26]John Byron, *Recent Research on Paul and Slavery*, Recent Research in Biblical Studies, ed. Alan J. Hauser (Sheffield, U.K.: Phoenix, 2008), p. 114.

In Paul's writings, believers are set free from the "elemental spirits of the world" (*stoicheia;* Gal 4:3; cf. Gal 4:9; Col 2:8, 20) and from the "rulers and authorities" (*archai* and *exousiai;* Col 2:15; cf. Col 1:16; 2:10). These terms are difficult to define with certainty. In Galatians 4, Paul seems concerned to liberate the Galatians from the rudimentary principles or basic teachings to which his opponents want to subject them. They are "observing special days, and months, and seasons, and years," (Gal 4:10) rather than claiming their freedom in Christ.[27] In Colossians 1–2, this theme is still present; the "elemental principles" are associated with "regulations" such as "Do not handle, Do not taste, Do not touch" (Col 2:20-21). However, the grounds for rejecting these elemental principles is that Christ "disarmed the rulers and authorities and made a public example of them, triumphing over them" by the cross (Col 2:15). Here the basic principles are associated with spiritual forces. These rulers and powers were created through Christ and for Christ (Col 1:16), but they have apparently become malign. Because of the cross, however, believers need not be bound by them or by the structures through which they exercise their influence.[28]

Interestingly, given the development of the ransom image in church history, Satan does not often appear in redemption passages. First John 3:8 asserts that the Son of God was revealed "to destroy the works of the devil." The word for "destroy" here is *lysē*, from *lyō*. The author of Hebrews similarly declares that Jesus redeems believers by destroying Satan: "Since, therefore, the children share flesh and blood, he himself likewise shared the same things, so that through death he might destroy the one who has the power of death, that is, the devil, and free [*apallaxē*] those who all their lives were held in slavery by the fear of death" (Heb 2:14-15). This is a key passage for the Christus Victor view of the atonement.[29] In this passage, Jesus frees people from Satan by releasing them from their fear of death. Jesus has conquered death, making it useless as a weapon of

---

[27]Richard N. Longenecker, *Galatians*, Word Biblical Commentary, ed. Bruce M. Metzger, David A. Hubbard and Glenn W. Barker (Dallas: Word, 1990), pp. 165-66; Ben Witherington III, *Grace in Galatia: A Commentary on Paul's Letter to the Galatians* (Grand Rapids: Eerdmans, 1998), pp. 284-87.

[28]Ralph P. Martin, *Colossians*, New Century Bible Commentary, ed. Ronald E. Clements and Matthew Black (Grand Rapids: Eerdmans, 1973), p. 56.

[29]On this view of the atonement, see Gustaf Aulén, *Christus Victor: An Historical Study of the Three Main Types of the Idea of the Atonement*, trans. A. G. Hebert (New York: Macmillan, 1969).

the devil to hold human beings captive to his will. In the context of Hebrews, the author is reassuring his audience that they need not turn away from the faith out of fear for their lives. They can face persecution and possible martyrdom knowing that Jesus has prepared the way for them into the presence of God.

Most commonly, New Testament writers assert that Jesus has redeemed believers from sin (Col 1:14). Through his death, Jesus has freed Gentiles from their bondage to pagan practices (1 Pet 1:18) and Jews from their sins committed under the old covenant (Heb 9:15).[30] Paul declares that Jesus "gave himself for our sins to set us free [*exelētai*] from the present evil age, according to the will of our God and Father" (Gal 1:4). First-century Jews expected to be delivered from the "present evil age" when God brought this age to an end and inaugurated the age to come. First-century Christians believed that Jesus had set them free from this age without yet bringing it to an end. He had delivered them from sin but had not yet delivered them from death. That final redemption—the redemption of their bodies—would take place at the resurrection (Rom 8:23). Jesus connects the eschatological redemption with his coming again: "Then they will see 'the Son of Man coming in a cloud' with power and great glory. Now when these things begin to take place, stand up and raise your heads, because your redemption is drawing near" (Lk 21:27-28). In Luke 21:31, he parallels the coming of this eschatological redemption with the coming of the kingdom of God.

No New Testament writer has more to say about salvation as liberation than the apostle Paul. He could be called "the apostle of freedom."[31] In Romans and Galatians, Paul argues at length that Jesus has redeemed people from "the curse of the law" (Gal 3:13)—that is, the destructive cycle of law-sin-death that held them captive (Rom 8:2). Romans 6–8, Paul's most extended treatment of this theme, has been the subject of much debate. Understanding it is critical for grasping Paul's view of the relationship between the law and freedom.

---

[30]The reference to "the futile ways inherited from your ancestors" in 1 Peter 1:18 indicates that the audience has come out of paganism. See J. N. D. Kelly, *A Commentary on the Epistles of Peter and of Jude* (Peabody, Mass.: Hendrickson, 1969), p. 74.

[31]Peter Richardson, *Paul's Ethic of Freedom* (Philadelphia: Westminster Press, 1979), pp. 164-65.

FREEDOM FROM LAW-SIN-DEATH

In Romans, Paul has set himself the task of explaining his gospel as the (Jewish) apostle to the Gentiles. He must justify his own claim that Gentiles can become members of God's covenant people without obeying the law that has marked that people until now. He must also explain how God can permit this without violating prior covenants. In Romans 3:28-31, he declares that God can justify both Jews and Gentiles apart from the law without violating the law: "For we hold that a person is justified by faith apart from works prescribed by the law. Or is God the God of Jews only? Is he not the God of Gentiles also? Yes, of Gentiles also, since God is one; and he will justify the circumcised on the ground of faith and the uncircumcised through that same faith. Do we then overthrow the law by this faith? By no means! On the contrary, we uphold the law."

Paul must explain how this paradoxical statement can be true. If his gospel is to be credible, he must explain the function of the law. He first argues in chapter 4 that faith, not law, has always been at the heart of covenant relationship with God, using Abraham as his example. He then explains in chapter 5 the new situation that obtains because of what Christ has done to deal with sin. Christ has undone what Adam did, bringing righteousness and life where Adam brought sin and death. But between Adam and Christ, "law came in, with the result that the trespass multiplied; but where sin increased, grace abounded all the more" (Rom 5:20).

Paul is now ready to tackle the relationship between law, sin and death. In chapters 6 and 7, he poses and answers four hypothetical questions: "Should we continue in sin in order that grace may abound?" (Rom 6:1); "Should we sin because we are not under law but under grace?" (Rom 6:15); "What then should we say? That the law is sin?" (Rom 7:7); and "Did what is good, then, bring death to me?" (Rom 7:13). He answers all four with "By no means!" First, we should not continue in sin, because we have died to sin and are no longer under its dominion (Rom 6:11, 14). Second, we should not sin, because we have been freed from our slavery to sin and have been enslaved to God; thus we owe our loyalty to our new master (Rom 6:18, 22). We have also been freed from the law, so that our new condition is regulated not by the law but by the Spirit (Rom 7:6). Third, the law is *not* sin, but sin uses the law to incite human beings to further sin (Rom 7:11-12). Finally, the law itself does not bring about death; sin does—although sin works through the law to do so (Rom 7:13).

Paul illustrates this last explanation with a description of someone who knows and loves the law but who is still in slavery to sin (Rom 7:14). This person desires to do good but is frustrated by indwelling sin: "For I delight in the law of God in my inmost self, but I see in my members another law at war with the law of my mind, making me captive to the law of sin that dwells in my members" (Rom 7:22-23). The identity of this "I" has been debated for many years, with no consensus in sight.[32] Interpreters disagree about whether the "I" is Paul himself or a persona assumed for the sake of illustration. More critically for our purposes, they disagree about whether or not the "I" is a Christian.

The assumed persona is plausible, since Paul has already used this rhetorical device in Romans 3:7: "But if through my falsehood God's truthfulness abounds to his glory, why am I still being condemned as a sinner?"[33] Whether autobiographical or not, however, the key issue in Romans 7:14-25 for our purposes is whether the "I" is a Christian. The most popular opinions are that the "I" represents Paul's Christian experience or that it represents Paul's view of the experience of non-Christian Jews, as seen from a Christian perspective.[34]

If the "I" is a Christian, Paul would seem to be saying that being freed from the cycle of law-sin-death results in a life that remains mired in sin. This passage depicts a hopeless struggle in which the "I" can find no victory. Presumably the "I" would not need to fear *death* in the sense of separation from God, but freedom from the power of *sin* would be out of reach until the eschaton. Interpreters advance four main reasons for taking this view. Some argue that no one can love the law without the indwelling Holy Spirit; thus the person must be a Christian. Others identify with the existential struggle experienced by the "I" and view that struggle as the

---

[32]For a survey of the options, see C. E. B. Cranfield, "Paul's Teaching on Sanctification," *The Reformed Review* 48, no. 3 (Spring 1995): 218.

[33]As Cranfield states, "The use of the first person here is simply rhetorical." C. E. B. Cranfield, *Romans: A Shorter Commentary* (Grand Rapids: Eerdmans, 1985), p. 63. James D. G. Dunn disagrees. *Romans 1–8*, Word Biblical Commentary, ed. David A. Hubbard and Glenn W. Barker (Dallas: Word, 1988), p. 136.

[34]For the former view, see Cranfield, "Sanctification," p. 218; and Dunn, *Romans 1-8*, p. 405. For the latter view, see J. Christiaan Beker, *Paul the Apostle: The Triumph of God in Thought and Life* (Minneapolis: Fortress, 1980), pp. 240-42; and N. T. Wright, *The Climax of the Covenant: Christ and the Law in Pauline Theology* (Minneapolis: Fortress, 1991), p. 199.

tension between "already" and "not yet" in the lives of Christians. All observe that Romans 7:14-25 are couched in present tense; thus if the "I" is Paul, the passage refers to his experience as a Christian. All point out that Paul's jubilant cry of liberation in the first half of Romans 7:25 ("Thanks be to God through Jesus Christ our Lord!") is followed by the grim realism in the second half ("So then, with my mind I am a slave to the law of God, but with my flesh I am a slave to the law of sin").[35]

The passage is indeed in present tense, but that fact does not resolve the question of whose present experience is being described. Paul uses first person and present tense in Romans 3:7 (above) to express the present experience of non-Christian Jews. The argument that only Christians can love the law seems to founder on the evidence of the Old Testament. To cite only one example, Psalm 119 was not written by a Christian. The existential argument, while compelling, seems somewhat anachronistic. The existential struggles of modern Christians (or Reformation era Christians) should not be read back into the life of an earlier believer who operated with a different psychology and who evidences no such struggle elsewhere in his writings.[36]

The final argument may be resolved by reading the second half of Romans 7:25 as part of a *logical* structure rather than a *chronological* one. Each of the four questions Paul raises in chapters 6 and 7 is answered, illustrated, and summarized before Paul moves on. Verse 25b is the summary of the answer to the question in Romans 7:13: Did the good law bring about my death? No; the law can capture my mind, but it cannot liberate my flesh from the dominion of sin, which causes my death. Paul's exclamation in the first half of verse 25 is the answer to this dilemma, but he does not unpack it until chapter 8. Paul is getting ahead of himself, so in 25b he summarizes the answer to the rhetorical question before moving on to the good news of chapter 8.[37]

Romans 7:14-25 illustrates the situation that Paul describes in Romans

---

[35]See Cranfield, "Sanctification," p. 218, and Dunn, *Romans 1-8*, pp. 404-12.

[36]See Robert A. Di Vito, "Old Testament Anthropology and the Construction of Personal Identity," *Catholic Biblical Quarterly* 61 (1999): 217-38; and Krister Stendahl, "Paul and the Introspective Conscience of the West," in *Paul Among Jews and Gentiles, and Other Essays* (Minneapolis: Fortress, 1976), pp. 78-96.

[37]Stendahl interprets Romans 7:25b as the answer to the rhetorical question of Romans 7:13. "Introspective Conscience," p. 212.

8:3: "the law, weakened by the flesh." The law, although good in itself, could not change the sinful inclinations of human beings and give them the power to do what God required. But now God has dealt with sin in Christ and has provided the Holy Spirit to empower believers to live the godly lives that the law demanded (Rom 8:3-4). Believers can now fulfill the "just requirement of the law"—not by keeping the law but by following the leading of the Spirit. Thus real freedom comes from the indwelling Spirit, as Paul declares in 2 Corinthians 3:17: "Where the Spirit of the Lord is, there is freedom."

Reading Romans 7 in this way allows Paul to be consistent in what he is saying about freedom in Christ. After arguing in chapter 6 that believers have been freed from their slavery to sin (Rom 6:14-22), he would not then in chapter 7 declare that Christians are still "sold into slavery under sin" (Rom 7:14). Although Christians do experience the tension between the "already" and the "not yet" (illustrated in the conflict between the Holy Spirit and the sinful orientation in Gal 5:16-26), they have a new identity in Christ and all the necessary power in the indwelling Spirit to live free of sin's dominion. Romans 7 more plausibly refers to those who know the law—and therefore know what they should do—but do not have the Holy Spirit and therefore do not have the power to do what they should. This critique of the law is shared by Paul and the author of Hebrews: the law was holy and good, but it lacked the power to transform people so that they could obey it (Rom 7:12; 8:3-4; Heb 9:9-14).

The Holy Spirit liberates believers by transforming their perception of reality: "The Spirit makes the reality of redemption *present* to us. . . . [The Spirit also] makes the reality of redemption *authoritative* to us." In other words, the Spirit brings the work of Christ into "critical opposition" to the false structures of the present evil age, grounds believers in the new reality in Christ, and enables them to live according to that new reality.[38]

THE NATURE OF CHRISTIAN FREEDOM

The linkage Paul establishes between freedom from the law and guidance by the Spirit shows that Paul is not advocating a freedom from all con-

---

[38]Oliver O'Donovan, *Resurrection and Moral Order: An Outline for Evangelical Ethics* (Grand Rapids: Eerdmans, 1986), pp. 102, 103, 104.

straint.[39] Believers have been freed from their slavery to sin, but they have
not become autonomous. They now belong to a new master:

> Do you not know that if you present yourselves to anyone as obedient slaves,
> you are slaves of the one whom you obey, either of sin, which leads to death,
> or of obedience, which leads to righteousness? But thanks be to God that
> you, having once been slaves of sin, have become obedient from the heart to
> the form of teaching to which you were entrusted, and that you, having
> been set free from sin, have become slaves of righteousness. I am speaking
> in human terms because of your natural limitations. For just as you once
> presented your members as slaves to impurity and to greater and greater
> iniquity, so now present your members as slaves to righteousness for sancti-
> fication. (Rom 6:16-19)

Believers definitively have been freed from sin and "enslaved" to God
(Rom 6:22). Thus, ironically, a certain kind of slavery is really true freedom. From Paul's perspective, human beings can never be autonomous;
they can only choose their master—and they are free to do that only because of Christ. Their slavery to God, unlike their slavery to sin, is volun-
tary. Paul's injunction to present themselves as slaves to righteousness indicates that believers have a choice. They can be obedient to the one who
has redeemed them, or they can continue to serve their former master.

Paul put a great deal of effort into defining and defending the freedom
that believers have in Christ (Gal 2:4). He urged Christians, especially
Gentile Christians, not to turn back to bondage under the law but to go
forward in the freedom that is granted and guided by the Spirit: "Now the
Lord is the Spirit, and where the Spirit of the Lord is, there is freedom"
(2 Cor 3:17); "For freedom Christ has set us free. Stand firm, therefore,
and do not submit again to a yoke of slavery" (Gal 5:1).[40] Paul had to distinguish Christian freedom from legalism on the one hand and license on
the other. While believers are under grace, rather than under the law,
they must not use their freedom to indulge their sinful inclinations. Instead, "through love" they should "become slaves to one another" (Gal
5:13; cf. 1 Pet 2:16). Rather than seeking their own advantage, they should

---

[39]Tolmie, "Salvation as Redemption," p. 265.
[40]Williams argues that Paul's "bought with a price" language derives from the purchase of a
slave by a new owner, while Galatians 5:1 derives from the practice of manumission. Slaves to
be set free were purchased "for freedom." Many inscriptions indicate that slaves freed by sacral
manumission could not be re-enslaved (*Paul's Metaphors*, pp. 116, 122).

serve one another as the Spirit directs (Rom 6:21-22).

Paul's understanding of Christian freedom governs his counsel concerning meat sacrificed to idols (see 1 Cor 8–10). He asserts that the issue generally falls within the sphere of Christian freedom. Believers may eat meat or abstain without affecting their spiritual lives (1 Cor 8:8). However, he makes two qualifications. Eating such meat in an idol temple would mean participating in the worship of the demonic, so he forbids it (1 Cor 8:10; 10:14-22). Eating such meat in other settings is permissible unless it would lead a fellow believer to violate his or her conscience. In such cases, the "free" believer should voluntarily limit his or her freedom and abstain from eating the meat to avoid destroying a brother or sister (1 Cor 8:10-13; 10:24-30).[41] Paul uses himself as an example: "For though I am free with respect to all, I have made myself a slave to all, so that I might win more of them" (1 Cor 9:19). Just as Jesus voluntarily took the form of a slave for the salvation of humanity (Phil 2:6-11), Paul voluntarily serves others to the same end (1 Cor 10:33).

Thus believers are not set free so that they can claim their rights or live as they please.[42] They are set free to become Christlike, as God intended in their creation. In short, they are set free to love. If they love others as they have been loved, they will experience true freedom while at the same time fulfilling the intention of the law (Rom 13:9-10). This is what James means by "the law of liberty": Christians are free to fulfill God's intentions for them (Jas 1:25; 2:12).[43] The New Testament clearly opposes any individualistic or self-centered interpretation of Christian freedom. Instead, Christians are freed from their own selfishness to live for Christ and for others.

FORGIVENESS: SET FREE FROM SIN

Forgiveness is not usually discussed in conjunction with the ideas of redemption and freedom, but it has both a verbal and a conceptual connection to those ideas. On the one hand, some instances of *lyō* and *apolyō* (to loose or release) express the idea of forgiveness. On the other hand, even if

---

[41]See the discussion in Gordon D. Fee, *The First Epistle to the Corinthians*, The New International Commentary on the New Testament, ed. Ned B. Stonehouse, F. F. Bruce and Gordon D. Fee (Grand Rapids: Eerdmans, 1987), pp. 357-92, 475-91.
[42]Ibid., pp. 369, 384-85.
[43]Blunck, "Freedom," in *NIDNTT* 1:717.

expressed in different words, the concept of forgiveness involves setting people free from sin. Ephesians and Colossians interpret redemption as forgiveness of sins: "In him we have redemption through his blood, the forgiveness of our trespasses, according to the riches of his grace" (Eph 1:7; cf. Col 1:14). Forgiveness is applied to debts (*opheilēmata*), sins (*hamartias*) and trespasses (*paraptōmata*).[44] This usage suggests that forgiveness typically deals with the objective offense standing between two people or between someone and God. To forgive someone is to release them from their obligation.

Forgiveness is related to redemption through the concept of binding and loosing. In the Gospels, *lyō* is sometimes used for breaking commandments (Mt 5:19; Jn 5:18; 7:23). Jesus declares that scripture cannot be broken or annulled (Jn 10:35). Similarly, binding and loosing relates to strictly applying or relaxing commandments. Jesus twice declares to his disciples, "Whatever you bind on earth will be bound in heaven, and whatever you loose on earth will be loosed in heaven" (Mt 16:19; 18:18). In the former instance, Jesus grants Peter the keys to the kingdom of heaven; in the latter, Jesus grants the disciples the authority to administer church discipline. A very similar passage substitutes "retain" and "forgive" for bind and loose: "If you forgive the sins of any, they are forgiven them; if you retain the sins of any, they are retained" (Jn 20:23).

The language of binding and loosing comes from the rabbinic practice of authoritative interpretation of the law to determine what behavior is permitted and what is forbidden. In the case of the disciples, it means that they are authoritative interpreters of the teaching of Jesus. As heralds of the kingdom, they proclaim the message that sets the conditions for entrance into the kingdom. As leaders of the church, they have authority to deal with cases of unrepentant sin in the community.[45] In both contexts, their application of the teaching of Jesus will determine whether or not someone experiences forgiveness in the community of faith. This authority is theirs because of the Holy Spirit they have received from Christ (Jn 20:22). All disciples are required to "loose" the sins of fellow believers in

---

[44]H. Vorländer, "Forgiveness," in *NIDNTT* 1:701.

[45]On binding and loosing in rabbinic practice and in relation to the disciples, see Donald A. Hagner, *Matthew 14–28*, Word Biblical Commentary, ed. Bruce M. Metzger, David A. Hubbard and Glenn W. Barker (Nashville: Nelson, 1995), pp. 473, 532.

order to receive divine forgiveness themselves: "Be merciful, just as your Father is merciful. Do not judge, and you will not be judged; do not condemn, and you will not be condemned. Forgive [*apolyete*], and you will be forgiven" (Lk 6:36-37).

Thus forgiveness includes the idea of releasing someone from their offense. Besides *lyō* and *apolyō*, other terms are used to express forgiveness. For example, *paresis* means to overlook an offense: "In his divine forbearance [God] had passed over [*paresin*] the sins previously committed" (Rom 3:25). Luke and Paul sometimes express forgiveness with the word *charizomai*, from *charis*, meaning grace. This word sometimes means to give freely or graciously (Rom 8:32; 1 Cor 2:12). Its use for forgiveness emphasizes that forgiveness is a gracious gift, whether bestowed by God or by a fellow believer (Eph 4:32; Col 3:13). The words most often used for forgiveness, *aphiēmi* and *aphesis*, bring us back to the idea of redemption. In its most common use, *aphiēmi* means to let, to leave or to allow. It can be used for release from oppression: "He has sent me to proclaim release [*aphesin*] to the captives and recovery of sight to the blind, to let the oppressed go free [*aphesei*]" (Lk 4:18). More often it refers to the forgiveness of sins, again suggesting that forgiveness includes the idea of freedom.

Forgiveness comes from God. Only God can forgive sins (Mk 2:7; Lk 5:21). In his parable of the lost son (Lk 15:11-32), Jesus pictures God as a loving father longing to forgive his wayward child. When the son realizes his situation, he returns to his father intending to confess his sin, but his father forgives him and celebrates his return even before he can complete his confession. While there is no indication that the wayward son receives any further inheritance, he is restored to relationship with his father. The point of the parable, like that of the others in Luke 15, is to depict God as seeking out those who need to be forgiven, rather than rejecting them as Jesus' audience wanted him to do (Lk 15:2).

Forgiveness is to be found in Christ. This is evident in his preaching and in his attitude toward sinners. When he heals the paralytic, he tells the man that his sins are forgiven (Mk 2:1-12; Mt 9:1-8; Lk 5:17-26). When the Pharisees protest that only God can forgive sins, Jesus declares that he has authority to forgive sins as the Son of Man. Thus his acts of forgiveness demonstrate his divine authority.

Although Jesus can forgive sins by declaration, his death has special

significance in making forgiveness available. Forgiveness is associated
with his blood (Eph 1:14). Sometimes his death is depicted as the sacrifice
that inaugurates the new covenant, whose purpose is the forgiveness of
sins. For example, at the Last Supper, Jesus proclaims, "This is my blood
of the covenant, which is poured out for many for the forgiveness of sins"
(Mt 26:28). In Jeremiah's prophecy of the new covenant, God declares, "I
will forgive their iniquity, and remember their sin no more" (Jer 31:34). At
other times, Jesus' death is depicted as a sacrificial offering for sin. Like
the blood of the sacrifices at Sinai, the blood of Christ purifies God's
people from their sins and grants them forgiveness (Heb 9:18-22). The
comprehensive forgiveness extended in the new covenant means that no
further offering for sin is needed (Heb 10:18).

Forgiveness is sometimes expressed in terms of releasing someone from
a debt: "God made you alive together with him, when he forgave us all our
trespasses, erasing the record that stood against us with its legal demands.
He set this aside, nailing it to the cross" (Col 2:13-14). The word for "record" here is *cheirographon*, which means a handwritten document, specifically a bond or "certificate of indebtedness."[46] The idea is that of can-
celling an IOU.[47] Matthew's version of the Lord's Prayer includes a petition
to "forgive us our debts" (Mt 6:12; Lk 11:4 has "sins"). Jesus illustrates
forgiveness with a parable of a creditor who cancels the debts that are owed
to him (Lk 7:41-43). This picture of sin as debt (a debt presumably owed
to God) suggests that forgiveness removes objective hindrances standing
between the sinner and God. Rather than claiming his due, God chooses
to write off the debt and absorb the cost of it himself.

The metaphor of debt forgiveness is one way to describe what happens
at the cross: in Christ, God bears the cost of human sin so that human
beings can be released from it. This is not quite the same thing as saying
that Jesus pays the penalty for human sin. In the model of penal substitution, for example, God receives his due through the penalty paid by Christ.
The debt owed to God is repaid, although not by the debtors. In the metaphor of debt forgiveness, by contrast, God is not repaid. Like the creditor
in Luke 7:41-43, God writes off the debt, "not counting [people's] tres-

---

[46]"χειρόγραφον," in *BAGD*, p. 880.
[47]Ralph P. Martin, *Colossians and Philemon*, The New Century Bible Commentary, ed. Ronald
E. Clements and Matthew Black (Grand Rapids: Eerdmans, 1973), p. 83.

passes against them" (2 Cor 5:19). God (through Christ) takes on himself the consequences of sin (separation from God and spiritual death) so that human beings do not have to experience them.[48]

The conditions for receiving forgiveness are repentance and faith. For new believers, these are expressed through water baptism. In his preparation for Jesus, John the Baptist offers a baptism of repentance for the forgiveness of sins (Mk 1:4; Lk 3:3). Jesus initiates his ministry with a call to repentance and faith (Mk 1:15) and carries on the practice of baptism (Jn 3:22). Forgiveness presupposes the admission that one has sinned—that is, confession or repentance.[49] The sermons in Acts associate forgiveness with both repentance (Acts 5:31) and faith in Christ (Acts 2:38; 10:43; 26:18). Peter's Pentecost sermon specifically links forgiveness with baptism (Acts 2:38).

Forgiveness, like redemption, is universal in its intent. The Synoptic Gospels identify only one sin that cannot be forgiven: blasphemy against the Holy Spirit (Mt 12:31; Mk 3:29; Lk 12:10). According to Matthew and Mark, Jesus refers to this sin in response to the accusation by his opponents that he is driving out demons through the agency of Beelzebul. In Matthew, Jesus counters that he casts out demons by the Holy Spirit (Mt 12:28). He declares that blasphemy against the Holy Spirit (or speaking against the Holy Spirit, Mt 12:32) will never be forgiven. In the context, his opponents are speaking against the Holy Spirit by attributing the Spirit's work to demons. Since Jesus states that the Spirit's agency demonstrates the presence of the kingdom of God (Mt 12:28), the unforgivable sin seems to be a rejection of the Spirit's testimony to Christ as the bringer of the kingdom.

If this interpretation is correct, it means that blasphemy against the Spirit is unforgivable not because God refuses to forgive it but because the one who commits it is rejecting the only means of forgiveness—Jesus Christ. This sin is less an action than a disposition of opposition to God's offer of salvation: "The sin is an ongoing state or attitude that cannot be forgiven so long as it persists."[50] This understanding has significant pastoral implications. As many have pointed out, people who are worried that

---

[48]See the discussion of cost vs. price, pp. 150-51.
[49]I. Howard Marshall, "'Sins' and 'Sin'," *Bibliotheca Sacra* 159 (January-March, 2002): 8.
[50]Ibid., pp. 8-9.

they may have committed this sin show by their spiritual sensitivity that they have not committed it.

The church has the task of proclaiming forgiveness through its preaching and its practices. The authority by which believers do this is not their own but Christ's; they forgive sins in Jesus' name or for his name's sake (Lk 24:47; 1 Jn 2:12). For example, Paul announces in Antioch that forgiveness (or freedom from sins) is found in Christ: "Let it be known to you therefore, my brothers, that through this man forgiveness of sins is proclaimed to you; by this Jesus everyone who believes is set free from all those sins from which you could not be freed by the law of Moses" (Acts 13:38-39).

Although forgiveness is received initially at conversion, further acts of sin should be confessed in order to receive forgiveness: "If we confess our sins, he who is faithful and just will forgive us our sins and cleanse us from all unrighteousness" (1 Jn 1:9). While John seems to assume the confession of sins to God, James envisions a situation where sins are confessed to other believers: "Are any among you sick? They should call for the elders of the church and have them pray over them, anointing them with oil in the name of the Lord. The prayer of faith will save the sick, and the Lord will raise them up; and anyone who has committed sins will be forgiven. Therefore confess your sins to one another, and pray for one another, so that you may be healed" (Jas 5:14-16). Believers thus have an important responsibility to serve as channels of the forgiving grace of God to one another.

FORGIVENESS: SETTING OTHERS FREE

As forgiven people, believers have an obligation to forgive others: "Be kind to one another, tenderhearted, forgiving one another, as God in Christ has forgiven you" (Eph 4:32; cf. Col 3:13). Jesus teaches his disciples to stand ready to forgive their brothers and sisters an unlimited number of times (Mt 18:21-22). According to Jesus' instructions on church discipline, believers are even to seek out offenders to try to bring them to repentance (Mt 18:15-20).[51]

Several passages seem to make God's forgiveness of the believer contingent upon the believer's forgiveness of others (Mt 6:14-15; 18:35; Mk 11:25-26). Believers assent to this condition when they pray the Lord's

---

[51]W. C. Morro and R. K. Harrison, "Forgiveness," in *ISBE* 2:341.

Prayer and ask God to forgive them in the same way that they have forgiven others (Mt 6:12; Lk 11:4). The parable of the unmerciful servant grimly underscores this correlation (Mt 18:23-35). When the servant refuses to forgive the debt of his fellow servant after his master has forgiven him, the master consigns him to be tortured until his debt is repaid. "So my heavenly Father will also do to every one of you, if you do not forgive your brother or sister from your heart" (Mt 18:35).

Extending forgiveness to another assumes that the offender has repented: "If another disciple sins, you must rebuke the offender, and if there is repentance, you must forgive. And if the same person sins against you seven times a day, and turns back to you seven times and says, 'I repent,' you must forgive" (Lk 17:3-4). The parallel passage in Matthew 18:21-22 does not specify repentance, but the parable of the unmerciful servant in the following verses describes apparent repentance in the case of both servants.[52] Indeed, when the repentance of the unmerciful servant is shown to be insincere, the master withdraws his forgiveness. What does this mean for believers who are called to forgive others? Should they forgive without repentance?

A great deal has been written on this question in recent years, most of it from a therapeutic perspective. Scientific studies have been conducted on the benefits of forgiveness to the one who forgives. Scholarly and popular writers advise Christians to forgive anyone who has offended them so that they will not become bitter and resentful. Even if there is no repentance or restoration, it is argued, the offended person will be released from bondage to the offense if he or she grants forgiveness.[53]

Modern Western psychological thinking tends to treat forgiveness as a subjective internal state, a feeling of good will toward the other person. For example, Elizabeth A. Gassin states that forgiveness as defined by psychologists "involves rooting out one's negative thoughts, feelings, and behaviors directed at an offender and developing positive thoughts, feelings, and behaviors towards him or her." She distinguishes forgiveness, understood in this sense, from legal pardon, reconciliation (restoration of

---

[52]Craig L. Blomberg argues that repentance is assumed in the Matthew passage. "On Building and Breaking Barriers: Forgiveness, Salvation, and Christian Counseling with Special Reference to Matthew 18:15-35," *Journal of Psychology and Christianity* 25, no. 2 (2006): 143.

[53]A seminal example is Lewis B. Smedes, *Forgive and Forget* (San Francisco: HarperSanFrancisco, 1996).

relationship) and rationalization of the offense. Given her definition of forgiveness, it is not surprising that she argues that Christians should forgive others even without repentance, citing studies that link such forgiveness with positive "mental health outcomes" for the one who forgives.[54]

To understand what forgiveness means in the New Testament, however, we should note that first century people were much less introspective than are modern Western people.[55] The New Testament seems to regard forgiveness not as an internal state or emotion but as an action that releases someone from an objective obligation. In Gassin's terms, it is not intrapersonal, as she suggests, but interpersonal.[56] While restoration of relationship is the ultimate goal, forgiveness seems to be the means to that end rather than the end itself, which might better be described as reconciliation.

A situation of offense, viewed from the perspective of the one who has been offended, has three dimensions: the internal state of the offended person, the objective offense, and the social context of the offense, including the relationship with the offender. The picture of sin as debt illustrates this point. An objective debt exists. The creditor's attitude toward—or relationship with—the debtor is separate from the existence of the debt itself. The creditor may choose to write off the debt while continuing to harbor ill will toward the debtor and refusing to have any further relations with him or her. Alternatively, the creditor may require the repayment of the debt while having no ill will at all toward the debtor. The restoration of relationship will require the efforts of both parties.

Forgiveness, in the biblical sense, seems to apply to the second of the three dimensions above—the release from objective debt. The words *lyō*, *apolyō* and *aphiēmi* certainly tend in this direction. When someone forgives, he or she agrees to absorb the cost of the offense rather than requiring repayment from the offender. God does not forgive anyone without repentance, nor does he expect believers to do so.[57] If God expected be-

---

[54]Elizabeth A. Gassin, "Are Christians Obliged NOT to Forgive? A Response to Martin (1997)," *Journal of Psychology and Theology* 28, no. 1 (2000): 36-37.

[55]For a discussion of how the developing introspection of Western culture has affected biblical theology, see Krister Stendahl's seminal essay, "Paul and the Introspective Conscience of the West," in *Paul Among Jews and Gentiles, and Other Essays* (Minneapolis: Fortress, 1976), pp. 78-96.

[56]Gassin, "Obliged NOT to forgive?" p. 41.

[57]W. C. Morro and R. K. Harrison, "Forgiveness," in *ISBE*, 2:341. The authors add, however, "Without the repentance of the one who has wronged him, [the believer] can have a forgiving state of mind."

lievers to grant universal, unconditional forgiveness, the authority to bind and loose would make no sense. In cases of church discipline, if the offender refuses to repent, he or she is not forgiven but excluded from the church (Mt 18:17).

This does not mean that Christians have no obligation to restore relationship or to deal with their own attitudes. In fact, the goal of church discipline is the restoration of the offender (cf. Gal 6:1-2). Sometimes forgiveness must be withheld temporarily so that reconciliation becomes possible. Jesus' command to forgive others from the heart (Mt 18:35) suggests that true forgiveness requires the appropriate attitude. The word *charizomai* suggests a gracious attitude toward the offender that issues in gracious actions. Believers should love even their enemies (Mt 5:44; Lk 6:27, 35), just as God loved them while they were his enemies (Rom 5:6-11). This love is less a feeling than a commitment to work actively for the good of the other, as God demonstrates by reconciling his enemies to himself through Christ. Jesus himself, despite his authority to forgive sins, does not grant forgiveness to those who are crucifying him but prays that his Father will grant it (Lk 23:34). Could this be because they have not yet repented? In any case, Jesus shows love for his enemies even as he suffers the fate that will make their restoration possible.

In an excellent article exploring forgiveness in biblical and psychological contexts, Craig L. Blomberg argues that complete forgiveness requires repentance on the part of the offender. Nevertheless, even where "conjunctive forgiveness" (i.e., reconciliation) is impossible, the offended party can offer "disjunctive forgiveness" (release and separation), as in the case of church discipline when the offender refuses to repent.[58] In the latter case, the offended party maintains a merciful attitude toward the offender and stands ready to reconcile if repentance ever occurs. This approach does justice to both the biblical emphasis on repentance and the psychological insight that an unforgiving spirit can harm the offended even more than the offender.

Similarly, Miroslav Volf describes an interdependent relationship be-

---

[58]Blomberg, "Building and Breaking Barriers," pp. 140, 146, 151. He is using terminology developed by J. M. Berecz. Ken Sande uses the terms "positional forgiveness" and "transactional forgiveness" for similar concepts. *The Peacemaker: A Biblical Guide to Resolving Personal Conflict*, 3rd ed. (Grand Rapids: Baker Books, 2004), pp. 190-91. See also the two small books printed back-to-back by David Augsburger, *Caring Enough to Forgive: True Forgiveness* and *Caring Enough to Not Forgive: False Forgiveness* (Ventura, Calif.: Regal, 1981).

tween forgiveness and repentance. The process of forgiveness has to start with the "will to embrace." This commitment must be unconditional; it creates a welcoming space in which the offender can acknowledge the offense. But "completed forgiveness" is conditional upon repentance:

> It is true that repentance—the recognition that the deed committed was evil coupled with the willingness to mend one's ways—is not so much a prerequisite of forgiveness as, more profoundly, its possible result. Yet repentance is the kind of result of forgiveness whose absence would amount to a refusal to see oneself as guilty and therefore a refusal to receive forgiveness as forgiveness. Hence an unrepentant wrongdoer must in the end remain an unforgiven wrongdoer—the unconditionality of the first step in the process of forgiveness notwithstanding.[59]

Forgiveness thus has an interdependent relationship with justice, as well. Volf argues that for complete reconciliation to take place, justice must be addressed.[60] However, "forgiveness presupposes that justice—full justice in the strict sense of the term—has not been done. If justice were fully done, forgiveness would not be necessary, except in the limited and inadequate sense of not being vindictive; justice itself would have fully repaid for the wrongdoing. Forgiveness is necessary because strict justice is not done and strictly speaking cannot be done." In fact, extending forgiveness may be the very act that brings the wrongdoer to a realization of the wrong he or she has done. Forgiveness both includes justice and transcends it: "More precisely, by forgiving we affirm the claims of justice in the very act of not letting them count against the one whom we forgive."[61]

The ultimate end of forgiveness is reconciliation: offender and offended come together to heal the breach between them. For a more detailed discussion of reconciliation, see chapter eight. Forgiveness not only grows out of love but fosters love (Lk 7:47). Like redemption, forgiveness requires a kind of substitution: one must identify with another, even put oneself in the place of the other, in order to set the other free. It is a costly and creative act that involves a kind of death to self.[62] In both redemption and

---

[59]Miroslav Volf, "Forgiveness, Reconciliation, and Justice," in *Stricken by God? Nonviolent Identification and the Victory of Christ*, ed. Brad Jersak and Michael Hardin (Grand Rapids: Eerdmans, 2007), pp. 280, 284.

[60]Ibid., p. 281.

[61]Ibid., p. 284.

[62]Moule, "Preaching the Atonement," pp. 22-23.

forgiveness, Jesus is the example, as well as the one who makes such freedom possible.

CONCLUSION

Thus in redemption Christ gives himself to set us free from sin, self and Satan. The freedom that is ours through redemption opposes both legalism and license. Although we are no longer bound to the law, we can fulfill its intention because we are empowered by the Spirit. As Spirit-led people, we are free to give ourselves in love and service to both God and others. As forgiven people, we can extend forgiveness to those who wrong us, in the hope that both we and they will be changed. These images of salvation have enormous implications, both theologically and practically.

Perhaps it is time to reconsider redemption—even ransom—as an understanding of salvation. Some recent writers have called for a recovery of this image, along with the *Christus Victor* theory of atonement with which it is associated. These scholars believe that ransom and *Christus Victor* depict Christ's defeat of evil without the violence that characterizes other atonement theories.[63] Darby Kathleen Ray has suggested that "a contemporary demythologization of the patristic model of atonement" could serve as model for unmasking evil and defeating it through creativity and compassion.[64] In an age of addiction, human trafficking and terrorism, people might be ready to hear that Christ has died to free them from their captivity and their fear. To a Western culture jaded by a freedom understood as license, we can proclaim a freedom that is Christ-centered, Spirit-empowered and other-focused. In a world of pain, we can model a forgiveness that deals realistically with sin and provides hope for lasting reconciliation.

Redemption offers hope to everyone who is bound. God is in the business of liberation. As Ernst Käsemann declares, "Jesus means freedom."[65]

---

[63]See, for example, the contributors to the volumes *Atonement and Violence: A Theological Conversation*, ed. John Sanders (Nashville: Abingdon, 2006); and *Stricken by God? Nonviolent Identification and the Victory of Christ*, ed. Brad Jersak and Michael Hardin (Grand Rapids: Eerdmans, 2007). The term *Christus Victor* was coined by Gustaf Aulén for his book of the same name: *Christus Victor: An Historical Study of the Three Main Types of the Atonement* (New York: Macmillan, 1969).

[64]Darby Kathleen Ray, *Deceiving the Devil: Atonement, Abuse, and Ransom* (Cleveland: Pilgrim, 1998), p. 142.

[65]Ernst Käsemann, *Jesus Means Freedom* (Philadelphia: Fortress, 1970). Käsemann surveys the theme of freedom in the New Testament in order to reflect on the state of the German church in his own day. Similarly, Michael Green, in *Jesus Spells Freedom* (Downers Grove, Ill.: Inter-

While we must insist that true liberation is spiritual first of all, it does not stop there. We should learn from liberation theologies to be more conscious of the relationship between our theology and our praxis. Does our theology lead to practices that are genuinely liberating? What would a theological emphasis on redemption have to say to issues such as immigration or economic policy?

Paradoxically (for Americans), freedom in Christ may not look like the freedom Americans are used to: "In the American context, the New Testament understanding of freedom would require a choice to live under the right set of both internal and external restraints with particular emphasis on duty to neighbor as demanded by subjection to God in Christ."[66] Sometimes to be free in Christ may not mean to stand on our rights but to yield our rights for the benefit of others.

The church has not had a spotless record on redemption. Christians have engaged in slavery, wars of conquest, colonialism, economic exploitation, racism, sexism, classism. Some Christians ignored or even opposed the civil rights movement in the United States. Many people today regard Christianity as an agent of oppression. If we want to regain our credibility, we need to demonstrate redemption in both our words and our lives. True freedom should be especially evident in the church.[67] Unfortunately, that is not always the case. Before we speak a word to the world, we should scrutinize ourselves.

The "already" and "not yet" dimensions of redemption explain why the Christian life is sometimes so hard. We must live as redeemed people in unredeemed bodies in the midst of an unredeemed world. As Paul says, we groan as we yearn for our final redemption—the resurrection of the body and the new creation. Even as Christians, we need the support of one another to break free from the wounds that still bind us. We must practice forgiveness with one another if we want to be truly free.

Varsity Press, 1972), brings the idea of freedom in the New Testament into dialogue with the ideas of freedom in modern Western societies.

[66]Malina, "Freedom," p. 83.

[67]"The freedom granted by God was given to operate above all in the communal life of the people of God. For the Christian church is the community of free men." Blunck, "Freedom," in *NIDNTT* 1:720. He contends that male and female behavior are still differentiated in the church, citing 1 Corinthians 14:34 on women's silence. Thus he apparently means "free men" in a restrictive rather than a generic sense, given that men have freedoms that women do not share.

As redeemed people, we should be concerned about redemption in all areas of life. Forms of slavery are everywhere. Congregations could offer support to those recovering from addictions or financial counseling to those trapped in debt. As citizens, Christians can work to change oppressive structures in our communities and in our societies. We should support restorative justice programs that work redemptively with both victims and perpetrators. Internationally, the persecuted church needs both our prayers and our influence. Christians should be in the forefront of the effort to stop human trafficking, while working to eliminate the extreme poverty that leads parents to sell their children into slavery. We can lend our voices to support international debt forgiveness to the poorest nations.

Christians have good news to proclaim to the world: there is a Redeemer who is longing to give people a freedom that no one can take away. But we must recognize that redemption is not simply an individual, spiritual matter. It is God's plan to set his groaning creation free. As the body of the redeemed, the church must show the way.

FOR FURTHER READING

Blomberg, Craig L. "On Building and Breaking Barriers: Forgiveness, Salvation and Christian Counseling with Special Reference to Matthew 18:15-35." *Journal of Psychology and Christianity* 25, no. 2 (2006): 137-54.

Bruce, F. F. *Apostle of the Heart Set Free*. Grand Rapids: Eerdmans, 2000.

France, R. T. "Liberation in the New Testament." *Evangelical Quarterly* 58, no. 1 (January 1986): 3-23.

Green, Michael. *Jesus Spells Freedom*. Downers Grove, Ill: InterVarsity Press, 1972.

Green, Joel B., and Mark D. Baker. *Recovering the Scandal of the Cross: Atonement in New Testament & Contemporary Contexts*. Downers Grove, Ill.: InterVarsity Press, 2000.

Käsemann, Ernst. *Jesus Means Freedom*. Translated by Frank Clarke. Minneapolis: Fortress, 1970.

Larsson, Göran. *Bound for Freedom: The Book of Exodus in Jewish and Christian Traditions*. Peabody, Mass.: Hendrickson, 1999.

Marshall, I. Howard. "The Development of the Concept of Redemption in the New Testament." In *Reconciliation and Hope: New Testament Essays on Atonement and Eschatology Presented to L. L. Morris on his 60ᵗʰ Birthday*. Edited by Robert Banks, pp. 153-69. Grand Rapids: Eerdmans, 1974.

Morris, Leon. *The Apostolic Preaching of the Cross*. 3rd ed. Grand Rapids: Eerdmans, 1965.

Moule, C. F. D. *Forgiveness and Reconciliation and Other New Testament Themes*. London: SPCK, 1998.

Ray, Kathleen Darby. *Deceiving the Devil: Atonement, Abuse, and Ransom*. Cleveland: Pilgrim, 1998.

Richardson, Peter. *Paul's Ethic of Freedom*. Philadelphia: Westminster Press, 1979.

Tolmie, D. Francois. "Salvation as Redemption: The Use of 'Redemption' Metaphors in Pauline Literature." In *Salvation in the New Testament: Perspectives on Soteriology*, pp. 247-69. Edited by Jan G. van der Watt. Supplements to Novum Testamentum. Leiden/Boston: E. J. Brill, 2005.

Volf, Miroslav. "Forgiveness, Reconciliation, and Justice," pp. 252-67. In *Stricken by God? Nonviolent Identification and the Victory of Christ*. Edited by Brad Jersak and Michael Hardin. Grand Rapids: Eerdmans, 2007.

8

NO LONGER STRANGERS

Reconciliation, Adoption, Peace

IN 2006, THE *WASHINGTON POST* reported on a study that found that the social isolation of Americans was rapidly increasing. Twenty-five percent of those surveyed (more than double the number of a 1985 study) reported that they had no one to confide in.[1] At a time when people can connect with one another in more ways than ever before—by phone, email, social networking sites, text messaging, Twitter—the hunger for meaningful relationships remains unsatisfied. The relationships people do have are threatened by estrangement, conflict and outright violence.

Salvation addresses this human longing for connection. "If we are in part who we are because we are embedded in a nexus of relations which make others to be part of ourselves, then we cannot be properly healed without our relationships being healed too."[2] The New Testament makes clear that while salvation is personal, it is more than individual. People are not saved in isolation but into relationship—with God, with others and with creation. This truth is best expressed in relational images such as reconciliation, adoption and peace.

The concept of reconciliation has been somewhat neglected in Protestant theology because of its traditional emphasis on justification. In fact,

---

[1]Shankar Vedantam, "Social Isolation Growing in U.S., Study Says," *Washington Post*, 23 June 2006, p. A03.
[2]Miroslav Volf, "Forgiveness, Reconciliation, and Justice," in *Stricken by God? Nonviolent Identification and the Victory of Christ*, ed. Brad Jersak and Michael Hardin (Grand Rapids: Eerdmans, 2007), p. 279.

reconciliation has often been treated as an appendage of justification, which has been understood in legal terms.[3] Theologians have assumed that once justification gives people a new legal standing before God, reconciliation takes place automatically.

However, there are other possible ways to understand the relationship between reconciliation and justification. For example, they could be two different ways to express the establishment of a right relationship with God. As I will argue in chapter nine, justification itself is a fundamentally relational term. Another possibility is that justification is the result of reconciliation: people can be declared righteous because they have been reconciled to God and are no longer God's enemies.[4]

Not all scholars believe that justification is more foundational than reconciliation. For instance, Ralph Martin has argued that reconciliation is the heart of Paul's theology.[5] Similarly, Peter Stuhlmacher contends that New Testament theology should begin with a discussion of the mission of Jesus defined as "messianic reconciliation." Through his death and resurrection, Jesus brought in the messianic era of peace promised by God to his people.[6] Other more recent works, such as Miroslav Volf's *Exclusion and Embrace* and Scot McKnight's *Embracing Grace*, have highlighted reconciliation as central to the gospel.[7]

If the primary human problem is defined as separation from God, reconciliation is the solution. Although the words for reconciliation are relatively rare in the New Testament, the concept is crucial, especially

---

[3]"Justification is the acquittal of the sinner from all guilt of sin; reconciliation is the restoration of the justified person to fellowship with God." George Eldon Ladd, *A Theology of the New Testament*, rev. ed., ed. Donald A. Hagner (Grand Rapids: Eerdmans, 1993), p. 492.

[4]Myron S. Augsburger argues that God's work of reconciliation is the "precondition" of justification. He states that justification by faith "would be empty without the reconciling work of Christ." *The Robe of God: Reconciliation, the Believers Church Essential* (Scottdale, Penn.: Herald, 2000), p. 15.

[5]Ralph P. Martin, *Reconciliation: A Study of Paul's Theology* (Grand Rapids: Zondervan, 1989). Martin argues that reconciliation is the way Paul expressed his gospel for Gentiles, while justification was how he expressed it for Jews (pp. 135, 153). While I agree with his emphasis on the importance of reconciliation, I believe that justification and reconciliation are comprehensive images that depict the good news (for *both* Jews and Gentiles) from different perspectives.

[6]Peter Stuhlmacher, "Jesus as Reconciler: Reflections on the Problem of Portraying Jesus Within the Framework of a Biblical Theology of the New Testament," in *Reconciliation, Law, & Righteousness: Essays in Biblical Theology* (Philadelphia: Fortress, 1986), pp. 4, 5, 10.

[7]Miroslav Volf, *Exclusion and Embrace: A Theological Exploration of Identity, Otherness, and Reconciliation* (Abingdon: Nashville, 1996); Scot McKnight, *Embracing Grace: A Gospel for All of Us* (Brewster, Mass.: Paraclete, 2005).

for Paul. It embraces not only reconciliation but other terms such as unity, adoption and peace. Its importance may be implied by Paul's customary greeting, which joins grace and peace (Rom 1:7; 1 Cor 1:3; 2 Cor 1:2; Gal 1:3).

TERMS AND CONCEPTS

Reconciliation (*katallagē*; verb form, *katallassō*) refers to the restoration of relationship between two parties that have been estranged. It usually refers to relations between human beings or between human beings and God. In the New Testament, only Paul uses these terms in a religious sense.[8] While reconciliation language was common in extrabiblical Greek, it was rarely used in reference to relationships between gods or between gods and humans.[9] It was used far more often in the context of diplomacy.[10] Reconciliation is closely related to peace, in that it describes the establishment of peace between parties that were at enmity. To reconcile is to make peace (see Eph 2:15-16). In biblical terms, peace means far more than the lack of conflict; it is a state of wholeness and well-being, expressed as *šālôm* in the Old Testament and *eirēnē* in the New. Peace is the most comprehensive biblical term for the goal of salvation.[11]

Šālôm has the sense of general well-being, including safety, health, prosperity, contentment and positive relationships. It can be used for alliances between peoples or individuals. It also describes the relationship that exists between parties to a covenant. It is the gift of God, which will be fully realized in the age to come.[12] *Šālôm* is not intended for "isolated, insulated individuals" but for "a whole community—young and old, rich

---

[8]H. Vorländer and C. Brown, "Reconciliation etc.," in *NIDNTT* 3:167. F. Büchsel, "ἀλλάσσω κτλ.," in *TDNT* 1:255.

[9]Cilliers Breytenbach, "Salvation of the Reconciled (With a Note on the Background of Paul's Metaphor of Reconciliation)," in *Salvation in the New Testament: Perspectives on Soteriology*, ed. Jan G. van der Watt. Supplements to Novum Testamentum, ed. M. M. Mitchell and D. P. Moessner (Boston: E. J. Brill, 2005), p. 276.

[10]I. Howard Marshall, *New Testament Theology: Many Witnesses, One Gospel* (Downers Grove, Ill.: InterVarsity Press, 2004), pp. 286, 441.

[11]For a comprehensive study of peace in the New Testament, see Willard M. Swartley, *Covenant of Peace: The Missing Peace in New Testament Theology and Ethics* (Grand Rapids: Eerdmans, 2006). Swartley's thesis is that "*peace* is integral to the *gospel* of the *kingdom* that Jesus proclaimed and brought in his own person" (p. 23, italics in original).

[12]G. von Rad, "εἰρήνη κτλ.," in *TDNT* 2:402-3, 405.

and poor, powerful and dependent."[13] This vision extends from the individual to the social order to all of creation.[14] In one important passage, Ezekiel prophesies that God will one day establish a "covenant of peace" with his people, restoring them to the land in safety and blessing (Ezek 34:25-30).[15]

Eirēnē in extrabiblical Greek refers to a state of rest, although because it was used to translate *šālôm* in the Septuagint, it took on the meanings associated with *šālôm*. In the New Testament, *eirēnē* can refer to an internal sense of peace, to healed relationships with God and others, and to the "salvation of the whole [person] in an ultimate eschatological sense."[16] Its primary sense is wholeness. *Eirēnē* occurs most frequently in the writings of Luke and Paul.[17]

Closely related to reconciliation is the image of adoption (in Greek, *huiothesia*). In its literal sense, this word refers to the legal transfer of someone from one family to another.[18] The English translation "adoption" stresses the act of transfer, while "sonship" stresses the resulting condition. Adoption was a common practice in the Greco-Roman context of Paul's day. In the New Testament, only Paul uses this word, and he seems to have been the first person to use it as a religious metaphor. While the word *huiothesia* does not occur in the Septuagint, the idea of adoption is present in the Old Testament. God names Israel his "firstborn son" at the exodus (Ex 4:22). Paul seems to have this event in mind when he says in Romans 9:4 that "the adoption" belongs to Israel.[19]

Besides Israel as a whole, the king is adopted as God's son: "I will tell of the decree of the LORD: He said to me, "You are my son; today I have begotten you" (Ps 2:7). The promised son of David will become God's son

---

[13]Walter Brueggemann, *Peace*, Understanding Biblical Themes (St. Louis, Mo.: Chalice, 2001), pp. 14-15.

[14]Ibid., pp. 15-19.

[15]Swartley argues that Jesus establishes this covenant of peace at the Last Supper (*Covenant of Peace*, p. 177).

[16]W. Foerster, "εἰρήνη κτλ.," in *TDNT* 2:406, 412, 415.

[17]H. Beck and C. Brown, "Peace," in *NIDNTT* 2:780.

[18]Trevor J. Burke, *Adopted into God's Family: Exploring a Pauline Metaphor*, New Studies in Biblical Theology, ed. D. A. Carson (Downers Grove, Ill.: InterVarsity, 2006), p. 27.

[19]For the New Testament context, see James M. Scott, *Adoption as Sons of God: An Exegetical Investigation into the Background of* ΥΙΟΘΕΣΙΑ *in the Pauline Corpus*, Wissenschaftliche Untersuchungen zum Neuen Testament 2.Reihe, ed. Joachim Jeremias and Otto Michel (Tübingen: Mohr Siebeck, 1992), pp. 61, 148.

in an everlasting relationship (2 Sam 7:14-16).[20] New Testament writers use the latter two passages, as well as passages about Israel's sonship (e.g., Hos 11:1), in reference to Christ. However, the word *huiothesia* is never applied to Jesus; Paul uses it exclusively in reference to God's adoption of believers in and through Jesus Christ.[21]

THE BASIS OF RECONCILIATION

The description of salvation as reconciliation and peace implies a prior state of discord and disorder that must be remedied. The New Testament writers assume that enmity exists throughout the created order, as well as between creation and the Creator. Human beings are at odds with God, with other spiritual forces, with one another, and with the rest of creation. In human life, hostility exists between Jew and Gentile, master and slave, rich and poor, male and female.[22]

In the Mediterranean world of the first century, the major claimant to the language of peace was Rome. The Pax Romana brought order and stability throughout the empire by unifying all its various peoples under the military power of Rome. The worship of Pax as a personified goddess began under the Emperor Augustus. This Roman version of peace was built upon the "pacification" (conquest) of the nations of the empire. According to Tacitus, the British chief Calgacus declared of Rome, "They make a desolation and call it peace." Emperor Vespasian even built a "peace temple" to commemorate the destruction of Jerusalem and the defeat of the Jewish uprising.[23] The order and prosperity established by Rome, derived from violence and exploitation, bore little relation to the *šālôm* or *eirēnē* that comes from God. The basis of reconciliation in the New Testament is the love of God expressed through the life, death and resurrection of Christ.

In the New Testament, as many scholars have pointed out, God is always the subject of reconciliation, never its object. God reconciles human

---

[20]Scott argues that all uses of *huiothesia* in Paul's writings are derived from the 2 Samuel 7:14 tradition except for Romans 9:4 (*Adoption*, p. 269). Most scholars posit a Greco-Roman background for the adoption image in Paul (Burke, *Adopted*, pp. 22n3, 29).

[21]Burke, *Adopted*, p. 123.

[22]Joel B. Green and Mark D. Baker, *Recovering the Scandal of the Cross: Atonement in New Testament & Contemporary Contexts* (Downers Grove, Ill.: InterVarsity Press, 2000), p. 107.

[23]For this overview of the Pax Romana, see Swartley, *Covenant of Peace*, pp. 37-40.

beings and the world to himself; God is never pictured as needing to be reconciled. This contrasts strikingly with the picture of divine-human relations in paganism and in some expressions of Hellenistic Judaism. For example, 2 Maccabees pictures God as being reconciled to human beings: "May [God] hear your prayers and be reconciled to you, and may he not forsake you in time of evil" (2 Macc 1:5).[24] In the New Testament, by contrast, God is always the initiator. Any acts of reconciliation by human beings—even repentance and faith—are responses to God's prior act of reconciliation in Christ.[25] In 2 Corinthians 5:19, Paul gives one of the most concise summaries of his understanding of the atonement: "God was in Christ reconciling the world to himself, not counting their trespasses against them" (NRSV mg.).

Like reconciliation, peace comes from God. God is the God of peace (Rom 15:33; 1 Thess 5:23), who grants peace to believers (Phil 4:6-7) and expects them to live in peace (2 Cor 13:11). Jesus is the Lord of peace who gives peace to his disciples (2 Thess 3:16; Jn 14:27). The Holy Spirit creates the unity of the church "in the bond of peace" (Eph 4:3). The expression "God of peace" is characteristic of Paul, who uses it seven times. Outside of Paul's writings, it occurs only in Hebrews 13:20 and in the *Testament of Dan* 5:2.[26]

Some scholars argue that God needs to be reconciled to human beings, in that his wrath against sin must be propitiated.[27] Jesus certainly does rescue believers from God's wrath, especially at the final judgment (Rom 5:9). But it is misleading to conceive of God's wrath as anger (in particular, anger toward sinners) that must be placated by Jesus. God is not an angry deity who must be persuaded to love human beings. In fact, God's unwavering love is the driving force behind reconciliation. This point is acknowledged even by scholars who strongly support the idea that God's wrath

---

[24]Breytenbach, "Salvation of the Reconciled," pp. 276-77. Joseph A. Fitzmyer similarly argues that the New Testament understanding of reconciliation is quite different from that in Josephus and 2 Maccabees. "Reconciliation in Pauline Theology," in *To Advance the Gospel: New Testament Studies* (New York: Crossroad, 1981), p. 168. See also Martin, *Reconciliation*, p. 106.

[25]Vorländer and Brown, "Reconciliation etc.," in *NIDNTT* 3:167.

[26]Swartley, *Covenant of Peace*, p. 208.

[27]Ladd, *Theology*, pp. 495-96. In his systematic theology, Millard J. Erickson discusses reconciliation briefly under the topic of adoption. He declares, "In adoption both sides are reconciled to one another." *Christian Theology*, 2nd ed. (Grand Rapids: Baker, 1998), p. 976.

must be propitiated. These writers believe that God's love leads him to appease his own wrath by sending his Son to suffer the penalty for sin.[28]

For example, while carefully presenting the evidence that human beings do not appease God's wrath, and that God is always the reconciler, never the reconciled, I. Howard Marshall argues that "when Paul says that God has reconciled us to himself, the meaning is thus that God has dealt with the sins which aroused his wrath and that there is no barrier on his side to the establishment of peace and friendly relations."[29] In other words, although Paul says that God reconciles us to himself, he really means that God has reconciled himself to us by appeasing his wrath toward our sin. Marshall acknowledges that this interpretation would mean that Paul has used "to reconcile" in a "highly unusual, and apparently unique, manner." In fact, this interpretation seems to require reading against the text. Although Marshall states that God does not have to change his feelings toward humanity, he interprets reconciliation consistently in terms of giving up one's anger toward another.[30] By contrast, Joseph Fitzmyer argues that reconciliation is not primarily about emotions at all, but about an alteration in the status of a relationship. The two parties who were at odds are now in accord. In the case of God and human beings, God takes the initiative and does not need to be appeased.[31]

Some scholars believe that God's wrath is not an emotion or attribute of God, like love, but is an action of God—namely, God's judgment on sin. Wrath has a relational context.[32] In the Old Testament, God's wrath

---

[28]Ladd, *Theology*, p. 493. Erickson, *Theology*, p. 835.

[29]I. Howard Marshall, "The Meaning of 'Reconciliation,'" in *Jesus the Savior: Studies in New Testament Theology* (London: SPCK, 1990), p. 264.

[30]Ibid., pp. 269, 272. In his more recent work, this emphasis on appeasing God's wrath is somewhat muted but still present. See his *New Testament Theology*, pp. 286, 310, 433, 441. He concludes, "Whether or not [God] sees himself as hostile to them, he cannot offer peace to them apart from Christ and his death" (p. 442). See also the discussion of reconciliation in Leon Morris, *The Apostolic Preaching of the Cross* (Grand Rapids: Eerdmans, 1956). Morris acknowledges that God is not said to be reconciled to humanity but calls that an "argument from silence" (p. 192). He asserts that the death of Christ is evidence enough of God's hostility toward sinners (p. 197). This conclusion seems self-evident to him: "It is this which gives point to the idea that God can be said to be reconciled to man, for it is *manifestly impossible* for God to regard man in quite the same way before the barrier [of sin] is removed as He does after that takes place" (p. 209, italics added).

[31]Fitzmyer, "Reconciliation," pp. 165, 166, 170. See also Martin, *Reconciliation*, p. 105.

[32]Stephen H. Travis, *Christ and the Judgment of God: The Limits of Divine Retribution in New Testament Thought* (Peabody, Mass.: Hendrickson, 2008), p. 69; Gary A. Herion, "Wrath of God (OT)," in *ABD* 6:991; Terence Fretheim, "Problematic Portraits of God in the Old Testament:

is aroused by violations of the covenant and by the actions of other nations to harm his covenant people.[33] According to Romans 1:18-32, God's wrath is God's response to people's refusal of relationship. Because people refuse to acknowledge God or give him thanks, God releases them to experience the consequences of their sinful choices. Wrath is thus personal and fitting but not retributive. As Karl Barth declares, "The enterprise of setting up the 'No-God' is avenged by its success."[34]

Thus wrath is not God's unresolved anger standing in the way of reconciliation, but rather is God's action ratifying the human refusal to reconcile. In *The Great Divorce*, C. S. Lewis expresses a similar idea, in words he places in the mouth of George MacDonald: "There are only two kinds of people in the end: those who say to God, 'Thy will be done,' and those to whom God says, in the end, '*Thy* will be done.' All that are in Hell, choose it."[35]

The New Testament declares that we are God's enemies, but it never says that God is ours. The difference is more than semantic, because it has a significant bearing on our image of God. The God of the Bible is not an angry Zeus preparing thunderbolts for those who displease him but a loving father longing to be reconciled to his prodigal sons and daughters. Although the injured partner, God actively seeks reconciliation.[36] He desires reconciliation so much that he bears the cost of it himself.

And reconciliation is very costly. God accomplishes it through Christ, by means of his death on the cross (Rom 5:10; Col 1:20). Because relationships have been broken by sin, reconciliation requires forgiveness on God's part—that is, not counting people's sins against them (2 Cor 5:19). Forgiveness, whether divine or human, requires the injured party to bear the cost of the sin rather than retaliating against the offender. "There is no forgiveness without the innocent suffering for the guilty."[37] In Christ's death, God has absorbed the cost of sin, freeing human beings to engage

---

Wrath and Judgment," Lecture at Ashland Theological Seminary, 22 October 2007.

[33]Herion, "Wrath of God," in *ABD* 6:994.

[34]Karl Barth, *The Epistle to the Romans* (London: Oxford University Press, 1933), p. 51; cited in Travis, *Judgment of God*, p. 61. Travis discusses the personal but nonretributive nature of God's wrath on pp. 61-62. He refers to this as "intrinsic punishment": by God's decision, sinful behavior carries within it its own consequences (p. 62).

[35]C. S. Lewis, *The Great Divorce* (New York: Macmillan, 1946), p. 72.

[36]James D. G. Dunn, *The Theology of Paul the Apostle* (Grand Rapids: Eerdmans, 1998), p. 229.

[37]Augsburger, *Robe of God*, p. 105. For a more detailed discussion of forgiveness, see chapter seven.

in restored relationships. Thus the work of Christ has brought about a new situation in which true reconciliation is possible.[38] Reconciliation is the solution to God's wrath, but not in the sense of appeasing God's anger through punishment. Since God's wrath consists of giving people over to experience the consequences of their rejection of God (Rom 1:18-32), those who have been reconciled do not experience God's wrath.

PEACE WITH GOD

Reconciliation and peace extend to all areas of life: internal, personal, interpersonal, social and even cosmic. In the thinking of the New Testament writers, the most fundamental dimension of reconciliation is a restored relationship with God:

> Therefore, since we are justified by faith, we have peace with God through the Lord Jesus Christ. . . . And hope does not disappoint us, because God's love has been poured into our hearts through the Holy Spirit that has been given to us. . . . But God proves his love for us in that while we were still sinners Christ died for us. Much more surely then, now that we have been justified by [Christ's] blood, will we be saved through him from the wrath of God. For if while we were enemies, we were reconciled to God through the death of his Son, much more surely, having been reconciled, will we be saved by his life. But more than that, we even boast in God through our Lord Jesus Christ, through whom we have now received reconciliation. (Rom 5:1, 5, 8-11)

This passage demonstrates the close relationship between reconciliation and justification, using the two terms in parallel. This parallelism does not requires us to subsume reconciliation into justification; instead, it indicates the relational character of justification. The entire context is relational: God takes the initiative to make peace with his enemies, reconciling them to himself through the death of Christ. God's love, which initiates the process, becomes a reality in the lives of believers through the gift of the indwelling Spirit.

Reconciliation is thus first of all an objective action of God in Christ, the benefits of which are offered to all human beings as a gift. To enjoy that gift, people must respond to God's offer: "In Christ God was recon-

---

[38]Vorländer and Brown, "Reconciliation etc.," in *NIDNTT* 3:168.

ciling the world to himself . . . and entrusting the message of reconciliation to us. So we are ambassadors for Christ, since God is making his appeal through us; we entreat you on behalf of Christ, be reconciled to God" (2 Cor 5:19-20). As James Dunn observes, "If Christ was the representative of God in effecting the atonement ('God was in Christ'), the apostles are the representatives of God in proclaiming it ('God makes his appeal through us')."[39]

Paul uses the familiar language of Hellenistic and Roman diplomacy to declare himself and others ambassadors for Christ.[40] Like Jesus himself, believers are called to proclaim a message of peace (Acts 10:36; Eph 2:17; 6:15). Through their preaching of the gospel, God entreats his estranged children to return to him. Strikingly, Paul turns the secular dynamic of reconciliation on its head. Instead of the defeated or helpless party begging for peace, God is begging human beings to accept the peace he offers.[41] Those who respond to God's entreaty and accept his gift are restored to fellowship with God and with one another.[42] The ministry of reconciliation thus makes God's reconciling act present to human beings, and as they accept it, makes reconciliation concrete in the life of the faith community.[43]

The difference between God's gift of reconciliation and human reception of it is well illustrated by a story recounted by Victor Paul Furnish. A Japanese soldier was discovered hiding on an island thirty years after World War II was over. Japan and the United States, the former enemies, had long been reconciled. That was an accomplished fact. But the message of reconciliation had never reached this soldier, so he lived as if peace had never been achieved.[44]

We normally think that only nonbelievers stand in need of reconciliation with God. In 2 Corinthians 5:20, however, Paul's call to be reconciled is addressed to the church. This suggests that reconciliation is not

---

[39]Dunn, *Theology of Paul*, pp. 229-30.

[40]Breytenbach, "Salvation of the Reconciled," pp. 273-76. He discusses at length the historical/cultural contexts of Paul's reconciliation language.

[41]Ibid., p. 284.

[42]Ladd, *Theology*, pp. 493, 494, 496; Marshall, "Meaning of 'Reconciliation,'" p. 264; Büchsel, "ἀλλάσσω κτλ.," in *TDNT* 1:256; Vorländer and Brown, "Reconciliation etc.," in *NIDNTT* 3:168.

[43]Victor Paul Furnish, "The Ministry of Reconciliation," *Currents in Theology and Mission* 4, no. 4 (August 1977): 217.

[44]Ibid., p. 218.

over and done with at conversion. Even those who have experienced a restored relationship with God must continue to allow that relationship to transform their lives.[45] They must live holy lives that are appropriate for those in covenant relationship with a holy God: "And you who were once estranged and hostile in mind, doing evil deeds, he has now reconciled in his fleshly body through death, so as to present you holy and blameless and irreproachable before him—provided that you continue securely established and steadfast in the faith, without shifting from the hope promised by the gospel that you heard, which has been proclaimed to every creature under heaven" (Col 1:21-23). God will continue to do the work of reconciliation in and through believers. For their part, believers must remain faithful to their relationship with God or forfeit the gift of reconciliation they have received.

ADOPTION

Paul also describes reconciliation with God in terms of adoption. Instead of God's enemies, believers are now God's children. Adoption is part of a cluster of family terms that describe the believer's relationship to God and to other believers. The idea of adoption stresses the familial character of these relationships while at the same time distinguishing the "sonship" of believers from that of God's natural son, Jesus Christ.[46] Paul may also have chosen this image because of its connection with inheritance. Many Greco-Roman adoptions took place to ensure that the adoptive parent would have an heir. In secular culture, the adopted heir was almost always male.[47] By contrast, when Paul alludes to the promise of adoption in 2 Samuel 7:14, he specifically inserts "daughters" into the verse: "I will be your father, and you shall be my sons and daughters, says the Lord Almighty" (2 Cor 6:18; cf. Is 43:6).[48] As adopted children, believers are co-heirs with the firstborn son (Rom 8:17).

Adoption has a trinitarian shape. Like reconciliation, adoption is initi-

---

[45]Martin, *Reconciliation*, p. 110. He notes that in the context of 2 Corinthians, Paul is also attempting to reestablish his apostolic relationship (and authority) with the Corinthians.

[46]Burke, *Adopted*, pp. 22, 89.

[47]Scott, *Adoption*, pp. 4-9; David J. Williams, *Paul's Metaphors: Their Context and Character* (Peabody, Mass.: Hendrickson, 1999), p. 64.

[48]James M. Scott, "Adoption," in *DPL*, p. 18.

ated by God the Father and is mediated by Christ (Eph 1:5).[49] God makes believers his children as an expression of the grace that he has bestowed on them in Christ. His love for his adopted children derives from his love for his Son. While Christ makes adoption possible, the Holy Spirit makes it real in the lives of believers. As John Stott observes, "First, God sent His Son into the world; secondly, He sent His Spirit into our hearts. . . . Thus, God's purpose was not only to secure our sonship by His Son, but to assure us of it by His Spirit. He sent His Son that we might have the *status* of sonship, and He sent His Spirit that we might have an *experience* of it."[50]

The "Spirit of adoption" (*pneuma huiothesias*) assures believers that they are God's children, intercedes for believers with their Father, and shapes believers into the family likeness by conforming them to Christ (Rom 8:14-16, 26-27, 29). The Spirit will bring about believers' final adoption by bringing life to their bodies in the resurrection (Rom 8:11, 23). The work of the Spirit shows that adoption is not merely a legal transaction. It involves a new identity and a new intimacy with God that enables believers to call God "Abba" (Rom 8:15; Gal 4:6).

Adoption also involves new responsibilities. Like all of Paul's salvation metaphors, adoption has ethical implications. In the Greco-Roman world, an adopted son left his old family behind and took on the honor and obligations of his new family. He owed allegiance to his new father, not to his biological father, and he was obligated to live in a way that would bring honor to his new family. Similarly, believers in Jesus are adopted into the family of God. Their allegiance to their new Father supersedes all prior allegiances, whether to their biological parents or even to the "divine father," the emperor.[51] They are obligated to follow the leading of God's Spirit (Rom 8:9, 12-14). Likewise, they take on new responsibilities to other believers, their brothers and sisters in Christ.

For Paul, adoption is more than a metaphor for individual salvation. It is also a metaphor of salvation history. The image is concentrated in Galatians and Romans where Paul is dealing with the role of the law in Jewish-Gentile relations before God. In both contexts, Paul contrasts adoption as

---

[49]Burke, *Adopted*, p. 195.
[50]John R. W. Stott, *The Message of Galatians*, The Bible Speaks Today (London: Inter-Varsity Press, 1968), p. 107.
[51]Burke, *Adopted*, pp. 42-43, 76, 81, 175.

sons with slavery under the law. In Galatians, Paul argues that "when the fullness of time had come, God sent his Son, born of a woman, born under the law, in order to redeem those who were under the law, so that we might receive adoption as children" (Gal 4:4-5). The coming of Christ means a new phase in God's relationship with his people. No longer will God deal with them as minors, who are no better than slaves, and who need the supervision of a disciplinarian (Gal 4:1; 3:24-25). Christ has set them free from the law, and the indwelling Spirit of Christ has made them children and heirs of God. Possession of the Spirit, not possession of the law, is now the indication of who is in the family (Rom 8:2, 9). If they live according to the Spirit, God's people can become the mature adult children that their Father always wanted them to be.

Adoption in Paul thus has an already/not yet character. Although believers already can experience a filial relationship to God, their final adoption awaits the resurrection. The completion of their adoption will mean the liberation of all creation (Rom 8:19-23). Until then, believers must bear with the suffering that results from this eschatological tension (Rom 8:17). One might say that the adoption papers have already been filed and the new relationship has been established, but the child has not yet gone to live in the new home, which is still under construction.

PEACE WITHIN

Other experiences of reconciliation and peace grow out of the fundamental reconciliation of human beings with God. While peace in the New Testament is not fundamentally a feeling but a new reality established by God,[52] there are passages in which believers are said to experience peace as a quality of life. In the Synoptic Gospels, peace is linked with salvation as forgiveness of sins and wholeness. After Jesus forgives the sinful woman who anoints him and heals the woman with the issue of blood, he says, "Your faith has saved you; go in peace" (Lk 7:50; 8:48, author's translation). Peace here is not a simple greeting but a new condition of well-being given to both of these women by Jesus. In John's Gospel, the peace Jesus gives to his disciples is a source of strength that will enable them to persevere through trials (Jn 14:27; 16:33).

---

[52]Martin, *Reconciliation*, p. 145.

While Paul attributes peace with God to the cross of Christ, he attributes peace in the believer's life to the presence of the Holy Spirit. Peace is one of the fruit of the Spirit (Gal 5:22). The experience of peace and joy produced in the believer by the Holy Spirit nurtures the hope that all of God's promises will be fulfilled (Rom 15:13). Human beings are not passive recipients of peace, however. They must train their minds to focus on spiritual things and follow the leading of the Spirit (Rom 8:6). They must pray diligently and trust in the Lord's care and protection:

> Do not worry about anything, but in everything by prayer and supplication with thanksgiving let your requests be made known to God. And the peace of God, which surpasses all understanding, will guard your hearts and your minds in Christ Jesus. Finally, beloved, whatever is true, whatever is honorable, whatever is just, whatever is pure, whatever is pleasing, whatever is commendable, if there is any excellence and if there is anything worthy of praise, think about these things. Keep on doing the things you have learned and received and heard and seen in me, and the God of peace will be with you. (Phil 4:6-9)

To experience peace, then, believers must practice not only prayer and mental discipline but obedience. The context (Phil 4:4) also suggests that they should cultivate the habit of rejoicing in the Lord.

PEACE WITH OTHERS

Reconciliation and peace should also govern human relationships. Jesus commands his disciples to practice in their own relationships the forgiveness they have received from God, and he blesses those who work for peace (cf. Mt 5:9, 23-24; 6:14-15). For Paul, reconciliation is a central pastoral concern. He tirelessly exhorts his congregations to pursue reconciliation and peacemaking (e.g., Rom 14:19; 15:5-13; Eph 4:1-6; Phil 2:1-2; 4:2-3). He urges them to foster unity through the practice of humility and mutual love, modeled on the attitude of Jesus himself (Phil 2:1-11). In concluding his advice to believers divided over whether to eat meat that had been sacrificed to idols, Paul declares that their ability to live at peace with one another despite their differences would be a sign of the kingdom of God (Rom 14:17). He even extends his call for peace beyond the bounds of the church: "If it is possible, so far as it depends on you, live peaceably with all" (Rom 12:18). Although he recognizes that peace with unbelievers may not always be possible, since unbelievers lack the foundation of true peace, Paul urges believers to do everything in their power to attain it.

Reconciliation in Christ has the power to overcome all social divisions, even the most fundamental division between Jews and Gentiles:

> For he is our peace; in his flesh he has made both groups into one and has broken down the dividing wall, that is, the hostility between us. He has abolished the law with its commandments and ordinances, that he might create in himself one new humanity in place of the two, thus making peace, and might reconcile both groups to God in one body through the cross, thus putting to death that hostility through it. So he came and proclaimed peace to you who were far off and peace to those who were near; for through him both of us have access in one Spirit to the Father. So then you are no longer strangers and aliens, but you are citizens with the saints and also members of the household of God. (Eph 2:14-20)

Jesus himself *is* peace, just as Gideon can declare, "The LORD is peace" (Judg 6:24). "Christ is the actualization of peace, and this peace remains tied to Jesus' fate and his person. But the peace itself is understood as reconciliation."[53] Through his death, Jesus abolished the law that kept Jews and Gentiles separate, becoming the source of a single new humanity. Now both Jews and Gentiles can live in covenant relationship with God. By virtue of their common relationship with God in Christ, Jews and Gentiles are also united with one another in Christ's body, the church. Peace with God entails peace with one another: "Peace is here defined as a comprehensive reconciling event connecting God and humanity and human beings to one another through Christ and personally represented in Christ."[54] In fact, the miraculous reconciliation of Jew and Gentile in Christ's new community is evidence that the messianic era of peace has begun.

Reconciliation across ethnic boundaries does not develop automatically, however. Paul's ministry demonstrates the hard work needed to create unity in a rapidly growing multicultural movement. He sometimes has to address this issue very directly, as when he confronts Peter about refusing to eat with Gentiles (Gal 2:11-14). He urges believers to "[make] every ef-

---

[53]Peter Stuhlmacher, "'He Is Our Peace' (Eph. 2:14): On the Exegesis and Significance of Eph. 2:14-18," in *Reconciliation, Law, & Righteousness: Essays in Biblical Theology* (Philadelphia: Fortress, 1986), p. 188.

[54]Ibid., p. 191. Stuhlmacher believes that Ephesians 2:13-18 is a christological exegesis of the promises of peace in Isaiah 9:5-6; 52:7; 57:19 (p. 187).

fort to maintain the unity of the Spirit in the bond of peace" (Eph 4:3).

But Paul believes in the power of the gospel to bring reconciliation. In Galatians 3:27-28, he declares that unity in Christ overcomes all divisions of race, class and gender: "As many of you as were baptized into Christ have clothed yourselves with Christ. There is no longer Jew or Greek; there is no longer slave or free; there is no longer male and female; for all of you are one in Christ Jesus." Those who have clothed themselves with Christ have a new identity by virtue of their solidarity with him. That new identity supersedes any previous identity, whether given by birth or by social circumstances. All of those in solidarity with Christ are therefore in solidarity with one another. The focus here is on unity rather than equality (believers are "one in Christ"), but such a unity has radical social consequences. It places Jews and Gentiles on equal footing in the church, it turns slave and master into brothers in Christ, and it enables women to work alongside men in the spreading of the gospel (Eph 2:19; Philem 16; Phil 4:3).

Just as reconciliation between God and human beings is costly, so is reconciliation between people. Although the foundation has been laid in Christ, the hard work is not over. As C. F. D. Moule explains, true reconciliation cannot be achieved without suffering on the part of both the offender and the offended. Like the suffering of Christ, however, that suffering is restorative rather than punitive:

> Suffering there is in plenty. If reconciliation could be effected without suffering, it would not be a reconciliation between persons. . . . A person is, by definition, responsible. If he has committed an offence, he cannot be restored to fellowship until he has accepted the pain of responsibility for his offence and (so far as possible) made reparation. . . . On the side of the injured party—who, ultimately, is God himself—the suffering of forgiveness is boundless. This too, is the cost involved in the structure of personal relationship, as God has created it.
>
> But, on both sides, the suffering is creative and restorative and healing, and in obedience not to abstract laws of justice but to the demands of the living organism of persons which is most characteristically represented by the Body of Christ.[55]

---

[55]C. F. D. Moule, "Punishment and Retribution: Delimiting Their Scope in N. T. Thought," in *Stricken by God? Nonviolent Identification and the Victory of Christ*, ed. Brad Jersak and Michael Hardin (Grand Rapids: Eerdmans, 2007), p. 266.

Reconciliation requires effort on both parts: "Thus, by the time the reconciliation is achieved—costly forgiveness responded to by costly repentance—two great expenditures of creative energy have taken place: the initial and initiating energy of forgiveness, without which the process could not begin—and the responsive energy of repentance, without which the reconciliation could not become a fact."[56] Forgiveness and repentance, each a kind of dying to self, thus work together to bring about reconciliation.

PEACE IN CREATION

Ephesians and Colossians offer a vision of cosmic reconciliation in Christ:

> He has made known to us the mystery of his will, according to his good pleasure that he set forth in Christ, as a plan for the fullness of time, to gather up all things in him, things in heaven and things on earth. (Eph 1:9-10)

> For in him all the fullness of God was pleased to dwell, and through him God was pleased to reconcile to himself all things, whether on earth or in heaven, by making peace through the blood of his cross. (Col 1:19-20)

Although reconciliation in the New Testament is generally concerned with human beings, God's reconciliation of all things (*ta panta*) in Christ suggests that God's purposes reach beyond human beings to embrace the rest of a fractured creation. The fundamental relationship between Creator and creation is being restored.[57] In these passages, Christ is both the one who orders and sustains creation and the one who rules over all hostile "principalities and powers" because of his death and resurrection.[58] Isaiah's vision of the messianic kingdom of peace (Is 11:6-9) likewise suggests that reconciliation will embrace the whole creation. This broader vision implies that believers, as ministers of reconciliation, have a responsibility to do all they can to live peaceably with the rest of creation as well.[59]

Peace is the normal life of the new creation. As such it is fundamentally eschatological, although (like other kingdom blessings) it can be experienced in part now.[60] Since the cross is the ground of reconciliation, Paul

---

[56]C. F. D. Moule, "Preaching the Atonement," in *Forgiveness and Reconciliation and Other New Testament Themes* (London: SPCK, 1998), p. 23.

[57]Dunn, *Theology of Paul*, p. 229.

[58]Martin, *Reconciliation*, pp. 120, 121-22.

[59]I am indebted for this insight to Ryan Patrick McLaughlin.

[60]Foerster, "εἰρήνη κτλ.," in *TDNT* 2:414; Beck and Brown, "Peace," in *NIDNTT* 2:780.

can describe cosmic reconciliation as a completed past event, just as he can call peace a present possession. But the application of the reconciling event is still being worked out in history; otherwise there would be no need for a ministry of reconciliation. According to Paul's eschatological vision in 1 Corinthians 15:24-28, in this time between the first and second comings, Christ must reign until he has become Lord of "all things" (*ta panta*, 1 Cor 15:28). Then he will complete his messianic mission by turning the kingdom over to the Father, so that God may be all in all.

CONCLUSION

As an image of salvation, reconciliation extends to all areas of life. As Joel Green and Mark Baker observe, "Salvation as portrayed in the Pauline concept of reconciliation, then, has personal and social, human and cosmic, spiritual and material, religious and ethnic meanings."[61] As such, it has far-reaching practical implications.

No image of salvation is more relevant to contemporary Western culture than reconciliation. In reconciliation, God desires to bring wholeness and peace to those who have been alienated and fractured by sin. God has borne the cost of reconciliation in Christ and now offers forgiveness to all who will respond. Besides being adopted as God's children, believers are joined to one another in Christ to form a new community empowered by the Spirit.

This image tells us a great deal about who God is and therefore who God expects us to be. God wants to bring about wholeness and peace; so should we. Because we have been reconciled, we are called to be reconcilers. Because we have been forgiven, we are called to forgive. Because we have peace with God, we are called to be peacemakers. Christians should be at the forefront of peacemaking at all levels—interpersonal, social, international—because we have been entrusted with the gospel message, the only basis on which authentic reconciliation and lasting peace can be achieved.[62]

---

[61]Green and Baker, *Scandal of the Cross*, p. 108.

[62]Many excellent resources exist to assist with peacemaking on an interpersonal level. The three books I have found most helpful are David Augsburger, *When Caring Is Not Enough: Resolving Conflicts Through Fair Fighting* (Ventura, Calif.: Regal, 1983); Roger Fisher, Bruce M. Patton and William L. Ury, *Getting to Yes: Negotiating Agreement Without Giving In*, 2nd ed. (Boston: Houghton Mifflin, 1991); and Ken Sande, *The Peacemaker: A Biblical Guide to Resolving*

Reconciliation demonstrates that salvation is inseparable from community. It calls us away from self-centeredness to other-centeredness. Because God wants to love people back to wholeness, the church must minister to whole people in the context of their relationships. Evangelism is not enough. The church must be a safe place where people can learn to trust one another and find healing. It has to teach, model and encourage healthy relationships for individuals and families. The church can even become a supportive family for those who have never experienced one.

God's desire for wholeness and restored relationships should inform how the church deals with difficult issues such as abortion, divorce, abuse and homosexuality. For example, as people who celebrate their adoption as God's children, Christians should support adoption both theologically and practically as one aspect of the church's response to abortion.[63] Too often Christians are known as people who oppose, rather than people who embrace. This reputation is a betrayal of the One who died to reconcile his enemies to himself.

Reconciliation does not require us to suppress biblical truth for the sake of unity; without truth, authentic reconciliation is impossible. It does, however, challenge us to be willing to bear the cost of reconciliation. This means taking the initiative to make peace with those who have offended us and with those we have offended (Mt 5:23-24; 18:15-17). It may also mean crossing social or theological boundaries and reaching out to others who make us uncomfortable. As the incarnation shows us, reconciliation cannot be accomplished at a distance.[64]

Reconciliation in Christ calls us to challenge the racism, sexism, classism and nationalism that still plague both church and society. It should lead us to question any strategy that aims to create peace through violence or oppression. It requires us to work toward the New Testament vision of the church as a multinational, multicultural people. Furthermore, the vision of Jews and

---

Personal Conflict, 2nd ed. (Grand Rapids: Baker, 1997). The first and third are written from a specifically Christian perspective. For an approach to war and peace that intends to unite both pacifists and just-war proponents, see Glen H. Stassen, *Just Peacemaking: Transforming Initiatives for Justice and Peace* (Louisville: Westminster John Knox Press, 1992); and Glen H. Stassen, ed., *Just Peacemaking: Ten Practices for Abolishing War* (Cleveland: Pilgrim Press, 2004).

[63]See the discussion by David V. Andersen, "When God Adopts," *Christianity Today*, July 19, 1993, pp. 36-39.

[64]Augsburger, *Robe of God*, p. 42.

Gentiles reconciled in Christ should motivate us to reflect carefully on the relations between Christians and Jews both past and present. In order to move forward in all these areas, the church may have to face some painful truths and repent of past and present sins, because without a foundation of truth and justice, peace cannot flourish.[65] God's vision of peace urges us outward to seek the stranger, befriend the alien, and restore the rest of creation.

In a contentious time, the church has an opportunity to show the world how to deal with others in a redemptive way, because we know how God has dealt with us. We have not always been very good at this, but we really have no choice. Regardless of what we say, our life will be a stronger witness than our words. The world will not take the gospel seriously unless they see that we do. We have no excuse. We can love—in deed and truth— because God has first loved us (1 Jn 3:18; 4:9-10, 19).

Finally, reconciliation in Christ gives us hope. Because it has already been accomplished, we can rejoice in our relationships with the Lord and with one another. Because it is not yet consummated, however, we must carry on the ministry of reconciliation that God has entrusted to us, anticipating the future day when God's kingdom of peace becomes a reality.

FOR FURTHER READING

Augsburger, Myron. *The Robe of God: Reconciliation, the Believers Church Essential*. Scottdale, Penn.: Herald, 2000.

Breytenbach, Cilliers. "Salvation of the Reconciled (with a Note on the Background of Paul's Metaphor of Reconciliation)." In *Salvation in the New Testament: Perspectives on Soteriology*. Edited by Jan G. van der Watt, pp. 271-86. Supplements to Novum Testamentum. Boston: E. J. Brill, 2005.

Brueggemann, Walter. *Peace*. Understanding Biblical Themes. St. Louis, Mo.: Chalice, 2001.

Burke, Trevor J. *Adopted into God's Family: Exploring a Pauline Metaphor*. Downers Grove, Ill.: InterVarsity Press, 2006.

Fitzmyer, Joseph A. "Reconciliation in Pauline Theology," pp. 162-85. In *To Advance the Gospel: New Testament Studies*. New York: Crossroad, 1981.

Furnish, Victor Paul. "The Ministry of Reconciliation." *Currents in Theology and Mission* 4, no. 4 (August 1977): 204-18.

Marshall, I. Howard. "The Meaning of Reconciliation," pp. 258-74. In *Jesus the Saviour: Studies in New Testament Theology*. London: SPCK, 1990.

---

[65]See especially Volf, "Forgiveness, Reconciliation, and Justice" and *Exclusion and Embrace*.

Martin, Ralph P. *Reconciliation: A Study of Paul's Theology.* Grand Rapids: Zondervan, 1989.

Moule, C. F. D. *Forgiveness and Reconciliation: And Other New Testament Themes.* London: SPCK, 1998.

———. "Punishment and Retribution: Delimiting their Scope in N. T. Thought," pp. 252-67. In *Stricken by God? Nonviolent Identification and the Victory of Christ.* Edited by Brad Jersak and Michael Hardin. Grand Rapids: Eerdmans, 2007.

Porter, Stanley E. *Katallassō in Ancient Greek Literature, with Reference to the Pauline Writings.* Córdoba: Ediciónes El Amendro, 1994.

Scott, James M. *Adoption as Sons of God: An Exegetical Investigation into the Background of ΥΙΟΘΕΣΙΑ in the Pauline Corpus.* Wissenschaftliche Untersuchungen zum Neuen Testament 2.Reihe. Edited by Joachim Jeremias and Otto Michel. Tübingen: Mohr Siebeck, 1992.

Spence, Alan. *The Promise of Peace: A Unified Theory of Atonement.* Edinburgh: T & T Clark, 2007.

Stuhlmacher, Peter. *Reconciliation, Law & Righteousness: Essays in Biblical Theology.* Philadelphia: Fortress, 1986.

Swartley, Willard M. *Covenant of Peace: The Missing Peace in New Testament Theology and Ethics.* Grand Rapids: Eerdmans, 2006.

Volf, Miroslav. *Exclusion and Embrace: A Theological Exploration of Identity, Otherness, and Reconciliation.* Nashville: Abingdon, 1996.

———. "Forgiveness, Reconciliation and Justice," pp. 268-87. In *Stricken by God? Nonviolent Identification and the Victory of Christ.* Edited by Brad Jersak and Michael Hardin. Grand Rapids: Eerdmans, 2007.

9

JUSTIFICATION BY
FAITH(FULNESS)

IN THE THEOLOGY OF REFORMATION TRADITIONS, justification by faith[1] came to be known as "the article [of doctrine] by which the church stands or falls."[2] It featured prominently in the theological divide between Protestantism and the Catholic Church. Since the Reformation, justification has been the primary model used by Protestants to describe salvation. Recent events, however, have reopened discussions about this important doctrine. Research by biblical scholars has called into question the traditional Protestant interpretation of Paul's writings, leading to the "New Perspective on Paul." In addition, conversations between the Roman Catholic Church and the Lutheran World Federation have resulted in a *Joint Declaration on the Doctrine of Justification* in which the two bodies declare that they are no longer at odds over this doctrine.[3]

Thus the time is ripe for an investigation of the biblical meaning of justification. In this chapter, we will look at justification in the New Testament, particularly in the writings of Paul. We will be focusing on the

---

[1]The expression "faith(fulness)" in the title is used by Richard B. Hays in reference to Christ in *The Faith of Jesus Christ: The Narrative Substructure of Galatians 3:1–4:11* (Grand Rapids: Eerdmans, 2002), p. 151.

[2]Alister E. McGrath, *Iustitia Dei: A History of the Christian Doctrine of Justification*, 2 vols. (Cambridge: Cambridge University Press, 1986), 2:1. McGrath discusses the origin of the phrase. Although not coined by Martin Luther, it reflects Luther's emphasis and resembles statements he made (2:193 n. 3).

[3]The text of the Declaration is available online. "Joint Declaration on the Doctrine of Justification" <www.vatican.va/roman_curia/pontifical_councils/chrstuni/documents/rc_pc_chrs tuni_doc_31101999_cath-luth-joint-declaration_en.html>.

biblical image of justification, not the *doctrine* of justification, which, as Alister McGrath has noted, "has come to develop a meaning quite independent of its biblical origins." While the image of justification is only one of the biblical pictures of salvation, the doctrine of justification has become a comprehensive term for the means by which human beings are brought into relationship to God.[4] Whether their perspective is "new" or "old," Protestants need to understand justification in order to come to terms with their own heritage. All believers need to understand it in order to comprehend what God has done for them in Christ.

THE TRADITIONAL VIEW AND THE "NEW PERSPECTIVE"

The traditional Protestant view of justification originates with Luther. Luther came to this view through his reading of Scripture and his personal struggle to find acceptance with God. He had inherited from medieval Catholicism the idea that the righteousness of God was God's personal holiness and justice, which required God to punish human sin. But he found theological resolution and personal freedom through his understanding that the righteousness of God was not a quality of God but the righteousness that God demanded of human beings, which God credited to them through the merit of Jesus Christ.[5] Justification, then, was God's declaration that human beings were not guilty of sin because they had been credited with the righteousness of Christ when they placed their faith in him.

Although Luther himself did not view justification in strictly legal terms, subsequent Protestant tradition has interpreted it that way. In this view, justification is forensic and purely declarative. Individuals, though sinners, are declared by God to be righteous, strictly on the basis of the righteousness of Christ, which is imputed to them. The righteousness involved is thus an "alien" righteousness—that is, alien to those being justified.[6] It is essential in this view that justification not be based on any ac-

---

[4]McGrath, *Iustitia Dei*, 1:2.
[5]Ibid., 2:4-8.
[6]Ibid., 2:23-25, 44-45, 12. McGrath attributes to Melanchthon the idea that Christ's righteousness is imputed to sinners. For contemporary statements of this view, see Millard Erickson, *Christian Theology*, 2nd ed. (Grand Rapids: Baker, 1998), p. 969; and John Piper, *The Future of Justification: A Response to N. T. Wright* (Wheaton, Ill.: Crossway, 2007), p. 9.

tual holiness in human beings. If it were, salvation would be by works rather than by faith alone.[7] By contrast, Catholic teaching holds that justification is a process that begins with "infused righteousness"—a holiness within the individual that is imparted by God's grace. Justification progresses as the individual grows in holiness.[8] For Protestants, the legal declaration of righteousness is the essence of salvation. It is effective whether the individual grows in actual holiness or not. Christians in this life always remain *justus et peccator simul*—justified and sinner at the same time.[9]

Building on the work of Krister Stendahl, in his essay "Paul and the Introspective Conscience of the West" (1963), and E. P. Sanders, in books such as *Paul and Palestinian Judaism* (1977), some recent scholars have argued that Luther's "insight" into justification actually resulted from reading the Reformation faith-works controversy back into the first century. They believe that Paul's view of justification should be understood in the context of the Jewish-Gentile issue in his ministry. These scholars, including James D. G. Dunn and N. T. Wright, represent what has been called the New Perspective on Paul.[10]

---

[7]Erickson states repeatedly that justification makes no change in someone's moral character (*Christian Theology*, pp. 969, 970, 971). These Reformation issues are still very much alive in evangelical circles.

[8]McGrath, *Iustitia Dei*, 2:80-86.

[9]Ibid., 2:12. For an illustration of Lutheran reluctance to discuss sanctification, see Gerhard O. Forde, "The Lutheran View," in *Christian Spirituality: Five Views of Sanctification*, ed. Donald L. Alexander (Downers Grove, Ill.: InterVarsity Press, 1988), pp. 13-32.

[10]The phrase was coined by N. T. Wright. See his *Justification: God's Plan and Paul's Vision* (Downers Grove, Ill.: InterVarsity Press, 2009), p. 28. The New Perspective is grounded in the rediscovery of the Jewish context and eschatological emphasis of Paul's theology by Albert Schweitzer and others. See, e.g., Schweitzer's *The Mysticism of Paul the Apostle*, trans. William Montgomery (Baltimore: Johns Hopkins University Press, 1998). See also the discussion in James D. G. Dunn, *The New Perspective on Paul*, rev. ed. (Grand Rapids: Eerdmans, 2007), especially the first two essays, "The New Perspective: Whence, What, and Whither?" and "The New Perspective on Paul" (1982). Wright notes that he and Dunn disagree on such matters as Christology, the interpretation of Romans 7, the meaning of *pistis christou*, and Wright's return from exile theme (*Justification*, pp. 28-29). A different perspective on the New Perspective is provided in John G. Gager, *Reinventing Paul* (Oxford: Oxford University Press, 2000). Gager does not cite Wright, but he disagrees with both Dunn and Wright concerning Paul's attitude toward the Judaism of his day. Gager believes that Paul critiqued only the Judaizers within Christianity, not Judaism itself, and that Paul expected the salvation of all Israel apart from Christ (pp. 141-42). Gager is concerned to refute the view that Paul is the founder of Christian anti-Semitism. While I agree with him on this point (and on many of the points he makes to critique the traditional view of Paul), I do not agree that Paul envisioned the salvation of Israel—or anyone—outside of Christ. Gager bases this conclusion on the fact that Paul does not explicitly mention Christ in Romans 11. While his purpose is admirable, his reading of Romans is idiosyncratic and unpersuasive.

In his seminal essay, Stendahl declares that Paul has too long been read through the lens of Luther's struggles in the sixteenth century. He contends that the central concern of Paul's ministry is not how individuals can find a gracious God but how Jews and Gentiles relate to one another now that Messiah has come. Paul's discussion of the law refers to the Mosaic law, not to legalism in general, and his treatment of justification apart from law is driven by his concern that Gentiles be included in the messianic community.[11]

For his part, Sanders argues that first-century Judaism was not a religion of works but of "covenantal nomism"—that is, a religion that regarded the law as an expression of Israel's covenant with God. In Sanders's terms, Jews did not follow the law in order to "get in" to a relationship with God but to "stay in" relationship with God. The law was not the way they obtained salvation, which they had by virtue of God's covenant with Israel, but the way they lived out that salvation. Sanders proposes that the central image in Paul's theology of salvation is not justification by faith but participation in Christ.[12]

James D. G. Dunn, N. T. Wright and others agree with Stendahl's critique and with Sanders's idea of covenantal nomism, although they do not agree with Sanders (or with one another) on everything else. Dunn has taken Sanders's analysis further by arguing that Paul's concern with "works of the law" was particularly focused on certain practices, such as circumcision and Sabbath, which served to mark off Israel from the Gentile nations. Paul's objection to "works of the law" was not that the Jews (and Jewish Christians) were using these as a means to earn their salvation but that they were clinging to the law as a badge of national identity and privilege, thereby excluding Gentiles from the covenant people.[13] Thus Paul was not arguing against Jewish works-righteousness but against Jewish exclusivism.

In the New Perspective, justification has a covenantal context. Paul dis-

---

[11]Stendahl, "Introspective Conscience," pp. 203-4, 206.

[12]E. P. Sanders, *Paul and Palestinian Judaism: A Comparison of Patterns of Religion* (Minneapolis: Augsburg Fortress, 1977), pp. 75, 93, 422. See also James D. G. Dunn, *Romans 1–8*, Word Biblical Commentary (Nashville: Nelson, 1988), pp. lxiii-lxxii; and N. T. Wright, *What Saint Paul Really Said* (Grand Rapids: Eerdmans, 1997), pp. 113-20, 129.

[13]James D. G. Dunn, "The New Perspective on Paul," in *Jesus, Paul and the Law: Studies in Mark and Galatians* (London: SPCK, 1990), pp. 191, 194.

cusses justification in Romans and Galatians because he must address the question of how both Jews and Gentiles can be part of the people of God. His answer is that membership in God's covenant people is not based on having the law (and thus open only to Jews) but on faith in Christ (and thus open to Gentiles also). According to Dunn, the righteousness of God is not the status of acquittal that God grants to human beings but God's own covenant faithfulness. Similarly, justification is not God's declaration that Christ's righteousness has been imputed to the sinner but "God's acknowledgement that someone is in the covenant." With the coming of Christ, the badge of covenant membership is now faith in Christ rather than possession of the law.[14]

N. T. Wright argues similarly that Paul understands the righteousness of God not as God's holiness or justice, and not as the righteousness that God demands of (and imputes to) human beings, but as God's covenant faithfulness. God demonstrates his righteousness, or covenant faithfulness, by sending Jesus to fulfill his covenant promises to rescue his people and deal with sin. Rather than the means by which individuals come into relationship with God, justification is God's vindication of the church, composed of both Jews and Gentiles, as his covenant people. Thus justification is primarily corporate rather than individual, and it applies not to conversion but to the ongoing life of faith. It is still forensic, but the context is covenant law, grounded in relationship, rather than an abstract legal code. Justification is still declarative, but rather than God's declaration that an individual is not guilty of sin, it is God's declaration that the church is his people. The basis of justification is faith in Christ, because Christ is the mediator of God's saving faithfulness. Membership in the covenant people of God comes only through him. Thus God's people are now to be identified by faith in Christ rather than by their possession of the law.[15]

The traditional view, according to Wright, sees justification as equivalent to conversion, the event at which God establishes a "personal" (individual) relationship with someone. For Wright, by contrast, justification is

---

[14]Ibid., pp. 190, 196. Dunn's view of justification seems to have shifted somewhat by the writing of his *Theology of Paul the Apostle*. In that work he states that justification is "the initial acceptance by God into restored relationship." It is "God accepting the sinner." James D. G. Dunn, *The Theology of Paul the Apostle* (Grand Rapids: Eerdmans, 1998), pp. 386, 387. These descriptions sound more like the traditional perspective on Paul.

[15]Wright, *Saint Paul*, pp. 113-33.

covenantal, not individualistic.[16] By "covenant," he means God's "single plan . . . through which he intended to rescue the world and the human race, and [which] was centered upon the call of Israel, a call which Paul saw coming to fruition in Israel's representative, the Messiah."[17] Justification is about membership in God's covenant people. For individuals, justification is not about "how someone becomes a Christian" or "gets in" to the people of God; instead, it is about "God's declaration that someone *is* in." It is God's eschatological verdict on someone's life, which can be announced in the present because that person has come to faith in Christ. Justification thus *follows* conversion and has to do with assurance or vindication.[18] Wright's understanding of how salvation takes place—by grace, through faith, on the basis of the work of Christ—is perfectly in line with traditional Protestantism. He simply argues that "justification" as Paul uses the term refers to a different part of that process.

The New Perspective has attained wide (but not universal) acceptance among biblical scholars.[19] Theologians have been slower to accept it, especially in those traditions that have been committed to a legal model of salvation. The discussion that follows is generally sympathetic to the New Perspective while attempting to retain some insights from the traditional perspective.

TERMS AND CONCEPTS

For English speakers, discussing justification in the Bible is hampered from the outset by terminology. The words that are translated "justify" and "righteousness" are from the same word group in both Hebrew and Greek, while the English words are from two different roots. Connections that are obvious in the original languages are obscured in English. Furthermore, in English, "justification" has legal connotations, while "right-

---

[16]N. T. Wright, "New Perspectives on Paul," in *Justification in Perspective: Historical Developments and Contemporary Challenges*, ed. Bruce L. McCormack (Grand Rapids: Baker, 2006), p. 255. For a discussion of justification as "how human beings enter into a right relation with God," see Alister McGrath, *Justification by Faith: What It Means for Us Today* (Grand Rapids: Zondervan, 1988), p. 27.

[17]Wright, *Justification*, p. 35. The original statement is italicized.

[18]Wright, "New Perspectives," pp. 260-61, 255-56.

[19]For an alternative view, see D. A. Carson, Peter T. O'Brien and Mark A. Seifrid, *Justification and Variegated Nomism*, vol. 1: *The Complexities of Second Temple Judaism* (Grand Rapids: Baker, 2001); and D. A. Carson, Peter T. O'Brien and Mark A. Seifrid, *Justification and Variegated Nomism*, vol. 2: *The Paradoxes of Paul* (Grand Rapids: Baker, 2004).

eousness" has moral connotations. We will have to set our English presuppositions aside as we examine the biblical words.

In the Old Testament, the most common words for justification are from the *ṣdq* root, including *ṣĕdāqâ* (straightness, justness, justice, honesty) and *ṣādaq* (vindicate, acquit, declare to be in the right). The noun form is less common than the verb, suggesting that justification/righteousness is thought of primarily as an action. The Old Testament concept of righteousness "emphasizes the relational aspect of God and humanity in the context of a covenant." It usually suggests God's "saving acts as evidence of God's faithfulness to the covenant."[20] The word *ṣĕdāqâ* is associated with concepts such as steadfast love, faithfulness and justice (Is 11:5; 16:5; Ps 85:7-13; 89:13-14; 98:2-3). To call on God's righteousness means to call on God for rescue or vindication (Ps 71:2; 143:11).[21] God's righteousness is thus his covenant faithfulness. Israel can call on God for deliverance because he has bound himself to them by covenant and has promised to come to their aid.

Similarly, a human being in the Old Testament is righteous if he or she acts in accordance with a particular covenant relationship.[22] This is why Judah acknowledges that his daughter-in-law Tamar is more righteous than he is after she dresses as a prostitute, seduces him and becomes pregnant by him (Gen 38:26). Her behavior hardly seems "righteous" to English-speaking Christians today, but she is faithfully carrying out her covenant obligation to raise up children for her dead husband. Judah had shirked his covenant obligation by refusing to marry Tamar to one of his other sons. For human beings, as for God, righteousness fundamentally means covenant faithfulness. Because of their different obligations in the covenant relationship, God's righteousness is expressed as redemption, reminder and judgment, while human righteousness is expressed as obedience.

In the New Testament, the word translated as justice or righteousness is *dikaiosynē*. It is used in the Septuagint to translate Hebrew words with the *ṣdq* root. It is also sometimes used to translate *ʾĕmet* (truth, faithfulness) and *ḥesed*, the word for God's covenant love.[23] The adjective form (*dikaios*)

---

[20]K. L. Onesti and M. T. Brauch, "Righteousness," in *DPL*, p. 828; see also H. Seebass, "Righteousness, Justification," in *NIDNTT* 3:355.

[21]Seebass, "Righteousness, Justification," in *NIDNTT* 3:355.

[22]Onesti and Brauch, "Righteousness," in *DPL*, p. 829.

[23]For *ʾĕmet*, see Gen 24:49; Josh 24:14; Is 38:19; 39:8; for *ḥesed*, see Gen 19:19; 20:13; 21:23;

is used most by Matthew and Paul; the other forms are used most by Paul, especially in Romans. Like *ṣdq* in the Old Testament, *dikaiosynē* has a relational or covenantal foundation.

Both God and human beings can be called righteous (*dikaios*). God's righteousness is associated with his judgment (2 Thess 1:5; 2 Tim 4:8; 1 Pet 2:23; Rev 16:7) and with his faithful forgiveness of sins (1 Jn 1:9). In both cases, God is carrying out his covenant responsibilities. Human righteousness is associated with doing God's will. People are sometimes called righteous in the formal sense of keeping the law (Mt 9:13; Mk 2:17), but Jesus says that their righteousness must be greater than that in order to enter the kingdom (Mt 5:20). He tells his followers to seek God's righteousness along with God's kingdom (Mt 5:6; 6:33).

Jesus himself is called the Righteous One (Acts 7:52; 1 Jn 2:1). In his ministry, he is concerned to "fulfill all righteousness" (Mt 3:15). Because he is the standard of righteousness for human beings, a righteous person is one who acts as Jesus did (1 Jn 2:6). Conformity to Christ is thus the New Testament counterpart to conformity to the law in the Old Testament. In both cases, such conformity is a faithful following that is motivated by love and gratitude for God's gracious act of redemption. According to Paul's analysis in Romans 1:18-21, unrighteousness originates in the failure to acknowledge God and results in greater and greater sin. That would imply that human righteousness begins in human responsiveness to God and issues in greater and greater obedience.

To express the verb form of *dikaiosynē* in English, translators use the word "justify," since "righteousness" has no verb form. Scholars have proposed other verbs, such as "rectify" and "rightwise," but these proposals have not been generally accepted. According to the Bauer, Arndt, Gingrich and Danker lexicon, the verb *dikaioō* means to justify, to vindicate, to acquit or to declare persons or things to be in the right and treat them as such.[24] In the New Testament, it often means to vindicate, such as when God's faithfulness is vindicated in spite of Israel's unfaithfulness (Rom 3:4) or when Jesus is vindicated by the Spirit (or in the spirit, 1 Tim 3:16).

24:27; 32:11; Ex 15:13; 34:7; Prov 20:28; Is 61:7. Seebass, "Righteousness, Justification," in *NIDNTT* 3:354.

[24]"δικαιόω," in *BAGD*, p. 197-98. The definitions reflect the influence of the traditional interpretation of Paul's letters.

Jesus says that wisdom is vindicated by her children (Lk 7:35). Paul expects that he will be vindicated at the last judgment (1 Cor 4:4).

In this last verse, "vindicated" seems a more appropriate translation than "acquitted" (NRSV), since Paul is defending his apostolic ministry rather than addressing any legal liability for sin. Because *dikaioō* comes from a forensic context, both vindication and acquittal are possible translations. The different nuances are significant, however. To be acquitted is to be absolved of all charges, whether guilty or innocent. It is possible for a judge to acquit a guilty person. To be vindicated, however, is to be proven to be in the right. This is the critical question for the traditional view and the New Perspective: when *dikaioō* refers to God's action toward human beings, is God acquitting the guilty or vindicating the righteous? We will begin to answer this question by exploring the righteousness of God.

THE RIGHTEOUSNESS OF GOD

Paul's concept of the righteousness of God (*dikaiosynē theou*) has been the subject of much debate. Paul describes it as central to the gospel: "For I am not ashamed of the gospel; it is the power of God for salvation to everyone who has faith, to the Jew first and also to the Greek. For in it the righteousness of God is revealed through faith for faith; as it is written, 'The one who is righteous will live by faith'" (Rom 1:16-17). The phrase *dikaiosynē theou* (in various forms) occurs ten times in the New Testament, all but two of them in Romans.[25] Like any genitive construction, this phrase is ambiguous. It could mean a quality of God (subjective genitive) or a quality that God requires of human beings (objective genitive). Protestants, following Luther, have read it as an objective genitive. Recent interpreters, however, have tended to see it as a subjective genitive referring either to God's character or God's actions.[26]

Chapter 3 of Romans, which contains five instances of the phrase, is the best place to go to attempt a definition. Romans 3:25-26 seem to indicate that the righteousness of God is God's own righteousness displayed in Jesus Christ: "God put [Jesus] forward as a sacrifice of atonement by his

---

[25]Rom 1:17; 3:5, 21, 22, 25, 26; 10:3 (2x); 2 Cor 5:21. The total of ten includes Mt 6:33, which can be read as either "his" (God's) or "its" (the kingdom's) righteousness. The total does not include Phil 3:9, which refers to a righteousness *from* God (*ek theou*).

[26]For a summary of interpretive approaches to this phrase, see the chart in N. T. Wright, *What Saint Paul Really Said* (Grand Rapids: Eerdmans, 1997), p. 101.

blood, effective through faith. He did this to show his righteousness, because in his divine forbearance he had passed over the sins previously committed; it was to prove at the present time that he himself is righteous and that he justifies the one who has faith in Jesus." God demonstrated his *dikaiosynē*—that is, demonstrated that he was *dikaios*—by offering Jesus as a sacrifice of atonement or a new mercy seat (*hilastērion*).[27]

Furthermore, the parallel constructions in Romans 3:3-7 suggest that God's righteousness is his covenant faithfulness:

3 What then? If some were unfaithful (*ēpistēsan*), their faithlessness (*apistia*) will not nullify the faithfulness (*pistin*) of God, will it?

4 May it never be! Let God be true (*alēthēs*), but every person false (*pseustēs*), just as it is written: "So that you may be vindicated (*dikaiōthēs*) by your words and prevail when you are judged (*krinesthai*)."[28]

5 But if our unrighteousness (*adikia*) highlights the righteousness (*dikaiosynēn*) of God, what shall we say? God is not unrighteous to inflict wrath, is he? I speak in human terms.

6 May it never be! For then how will God judge (*krinei*) the world?

7 But if by my falsity (*pseusmati*) the truthfulness (*alētheia*) of God abounds to his glory, why am I still being condemned (*krinomai*) as a sinner? (author's translation)

In these verses, Paul uses three pairs of terms to draw a contrast between God and human beings:

Verse 3:	faithfulness (*pistis*) vs. unfaithfulness (*apistia*)
Verses 4, 7:	truth (*alētheia*) vs. falsity (*pseusma*)
Verse 5:	righteousness (*dikaiosynē*) vs. unrighteousness (*adikia*)

Verse 5 is clearly a restatement of the comparison made in verses 3 and

---

[27]Onesti and Brauch define the righteousness of God as "God's relation-restoring love." They note that "the concrete historical expression of 'God's righteousness' is the event of Christ." "Righteousness," in *DPL*, p. 836.

[28]Most interpreters read this quotation from Psalm 51:4 (LXX) as a reference to God's justice in rendering judgment. This makes sense in the context of the psalm. In the context of Paul's argument, however, it seems more appropriate to read it as a reference to God's vindication. God's faithfulness to his promises will be vindicated regardless of the faithlessness of his covenant partners. See the discussion in Dunn, *Romans 1–8*, p. 134; and C. K. Barrett, *The Epistle to the Romans*, Harper's New Testament Commentaries (1957; reprint, Peabody, Mass.: Hendrickson, 1987), p. 63.

4. These parallels suggest that God's righteousness is God's faithfulness or God's truthfulness, in the sense of integrity or dependability.[29] In the context of chapter 3, Paul is concerned to establish that God was faithful to his covenant promises, even though Israel was not. The frequent occurrence of *dikaiosynē theou* in Romans makes sense because of Paul's concern to defend God's covenant faithfulness to Israel in light of his allowing Gentiles to be members of the covenant people. When Paul refers to a righteousness that people have *from* God, he uses a different expression: "the righteousness from God [*tēn ek theou dikaiosynēn*] based on faith" (Phil 3:9). The preposition *ek* indicates "from."[30]

The traditional Protestant understanding of justification regards Romans 3:25-26 as a paradox. How can God be just and justify (acquit) the guilty? In the Old Testament, acquitting the guilty is the mark of an unjust judge (Ex 23:7). The traditional answer is that God can declare people not guilty because Jesus has paid the penalty for their sins. Their guilt has been credited to him, and his innocence has been credited to them because of their faith in him.[31] But this exchange does not really resolve the tension. How has justice been done if the innocent has been punished and the guilty have been freed?

However, if God's *dikaiosynē* is his covenant faithfulness, Romans 3:25-26 is not a paradox. God demonstrates his covenant faithfulness by sending Jesus to deal with sin as he had promised. Although he had "passed over" sins previously, without bringing judgment upon his people, he has now sent Jesus to deal with sin decisively and finally. In fact, these verses can be seen as a threefold declaration of covenant faithfulness: God demonstrates his own faithfulness by sending Jesus, and he vindicates those who are of the same faith(fulness) as Jesus (*ek pisteōs Iēsou*).[32]

The final phrase is usually translated "faith in Jesus," although the NRSV notes "faith of Jesus" in the margin as an alternative translation. The usual translation is not a natural rendering of the Greek, but it fits well with the

---

[29]See "ἀλήθεια," in *BAGD*, p. 35; and "ψεῦσμα," in *BAGD*, p. 892.

[30]Paul seems to use "righteousness of God" to mean God's own righteousness; when he wants to talk about a righteousness *from* God, he uses a different expression. Wright, *Saint Paul*, p. 104.

[31]George Eldon Ladd, *A Theology of the New Testament*, ed. Donald A. Hagner, rev. ed. (Grand Rapids: Eerdmans, 1993), pp. 473, 489-90.

[32]Hays, "Πίστις and Pauline Christology," in *Faith of Jesus Christ*, p. 284; Wright, *Justification*, pp. 201-4.

traditional view of justification. However, a relational or covenantal understanding of justification can read the phrase as it stands. God demonstrates his faithfulness through the faithfulness of Jesus, who makes possible an answering faithfulness in those who follow him.[33] As Richard Hays points out, Romans 3:26 is parallel to Romans 4:16. Since the latter verse refers to those who share the "faith(fulness) of Abraham" (*ek pisteōs Abraam*), it makes sense to regard the former as those who share the "faith(fulness) of Jesus" (*ek pisteōs Iēsou*).[34]

As I have noted previously, the Greek word *pistis* can mean both "faith" and "faithfulness." The nuance of any particular instance must be decided from the context. Romans 3:3, above, clearly deals with faithfulness and faithlessness rather than belief and unbelief. This is why I will use the phrase "justification by faith(fulness)," since the idea of faithfulness may be implied in any instance of the word *pistis*.

Two other passages in Romans suggest a threefold pattern of faithfulness. In Romans 3:21-22, Paul declares, "But now, apart from law, the righteousness of God has been disclosed, and is attested by the law and the prophets, the righteousness of God through faith in Jesus Christ [NRSV note reads "through the faith of Jesus Christ"] for all who believe." The gospel reveals the covenant faithfulness of God (*dikaiosynē theou*) through the faithfulness of Christ (*dia pisteōs Iēsou Christou*) to all who have faith (or are faithful, *tous pisteuontas*). Similarly, in Romans 1:16-17, Paul says that the gospel is "the power of God for salvation to everyone who has faith [or is faithful, *panti tō pisteuonti*], to the Jew first and also to the Greek. For in it the righteousness of God is revealed through faith for faith [*ek pisteōs eis pistin*]." The gospel reveals God's covenant faithfulness through the faith(fulness) of Christ, to benefit all those who have the same faith(fulness) as Christ.[35]

In both of these passages, Paul states that God's righteousness has been revealed apart from of law, although it is "attested by the law and the prophets." God had promised his people through the law and the prophets

---

[33]This understanding of *pistis christou* was largely pioneered by Richard B. Hays. For his own work, as well as an overview of scholarship on the topic, see his *Faith of Jesus Christ*. See also Michael F. Bird and Preston M. Sprinkle, eds., *The Faith of Jesus Christ: Exegetical, Biblical, and Theological Studies* (Peabody, Mass.: Hendrickson, 2010).

[34]Hays, "Πίστις and Pauline Christology," p. 284.

[35]See Wright, *Justification*, pp. 181, 203-4.

that he would redeem them, and Jesus was the fulfillment of that promise. But although the law attests to the redeemer, the law is not the means of redemption. For that reason, since it is apart from the Mosaic law, redemption is available to both the Jew and the Greek.

However, in Romans 10:3-4, Paul declares that Israel has not been willing to accept covenant membership on God's terms: "For, being ignorant of the righteousness that comes from God [actually, "the righteousness of God," *tou theou dikaiosynēn*], and seeking to establish their own, they have not submitted to God's righteousness [*dikaiosynē tou theou*]. For Christ is the end of the law so that there may be righteousness for everyone who believes." Israel is ignorant of God's covenant faithfulness, in that they have failed to recognize Jesus as the fulfillment of God's promises. Instead, they want to have a righteousness of "their own"—that is, belonging only to them.[36] Christ is both the goal and the completion (*telos*) of the law, in that he fulfills the purpose of the law to enable human beings to be God's faithful covenant partners. As Paul argues in Romans 8:1-4, Jesus, by dealing with sin and sending the Spirit, has enabled believers to live as the law had commanded them to live. Covenant membership is therefore now open to everyone who believes, whether Jew or Gentile.

The most significant instance of *dikaiosynē theou* outside of Romans occurs in 2 Corinthians 5:21: "For our sake he made him to be sin who knew no sin, so that in him we might become the righteousness of God." In the traditional view of justification, this verse is read as an exchange in which Christ's righteousness is imputed to human beings while their sin is imputed to him.[37] However, this verse does not say that *we receive* the righteousness of God or Christ or that *we are credited with* such righteousness. It says *so that we might become* (*hina hēmeis genōmetha*) the righteousness of God. How is that possible? If God's righteousness is his covenant faithfulness, we become the righteousness of God as we become agents of God's saving faithfulness by sharing the gospel.[38] This interpretation of

---

[36]Dunn, *Romans 9-16*, p. 595.
[37]Ladd, *Theology*, p. 491.
[38]See the discussion in N. T. Wright, "On Becoming the Righteousness of God: 2 Corinthians 5:21," in *Pauline Theology, Volume II*, ed. D. M. Hay (Minneapolis: Augsburg Fortress, 1993), pp. 200-208. Wright summarizes Paul's argument here by saying that "the apostolic ministry, including its suffering, fear and apparent failure, is itself *an incarnation of the covenant faithfulness of God.*" *Saint Paul*, pp. 104-5 (italics in original).

the verse fits the context, in which Paul declares that we are ambassadors of Christ, entreating others to be reconciled to God (2 Cor 5:18-21).

JUSTIFICATION

So, then, what does it mean when God justifies human beings? Let's return to Romans 3. First, Paul declares that all human beings are in need of justification:

> We have already charged that all, both Jews and Greeks, are under the power of sin, as it is written: "There is no one who is righteous, not even one." . . . For there is no distinction, since all have sinned and fall short of the glory of God; they are now justified by his grace as a gift, through the redemption that is in Christ Jesus, whom God put forward as a sacrifice of atonement [or place of atonement] by his blood, effective through faith. (Rom 3:9-10, 22-25)

Neither Jews nor Greeks are *dikaios*, because they have fallen short of God's expectations, whether revealed through the Mosaic covenant (in the case of Jews) or through general revelation and conscience (in the case of Gentiles). They can become *dikaios* only by God's gracious action on their behalf.

Second, people are "justified by [God's] grace as a gift, through the redemption that is in Christ Jesus" (Rom 3:24). God's grace is extended to all through the blood (death) of Christ (Rom 3:25). Paul insists that God is the one who justifies (Rom 8:33). While he attributes justification to the cross in chapter 3, he attributes it to the resurrection in chapter 4: Jesus "was handed over to death for our trespasses and was raised for our justification [*dikaiōsin*]" (Rom 4:25). The traditional understanding of Paul tends to see the resurrection as a mere affirmation of the work of justification accomplished by the cross.[39] However, Romans 4:25 describes a causal relationship between the resurrection and justification. In this instance, *dikaiōsis* seems to mean vindication. Just as Jesus was vindicated through his resurrection, those who are identified with him are vindicated also (cf. Rom 6:4-5).[40]

---

[39]See the discussion in Frank D. Macchia, "Justification through New Creation: The Holy Spirit and the Doctrine by Which the Church Stands or Falls," *Theology Today* 58, no. 2 (July 2001): 209-10.

[40]Wright, *Justification*, p. 106.

Jesus makes human *dikaiosynē* possible by undoing what Adam did: "Therefore just as one man's trespass led to condemnation for all, so one man's act of righteousness leads to justification and life for all. For just as by the one man's disobedience the many were made sinners, so by the one man's obedience the many will be made righteous" (Rom 5:18-19). Jesus' "act of righteousness" (*dikaiōma*), or his faithful obedience unto death, enables faithless sinners to find life in covenant relationship with God.

Third, justification is primarily relational and only secondarily forensic. Jesus' death on behalf of human beings demonstrates God's love for the ungodly (Rom 5:6-8). It also makes possible a restored relationship with God: "Much more surely then, now that *we have been justified* by his blood, will we be saved through him from the wrath of God. For if while we were enemies, we were reconciled to God through the death of his Son, much more surely, *having been reconciled*, will we be saved by his life" (Rom 5:9-10, italics added). The "for" (*gar*) in Romans 5:10 indicates that this verse is an explanation of the previous statement. The parallel between justification and reconciliation (both aorist passive participles) suggests that justification is fundamentally relational. The decisive event of reconciliation and justification took place at the cross, when "we were reconciled" (aorist passive indicative) to God by the death of Christ. The cross made possible restored relationship between God and human beings, a new covenant mediated by Christ. The forensic aspect of justification must be understood in the context of this covenant relationship.

A forensic understanding of justification probably became inevitable when the Western church began to do theology in Latin rather than in Greek. It would be difficult to read the word *iustitia* without thinking in legal terms. Nevertheless, David deSilva has shown that even *iustitia* had a relational context. According to Pseudo-Cicero, *iustitia* is demonstrated where "faith" is "zealously kept," "alliances and friendships . . . scrupulously honoured," and "ties of hospitality, clientage, kinship, and relationship by marriage . . . inviolably cherished."[41]

Fourth, justification is basically eschatological, but it can be experienced in the present because of Christ. Matthew 12:36-37 connects justi-

---

[41]Pseudo-Cicero *Rhet. ad Her.* 3.3.4; quoted in David deSilva, *An Introduction to the New Testament: Contexts, Methods & Ministry Formation* (Downers Grove, Ill.: InterVarsity Press, 2004), pp. 610-11.

fication with the eschaton: "I tell you, on the day of judgment you will have to give an account for every careless word you utter; for by your words you will be justified, and by your words you will be condemned." Similarly, the parable of the sheep and the goats describes the final judgment, in which the righteous are vindicated because of their works (Mt 25:31-46). Paul, in Galatians 5:4-5, describes righteousness as a future reality for Christians: "You who want to be justified by the law have cut yourselves off from Christ; you have fallen away from grace. For through the Spirit, by faith, we eagerly wait for the hope of righteousness" (Gal 5:4-5). At the last judgment, the righteous will be vindicated on the basis of their faith(fulness), their Spirit-empowered, obedient lives that derive from their trust in God through Christ.[42]

This same faith(fulness) marks in the present those who are in covenant relationship with God. Romans 5:9-10, above, describes both justification and reconciliation as an accomplished fact. While the atonement seems to be in view in those verses, the beginning of the same chapter lists blessings that believers already have by virtue of their justification:

> Therefore, since we are justified by faith, we have peace with God through our Lord Jesus Christ, through whom we have obtained access to this grace in which we stand; and we boast in our hope of sharing the glory of God. And not only that, but we also boast in our sufferings, knowing that suffering produces endurance, and endurance produces character, and character produces hope, and hope does not disappoint us, because God's love has been poured into our hearts through the Holy Spirit that has been given to us. (Rom 5:1-5).[43]

Because believers have been justified, they have peace with God—again emphasizing the relational character of justification. They experience God's grace, and they have the hope of sharing God's glory. They can

---

[42]Wright concludes that final judgment will be on the basis of works—that is, "the entirety of a life led" ("New Perspectives," p. 253). By contrast, Piper says final justification is "an act of public confirmation of a past, once-for-all, imputed righteousness received in this life at the first act of faith" (*Future of Justification*, p. 101). For Wright, then, justification is an eschatological verdict anticipated in the present, while for Piper, it is God's declaration in the present, which will simply be affirmed in the eschaton.

[43]The manuscript variant in verse one ("let us have peace with God"; see NRSV mg.) does not substantially change my point. Even if peace with God is a hope rather than a present possession, believers still experience God's grace and the presence of the Spirit because they have already been justified.

persevere through their sufferings because they experience God's love through the Holy Spirit. These verses seem to describe a causal relationship between being justified and receiving the blessings of salvation: peace with God, access to grace, the experience of the Spirit. This connection makes more sense if we understand justification here as the initiation of covenant relationship rather than as the vindication of a relationship that has already been established.

Similarly, Paul describes justification as past tense for the Corinthians: "But you were washed, you were sanctified, you were justified in the name of the Lord Jesus Christ and in the Spirit of our God" (1 Cor 6:11). Justification here is associated with sanctification (in the sense of being set apart for God), and cleansing or baptism, which again suggest initial salvation rather than vindication. In Titus 3:4-7, after connecting justification with regeneration and the reception of the Spirit, Paul adds, "so that, having been justified by his grace, we might become heirs according to the hope of eternal life." If justification makes one an heir of eternal life, it would seem to take place at conversion.

Thus justification is both past and future for Christians. While the future sense seems to refer to the vindication of God's covenant people, the past sense seems to refer to coming into covenant relationship with God. This would mean that justification (in the past sense) is not merely the declaration of a new legal status but the creation of a new relationship.

Finally, human beings are justified—whether in the past or the future sense—by faith(fulness). Paul insists that justification is by faith and not by works of the law. He demonstrates this point thoroughly in Romans 4 with the example of Abraham, who "believed God, and it was reckoned to him as righteousness" (Rom 4:3). Since Abraham was considered righteous before he was circumcised, his righteousness could not be based on the law. God's promise comes not through the law but through "the righteousness of faith" (Rom 4:13). Paul declares further in Galatians 2:16 that no one can be justified by works of the law.

However, while believers are justified by faith rather than by works of the law, to say that they are justified by faith *alone* is somewhat misleading. The phrase "faith alone" might imply—and for some, does imply—that obedience is irrelevant to salvation. However, we have already seen that *pistis* can mean both faith and faithfulness. Paul declares that the aim of his gospel is to bring the Gentiles to "the obedience of faith" (Rom 1:5; 16:26). Thus the "righteousness of faith" in Romans 4:13 is matched by the "obedience of faith" in Romans 1:5 and 16:26. Faith in Christ entails faithfulness made possible by the Holy Spirit (Rom 8:1-4).

For Protestants, who traditionally have insisted on justification by faith alone (*sola fide*), it may be startling that the only mention in the New Testament of "faith alone" (*pisteōs monon*) is by James, who rejects it: "You see that a person is justified by works and not by faith alone" (Jas 2:24). In 2:14-26, James is arguing that true faith will demonstrate itself in action. The faith is "brought to completion" by works (Jas 2:22). Paul would agree. Taking a stand on "faith alone," while a helpful reminder of our dependence on God's grace, has unfortunately led to a weak foundation for ethics in much Protestant theology.

Paul's insistence that justification depends upon faith rather than on works of the law is directed against Jewish claims to exclusivity: "For we hold that a person is justified by faith apart from works prescribed by the law. Or is God the God of Jews only? Is he not the God of Gentiles also? Yes, of Gentiles also" (Rom 3:28-29). Paul's logic runs as follows: If people are justified on the basis of the law, only Jews can be God's people. But God is not simply the God of the Jews, but the God of all nations. Therefore, justification cannot depend upon the law.[44]

Justification in the past sense (reconciliation) depends upon the faithfulness of Jesus in carrying out his mission and on the individual's faith in Christ as the fulfillment of God's promise. Justification in the future sense (vindication) depends upon the works of faithfulness that issue from an ongoing relationship with Christ (cf. Rom 2:13; 14:10-12; 1 Cor 3:13-15; 2 Cor 5:10). Thus when God justifies the ungodly (Rom 4:5), he is not acquitting the guilty. In the past, God reconciles the estranged; in the future, God vindicates the faithful.

Believers' faith, like Abraham's, is "reckoned" as righteousness (Rom 4:20-25). The word *logizomai* can mean to calculate, to take into account, to evaluate, to consider, or even to believe.[45] The traditional view interprets this expression as legal imputation: believers are not righteous, but because of their faith in Christ, Christ's righteousness is credited to their

---

[44]See the discussion in Wright, *Justification*, p. 212.
[45]"λογίζομαι," in *BAGD*, pp. 475-76.

account.[46] Notice, however, that *faith*, not *Christ's righteousness*, is reckoned as human righteousness. Paul is emphasizing that Abraham's faith, not his law-keeping, was the basis of his relationship with God. Paul's argument seems to be as follows: Just as law-keeping was the mark of covenant faithfulness under the old covenant, faith in Christ is the mark of covenant faithfulness under the new. Moreover, faith actually trumps the law, since faith has been the foundation of relationship between God and humanity since before the law was given. When people respond to God in faith, they are regarded as righteous because they have taken the first trusting step in a journey of covenant partnership that will require ongoing faithfulness. This understanding of "reckoning" has been beautifully expressed by Markus Barth:

> A trusting faithfulness on man's part is the right answer to the faithfulness God has shown in sending and resurrecting the intercessor. Believing means taking refuge in Jesus Christ's obedience and love, that is, in his faith. It means to live from it, with it, and according to it. . . . The "reckoning of faith as righteousness" is not a matter of bookkeeping, not a matter of carrying over an alien credit into an overdrawn bank account, surely not a matter of treating a man according to the fiction that he is in the right. Rather, it is the expression of the pleasure that God takes in a man's complete trust and obedience.[47]

To live faithfully in covenant relationship with God means also to live faithfully with others. Frank J. Matera urges us to "recover the social dimension of justification," expressed in the New Testament as the reconciliation of Jews and Gentiles to God and to one another. He points out that the justified "live in the sphere of God's Spirit," who empowers them to live as God desires.[48] According to Wright, justification is about God "putting the world to rights." Those who have been justified are called to be agents of God's restorative justice in the world.[49] Living righteously, in the biblical sense, means doing justice and showing mercy (Micah 6:8). "One is *made*

---

[46]Ladd, *Theology*, p. 491.

[47]Markus Barth, *Justification: Pauline Texts Interpreted in Light of the Old and New Testaments* (Grand Rapids: Eerdmans, 1971), pp. 66-67.

[48]Frank J. Matera, "Galatians and the Development of Paul's Teaching on Justification," *Word and World* 20, no. 3 (Summer 2000): 247, 248.

[49]Wright, *Justification*, p. 264.

righteous in order that one may *do* justice and righteousness."[50] When justification is understood in this way, it does not divide salvation from ethics.

God's *dikaiosynē* is not merely declarative but transformative. The end point of justification is "new heavens and a new earth, where righteousness is at home" (2 Pet 3:13). What began as the justification of Jews and Gentiles ends with the putting right of creation itself: "The Last Day discloses that in his judgment of Jews and Gentiles God was thinking of his whole creation and took mercy on all his works. . . . Now in the Last Judgment, the conclusive subordination of all powers proves that God's judging is in the end edification, building up; that in setting things *right* he has set them *upright* and saved his whole creation."[51]

CONCLUSION

This exploration has affirmed much of the New Perspective. God's righteousness is his covenant faithfulness, while human righteousness is faith(fulness) in response to God's grace. Justification is the eschatological vindication of the church as the true people of God. Those who will be vindicated can be recognized in the present by their faith in Christ rather than by their possession of the law. However, justification also refers to the way in which individuals become part of the people of God, as God reconciles them to himself through the death and resurrection of Christ. Justification is not simply declarative; it is the creation and fulfillment of a relationship sustained by God's grace. To live out this relationship, human beings place their trust in Christ, yield themselves to God for his righteous purposes, and cooperate with the Holy Spirit, who produces faithfulness in their lives (Gal 2:16; Rom 6:13; Gal 5:22-23).

The image of justification demonstrates that relationship is the essence of salvation. Like any relationship, our relationship with God begins with the decision to trust and grows through mutual faithfulness. While the relationship is not based upon our works but upon God's grace, our obedience is not optional but integral to the relationship. In fact, rather than separating faith and works, justification shows that faith is fulfilled and completed by works.

---

[50]James K. Bruckner, "Justice in Scripture," *Ex Auditu* 22 (2006): 4. See also the discussion in Kathryn Tanner, "Justification and Justice in a Theology of Grace," *Theology Today* 55, no. 4 (January 1999): 510-23.

[51]Barth, *Justification*, p. 77.

This image pictures God not as a lawgiver and judge, but as a covenant maker and covenant keeper. He extends to everyone, both Jews and Gentiles, the offer of covenant relationship with him through Christ. Justice is indispensable to this image—not a retributive justice that metes out appropriate punishment for sins, but a restorative justice that reconciles and heals. Instead of a criminal trial, perhaps the best modern analogy for justification would be family court, in which the ideal outcome is the restoration of relationships. As God's covenant partners, Christians should both practice and pursue God's kind of justice in the world.

This understanding of justification makes the best sense of Paul's argument in Romans. Chapters 9–11, which focus on Israel and the nations in God's plan, are not a lengthy digression in a book about individual salvation but the climax of the book. This is why chapter 11 ends with Paul's doxology to God's wisdom and mercy. Although the Jewish-Gentile issue may seem remote to modern Western Christians, Paul's solution to it is the spiritual heritage of every Gentile believer. It should inspire us to worship, as it did Paul.

Viewed in this way, justification has a more corporate emphasis than Protestants are accustomed to. It elevates the church to a degree that is not often found in Protestant theology. It may be less appealing to some than the traditional view, because Protestants are accustomed to thinking in individualistic terms. A gospel about Jews and Gentiles in the people of God may seem less immediate than a gospel about how I can get right with God. Nevertheless, justification shows God's loving faithfulness to all of us—and each of us—in a profound and personal way.

As Western society becomes more postmodern and pluralistic, Christians will need to consider carefully how they can work together for the sake of the kingdom. The covenantal context of the New Perspective may provide a framework for greater understanding between Catholics and Protestants.[52] It holds together the Protestant emphasis on grace and the

---

[52]Some evangelicals may regard this as a danger rather than an advantage of the New Perspective. One of Piper's objections to Wright's presentation of justification is that it does not clearly demonstrate the falsity of the Catholic understanding of final salvation: "Wright's statements about future justification are so similar to [the Catholic view] (even if his meaning isn't) that it is doubtful his paradigm will set Roman Catholics on a new conceptual playing field." *Future of Justification*, p. 183.

Catholic concern for the moral life.[53] Because the New Perspective does not divorce justification from sanctification, the New Perspective may help the church maintain its commitments to both evangelism and social concern.[54]

Paul's vision is also essential for a modern church that is becoming increasingly multicultural. Like the first-century Jewish believers, European and American Christians may need to be challenged by Paul's description of an ever-faithful God who keeps his promises in creative and surprising ways. What badges of covenant membership might God want us to give up so that he can welcome new people into his family? As the center of gravity for the church moves from Europe and America to the Two-Thirds World, can we welcome the moving of God's Spirit and willingly yield our privileged position? It will require humility for those who have been teachers to become learners again. But if we truly understand God's grace toward us, we can do no less.

FOR FURTHER READING

Barth, Markus. *Justification: Pauline Texts Interpreted in the Light of the Old and New Testaments*. Translated by A. M. Woodruff III. Grand Rapids: Eerdmans, 1971.

Bird, Michael F. *The Saving Righteousness of God: Studies on Paul, Justification and the New Perspective*. Milton Keynes, U.K.: Paternoster, 2007.

Bird, Michael F., and Preston Sprinkle, eds. *The Faith of Jesus Christ: Exegetical, Biblical, and Theological Studies*. Peabody, Mass.: Hendrickson, 2010.

Campbell, Douglas. *The Deliverance of God: An Apocalyptic Rereading of Justification in Paul*. Grand Rapids: Eerdmans, 2009.

Carson, D. A., Peter T. O'Brien and Mark A. Seifrid. *Justification and Variegated Nomism*. Vol. 1: *The Complexities of Second Temple Judaism*. Grand Rapids: Baker, 2001.

———. *Justification and Variegated Nomism*. Vol. 2: *The Paradoxes of Paul*. Grand Rapids: Baker, 2004.

Dunn, James D. G. *The New Perspective on Paul*. Rev. ed. Grand Rapids: Eerdmans, 2007.

---

[53]Matera expresses enthusiasm for the New Perspective in the context of the Lutheran/Catholic *Joint Declaration on the Doctrine of Justification*. "Paul's Teaching on Justification," pp. 239-48.

[54]Although not an advocate for the New Perspective, Frank Macchia connects the traditional split between justification and sanctification with the lack of integration "between the kerygmatic and the social missions of the church." "Justification through New Creation," p. 216.

Hays, Richard. *The Faith of Jesus Christ: The Narrative Substructure of Galatians 3:1–4:11*. Grand Rapids: Eerdmans, 2002.

Husbands, Mark, and Daniel J. Treier, eds. *Justification: What's at Stake in the Current Debates*. Downers Grove, Ill.: InterVarsity Press, 2004.

Ladd, George Eldon. *A Theology of the New Testament*. Edited by Donald A. Hagner. Rev. ed., Grand Rapids: Eerdmans, 1993, pp. 478-98.

Matera, Frank J. "Galatians and the Development of Paul's Teaching on Justification." *Word and World* 20, no. 3 (Summer 2000): 239-48.

———. "Galatians in Perspective: Cutting a New Path through Old Territory." *Interpretation* 54, no. 3 (July 2000): 233-45.

McGrath, Alister E. *Iustitia Dei: A History of the Christian Doctrine of Justification*. 2 vols. Cambridge: Cambridge University Press, 1986.

Piper, John. *The Future of Justification: A Response to N.T. Wright*. Wheaton, Ill.: Crossway, 2007.

Sanders, E. P. *Paul and Palestinian Judaism: A Comparison of Patterns of Religion*. Minneapolis: Augsburg Fortress, 1977.

Stendahl, Krister. "Paul and the Introspective Conscience of the West," pp. 78-96. In *Paul Among Jews and Gentiles, and Other Essays*. Minneapolis: Fortress, 1976.

Stuhlmacher, Peter, and Donald A. Hagner. *Revisiting Paul's Doctrine of Justification: A Challenge to the New Perspective*. Downers Grove, Ill.: InterVarsity Press, 2001.

Wax, Trevin. "The Justification Debate: A Primer." *Christianity Today*, June 2009, pp. 34-35.

Wright, N. T. *Justification: God's Plan & Paul's Vision*. Downers Grove, Ill.: InterVarsity Press, 2009.

10

ELECTION IN CHRIST
FOR THE SAKE
OF THE WORLD

NO TOPIC ENGENDERS LIVELIER DISCUSSION in my theology classes than election. Some students regard it as the key that unlocks the doctrine of salvation. Others regard it with deep suspicion. Still others wonder what all the fuss is about. At least once during the conversation, someone (on one side or the other) usually asks, "People don't really believe that, do they?" Believable or not, our view of election significantly influences our view of God and our understanding of God's purposes in salvation. Very different theologies claim the writings of Paul as their foundation.

Any discussion of election in the New Testament faces two critical issues: where should the discussion start, and what passages should be included? The interpreter's response to these two issues will strongly influence the outcome. For example, while William MacDonald begins an essay on election by recounting God's choices throughout salvation history, culminating in Jesus as the perfect revelation of God; Wayne Grudem, in his systematic theology, goes immediately to Paul's discussion of election in Romans.[1] These starting points are more amenable to Arminian and Calvinist interpretations, respectively.

---

[1]William G. MacDonald, "The Biblical Doctrine of Election," in *The Grace of God, the Will of Man: A Case for Arminianism*, ed. Clark H. Pinnock (Grand Rapids: Zondervan, 1989), pp. 207-29; and Wayne Grudem, *Systematic Theology* (Grand Rapids: Zondervan, 1995), p. 673. Grudem quotes Acts 13:48 before turning to Romans 8–9.

Moreover, distinguishing on a priori grounds between religious and nonreligious instances of choosing can allow interpreter to exclude passages that do not support their perspective. When Jesus says that he has chosen the Twelve, yet one of them is a devil (Jn 6:70), is he speaking about election as his apostle or election to salvation, or both? If the interpreter assumes that the elect always persevere, he or she can avoid dealing with contrary data by declaring that this verse is not relevant to a discussion of election to salvation.[2] In this chapter, I will try to avoid this problem by examining the range of passages that deal with choosing to see what they might say about election.

TERMS AND CONCEPTS

The main Hebrew word for election is *bāhar*, meaning to select or prefer. In the Old Testament, this word is always found as a verb, never as a noun. This suggests that election is thought of as an action rather than as a condition. The verbal forms emphasize the one doing the choosing and the one chosen.[3] Sometimes a human being chooses a person, a place, a teaching or a way of life. For example, Israel can choose life or death (Deut 30:9); choose to serve God or idols (Josh 24:15); choose to serve the Lord and make a covenant with him (Josh 24:22); or choose their own way and delight in abominations (Is 66:3).

Usually God is the one doing the choosing. God chooses Israel to be his people (Deut 7:6-11). He also chooses individuals within Israel, especially prophets and kings: Moses and Aaron (Ps 105:26), David and Solomon (1 Sam 16:7-13; 1 Chron 28:5-6), Isaiah and Jeremiah (Is 49:1; Jer 1:5). God chooses Saul, but later rejects him (1 Sam 10:24; 16:1). Being chosen by God is often spoken of in terms of servanthood (Ps 105:26; Is 45:4). God also chooses people outside of Israel, including the Chaldeans (Hab 1:12), and raises up Cyrus of Persia, his "anointed" (Is 45:1, 4).[4] Finally, God chooses a special Servant (Is 42:1, 6).

---

[2] See for example, Bruce Demarest, *The Cross and Salvation*, Foundations of Evangelical Theology Series (Wheaton, Ill.: Crossway, 1997), p. 119. Demarest states (without supporting the point) that John 13:18, which excludes Judas, refers to election to salvation, while John 6:70 refers to election to service.

[3] L. Coenen, "Elect, Choose," in *NIDNTT* 1:537.

[4] Although Cyrus is called God's anointed, the word for choosing does not occur in this passage. Nevertheless, given the significance of anointing in the Old Testament, it seems appropriate to include him.

In all of these cases, God chooses people to serve him and carry out his will. His choice often entails special privilege but always entails special responsibility.[5] These Old Testament examples suggest that the often-asked question of whether election is to a task or to salvation is misleading. Being chosen by God means being called to service, but God takes care of his servants. He rewards their faithfulness, but he can also reject them if they are faithless. In Jeremiah 18:6-12, God promises that he will withdraw his blessings from nations if they turn away from him. In Ezekiel 18:1-32, he promises the same for individuals. However, both of these passages declare that those under God's judgment can be restored if they repent. Isaiah prophesies that God will again choose Israel when he brings them back from exile (Is 14:1; 41:8-9). These passages suggest that election in the Old Testament is not God's pretemporal choice of an individual's eternal destiny but God's temporal choice of people for privilege and service. Election can be forfeited, but even this condition need not be permanent.

The primary word for election in the New Testament is *eklegomai*, which means to select or choose or pick out for oneself.[6] Sometimes people choose a thing or course of action, as when guests choose the places of honor at a banquet (Lk 14:7) or Mary chooses the "better part"—sitting at Jesus' feet (Lk 10:42). People also choose leaders or representatives (Acts 6:5; 15:22). As in the Old Testament, however, God or Jesus usually chooses. God chooses the weak and foolish things to shame the strong and wise (1 Cor 1:27-28). He chooses Jesus (Lk 9:35; 23:35; 1 Pet 2:4, 6). He chooses Israel (Acts 13:7; Rom 11:28). He chooses believers in Christ, almost always as a corporate reference (Lk 18:4; Rom 8:33; Col 3:12; 2 Tim 2:10). Rufus in Romans 16:13 is also "chosen in the Lord," although Paul may simply be saying that he is a choice or precious Christian.[7] The "elect lady" of 2 John 1 is probably a congregation. God's choice of Jacob over Esau (Rom 9:11) will be explored in detail below. In 1 Timothy 5:21, angels are called elect. Jesus chooses his disciples, including Judas (Mk 3:14-

---

[5]Harold H. Rowley, *The Biblical Doctrine of Election* (Eugene, Ore.: Wipf & Stock, 2009), p. 45.

[6]Coenen, "Elect, Choose," in *NIDNTT* 1:536.

[7]C. K. Barrett renders this phrase as "outstanding Christian." *A Commentary on the Epistle to the Romans*, Harper's New Testament Commentaries, ed. Henry Chadwick (1957; reprint, Peabody, Mass.: Hendrickson, 1987), p. 285.

15; Lk 6:13; Jn 6:70). One passage seems to imply that he has not chosen Judas: "I am not speaking of all of you; I know whom I have chosen" (Jn 13:18). However, Raymond Brown renders the second part of the sentence as "I know the kind of men I chose"—meaning that Jesus had chosen Judas even knowing the kind of person he was, because it was necessary for the Scriptures to be fulfilled.[8] Jesus also chooses Paul to be apostle to the Gentiles (Acts 9:15).

In the New Testament, as in the Old, God chooses people to belong to him and serve him. While election does not always entail salvation, the salvific associations of election are stronger in the New Testament than in the Old, if only because the concept of salvation is more fully developed. All instances in which people are identified as "elect" refer to people already in relationship with God. "The elect" seems to be a way to refer to the church as God's chosen people, like Israel in the Old Testament. This may explain the elect angels of 1 Timothy 5:21—not angels who have been selected to receive salvation, but angels who are in fellowship with God. The expectation of service is inherent in election in the New Testament, as in the Old. H. H. Rowley declares that by claiming to be "the heir of Israel's election," the church took on "the obligation of Israel's mission."[9]

While elect is used to refer to those already in relationship with God, Paul uses the word *kaleō* (to call) for God's invitation to human beings to join him in his kingdom purposes.[10] In some instances, people are called out of the kingdom of darkness into the kingdom of God (1 Thess 2:12; 1 Pet 2:9). In other instances, they are called to belong to Jesus Christ or are called into his fellowship (Rom 1:6; 1 Cor 1:9). Romans 9:11-12 identifies God's call as the basis of election. Like "the elect," "the called" is a term for Christians collectively (Rom 8:28; 1 Cor 1:24; Jude 1:1). The word *kaleō* is useful because it suggests both invitation and vocation. Paul

---

[8]Raymond E. Brown, *The Gospel According to* John, 2 vols., Anchor Bible, ed. William Foxwell Albright and David Noel Freedman (New York: Doubleday, 1970), 2:549, 553. The perspective of the Fourth Gospel is sharply dualistic. Events in Jesus' ministry are the visible manifestations of a spiritual struggle between light and darkness, God and Satan. Just as Jesus is from God, his Father, his opponents are from Satan, their father (Jn 8:44). Judas has become an agent of Satan in this struggle (Jn 13:2, 27).

[9]Rowley, *Election*, p. 161.

[10]I. Howard Marshall, "Election and Calling to Salvation in 1 and 2 Thessalonians," in *The Thessalonian Correspondence*, ed. Raymond F. Collins, Bibliotheca Ephemeridum Theologicarum Lovaniensium (Louvain: Leuven University Press, 1990), p. 269.

is called to be an apostle (Rom 1:1); then the Thessalonians are called to salvation through his apostolic ministry (2 Thess 2:13-14). Paul's own calling on the Damascus Road seems to be both an invitation to salvation and a vocation (Gal 1:15-16).

Calling is divinely initiated but requires human response. I. Howard Marshall has identified four elements of calling in 1 and 2 Thessalonians: "a. the initial call through the gospel and the continuing call to faith; b. the goal of the call, which is final salvation; c. the need for a response in a way of life which is appropriate to the God who calls; and d. the promise that the God who calls is faithful in providing the means for his people to respond."[11] Like election, calling involves both privilege and responsibility. Paul often refers to God's call in order to emphasize the believer's responsibility to live a life worthy of that call (Eph 4:1; 1 Thess 2:12). He says that believers are called to be holy (Rom 1:1), to live in freedom (Gal 5:13), and to practice peace in their relationships (1 Cor 7:15). He exhorts Timothy, "But as for you, man of God, shun all this; pursue righteousness, godliness, faith, love, endurance, gentleness. Fight the good fight of the faith; take hold of the eternal life, to which you were called and for which you made the good confession in the presence of many witnesses" (1 Tim 6:11-12). God called Timothy to eternal life; now Timothy must exert himself to take hold of that life by avoiding sin and pursuing righteousness. Since Paul has just warned Timothy about the destructive power of materialism to draw people away from the faith, he seems to be suggesting that Timothy's actions will influence whether or not he attains the eternal life to which he has been called.

The term *helkō* (to draw) is a concept similar to calling that appears in the Gospel of John. Jesus draws people to himself universally through the cross: "And I, when I am lifted up from the earth, will draw all people to myself" (Jn 12:32). God also draws people to Jesus. This drawing is so critical that no one can come to Jesus without it (Jn 6:44, 65). It appears to be not a private work of the Holy Spirit upon individuals but God's public testimony through Scripture (Jn 5:37-40), the ministry of John (Jn 5:33), and the miracles and teaching of Jesus himself (Jn 5:36; 7:16). God gives to Jesus those who belong to God—that is, those who have "heard and

---

[11] Ibid., p. 270.

learned from the Father" (Jn 6:37-39, 45-46).

The Greek word *proorizō* (predestine) occurs six times in the New Testament. In two instances, God predestines the work of Christ in salvation (Acts 4:28; 1 Cor 2:7). In the other four instances, God predestines people. Rather than God's choice of some for salvation, however, these instances seem to refer to the destiny God has prepared for his people: conformity to the image of Christ (Rom 8:29-30), adoption (Eph 1:5) and inheritance (Eph 1:11). The decisive event to secure this destiny was the cross and resurrection of Christ: "God predestines from the cross and resurrection of Jesus to future Glory and not from pre-historical time to our conversion."[12] Thus God has determined beforehand that Christ would accomplish salvation and that those in Christ would be conformed to his image and would share in his blessings.

A possibly similar word, *tetagmenoi*, occurs in Acts 13:48. After Paul and Barnabas had preached at Pisidian Antioch, "as many as had been destined [*tetagmenoi*] for eternal life became believers." The word *tetagmenoi* is the perfect middle or passive participle of *tassō*, which means to place or station or appoint or classify.[13] Some read this instance of the word as a divine passive: those whom God had previously appointed to eternal life became believers at this time. By contrast, reading *tetagmenoi* as a middle would mean that the persons in question positioned *themselves* for eternal life. Most English translations (like the NRSV above) opt for the passive. Even as a passive, however, the word need not imply divine selection to salvation. The *BAGD* lexicon renders the word in Acts 13:48 as a passive with the sense of "belong to, be classed among those possessing."[14] In this view, those who belonged to eternal life became believers. The reason for their "belonging" is not stated.

The context of Acts 13:48 seems to militate against reading *tetagmenoi* as a divine passive. Paul and Barnabas have been preaching the gospel in Pisidian Antioch for over a week and have encountered opposition from some of the Jews. As they address the crowds on the second Sabbath, they

---

[12]Carey C. Newman, "Election and Predestination in Ephesians 1:4-6a: An Exegetical-Theological Study of the Historical, Christological Realization of God's Purpose," *Review and Expositor* 93 (1996): 241.

[13]"τάσσω," in *BAGD*, pp. 805-6.

[14]Ibid., p. 806. The authors list the verse under definition 1b along with 1 Corinthians 16:15 ("they have devoted themselves [*etaxan heautous*] to the service of the saints").

declare that since the Jews are rejecting the gospel, they will turn to the Gentiles. A clear contrast is drawn between the Jews who "reject" the word of God and "judge [them]selves to be unworthy of eternal life" (Acts 13:46) and the Gentiles who "were glad and praised the word of the Lord" (Acts 13:48). Unlike the Jews, these Gentiles have taken Paul's message to heart and are ready to respond to the gospel. The emphasis on human volition for both Jews and Gentiles makes it unlikely that the narrator would say in Acts 13:48 that God had predetermined who would believe. The best translation of Acts 13:48 might be something like "as many as were positioned for eternal life became believers." This rendering opts for the passive (suggested by *ēsan tetagmenoi*) but makes room for the confluence of divine and human agency (the preaching of the gospel and the receptivity of the audience) that is suggested by the context.[15]

The word *proginōskō* (to foreknow) and its noun form, *prognōsis* (foreknowledge), occur seven times in the New Testament. Twice people foreknow facts (Acts 26:5; 2 Pet 3:17). Once God foreknows events (Acts 2:23). Four times God foreknows people (Israel in Rom 11:2; Christ in 1 Pet 1:20; and believers in Rom 8:29 and 1 Pet 1:2). *Proginōskō* can mean not only to know something or someone beforehand but also to know someone or something previously (that is, before the time in question). For example, in Acts 26:5 Paul says that the Jews "have known for a long time" (*proginōskontes*) that he was a practicing Pharisee. Peter tells his readers that they are "forewarned" (*proginōskontes*) about God's coming judgment of the earth (2 Pet 3:17).

In his Pentecost sermon, Peter tells the Jews that the crucifixion took place "according to the definite plan and foreknowledge of God" (Acts 2:23). Thus God both predestines and foreknows the work of Christ in salvation. It certainly makes sense that God knows beforehand about events that he plans to bring about.

But what does it mean when God foreknows people? Peter's statement that Jesus was "destined [literally, "foreknown" (*proegnōsmenou*)] before the foundation of the world" (1 Pet 1:20) seems to be a reference to Christ's

---

[15]See also the discussions in I. Howard Marshall, *The Acts of the Apostles: An Introduction and Commentary*, Tyndale New Testament Commentaries, ed. R. V. G. Tasker (Grand Rapids: Eerdmans, 1986), pp. 230-31; Robert Shank, *Elect in the Son: A Study of the Doctrine of Election* (Minneapolis: Bethany House, 1989), pp. 183-88; and MacDonald, "Election," pp. 226-28.

preexistence—in other words, God has known Jesus since the before the world was created. It may also refer to God's plan for Jesus to accomplish salvation. According to Romans 11:2, God also foreknew Israel: "God has not rejected his people whom he foreknew [*proegnō*]." Paul is defending God's faithfulness to Israel, as he has been in chapters 9 and 10. In view of the context, which has rehearsed God's history with Israel, it seems preferable to translate *proegnō* as "has known for a long time." God has not been faithful to his people for over a thousand years only to abandon them now.

The two instances in which God foreknows believers are connected with election and predestination. Peter describes his audience as those "who have been chosen and destined by [literally "chosen according to the foreknowledge of" (*kata prognōsin*)] God the Father and sanctified by the Spirit to be obedient to Jesus Christ and to be sprinkled with his blood" (1 Pet 1:2). Paul argues that God works for good in the lives of believers: "For those whom he foreknew [*proegnō*] he also predestined to be conformed to the image of his Son, in order that he might be the firstborn within a large family" (Rom 8:29).

These passages clearly state that foreknowledge logically precedes election and predestination. Arminians usually understand this to mean that God's choice of individuals for salvation is based upon his knowledge of how they will respond to the gospel.[16] Calvinists usually interpret foreknowledge as God's intimate personal knowledge of the individuals he has chosen for salvation.[17] Given the other uses of foreknowledge, which are more informational than relational, the Arminian position seems to be stronger. However, if election generally refers to those in God's service, foreknowledge may simply mean that God knows people before they enter his service. For example, Jesus explains to Nathaniel that he knew him before Philip called him because he saw him sitting under the fig tree (Jn 1:47-48). God is involved in people's lives before they hear and respond to his call.

---

[16]For a recent statement of the classical Arminian position, see Robert E. Picirilli, *Grace, Faith, Free Will: Contrasting Views of Salvation: Calvinism & Arminianism* (Nashville: Randall House, 2002). Picirilli prefers to say that God elects individuals to salvation based upon his foreknowledge, and he elects these individuals as believers. He acknowledges, however, that "election according to foreseen faith" may be "the best we can do while we continue to face the problem of eternity and time" (pp. 55-56).

[17]See Grudem, *Systematic Theology*, p. 1242.

CORPORATE ELECTION IN CHRIST

Election in the Bible is primarily corporate and covenantal.[18] Of central importance to the New Testament concept of election is the election of Israel:

> For you are a people holy to the LORD your God; the LORD your God has chosen you out of all the peoples on earth to be his people, his treasured possession. It was not because you were more numerous than any other people that the LORD set his heart on you and chose you—for you were the fewest of all peoples. It was because the LORD loved you and kept the oath that he swore to your ancestors, that the LORD has brought you out with a mighty hand, and redeemed you from the house of slavery, from the hand of Pharaoh king of Egypt. Know therefore that the LORD your God is God, the faithful God who maintains covenant loyalty with those who love him and keep his commandments, to a thousand generations, and who repays in their own person those who reject him. He does not delay but repays in their own person those who reject him. Therefore, observe diligently the commandment—the statutes and the ordinances—that I am commanding you today. (Deut 7:6-11)

God has chosen Israel not because of their merit but because of his love. God's choice of Israel means that Israel has a special relationship with God, as God's "treasured possession." Israel's election was initiated by God's gracious act of redemption (the exodus) but entails human responsibility (keeping God's commandments). God and Israel have a covenant relationship that requires faithfulness on both sides. Although God's covenant faithfulness is assured, Israel must reciprocate with love and obedience; otherwise they run the risk of being "repaid" for their rejection of God. Election here is clearly a corporate concept. Individuals participate in the election as members of the people of Israel. Non-Israelites such as Caleb, Rahab and Ruth can become part of God's people. Individuals who do not keep the covenant can be cut off from God's people (Gen 17:16; Lev 20:6; 23:29).

Election in the New Testament is also corporate. New Testament writers describe the church as God's chosen people: "You are a chosen race, a royal priesthood, a holy nation, God's own people, in order that you may

---

[18]See the discussion in William W. Klein, *The New Chosen People: A Corporate View of Election* (Grand Rapids: Zondervan, 1990), pp. 257-74 and *passim*.

proclaim the mighty acts of him who called you out of darkness into his marvelous light" (1 Pet 2:9). As Paul explains in Romans 11:11-24, God has not broken his covenant with Israel, but Jewish participation in his chosen people, like Gentile participation in that people, is based on their faith(fulness)—in particular, on their trust in Christ as the fulfillment of God's promises. First Peter, which begins with an address to the Christian Diaspora who are chosen by God, ends with a greeting from "your sister church [literally, "she who is"] in Babylon, chosen together with you" (1 Pet 5:13). The idea of being "chosen together with" someone else, whether a congregation or an individual, is more consistent with a corporate view of election than with an individual view. Furthermore, a corporate view of election reflects the more corporate sense of personal identity in the first century Mediterranean world.[19]

Besides being corporate, election in the New Testament is in Christ.[20] As Karl Barth has observed, "God's eternal election of grace is concretely the election of Jesus Christ."[21] Ephesians 1:4 makes this point clearly: God "chose [believers] in Christ before the foundation of the world to be holy and blameless before him."[22] This statement echoes God's command to Abram in Genesis 17:1: "I am God Almighty; walk before me, and be blameless." Jesus is the Elect One, the Beloved (Eph 1:6). Individual believers participate in the election by participating in him.

It is only in Christ that believers are elect "before the foundation of the world." Because the pre-existent Christ is elect from eternity past, the church can be said to participate in his pretemporal election.[23] Ephesians

---

[19]See the discussion in chapters two and three.

[20]Robert Shank has argued this point at length and with extensive exegetical support in *Elect in the Son*, pp. 27-55 and *passim*. "In God's eternal purpose the believers are contemplated as existing in Christ, as the Head, the Summary, of the race. The *ekloge* . . . has no separate existence independently of the *eklektos*. . . . The election of Christ involves implicitly the election of the Church" (p. 43).

[21]Karl Barth, *Church Dogmatics*, ed. G. W. Bromiley and T. F. Torrance, trans. G. W. Bromiley (Edinburgh: T & T Clark, 1958), 4/2:31. I agree with Barth that election is solely in Christ, but I differ from him in believing that individuals must place their faith in Christ in order to participate in the election.

[22]J. B. Lightfoot comments on "in Christ" in Ephesians 1:4: "by virtue of our incorporation in, our union with, Christ." *Notes on the Epistles of St. Paul* (Grand Rapids: Zondervan, 1957), p. 312. According to Roger Forster and Paul Marsten, "We are chosen in Christ. The church is elect because it is in Christ and he is elect." Roger T. Forster and V. Paul Marsten, *God's Strategy in Human History* (Wheaton, Ill.: Tyndale House, 1973), p. 130.

[23]Carey Newman, "Election and Predestination," pp. 239-40. Newman insists, however, that

1:13 implies that believers become part of the elect body when they hear
the word and place their trust in Christ: "In him you also, when you had
heard the word of truth, the gospel of your salvation, and had believed in
him, were marked with the seal of the promised Holy Spirit." The NIV
translation of this verse suggests corporate election in Christ even more
strongly: "And you also were *included in Christ* when you heard the word of
truth, the gospel of your salvation. Having believed, you were marked in
him with a seal, the promised Holy Spirit" (emphasis mine). As the Chosen One, Jesus mediates the blessings of salvation to all those who belong
to him. Chapter eleven explores more fully the blessings believers have
through participation in Christ.

As in the Old Testament, election is not based on merit but on God's
grace. Paul takes pains to point out that the Corinthians are not elect because of any nobility or accomplishments of their own; they are among the
"weak" and "foolish" things chosen by God to confound the powerful and
wise (1 Cor 1:26-31). K. K. Yeo argues that Paul uses the rhetoric of election
and calling to restructure the Thessalonians' notions of honor and shame.
This language confers honor upon them and gives them both purpose and
hope. It thereby motivates them to live in a way that honors God.[24]

All of the concepts we have examined—election, calling, drawing, predestination, positioning, foreknowledge—emphasize divine initiative. Jesus enacts this divine initiative in his calling of the disciples: "You did not
choose me but I chose you" (Jn 15:16). However, none of these concepts
precludes the need for human response. As Rowley observes, "They were
chosen and called for service. It was realized that the grace of God became
effective for them when they yielded to that grace, and that it can only become effective for those who do so yield."[25] Paul tells the Thessalonians,
"God chose you as the first fruits for salvation through sanctification by the
Spirit and through belief in the truth" (2 Thess 2:13).[26] God had decided

---

election is accomplished in the historical events of the life, death and resurrection of Christ.
Individuals are included in the election when they respond to the gospel in faith.

[24]K. K. Yeo, "The Rhetoric of Election and Calling Language in 1 Thessalonians," in *Rhetorical Criticism and the Bible*, ed. Stanley E. Porter and Dennis L. Stamps, Journal for the Study
of the New Testament Supplement Series (London: Sheffield, 2002), pp. 527, 532, 533, 538,
546.

[25]Rowley, *Election*, p. 170.

[26]The word for choosing here is not *eklegomai* but *haireomai*. Manuscript variants result in different renderings: NRSV and TNIV say that God has chosen the Thessalonians as "first fruits,"

that they were to be among the first people reached by the gospel, but both the work of the Holy Spirit and their own response of faith were necessary for their salvation. Similarly, Paul tells the Thessalonians that he knows that they are chosen because he witnessed both the power of the gospel he preached to them and the authenticity of their response (1 Thess 1:4-10).

It is significant that people are not called elect before they become believers. I. H. Marshall has noted that if election were decided pretemporally, we would expect to find some instances in which persons were called "elect" before they came to faith. But this is not the case either in the Bible or in pre-Christian Jewish literature.[27] Elect and non-elect are not eternal categories predetermined by God but temporal categories created by the gospel proclamation: those who accept the gospel become the elect, while those who reject it become the non-elect. As Carey Newman states, "*Election is historical. . . . Further, our incorporation into the electing purposes of God is an historical event.*"[28]

One passage that seems to contradict this idea is 2 Timothy 2:10: "Therefore I endure everything for the sake of the elect, so that they may also obtain the salvation that is in Christ Jesus, with eternal glory." Paul here describes the elect as those who have not yet received salvation. However, since Paul seems to have final salvation in mind, as implied by "eternal glory," he is likely saying that he endures suffering so that the church may persevere. Revelation 17:14, which refers to those with the Lamb as "called and chosen and faithful," may imply a brief order of salvation: God's call, the formation of a covenant relationship as part of God's chosen people, and a faithful life growing out of that relationship.

God's calling can be resisted, and election can be forfeited. In the Old Testament, both Saul and Israel were chosen and then rejected by God. In the New Testament, numerous passages state or imply that people can resist God's purposes. For example, in Matthew 23:37, Jesus laments that he wants to gather the people of Jerusalem but they are not willing. His apoc-

---

while NIV and NASB say that God has chosen them "from the beginning." The 4th edition of the United Bible Society's *Greek New Testament* chooses ἀπαρχήν (first fruits). *The Greek New Testament*, ed. Barbara Aland et al., 4th rev. ed. (Stuttgart: Deutsche Bibelgesellschaft and United Bible Societies, 1998). The two expressions are very close in Greek: ἀπαρχήν (first fruits) vs. ἀπ' ἀρχῆς (from the beginning). In early uncial manuscripts, which had no punctuation or word divisions, the difference would be a single letter.

[27]Marshall, "Election and Calling," pp. 263-65, esp. p. 263 n. 13 and p. 264 n. 14.

[28]Newman, "Election and Predestination," pp. 238-39 (italics in original).

alyptic warning in Matthew 24:24 (=Mk 13:22) implies that the elect can be led astray. Similarly, Luke declares that the Pharisees and lawyers have "rejected God's purpose for themselves" by refusing to be baptized by John (Lk 7:30). He further states that Judas "turned aside" from his apostleship (Acts 1:25). In Acts 7:51, Stephen accuses his audience of "forever opposing the Holy Spirit" as their ancestors had done. Paul implies that attempting to be justified by works of the law, as the Galatians were doing, would be to nullify the grace of God extended in Christ (Gal 2:21). Peter describes false teachers who "deny the Master who bought them" (2 Pet 2:1). He urges believers to make their calling and election certain by "[making] every effort" to grow in godly character (2 Pet 1:5-11). Finally, God's desire to save all people (2 Pet 3:9) apparently will not be fulfilled, if the numerous references to hell in the New Testament are any indication.

The possibility of forfeiting election makes sense if election is primarily to service. Persistent refusal to carry out God's mission would mean the end of election.[29] However, in Romans 11:29, Paul declares that "the gifts and the calling God are irrevocable." The word translated "irrevocable" in the NRSV, *ametamelēta*, means "not to be regretted." It refers to something that one will not take back.[30] Paul is emphasizing God's faithfulness; God will not be false to his word and withdraw his offer of grace. Barrett renders this statement as "God does not go back on his acts of grace and his calling."[31] This verse does not say that the status of election, as such, is irrevocable.

The parable of the great banquet (Mt 22:1-14; Lk 14:15-24) illustrates divine/human interaction in calling and election. The host has prepared his guest list and calls his guests to the banquet, but the guests refuse to come. In response, the master tells his servants to invite as many people as they can find, whether reputable or disreputable. In Luke's version, the master expresses his desire that his house may be full, and adds, "None of those who were invited [literally, called (*keklēmenōn*)] will taste my dinner" (Lk 14:24). In Matthew, the king fills the house but ejects one guest who is not wearing a wedding garment. He adds, "For many are called, but few are chosen" (Mt 22:14). In both versions, the initiative lies with the host, but the host's invitation can be rejected. The host is determined to

[29]Rowley, *Election*, p. 68.
[30]"ἀμεταμέλητος," in *BAGD*, p. 45.
[31]Barrett, *Romans*, pp. 221, 225.

have a banquet, so he throws away the guest list in order to include as many people as possible. However, the episode of the wedding garment reminds us that participation must be on the host's terms.

As a parable of the kingdom, the great banquet illustrates the inclusiveness of the gospel invitation. It suggests a call to salvation that is both universal and resistible. In Jesus' ministry, the original guests—the leaders of Israel—were rejecting his invitation, while others, both reputable and disreputable, were responding to it. Although Matthew's version says that few are chosen, the house is at least as full by the end as it would have been if the original guests had come. The point may be that receiving a call from God does not guarantee salvation; those who hear the gospel must respond and accept God's terms in order to become members of the elect.

Robert Shank argues that election is unconditional for the church but conditional for individuals in the church. He bases his conclusion on passages in Ephesians and Colossians that describe God's purpose to create a people who are holy and blameless (*hagious kai anōmous*). Ephesians 1:3-4 describes God's purpose; Ephesians 5:25-27 describes its unconditional fulfillment for the church, and Colossians 1:21-23 describes its conditional fulfillment for individuals:

> Blessed be the God and Father of our Lord Jesus Christ, who has blessed us in Christ with every spiritual blessing in the heavenly places, just as he chose us in Christ before the foundation of the world to be *holy and blameless* before him in love. (Eph 1:3-4)

> Husbands, love your wives, just as Christ loved the church and gave himself up for her, in order to make her holy by cleansing her with the washing of water by the word, so as to present the church to himself in splendor, without a spot or wrinkle or anything of the kind—yes, so that she may be *holy and without blemish*. (Eph 5:25-27)

> And you who were once estranged and hostile in mind, doing evil deeds, he has now reconciled in his fleshly body through death, so as to present you *holy and blameless* and irreproachable before him—provided that you continue securely established and steadfast in the faith, without shifting from the hope promised by the gospel that you heard, which has been proclaimed to every creature under heaven. (Col 1:21-23)[32]

---

[32]Shank, *Elect in the Son*, p. 49. I have quoted the verses from the NRSV rather than reproducing Shank's paraphrase (emphasis mine).

Thus God has chosen the church in Christ and has prepared a glorious destiny for its members, but he has not predetermined who those members will be. The election of Christ, and the church in Christ, takes place *in eternity*; the election of individuals to salvation takes place *in time* as those individuals respond to the gospel and become part of the chosen people of God.

Some scholars argue that God cannot elect the church without electing to salvation every individual within it. However, even with the limited foreknowledge available to human beings, I can elect to teach a course and predestine that the course will be worth four credits without predetermining which students will take it. Concern is sometimes expressed that the idea of corporate election does not ensure that anyone will actually be saved. However, since the New Testament seems to indicate that some will be (and Hebrews 11 suggests that some already have been), this objection does not seem to have much practical force.

ELECT FOR THE SAKE OF THE WORLD

Election has several purposes. As already mentioned, the elect enjoy God's favor and carry out his will. The elect should also demonstrate God's character: "As God's chosen ones, holy and beloved, clothe yourselves with compassion, kindness, humility, meekness, and patience" (Col 3:12). Finally, as God's people, the elect will be rescued and blessed by God. However, the blessing of the elect is not the only goal of election.

Perhaps surprisingly, one of the central purposes of election is *to benefit the non-elect*. God chooses individuals and nations so that they will be channels of his blessing to the world. This is very clear in God's election of the patriarchs. For example, God tells Abram, "In you all the families of the earth shall be blessed" (Gen 12:2-3; cf. Gen 18:18; 22:18). God repeats both his promise of blessing and his commission to bless all nations in his election of Isaac (Gen 26:4) and Jacob (Gen 28:14). At Sinai, God declares to Israel, "Now therefore, if you obey my voice and keep my covenant, you shall be my treasured possession out of all the peoples. Indeed, the whole earth is mine, but you shall be for me a priestly kingdom and a holy nation" (Ex 19:5-6). God has chosen Israel "out of all the peoples," but for the benefit of all the peoples. They are to serve God as priests to mediate the knowledge of God to the nations.[33] In the words of Terrance Fretheim, "God's initially exclusive move is for the sake of a maximally inclusive end."[34]

Walter Brueggemann observes, "In these traditions of promise, Israel, by its life and its obedience, is entrusted with the well-being of the nations."[35] God intends that the blessing extended to the world through Israel will counteract the curse that has resulted from the fall, so that creation can enjoy the well-being God intended.[36] New Testament writers quote Genesis 26:4 and 28:14 as they declare that God's commission is being fulfilled in the spreading of the gospel to both Jews (Acts 3:8) and Gentiles (Gal 3:8). The commission is finally fulfilled in the vision of Revelation 7:9, when "a great multitude . . . from every nation, from all tribes and peoples and languages" gathers before the throne of God in worship.·

This theme of election for the sake of the world continues through the rest of the Old Testament. The Mosaic law includes provisions to benefit foreigners living in Israel (e.g., Lev 23:22; Deut 10:17-19). The prophets envision Israel as a magnet drawing all nations to the worship of the Lord (Is 2:2; Jer 3:17; Mic 4:2; Zech 8:22). Sometimes the responsibility to bless the nations is concentrated in a representative figure, such as the king (Ps 72:17). This representation culminates in Isaiah's figure of the Servant, who sometimes is identified as Israel (Is 49:3) but other times seems to be an individual who represents Israel:

> Here is my servant, whom I uphold, my chosen, in whom my soul delights; I have put my spirit upon him; he will bring forth justice to the nations. He will not cry or lift up his voice, or make it heard in the street; a bruised reed he will not break, and a dimly burning wick he will not quench; he will faithfully bring forth justice. He will not grow faint or be crushed until he has established justice in the earth; and the coastlands wait for his teaching. . . . I am the Lord, I have called you in righteousness, I have taken you by the hand and kept you; I have given you as a covenant to the people, a light to the nations, to open the eyes that are blind, to bring out the prisoners from the dungeon, from the prison those who sit in darkness. (Is 42:1-7)

---

[33]Göran Larsson, *Bound for Freedom: The Book of Exodus in Jewish and Christian Traditions* (Peabody, Mass.: Hendrickson, 1999), pp. 130-33. See also Rowley, *Election*, pp. 59-60.

[34]Terrance Fretheim, *The Pentateuch* (Nashville: Abingdon, 1996), p. 118.

[35]Brueggemann, *Theology of the Old Testament*, p. 168.

[36]Walter Brueggemann, *An Introduction to the Old Testament: The Canon and Christian Imagination* (Louisville, Ky.: Westminster John Knox Press, 2003), p. 46.

The Servant is God's Chosen One, God's Beloved, who bears God's Spirit. He will fulfill the purpose of Israel's election to be "a light to the nations." He will be righteous and he will "bring forth justice" in the world. He himself will be God's covenant to the people, suggesting that he will mediate relationship with God. He will accomplish this through a ministry of teaching, healing and liberation. In Isaiah 49:6, God declares, "It is too light a thing that you should be my servant to raise up the tribes of Jacob and to restore the survivors of Israel; I will give you as a light to the nations, that my salvation may reach to the end of the earth."

New Testament writers identify Isaiah's Servant as Jesus. Matthew 12:17-21 declares that Jesus has fulfilled the prophecy in Isaiah 42:1-4

> This was to fulfill what had been spoken through the prophet Isaiah: "Here is my servant, whom I have chosen, my beloved, with whom my soul is well pleased. I will put my Spirit upon him, and he will proclaim justice to the Gentiles. He will not wrangle or cry aloud, nor will anyone hear his voice in the streets. He will not break a bruised reed or quench a smoldering wick until he brings justice to victory. And in his name the Gentiles will hope."

Other passages identify Jesus as God's beloved or chosen Son (Mt 17:5; Lk 9:35). In Luke 4:16-20, Jesus claims to fulfill the servant passage in Isaiah 61:1-2. As the Chosen One, Jesus will fulfill the role of the Servant—representing Israel—to bring God's salvation to the ends of the earth. In Jesus' case, it is obvious that he is elect for the sake of the world's salvation, not for the sake of his own. I would argue that the same thing is true for those who believe in Jesus.[37] Although those who are elect in Christ are blessed by God's favor, the greater purpose of their election is to extend God's offer of salvation to the world.

Sometimes the elect are called to suffer in order to bring salvation to others. Isaiah's Servant (Is 53:4-6, 11-12) and Jesus (Mk 10:45) are the most obvious examples. Prophets such as Elijah and Jeremiah were persecuted for delivering God's message. Hosea was required to live out in his own marriage God's heartbroken love for his people. Similarly, Christians,

---

[37]Thomas B. Talbott has also argued that "the election of one person is always on behalf of others." "Universal Reconciliation and the Inclusive Nature of Election," in *Perspectives on Election: Five Views*, ed. Chad Owen Brand (Nashville: Broadman & Holman, 2006), p. 241. While I agree with his statement and appreciate his arguments, I do not agree that the New Testament concept of election leads to universalism. The possibility of rejecting or forfeiting election militates against that.

those chosen in Christ, are called to endure suffering so that the world may hear the gospel. Jesus declares that those who are persecuted for his sake should rejoice because they are following in the footsteps of the prophets (Mt 5:10-12). In John 17, Jesus prays for God to protect and sustain his disciples in the face of the world's hatred "so that the world may believe that you have sent me" (Jn 17:21). Paul claims that his own sufferings as an apostle are completing what is lacking in the sufferings of Christ (Col 1:24). Calvin Roetzel observes that in 1 Thessalonians 1:4-6, "the *modus vivendi* of the elect is suffering."[38]

The biblical theme that election is for the benefit of the non-elect stands in stark contrast to theological views that limit God's love to the elect. Rather than a fixed category (defined in eternity past) consisting of those whom God determines to save, "the elect" is an open category whose members have *become* elect by responding to the gospel and joining with God's people. Instead of being God's instruments to reach the elect with the gospel, believers are instruments of God's universal salvific will. They serve and suffer for the non-elect (unbelievers) so that as many as possible of the non-elect may be saved.

Figure 2 traces the development of election through salvation history as God's plan to restore his creation to the blessings he always intended for it. God chose Israel to begin to undo the damage to creation caused by the fall. When Israel failed in its calling, God worked with a faithful remnant, which would ultimately be represented by Isaiah's Servant. The pivotal figure—and the focal point of election—is that Servant, Jesus Christ, who fulfills the purpose of God's chosen ones in the Old Testament and makes possible the expansion of God's invitation through the church to the whole world.[39]

---

[38]Calvin J. Roetzel, "Election/Calling in Certain Pauline Letters: An Experimental Construction," *Society of Biblical Literature 1990 Seminar Papers*, ed. David J. Lull (Atlanta: Scholars Press, 1990), p. 556. He describes a scholarly consensus on the connection between election and suffering in Paul (p. 556 n. 11).

[39]This summary and the accompanying chart are an adaptation and extension of N. T. Wright's description of the view of salvation history held by the early church: "It was the entire narrative, the complete story-line, the whole world of prayer and hope, focused on Israel as the bearer of God's promises for the world, then focused on the remnant as the bearer of Israel's destiny, and focused finally on Israel's true king as the one upon whom the task even of the remnant would finally devolve. He had been the servant for the servant-people." *The Challenge of Jesus: Rediscovering Who Jesus Was and Is* (Downers Grove, Ill.: InterVarsity Press, 1999), p. 162.

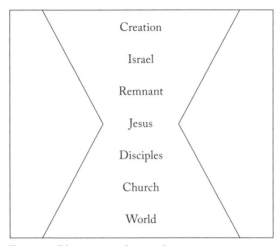

Figure 2. Election in salvation history

ELECTION IN ROMANS 9–11

The critical passage for Paul's understanding of election is Romans 9–11. These chapters have often been read as a description of God's choice of individuals for salvation—and sometimes, depending on the reader's perspective, for damnation. It is certainly possible to read these chapters in that way if we view them through the lens of Western individualism. Paul's quotation of "I have loved Jacob, but I have hated Esau" (Rom 9:13, quoting Mal 1:2-3) seems to describe God's sovereign choice to save one individual and condemn another. This reading also seems consistent with the traditional Protestant interpretation of Romans as a book about how individuals can get right with God.

However, Romans is not primarily about how individuals get right with God but about how Jews and Gentiles relate to one another in the plan of God. Justification is not first about individual salvation but about identifying who are the true covenant people of God (see chapter nine). Because Paul has separated justification from the "ethnic boundary markers" of Israel, he now must explain what has happened to the election of Israel.[40]

---

[40]Michael Cranford, "Election and Ethnicity: Paul's View of Israel in Romans 9:1-13," *Journal for the Study of the New Testament* 50 (1993): 29. Cranford argues that Paul uses the idea of the faithful remnant to distinguish between the sociological and soteriological boundaries of the people of God so that he can both defend God's faithfulness to his promises and allow for the expansion of God's people to include Gentiles (p. 41).

Has God been faithful to his chosen people?

To understand Paul's view of election, it is important to follow his argument in Romans 9. His discussion of election is prompted by his concern for God's covenant people: "I have great sorrow and unceasing anguish in my heart. For I could wish that I myself were accursed and cut off from Christ for the sake of my own people, my kindred according to the flesh. They are Israelites, and to them belong the adoption, the glory, the covenants, the giving of the law, the worship, and the promises; to them belong the patriarchs, and from them, according to the flesh, comes the Messiah, who is over all, God blessed forever" (Rom 9:2-5). If the covenants and the promises belong to Israel, why are they not following Jesus, the fulfillment of God's covenant promises? Paul answers this question in a creative dialogue with the Old Testament.

Paul discusses election in order to defend God's covenant faithfulness. He affirms both God's faithfulness to his promises and God's sovereign right to reach the promised goal by whatever route he chooses. God chooses individuals and nations to be bearers of his promise and therefore channels of his blessing. Paul immediately asserts that God has not broken his promise: "It is not as though the word of God had failed" (Rom 9:6). Paul had demonstrated in Romans 4 that membership in God's covenant people had always been based on faith; thus Abraham's true descendants, the chosen people of God, are those who share his faith. Now in Romans 9, Paul returns to Abraham to trace the fulfillment of God's promise through salvation history. He recounts three events that show how God works through selected people to maintain his promise despite human failure and opposition.

Paul first turns to the story of Isaac and Ishmael. Abraham's descendants will be named not through his firstborn, Ishmael, but through the child of the promise, Isaac (Rom 9:7-9). God carries out his promise to give a son to Sarah despite the efforts of Abraham and Sarah to arrange for offspring by other means. In the Genesis story, God even redeems the disaster they cause by rescuing Hagar and promising to bless Ishmael with many descendants (Gen 21:9-21).

Then Paul turns to the most debated section in Romans 9, God's choice of Jacob rather than Esau: "Even before they had been born or had done anything good or bad (so that God's purpose of election might continue, not by works but by his call) she was told, 'The elder shall serve the younger.' As it is written, 'I have loved Jacob, but I have hated Esau'" (Rom 9:11-13). Despite his birthright as the firstborn, Esau is not chosen to carry on the promise; Jacob is. The story in Genesis attributes this overturning of expectations to a combination of Esau's impulsive selling of his birthright (Gen 25:29-34) and deception by Rebekah and Jacob (Gen 27:1-40). Paul uses the story to demonstrate God's right to show mercy to the undeserving Jacob by choosing him to carry out his will (Rom 9:14-15). As H. H. Rowley comments, "Sometimes God chooses those who are not particularly choice."[41]

Jacob and Esau are useful illustrations for Paul's purpose because they are the progenitors of nations. In fact, Paul's quotation "I have loved Jacob, but I have hated Esau," in its original context in Malachi 1:1-5, refers to Israel and Edom rather than to Jacob and Esau as individuals. Pharaoh, in the following verses, represents Egypt by virtue of his kingship. The dual identities of Jacob, Esau and Pharaoh as both individuals and nations help Paul construct his defense of God's right to work with the Gentiles.

God chooses people so that "God's purpose of election might continue" (Rom 9:11)—that is, so that God can form a people to love and serve him, and through whom he can bless the world. This people will come from Jacob rather than from Esau. As is the case with Israel in Deuteronomy 7:6-11, God's choice of Jacob demonstrates that election is due to God's grace, not human merit. God does not literally hate Esau, any more than Jesus literally wants believers to hate their families (Lk 14:26). This is a figurative expression meaning to love or honor less than another (see the parallel in Matthew 10:37). In Genesis, Esau prospers, as Jacob does, but he does not serve as the channel of God's promise.

The third event Paul refers to is the exodus. God's promise is threatened by Pharaoh's refusal to let the Israelites leave Egypt. Genesis attributes the hardening of Pharaoh's heart first to Pharaoh and then to God (e.g., Ex 8:15, 32; 9:12, 34; 10:20, 27). Paul uses the story as another illustration of God's ability to keep his promises despite opposition. God has mercy on the insignificant Israelites and uses the mighty Pharaoh as an instrument to accomplish his purposes. Paul is not talking about the possibility of Pharaoh's salvation here but about God's rescue of the Israelites from slavery. God confirms Pharaoh's opposition to him in order to

---

[41]Rowley, *Election*, p. 35.

demonstrate his own power in liberating his people (Rom 9:17-18). Furthermore, in the Genesis story, Pharaoh is said to repent only *after* God begins to harden his heart (Ex 9:27; 10:16).[42] This suggests that God's hardening is not a sovereign act that determines one's eternal destiny but a temporal act for a particular temporal purpose (in this case, the exodus).

Paul relates these three stories because they are important to the continuation of God's promise. In all three cases, God's promise is threatened, and in all three cases God chooses fallible human beings to carry on his promise in surprising ways.[43] As Paul makes clear in Romans 9:24-29, he has been talking about Israel and the Gentiles. As with Isaac and Jacob, God has chosen to work not through his "firstborn" (Israel) but through the second child (the Gentiles). As with Pharaoh, God has temporarily "hardened" Israel so that the Gentiles might become his people (see Romans 11:7-10, where Paul argues this explicitly). Thus even God's hardening is ultimately for a redemptive purpose. Notice that Paul cites Pharaoh, not Esau, as an example of God hardening an individual's heart. God's choice of Jacob does not mean that Esau was hardened, but merely that Esau's line would not be the channel of God's promised blessing.

Paul's potter analogy in Romans 9:19-24 has been read by some interpreters as Paul's assertion of God's right to determine the destiny of every individual. However, it would be more consistent with Paul's argument to see this as a defense of God's prerogative to work through the Gentiles as well as through the Jews:

> You will say to me then, "Why then does he still find fault? For who can resist his will?" But who indeed are you, a human being, to argue with God? Will what is molded say to the one who molds it, "Why have you made me like this?" Has the potter no right over the clay, to make out of the same lump one object for special use and another for ordinary use? What if God, desiring to show his wrath and to make known his power, has endured with much patience the objects of wrath that are made for destruction; and what if he has done so in order to make known the riches of his glory for the objects of mercy, which he has prepared beforehand for glory—including us whom he has called, not from the Jews only but also from the Gentiles?

---

[42]I am indebted for this insight to Ryan Patrick McLaughlin.
[43]See David J. A. Clines, *The Theme of the Pentateuch* (Sheffield, U.K.: JSOT Press, 1982). He traces through the Pentateuch the theme of God's promise as it is threatened and fulfilled.

Paul imagines someone raising a question: If God can harden and show mercy as he wishes, then why should anyone be held accountable? Paul answers with an allusion to Jeremiah's visit to the potter's house, when God declared that it was his right as the potter to remake any spoiled vessel to serve another purpose. If he promised blessing to a nation, but the nation turned to evil, he would change his mind about bringing that blessing. If he promised disaster to another nation, but the nation repented, God would change his mind about bringing the disaster he had promised. Thus God can change his plans when nations change their behavior toward him. God is warning Israel through the prophet to repent in order to avoid God's judgment (Jer 18:1-11).

The analogy of God as potter has a rich history in the Old Testament and intertestamental literature (Is 45:9; Wisd 15:7). The law stipulated that a pottery vessel that became unclean must be broken (Lev 11:33; 15:12). The breaking of such a vessel became a common metaphor for God coming against an individual or nation in judgment (Ps 2:9; Is 30:14; Jer 19:11; 48:38).

In Paul's use of the potter analogy, Israel is a vessel made for special (literally, "honorable") use, and the Gentiles are vessels made for ordinary use. Both have had their uses in God's economy, but both have made themselves objects of wrath fit for destruction. The word *katartizō* ("prepared" or "fit") could be understood as either a passive or a middle. In the first case, someone (usually understood as God) designed or prepared these vessels for destruction. In the second case, the vessels have "fitted themselves" for destruction. Given the context of Paul's argument, the second case seems more likely.[44] Neither the ordinary nor the special vessels were created for destruction, but both have made themselves worthy of it.[45]

Paul has described this process in Romans 1–2. The Gentiles have not honored what they know of God, so God demonstrates his wrath by giving them over to experience the consequences of their sin (Rom 1:18-32).

---

[44]James D. Strauss, "God's Promise and Universal History: The Theology of Romans 8," in *Grace Unlimited*, ed. Clark H. Pinnock (Eugene, Ore.: Wipf & Stock, 1999), pp. 199-201.

[45]Rowley argues similarly in *Election*, pp. 40-42, although he believes that this passage has to do with service rather than with salvation. He states that both special and ordinary vessels are intended by the potter to serve a constructive purpose, not to be destroyed. He notes that God is not "a crazy potter, who made vessels with no other thought than that he would afterwards knock them to pieces."

God's own people have been "storing up wrath for [themselves]" through their disobedience to the law (Rom 2:5). Both "vessels" deserve to be broken and discarded. But instead, Paul turns to a metaphor of remaking. God, as the potter, has chosen to be patient with his spoiled vessels and remake them into vessels of mercy, composed of believing Jews and Gentiles. Unlike the objects of wrath, who have prepared themselves for destruction, the objects of mercy have been "prepared beforehand for glory" (Rom 9:23) by God's patient work with his people throughout salvation history. God has the right to do with his creation as he wishes. Who is qualified to question him?[46]

In 2 Timothy 2:20-21, Paul uses the pottery imagery in an individual context. He declares that those who cleanse themselves from the practices he has mentioned will become special vessels that are consecrated for the use of the master. The notion that one can *become* an honorable vessel supports the idea that the ordinary and special vessels in Romans 9:21 are not eternal categories (the elect and the reprobate) but instead are provisional categories that permit movement from one to the other. In any case, whether special or ordinary, both Jews and Gentiles have failed to fulfill God's intentions. They deserve destruction, but God chooses to be patient with them in order to give the vessels of wrath time to repent and become vessels of mercy.

Thus Paul's discussion of election in Romans 9–11 deals primarily with how God is working with Israel and the nations to carry out his merciful plan. In Romans 10:8-17, Paul indicates how individuals come to participate in the election: the church sends messengers to proclaim the gospel; then people hear the gospel, respond with faith, and express their faith by committing themselves to Christ as Lord. Similarly, in Romans 11:17-24, Paul explains that individual branches may be grafted into or cut off from the olive tree (the people of God) on the basis of their faith(fulness) or lack thereof.

---

[46]The potter analogy plays a critical role in the Reformed understanding of election: because God is sovereign, he can choose individuals for salvation (the "objects of mercy") and pass over others (the "objects of wrath") solely on the basis of his sovereign will. Paul certainly does argue here for God's sovereign rights as creator. However, just because God can exercise his power through apparently arbitrary choice, nothing in the passage indicates that he must do so. In fact, Paul says that God has chosen instead to be patient and show mercy so that some of the "objects of wrath" might become "objects of mercy."

If God has opened his people to Gentiles, what has happened to Israel's election? To this question, Paul gives two answers. First, a "remnant" within Israel, including Paul himself, has believed in Christ. This chosen remnant carries on the election of Israel, while the rest of Israel has been hardened (Rom 11:1-10).[47] Second, God's rejection of Israel is not permanent. Israel is still the object of God's love. God is using the Gentiles to make Israel jealous, so that when they turn from their faithlessness, they can rejoin God's people. The ones who were hardened can be grafted in again, so that finally "all Israel" will be saved (Rom 11:11-16, 23-29). As was the case with Pharaoh, the hardening of the majority of Israel cannot mean that they are destined for damnation, because the possibility of repentance remains open to them. In fact, Paul is confident that Israel as a whole will eventually be God's people again. The function of the chosen people of God—Jews as well as Gentiles—is to be a channel of God's blessing so that the non-elect can be won to God.

The referent of Paul's declaration that "all Israel will be saved" has been vigorously debated. Since Paul has been concerned with the election of ethnic Israel, he probably means ethnic Israel here. In the present, only a remnant of Israel is faithful, but in the future, once "the full number of the Gentiles has come in" (Rom 11:25), ethnic Israel will come to faith in Jesus the Messiah.[48] Thus the church does not replace Israel. As Bruce Longenecker has argued, the interplay between Israel and the Gentiles relates to the progress of salvation history. Despite being Apostle to the Gentiles, Paul believes that Israel is still central to God's plan, and God will ensure that Israel plays its part: "All of salvation history is rooted in the history of Israel and will be completed with Israel. In the process, God will have mercy on all humanity, and Israel will have been the instrument of his grace. Thus, whether by their present faith or disobedience, Israel will have fulfilled the task which God commissioned her to do."[49]

For their part, Gentile members of the people of God should not "boast" over the Jewish branches that are presently cut off (Rom 11:18). Gentiles

---

[47]Cranford argues that God's promises to Israel were always to the obedient within Israel—that is, the faithful remnant. "Election and Ethnicity," *passim.*

[48]Bruce L. Longenecker, "Different Answers to Different Issues: Israel, the Gentiles and Salvation History in Romans 9–11," *Journal for the Study of the New Testament* 36 (1989): 97, 99-100.

[49]Ibid., pp. 101-3, 113.

are the wild olive branches who have been "grafted in" to God's people (Rom 11:17). They cannot afford to become arrogant. As Shirley Guthrie reminds us, "Any assertion that Christians are superior because of their 'true religion' or 'deeper morality'—an assertion that has been typical of many Christians throughout subsequent history—can only lead them to repeat the sin of Israel, make themselves to be the 'enemies of God,' and suffer the same consequences Israel suffered (Rom 11:21). Gentile Christians cannot hear the good news of their election without hearing at the same time the word of judgment that goes with it."[50]

CONCLUSION

Election is the story of God working throughout salvation history to form a people who will reflect his character and offer his salvation to the world. God calls individuals and moves entire nations to bring about his redemptive purposes. Paul's sweeping vision of God's mercy to all (Rom 11:32) cannot be reduced to a narrow prospect of God's mercy to a few.

Paul's picture of election demonstrates the interdependence of Jews and Gentiles in God's plan. If the church had taken his vision seriously, the tragic history of Christian anti-Semitism could have been avoided. As Christians, we should be grateful for the heritage of Israel, and we should honor the Jewish people, knowing that they are still loved by God (Rom 11:28). This does not mean that the modern state of Israel deserves our unconditional support. But it does mean, in this post-Holocaust era, that we should engage in interfaith dialogue with great sensitivity, repenting of our past sins while continuing to testify to our belief that Messiah has come and will return.[51]

The image of election reminds us of the centrality of Christ in salvation. Outside of Christ, there is no election. He is the Elect One; we are chosen in him. Our election is grounded not in an immutable eternal decree but in the redemptive work of Christ. It is experienced as an ongoing relationship with God made possible by Christ and made actual by his Spirit.

This understanding of election also emphasizes the importance of the community. We are chosen not as isolated individuals but as members of

---

[50]Shirley C. Guthrie, "Romans 11:25-32," *Interpretation* 38, no. 3 (July 1984): 288.

[51]Shirley Guthrie, in the article cited above, has a sensitive discussion of the attitudes Christians should have toward Jews in light of the New Testament teaching on election.

the community of faith. We could say, then, that the community is the vehicle of salvation for all those who participate in it. People who place their faith in Christ are joined to Christ's community and thereby participate in the election.

Election assures us of God's love for us. We are God's choice and precious people, the objects of his mercy. We can be confident of our value to God and can trust in his provision and care. Nevertheless, the image of election should not turn us inward in self-centered satisfaction but outward in love and mercy toward others. In particular, the emphasis on the calling of the elect to suffer for the sake of others is a helpful counterbalance to the triumphalism that sometimes accompanies the doctrine of election in the church. In this sense, election is not exclusive but inclusive: we who have experienced God's grace become channels of that grace to others, so that the number of the elect may continue to grow.

Election demonstrates the dance of divine initiative and human response that is at the heart of salvation. Election is established by grace, but it brings with it significant responsibility. Although, as God's elect, we may have confidence in God's love and faithfulness, we must not become complacent. We need God's ongoing grace, personal diligence, and the help of one another to make our calling and election sure. As we live out our election, may our contemplation of God's wisdom and mercy move us, like Paul, to thanksgiving and praise.

FOR FURTHER READING

Basinger, David, and Randall Basinger, eds. *Predestination & Free Will: Four Views of Divine Sovereignty & Human Freedom*. Downers Grove, Ill.: InterVarsity Press, 1986.

Brand, Chad, ed. *Perspectives on Election: Five Views*. Nashville: Broadman & Holman, 2006.

Cranford, Michael. "Election and Ethnicity: Paul's View of Israel in Romans 9:1-13." *Journal for the Study of the New Testament* 50 (1993): 27-41.

Demarest, Bruce. *The Cross and Salvation*. Foundations of Evangelical Theology Series. Wheaton, Ill.: Crossway, 1997.

Forster, Roger T., and V. Paul Marsten. *God's Strategy in Human History*. Wheaton, Ill.: Tyndale House, 1973.

Guthrie, Shirley C. "Romans 11:25-32." *Interpretation* 38, no. 3 (July 1984): 286-91.

Klein, William W. *The New Chosen People: A Corporate View of Election.* Grand Rapids: Zondervan, 1990.

Longenecker, Bruce L. "Different Answers to Different Issues: Israel, the Gentiles and Salvation History in Romans 9–11." *Journal for the Study of the New Testament* 36 (1989): 95-123.

Marshall, I. Howard. "Election and Calling to Salvation in 1 and 2 Thessalonians." In *The Thessalonian Correspondence.* Edited by Raymond F. Collins. Bibliotheca Ephemeridum Theologicarum Lovaniensium. Louvain: Leuven University Press, 1990.

Newman, Carey C. "Election and Predestination in Ephesians 1:4-6a: An Exegetical-Theological Study of the Christological Realization of God's Purpose." *Review and Expositor* 93 (1996): 237-47.

Picirilli, Robert E. *Grace, Faith, Free Will: Contrasting Views of Salvation: Calvinism & Arminianism.* Nashville: Randall House, 2002.

Pinnock, Clark H., ed. *Grace Unlimited.* Minneapolis: Bethany House, 1975.

———. *The Grace of God, the Will of Man: A Case for Arminianism.* Grand Rapids: Zondervan, 1989.

Rowley, Harold H. *The Biblical Doctrine of Election.* Eugene, Ore.: Wipf & Stock, 2009.

Schreiner, Thomas R., and Bruce A. Ware, eds. *Still Sovereign: Contemporary Perspectives on Election, Foreknowledge, and Grace.* Grand Rapids: Baker, 2000.

Shank, Robert. *Elect in the Son: A Study of the Doctrine of Election.* Minneapolis: Bethany House, 1989.

II

TRANSFORMATION BY PARTICIPATION

Being in Christ, Glorification, Theosis

MODERN PEOPLE HAVE AN IDENTITY PROBLEM.[1] Scientists, social scientists, philosophers and theologians offer a variety of competing definitions of what it means to be human. Studies of animal cognition are challenging the old definitions of human beings as tool-using or problem-solving animals. Advances in artificial intelligence lead people to wonder if the definition of humans as thinking beings (implied by the term *homo sapiens*) will soon be outdated.

Presumably neither animals nor computers ask, "Who am I?" But for human beings, the question of identity is a fundamental existential question. This question is exacerbated in modern societies as mobility and rapid social change isolate people from the structures, relationships and traditions by which they have defined themselves. It is becoming critical in the postmodern era, as the modern confidence in the autonomous self is eroding.

The biblical answer to the question of identity is that human beings are creatures made in God's image who have been damaged by sin. They do indeed have an identity problem, in that they are not who they were created to be. But God has provided a remedy: human beings can find their true identity in Christ, the image of God (2 Cor 4:4). Believers become their tru-

---

[1]Stanley J. Grenz, *Theology for the Community of God* (1994; reprint, Grand Rapids: Eerdmans, 2000), pp. 127-29. References are to the 2000 edition.

est selves in Christ, with whom they have a relationship that defines their entire existence. They experience the blessings of salvation in their lives because they participate in his life. Because they are in Christ, they can be confident that no matter what trials they face, they will never be alone.

SALVATION AS PARTICIPATION

This picture of salvation through participation has a strong foundation in the New Testament, particularly in the writings of John and Paul. The Gospel of John describes a mutual indwelling between Christ and believers, while Paul talks about being "in Christ" (*en Christō*). For example, John declares that believers are in Christ just as Christ is in them (Jn 17:20-26). To receive eternal life, people must believe in Christ (*eis auton*; Jn 3:16). Through the Holy Spirit, who will indwell believers, both the Father and the Son will be in them (Jn 14:17; 17:21-23).

The idea of mutual indwelling in the Gospel of John is clearest in the allegory of the vine and the branches (Jn 15:1-11). Jesus tells his disciples that they must abide or remain (*menō*) in him, the true vine. In union with him, they will be fruitful and effective in prayer; without the strength and nourishment they draw from him, however, they can do nothing. The allegory does not specify how Jesus' disciples come to be in him. It may be that the theme of believing in Christ, which is so strong in the Gospel, answers this question. However, the Old Testament background of the vineyard as a metaphor for Israel (cf. Is 5:1-7) suggests that the vine and branches may be a corporate image before it is individual. Jesus' disciples, as Jews, are already members of Israel. What is new is that Jesus, the true vine, has cleansed them by his word (Jn 15:3). They now are prepared to produce the kind of fruit the Gardener (God) desires.

Jesus has reinterpreted a traditional metaphor by replacing Israel with himself.[2] He is the true, faithful Israelite who will give life to God's people. As long as Jesus' disciples remain in his love (Jn 15:9) and keep his commandments (allow his words to remain in them, Jn 15:7, 10), they will flourish and experience fullness of joy (Jn 15:11). But the message of Jesus brings judgment as well as cleansing. Any branches that do not remain in him will be cast aside to be burned (Jn 15:6). Participation in Christ is thus

---

[2]See the discussion in D. A. Carson, *The Gospel According to John* (Grand Rapids: Eerdmans, 1991), pp. 513-14.

the only source of life. Although Jesus does not emphasize this, the vine image suggests that those who participate in his life are also connected to one another. Some have seen this image a resemblance to Paul's metaphor of the body of Christ.[3]

Salvation as participation in Christ occurs most often in Paul, who expresses it as "being in Christ." This phrase, or variations on it, is pervasive in Paul's letters. According to James D. G. Dunn, "[A] continuing identification with Christ in, through, and beyond his death . . . is fundamental to Paul's soteriology."[4] A search of the Greek New Testament turns up over 150 instances of "in Christ," "in the Lord," or "in him" (in reference to Christ).[5] In many other instances, Paul talks about believers doing something in solidarity with Christ, such as being crucified, buried and raised with Christ (Rom 6:1-11). E. P. Sanders has argued that participation in Christ is the most fundamental idea in Paul's understanding of salvation: "Paul's soteriology is basically cosmic and corporate or participatory."[6]

Scholars have debated what Paul means by "in Christ." Some understand the phrase as legal representation. Christ serves as the legal representative of believers collectively, just as the president of the United States represents the American people. In the same way that Adam's sin was credited to all those he represented (the human race), Christ's righteousness is credited to all those he represents (believers in him). Other scholars believe that "in Christ" refers to the mystical union or experiential fellowship that believers have with Christ. Still others believe that Paul is presenting Christ as a corporate personality who includes others within himself. Finally, some understand the phrase eschatologically. They argue that "in Christ" is a shorthand way of saying "in the new era brought about by the work of Christ."[7]

---

[3]Raymond E. Brown, *The Gospel According to John*, 2 vols., Anchor Bible (New York: Doubleday, 1970), 2:670.

[4]James D. G. Dunn, *The Theology of Paul the Apostle* (Grand Rapids: Eerdmans, 1998), p. 223.

[5]Scholars have long cited the estimate of Adolf Deissmann, who found 164 instances of these phrases in Paul's letters, not counting the Pastorals, Colossians and Ephesians, which he believed were pseudonymous. For example, see J. A. Allan, "The 'In Christ' Formula in Ephesians," *New Testament Studies* 5 (October 1958): 54.

[6]E. P. Sanders, *Paul and Palestinian Judaism: A Comparison of Patterns of Religion* (Minneapolis: Augsburg Fortress, 1977), p. 508; see also p. 502.

[7]Millard Erickson believes that the relationship between Christ and believers is one of federal headship (legal representation). He calls it "judicial in nature." *Christian Theology*, 2nd ed.

In the discussion that follows, I will suggest that the idea of legal representation misses the mark as an explanation of what Paul means by being in Christ. For Paul, "being in Christ" is not a transaction but a real spiritual union between Christ and the believer that determines the believer's identity and shapes all of the believer's life. While it does have an experiential dimension, it is fundamentally objective rather than mystical. It is eschatological, but it is not merely shorthand for the new era. Rather, it is a relationship made possible in the new era by the indwelling of the eschatological Spirit.

THE NEW ERA IN CHRIST

The phrase "in Christ" seems to have several different shades of meaning.[8] Paul sometimes uses it as a synonym for "Christian" or "in a Christian manner." For example, when he says that he knows a man in Christ (2 Cor 12:2), he probably means simply that the man (whether himself or another) is a Christian. Similarly, he says that Andronicus and Junia "were in Christ before I was," meaning that they have been Christians longer (Rom 16:7). He counsels widows to marry "in the Lord," meaning that they should marry Christian men (1 Cor 7:39). Paul regards both individuals and churches as being "in Christ" (Gal 1:22; Phil 4:21).

Sometimes the phrase focuses more specifically on the spiritual life. For example, Paul considers Timothy and the Corinthians to be his children in the Lord, or his spiritual children (1 Cor 4:15, 17). Life in Christ extends from infancy to maturity (1 Cor 3:1; Col 1:28). Paul considers it his

---

(Grand Rapids: Baker, 1998), p. 965. The mystical approach was pioneered by Adolf Deissmann and Albert Schweitzer, who dubbed it "Christ-mysticism." Adolf Deissmann, *Paul: A Study in Social and Religious History*, trans. William E. Wilson (New York: Harper & Brothers, 1957), pp. 138, 147-57. Schweitzer added an eschatological emphasis. Albert Schweitzer, *The Mysticism of Paul the Apostle*, trans. William Montgomery (Baltimore: Johns Hopkins University Press, 1998), pp. 13, 37-40, 122-30. Similarly, Richard N. Longenecker states, "Paul's emphasis . . . was on the nearness of the Lord in the experience of the Christian." *The Christology of Early Jewish Christianity* (Grand Rapids: Baker, 1970), p. 135. Ernest Best argues for corporate personality: believers "as a corporate whole dwell 'in Christ.'" "Appendix: Prepositions and Theology in the Greek New Testament," in *NIDNTT* 3:1192. George Eldon Ladd takes the eschatological approach: "Therefore to be 'in Christ' means to be in the new sphere of salvation. To be in Christ means to experience the newness of the new aeon." *A Theology of the New Testament*, ed. Donald A. Hagner, rev. ed. (Grand Rapids: Eerdmans, 1993), p. 525.

[8]For a survey of categories, see A. Oepke, "ἐν," in *TDNT* 2:541-42; Best, "Appendix: Prepositions and Theology in the Greek New Testament," in *NIDNTT* 3:1191-93; and "ἐν," in *BAGD*, pp. 259-60. My categories will have some overlap with theirs.

responsibility to help his spiritual children grow to maturity in the Lord. Christ is both the source of their life and the endpoint of their growth (Eph 4:15).

Paul often uses "in Christ" in an instrumental or causal sense—that is, by means of Christ or because of what Christ has done.[9] This sense is clearest in Paul's descriptions of the atonement. He declares that "in Christ God was reconciling the world to himself, not counting their trespasses against them" (2 Cor 5:19). Because all have sinned, "they are now justified by his grace as a gift, through the redemption that is in Christ Jesus" (Rom 3:24).

Christ is the mediator of God's grace toward sinners (1 Cor 1:4; Eph 2:7; 2 Tim 1:9). In particular, Paul emphasizes that Christ is the mediator of covenant membership for the Gentiles: "Christ redeemed us from the curse of the law by becoming a curse for us . . . in order that in Christ Jesus the blessing of Abraham might come to the Gentiles" (Gal 3:13-14; cf. Eph 2:13; 3:6). Christ has inaugurated a new era, the age of fulfillment. He is the fulfillment of all of God's promises (2 Cor 1:19-20). He has fulfilled the law so that its purpose as disciplinarian is no longer needed, "for in Christ Jesus you are all children of God through faith" (Gal 3:26). Because of his pivotal role, Jesus is the key to understanding even the old covenant (2 Cor 3:14-16).

This eschatological dimension of being in Christ is probably the most foundational. Because of what God has done in Christ, reality has been changed. The age to come has dawned, and God has begun to reassert his rule over creation. Believers in Christ take part in this new era while living in the midst of the old one. Before their conversion, they were enslaved by the powers of the old era—Satan, sin and death. They were "in Adam" or "in sin" (Rom 6:1-2; 1 Cor 15:22). But now they are free from bondage and empowered for godly living. They are "in Christ." Essentially, Paul views Christ and sin as different dominions to which the person could belong.[10] At conversion, people are transferred from the dominion of sin to the do-

---

[9]A. J. M. Wedderburn argues that most instances of "in Christ" can be understood in this way. "Some Observations on Paul's Use of the Phrases 'in Christ' and 'with Christ,'" *Journal for the Study of the New Testament* 25 (1985): 89-91. His article includes an extensive grammatical survey of the phrases in the title.

[10]Victor Paul Furnish interprets "in Christ" as belonging to Christ. *Theology and Ethics in Paul* (Nashville: Abingdon, 1968), p. 176. While ownership is certainly one dimension of being in Christ, it does not exhaust the meaning of the expression.

minion of Christ. "Being 'in Christ' means being within the dominion of Christ, under Christ's lordship as it is made good on earth by the Spirit."[11]

For Paul, being in Christ expresses the new reality in general and comprehends every dimension of the Christian's life in particular: "So if anyone is in Christ, there is a new creation: everything old has passed away; see, everything has become new!" (2 Cor 5:17). Paul certainly means that every individual Christian is being renewed, but he also means that each individual renewal is part of God's grand project to restore creation. Each person who is "in Christ" demonstrates that the new creation is underway.

Being in Christ carries with it behavioral obligations. Believers should live like participants in the new era. Paul tells the Thessalonians to rejoice, pray and give thanks, "for this is the will of God in Christ Jesus for you" (1 Thess 5:18). He urges the Roman believers to welcome Phoebe "in the Lord as is fitting for the saints" (Rom 16:2; cf. Phil 2:29). Evidently he expects them to receive her with Christian hospitality. Even this modest sense of "in Christ" can carry significant theological weight. When Paul urges Euodia and Syntyche to "be of the same mind in the Lord" (Phil 4:2), his words echo his exhortation (two chapters earlier) to be of the same mind, on the example of Christ himself (Phil 2:2, 6-11). Similarly, he exhorts believers to forgive one another "as God in Christ has forgiven you" (Eph 4:32).

Because they are identified with Christ, believers are to live Christlike lives: "As you therefore have received Christ Jesus the Lord, continue to live your lives [literally, "walk"] in him" (Col 2:6). When Paul instructs the members of Christian households how to behave toward one another, he transforms the standard Greco-Roman "household code" by saying that everyone involved should fulfill their responsibilities "in the Lord" (Eph 6:1; Col 3:18). Because they participate in Christ, Christ participates in each of their relationships, which must now be governed by Christian values and priorities. The socially dominant party (the adult male) has new responsibility and accountability, while the socially subordinate parties have the added dignity of their standing in Christ.

Although Paul does not call for the overthrow of the social order, his understanding of the new reality of being in Christ carries within it the

---

[11]Lewis B. Smedes, "Being in Christ," in *Major Themes in the Reformed Tradition*, ed. Donald K. McKim (Grand Rapids: Eerdmans, 1992), p. 149. See also Dunn, *Theology of Paul*, p. 400.

seeds of revolutionary change: "There is no longer Jew or Greek, there is no longer slave or free, there is no longer male and female; for all of you are one in Christ Jesus" (Gal 3:28). While Paul's concern here is unity, rather than equality, he is still asserting that the most fundamental human divisions have been overcome in Christ. The social implications of this unity are far-reaching. The new reality is most apparent when Paul tells Philemon that Onesimus, his runaway slave, is now no longer a slave but a "beloved brother . . . both in the flesh and in the Lord" (Philem 16). He seems to be making a distinction between relationships established by society ("in the flesh") and relationships transformed by Christ. Paul adroitly requests Onesimus's services as a benefit from Philemon "in the Lord" (Philem 20).

BLESSINGS AND DISCERNMENT IN CHRIST

Sometimes Paul describes Christ as the location where the Christian's blessings are found. Paul's use of "in Christ" rather than "through Christ" or "from Christ" suggests that believers enjoy these blessings because of their union with Christ rather than because of a legal transaction. Believers are taught in Christ (Eph 4:21), justified in Christ (Gal 2:17), sanctified in Christ (1 Cor 1:2), glorified in Christ (2 Thess 1:12), enriched in every way in Christ (1 Cor 1:5). They have hope in Christ (1 Cor 15:19), encouragement in Christ (Phil 2:1), freedom in Christ (Gal 2:4), faith and love in Christ (Rom 8:39; 1 Tim 1:14), eternal life in Christ (Rom 6:23), and the riches of God's glory in Christ (Phil 4:19). According to 2 Timothy, salvation, God's grace, and the promise of future life are found in Christ (2 Tim 1:1; 2:1, 10).

Ephesians 1 envisions a panorama of blessings: Christians have been "blessed . . . in Christ with every spiritual blessing in the heavenly places" (Eph 1:3). In Christ, they have election (Eph 1:4), God's grace (Eph 1:6), redemption and forgiveness (Eph 1:7), inheritance (Eph 1:11), hope (Eph 1:12), and sealing by the Holy Spirit (Eph 1:13). All the blessings of salvation are to be found in him, because he embodies salvation: "By his doing you are in Christ Jesus, who became to us wisdom from God, and righteousness and sanctification, and redemption" (1 Cor 1:30 NASB). Paul can say to believers, simply, "Christ . . . is your life" (Col 3:4). Paul's profound sense of indebtedness to Christ explains his frequent theme of boasting in the Lord rather than in his own accomplishments (Rom 15:17; 1 Cor 1:31; 15:31; 2 Cor 10:17; Phil 1:26; 3:3).

Some instances of "in Christ" are experiential. As A. M. Hunter has suggested, "Whatever else it means, 'in Christ' must mean 'in communion with Christ.'"[12] Because of their conscious fellowship with Christ, Christians can draw upon his resources to live the Christian life. Paul tells the Ephesians to "be strong in the Lord and in the strength of his power" (Eph 6:10). The experiential dimension of being in Christ is especially strong in Philippians. Paul seems to have had an ongoing sense of Christ's presence, out of which he lived and ministered.[13] Paul is bold in Christ (Phil 1:8); he hopes in the Lord to send Timothy to them (Phil 2:19); he trusts in the Lord that he will come to them soon (Phil 2:24). He claims that he can endure any circumstances in Christ (Phil 4:13). He says that other Christians have been made confident in the Lord by his imprisonment (Phil 1:14). He urges the Philippians to stand firm in the Lord (Phil 4:1) and most notably to rejoice in the Lord (Phil 3:1; 4:4, 10). He instructs them to pray about everything: "And the peace of God, which surpasses all understanding, will guard your hearts and your minds in Christ Jesus" (Phil 4:7).

For Paul, being in Christ extends to matters of conscience and spiritual discernment. Being united to Christ through the Holy Spirit makes it possible for believers to discern the mind of Christ (1 Cor 2:6-16). This spiritual insight enables Paul to be confident about the Galatians "in the Lord" (Gal 5:10) and to recognize that an opportunity for ministry has been opened for him "in the Lord" (2 Cor 2:12). It enables him to decide what to do about meat sacrificed to idols: "I know and am persuaded in the Lord Jesus that nothing is unclean in itself; but it is unclean for anyone who thinks it is unclean" (Rom 14:14). Such discernment is not merely a matter of knowing the commands of Christ but of seeking the will of Christ in new situations. In 1 Corinthians 7, for example, Paul carefully distinguishes between what Jesus has specifically commanded and what Paul himself has discerned (1 Cor 7:6, 10, 12, 25, 40).

Being in Christ is the context of both authority and accountability. As

---

[12]Archibald M. Hunter, *The Gospel According to St. Paul* (Philadelphia: Westminster Press, 1966), p. 33.

[13]Dunn, *Theology of Paul*, p. 400.

we saw above, Paul does not hesitate to describe his pastoral counsel as "the will of God in Christ Jesus" for his churches (1 Thess 5:18). Regarding idlers, he declares, "Now such persons we command and exhort in the Lord Jesus Christ to do their work quietly and to earn their own living" (2 Thess 3:12). He insists to the Thessalonians and Ephesians "in the Lord" that they must live lives that are pleasing to God (Eph 4:17; 1 Thess 4:1). He expresses a similar command "by the Lord" in 1 Thessalonians 5:27.

Paul also acknowledges his own accountability to Christ. He calls Christ to witness to his sincerity: "I am speaking the truth in Christ—I am not lying; my conscience confirms it by the Holy Spirit" (Rom 9:1). He resorts to this especially when he is defending his apostolic authority: "In Christ we speak as persons of sincerity, as persons sent from God and standing in his presence" (2 Cor 2:17). More briefly, he asserts, "We are speaking in Christ before God" (2 Cor 12:19). These statements are more than assertions that Paul has been faithful to Christ's commands. He seems to have the sense that he is conducting his ministry in the presence of Christ, to whom he is accountable and by whom he will be judged (1 Cor 4:1-5).

Paul also lives out his Christian calling in Christ. People are called to salvation and service "in Christ" or "in the Lord" (Phil 3:14; 1 Cor 7:22). Paul's frequent use of the title "Lord" rather than "Christ" in these passages suggests that he is emphasizing the status of believers as servants of Christ. Paul holds his apostleship in the Lord, and the people he serves are his work in the Lord (1 Cor 9:1-2). He identifies others as ministers or coworkers in the Lord, who have their own tasks to complete in him (Eph 6:21; Col 4:7, 17). He assures the Corinthians that because of the resurrection, their work in the Lord is not in vain (1 Cor 15:58).

Paul even regards his imprisonment as a dimension of his calling; he identifies himself as a prisoner in the Lord (Eph 4:1; cf. "for Christ" in Phil 1:13; "of Christ Jesus" in Philem 1). He draws an explicit parallel between God's work of redemption and believers' participation in God's redemptive purposes. Just as God was "in Christ" reconciling the world to himself, believers become the righteousness of God "in him" as they proclaim God's message of reconciliation (2 Cor 5:19, 21).[14]

---

[14]See chapter nine for a detailed discussion of the righteousness of God.

DWELLING IN CHRIST

Believers and Christ are so closely identified with one another that Paul describes Christ as the location where believers are found: "For his sake I have suffered the loss of all things, and I regard them as rubbish, in order that I may gain Christ and be found in him . . ." (Phil 3:8-9). Christ is the ground of the believer's existence, the sphere in which he or she lives. Believers have been newly "created in Christ Jesus" (Eph 2:10). Their identity is now bound up with his: "I have been crucified with Christ; and it is no longer I who live, but it is Christ who lives in me. And the life I now live in the flesh I live by faith in the Son of God, who loved me and gave himself for me" (Gal 2:19-20). Paul has found new life and identity in Christ, but he has not lost himself in this union.[15] Just as Christ identified with him, he now identifies with Christ and lives his new life in solidarity with him.

Similarly, Paul urges believers to "put on" Christ (Rom 13:14) as they put on the new self created in the divine likeness (Eph 4:24). This "putting on" takes place definitively in baptism, the act that most strikingly represents the believer's identification with Christ: "As many of you as were baptized into Christ have clothed yourselves with Christ" (Gal 3:27). In baptism, believers identify with Christ's death and resurrection on their behalf (Rom 6:3-4). But Paul's exhortation to *Christians* to put on Christ implies that believers must continually reaffirm their new identity in Christ. In the same way, although believers have been transferred through baptism from the dominion of sin to the dominion of Christ, they still must stop offering themselves to sin and offer themselves to God (Rom 6:12-14). The union between Christ and the believer thus does not erase the believer's individuality, and it depends at least in part on the believer's cooperation.

Galatians 2:19-20, above, illustrates that the indwelling between Christ and the believer is reciprocal: Christ is in the believer, just as the believer

---

[15]Many interpreters have rejected a "mystical" understanding of being in Christ on the grounds that the believer's identity is not merged with Christ's or lost in Christ's. See, e.g., Ernest Best, *One Body in Christ: A Study in the Relationship of the Church to Christ in the Epistles of the Apostle Paul* (London: SPCK, 1955), p. 23; and J. K. S. Reid, "The Phrase 'in Christ,'" *Theology Today* 17 (1960): 360. While Paul's use of "in Christ" is certainly not "mystical" in this sense, it does seem to point to a union with Christ that is personal and experiential, not simply objective or forensic.

is in Christ (see also Rom 8:10; Eph 3:17). This reciprocity demonstrates that being in Christ means more than benefiting from the work of Christ. Such a transaction would not be reciprocal. It is rare for Paul to say that Christ is in the believer; he usually says instead that the Holy Spirit is in the believer. Nevertheless, he draws a very close connection between the Holy Spirit and the exalted Christ. In Romans 8:9-11 he equates "the Spirit," "the Spirit of God," "the Spirit of Christ," "Christ" and "the Spirit of him who raised Jesus from the dead." By implication, it is the Holy Spirit, dwelling in the believer, who effects this union between the believer and Christ, which is symbolized by water baptism (1 Cor 12:13). The freedom from sin brought into the believer's life by the indwelling Spirit means that there is no condemnation for those who are in Christ (Rom 8:1-2). Even after death, believers are still in Christ (1 Cor 15:18; 1 Thess 4:16), because even death cannot separate them from God's love in Christ (Rom 8:38-39).

The most important metaphor of incorporation in Christ is Paul's metaphor of the body of Christ. Believers are baptized into the body of Christ, the church, by the Holy Spirit at conversion (1 Cor 12:12-13). Because believers are members of the body of Christ, they are members of Christ and members of one another (Rom 12:5). According to Smedes, "The person in Christ is never there by himself or herself; being in Christ is always an existence in communion."[16] Paul uses this "body" language both individually and corporately to express the intimate union between Christ and his own. A believer who is united with Christ "becomes one spirit with him" (1 Cor 6:17).

Modern Western Christians tend to think of the physical as more "real" than the spiritual.[17] Paul does not. For him, the spiritual union between Christ and Christians is as real as becoming "one body" with a prostitute through a physical union (1 Cor 6:16). Moreover, the spiritual union with Christ must govern all other unions. Uniting the members of Christ to a

---

[16]Smedes, "Being in Christ," p. 146.

[17]For example, in his seminal study of the body in Paul, Robert H. Gundry seems to equate the real with the physical. He rejects any physical understanding of the union between Christ and believers as follows: "The terms 'mystical' and 'spiritual' tend to take back what the term 'real' offers; but they fail to cover up the difficulty in carrying through the 'real' with consistent literalness to the end. We might just as well have the courage to say 'metaphorical.'" *Soma in Biblical Theology, with Emphasis on Pauline Anthropology* (Cambridge: Cambridge University Press, 1976), p. 228.

prostitute would be unthinkable. As Sanders has observed, "The argument is that one participatory union can destroy another, even though the two are not on precisely the same level. A person cannot participate in two mutually exclusive unions. . . . The participatory union is not a figure of speech for something else; it is, as many scholars have insisted, real."[18] Similarly, Ephesians 5:21-32 compares the union between Christ and the church to the sexual union between husband and wife. These descriptions express intimacy in the strongest possible terms.

The language of participation includes the familiar word *koinōnia*. While this word is often rendered as fellowship, it actually means participation, a personal sharing in something with someone else.[19] Paul tells the Corinthians that God has called them into *koinōnia* with Christ (1 Cor 1:9). Because they participate in Christ, they also share in Christ's sufferings (Phil 3:10).

The Eucharist signifies a *koinōnia* in the body and blood of Christ (1 Cor 10:16). The communion service both represents and facilitates the union of believers with Christ and with one another: "Because there is one bread, we who are many are one body, for we all partake of the one bread" (1 Cor 10:17). Paul warns the Corinthians that their *koinōnia* with Christ precludes any *koinōnia* with demons. They cannot eat at Christ's table and then eat at the table of demons (1 Cor 10:21). The language again suggests a real spiritual union, although it does not necessarily require a real presence of Christ in the communion elements per se. Paul is contrasting the real participation of believers in Christ and the potentially real participation of believers in the demonic, not the real participation of believers in Christ at communion and their lack of participation in Christ at other times (1 Cor 10:20).

Paul commonly associates *koinōnia* with the Holy Spirit: "The grace of the Lord Jesus Christ, the love of God, and the communion of the Holy Spirit be with all of you" (2 Cor 13:14; cf. Phil 2:1). This is because the Holy Spirit facilitates the participation of believers in Christ and in one another. Believers have *koinōnia* with one another both spiritually and materially. It is because of their spiritual bond in Christ that Paul exhorts Gentile believers to give material aid to the poor in Jerusalem (Rom

---

[18]Sanders, *Palestinian Judaism*, pp. 454-55.
[19]J. Schattenmann, "Fellowship etc.," in *NIDNTT* 1:643-44.

15:27). By contrast, he tells Timothy not to participate in the sins of others (1 Tim 5:22). The idea of *koinōnia*, therefore, signifies more than mere association.[20]

Some scholars believe that Paul sees Christ as a corporate personality, an individual who can in some sense include others within himself or herself, so that what he or she does applies to those others: "The first and the second Adam are progenitors initiating two races of men. Each implies a whole world, an order of life or death. Each includes his adherents in and under himself."[21] Whether or not he sees Christ as a corporate personality, Paul is certainly working with some concept of corporate solidarity. This is clearest in his image of Christ as the Last Adam. Such solidarity would be a natural assumption in first-century Mediterranean culture, in which personal identity was primarily corporate.[22]

In Romans 5:12-21, Paul compares Adam and Christ in light of sin and grace. Each is one man whose actions affected all those affiliated with him. Adam's act of disobedience (sin) made many people sinners and led to judgment, condemnation and death. Christ's act of obedience made many people righteous and led to justification and life. Paul does not specify how sin, which started with one man, became universal (Rom 5:12). Any attempt to fill in this gap is speculation. However, Paul does emphasize that life in Christ is a gift of God's grace (Rom 5:15). He also claims that Christ has accomplished "much more" than Adam did (Rom 5:15, 17). If the effects of Adam's sin have been significant and far-reaching, the effects of Christ's righteousness will be even more so. However we understand the statements about "all" and "many" here, it is difficult to reconcile this passage with views of salvation that limit God's salvific will to only a few.

In 1 Corinthians 15, Paul compares Adam and Christ in terms of mortal life and resurrection life: "For as all die in Adam, so all will be made alive in Christ" (1 Cor 15:22). Once again, Christ is far superior to Adam. Adam was merely a "living being," while the Last Adam, Christ, is a "life-giving spirit" (1 Cor 15:45). Adam was from the earth and bequeathed to

---

[20]The author of Hebrews declares that it was necessary for the Son to "share" flesh and blood in order to redeem human beings who also "share" flesh and blood (Heb 2:14).

[21]Oepke, "ἐν," in *TDNT* 2:542.

[22]See the discussion in chapters two and three.

his posterity a perishable earthly body. Christ is from heaven and gives to his own an imperishable resurrection body (1 Cor 15:42, 47-48). The latter is as certain as the former: "Just as we have borne the image of the man of dust, we will also bear the image of the man of heaven" (1 Cor 15:49).

Both Adam and Christ, like the patriarchs of Genesis, are the progenitors of families of human beings.[23] Both take actions that affect the rest of their families. Both provide their families with an inheritance that shapes their destinies. Paul has identified a typological relationship that lets him make important points about the new age that has begun with Christ. But Paul's Adam/Christ typology is not just a literary device. Once again, he envisions a connection between Christ and believers that is at least as strong as the relationship between Adam and his biological descendants. His language creates a strong sense of corporate solidarity. "'Being in Christ' is therefore a social experience. What Paul has in mind is changed men and women living in a changed society, with Christ the author of the change in the individual, and Christ the living centre of the new environment in which they live."[24]

THE IMAGE OF GOD AND GLORIFICATION

The "image" language used in the Adam/Christ comparison interprets the believer's solidarity with Christ in terms of the restoration of the divine image. Human beings, both male and female, were created in the image of God (Gen 1:27), but that image was damaged by the fall. Something still remains of the divine image, since it is used as the rationale for biblical commands against murder and cursing others (Gen 9:6; Jas 3:9-10). But because of sin, Paul can say that human beings bear the image of Adam (*eikōn*; 1 Cor 15:49).

---

[23]Wedderburn sees the key to Paul's "in Christ" language in Galatians 3, where Paul says that "in Christ" the blessing of Abraham has come to the Gentiles. He believes that Paul sees both Abraham and Christ as "representative figures through whom God acts toward the human race." "Some Observations," pp. 88, 91. Herman Ridderbos identifies Paul's Adam/Christ typology as a Semitic understanding of corporate personality similar to the Old Testament kings or patriarchs who represented their people. *Paul: An Outline of His Theology*, trans. John Richard DeWitt (Grand Rapids: Eerdmans, 1975), pp. 38, 62. C. F. D. Moule argues that Paul's application of collective Old Testament figures to Jesus "seems to imply that Christian experience found in Christ not only an individual revelation of God but also the very society or corporate entity to which they belonged." *The Origin of Christology* (Cambridge: Cambridge University Press, 1977), pp. 95, 94; see also p. 50.

[24]Hunter, *Gospel According to St. Paul*, p. 34.

Jesus Christ is the perfect image of God in a human being (2 Cor 4:4; Col 1:15). Through their relationship with Christ, the Holy Spirit is progressively conforming believers to Christ's image: "Now the Lord is the Spirit, and where the Spirit of the Lord is, there is freedom. And all of us, with unveiled faces, seeing the glory of the Lord as though reflected in a mirror, are being transformed into the same image from one degree of glory to another; for this comes from the Lord, the Spirit" (2 Cor 3:17-18). God predestined this transformation for those in Christ (Rom 8:29-30). The inward dimension of this change is already underway: believers have received a new self that is being renewed in God's image (Col 3:10). The outward change will be complete at the resurrection, when they will fully bear the image of Christ (1 Cor 15:49-53). In the meantime, they are called to live as God's image-bearers, reflecting God's character (Col 3:1-11).

The passage from 2 Corinthians 3, above, indicates that believers' participation in Christ includes sharing Christ's glory. This is an extraordinary theme in the New Testament. In the Old Testament, glory belongs to God, who proclaims that he will not yield his glory to another (Is 42:8; 48:11). Human beings have a derived glory by virtue of their status as the stewards of God's creation (Ps 8:5). However, according to Paul, all human beings have fallen short of God's glory because of their sin (Rom 3:23). In redemption, through their solidarity with Christ, believers come to share the glory of God (Rom 5:2).

The glorification of believers is modeled on that of Christ and is received by participating in his life. When Christ returns in glory, believers will be glorified along with him (Mt 25:31; Col 3:4; 2 Thess 2:14). However, in order to share his glory, they must first share his sufferings (Rom 8:17). The glory of the incarnate Word was manifested most fully at the cross (Jn 1:14; 12:23-24; Heb 2:9-10). Like Jesus, believers must accept that the way to glory is through the cross. Only by being fully conformed to the image of Christ will believers come to share his glory. Even glorification has more than individual scope; the glorification of believers will result in the renewal of creation.[25]

---

[25]Bernard Ramm, *Them He Glorified: A Systematic Study of the Doctrine of Glorification* (Grand Rapids: Eerdmans, 1963), p. 105.

ALL OF CREATION IN CHRIST

The books of Ephesians and Colossians take the inclusiveness of Christ to cosmic proportions. Ephesians proclaims that God's plan for creation has been set forth in Christ—namely, his plan to sum up everything in Christ (Eph 1:9-10). Christ is both the revelation and the goal of God's salvation plan. James Dunn argues that "Paul's language indicates . . . a quite profound sense of participation with others in a great and cosmic movement of God centred [sic] on Christ and effected through his Spirit." This sense of participation is expressed not only by the phrase "in Christ" but also by the forty or so "with"-compounds (*syn-*) that Paul uses to describe believers' solidarity with Christ, about half of which are used only by Paul in the New Testament.[26]

Jesus sums up God's work with human beings through salvation history by becoming the origin of a new humanity established through the union of Jews and Gentiles in him: "For he is our peace; in his flesh he has made both groups into one and has broken down the dividing wall, that is, the hostility between us. He has abolished the law with its commandments and ordinances, that he might create in himself one new humanity in place of the two, thus making peace, and might reconcile both groups to God in one body through the cross, thus putting to death that hostility through it" (Eph 2:14-16). Through one body (the body of Jesus), Jews and Gentiles can now form one body (the body of Christ). The same point is made through a building metaphor. Both Jews and Gentiles are now members of the household of God: "In him the whole structure is joined together and grows into a holy temple in the Lord" (Eph 2:21).

In Colossians, Christ seems to be the ground of unity for creation itself: "He is the image of the invisible God, the firstborn of all creation; for *in him* all things in heaven and on earth were created, things visible and invisible, whether thrones or dominions or rulers or powers—all things have been created through him and for him. He himself is before all things, and *in him* all things hold together. . . . For *in him* all the fullness of God was pleased to dwell . . ." (Col 1:15-17, 19, italics added). The universe was created in Christ and is sustained in Christ. This is possible because he embodies the fullness of God—one instance of "in Christ" that excludes

---

[26]Dunn, *Theology of Paul*, pp. 404, 402, 402 n. 61.

believers![27] In his own body, Jesus unites Jews and Gentiles (Col 1:22). This aspect of God's plan is a great mystery, which has been revealed at last in the mission to the Gentiles: "Christ in you, the hope of glory" (Col 1:27). Because the fullness of deity dwells in Jesus, believers come to fullness in him (Col 2:9-10). Organic and building metaphors come together in Colossians 2:6-7: "As you therefore have received Christ Jesus the Lord, continue to live your lives in him, rooted and built up in him and established in the faith." Christ is the ground of unity from creation to consummation.

For Paul, participation in Christ is a comprehensive image for the new reality brought into existence by the work of Christ and experienced by the church as Christ's body. It expresses many dimensions of this new reality: identity, relationship, character, ethics, experiential intimacy, spiritual discernment, vocational calling and corporate solidarity. Being in Christ integrates conversion and the Christian life, salvation and ethics, theology and spiritual formation. It reminds us that salvation from beginning to end is centered on Christ, and it underscores our complete dependence upon him.

2 PETER AND THEOSIS

What we have seen in both John and Paul suggests that the result of participating in Christ is becoming like Christ. Morna Hooker prefers the term "interchange" for this idea in Paul: "Now 'interchange' is a term which some of us have used for the idea which Paul sometimes uses, but which can perhaps best be summed up in some words of Irenaeus: 'Christ became what we are, in order that we might become what he is'." In other words, Christ shared human experience in the incarnation and thereafter enabled human beings to share his. "It is not a matter of substitution, whereby Christ dies and we live. Rather, he shares our life and our death; and we, in turn, share his death and his life, by dying to sin and living to God."[28]

The idea of sharing Christ's life finds exalted expression in 2 Peter: "His divine power has given us everything needed for life and godliness, through the knowledge of him who called us by his own glory and goodness. Thus he has given us, through these things, his precious and very

---

[27]Best, *One Body in Christ*, p. 6.
[28]Morna Hooker, "Interchange in Christ and Ethics," *Journal for the Study of the New Testament* 25 (1985): 6, 7.

great promises, so that through them you may escape from the corruption that is in the world because of lust, and may become participants of the divine nature" (2 Pet 1:3-4). Christ has given believers all they need for godly living now, along with promises that will lead eventually to incorruption and participation in divinity. Through this participation in Christ, believers are empowered to escape the corruption of sin that leads to death.

This passage is the most important biblical foundation for the doctrine of *theosis*, usually translated divinization or deification.[29] Irenaeus's aphorism on Christ, quoted above, is one version of this doctrine. A more familiar version is that of Athanasius of Alexandria, the fourth-century bishop, who declared that in Christ, God became human so that human beings might become divine.[30] This idea sounds strange, even heretical, to modern Western ears. Yet *theosis* is the primary way in which the church fathers understood salvation, and it is the primary view in Eastern Orthodox Christianity today. In the incarnation, divinity unites with humanity in the person of Jesus Christ. Then as human beings are united with Christ through the Holy Spirit, they are healed, restored and brought to share in the life and character of God.

What does it mean that believers "become participants of the divine nature"? Besides life (2 Pet 1:3), the context in 2 Peter 1 suggests that Peter primarily has moral qualities in mind.[31] The following verses illustrate what godliness (2 Pet 1:3) looks like: "For this very reason, you must make every effort to support your faith with goodness, and goodness with knowledge, and knowledge with self-control, and self-control with endurance, and endurance with godliness, and godliness with mutual affection, and mutual affection with love. For if these things are yours and are increasing among you, they keep you from being ineffective and unfruitful

---

[29]For a summary of the biblical evidence for *theosis*, see Veli-Matti Kärkkäinen, *One with God: Salvation as Deification and Justification* (Collegeville, Minn.: Liturgical Press, 2004), pp. 18-19.

[30]Athanasius, *On the Incarnation* 54, in *Christology of the Later Fathers*, ed. Edward Rochie Hardy, Library of Christian Classics (Philadelphia: Westminster Press, 1954), p. 107. Although I have cited Athanasius, many other church fathers expressed the same idea.

[31]James Starr identifies five qualities associated with divine nature in 2 Peter 1:1-4: incorruptibility, power, glory, excellence or virtue, righteousness or justice (also understood in moral terms). "Does 2 Peter 1:4 Speak of Deification?" in *Partakers of the Divine Nature: The History and Development of Deification in the Christian Tradition*, ed. Michael J. Christensen and Jeffery A. Wittung (Grand Rapids: Baker, 2007), p. 82.

in the knowledge of our Lord Jesus Christ" (2 Pet 1:5-8). While they have received from God "everything needed" for godliness, believers must cultivate these virtues as a support for their faith, so that their lives will be effective and fruitful. Their growth in Christ will "confirm" God's call upon their lives and ensure their final salvation: "Therefore, brothers and sisters, be all the more eager to confirm your call and election, for if you do this, you will never stumble. For in this way, entry into the eternal kingdom of our Lord and Savior Jesus Christ will be richly provided for you" (2 Pet 1:10-11).

Clearly, then, Peter is not talking about human beings becoming gods—or God—but about their taking on particular divine moral qualities that are characteristic of Christ.[32] The key to this process of transformation is "the knowledge of our Lord Jesus Christ."[33] This knowledge is more than a factual knowledge about Christ; it is a personal knowledge of him. Starr calls it "an *effective* knowledge of Christ, received at conversion, that leads ultimately to eternal life."[34] Through their relationship with Christ, believers become like him. They share in his character and in his life, the life of the "eternal kingdom."

Like being in Christ, participating in the divine nature has both present and future dimensions. Believers can grow in Christlike virtues in the present, and they can look forward to a future of incorruption and eternal life. They do not achieve this future by their own efforts, however; they receive it only because of their knowledge of Christ.[35]

CONCLUSION

The image of salvation as participation focuses not on what we have done and how we can do better, but on who we are and how we can become the people God has always intended us to be. This view is well expressed in the title of the book by John Zizioulas *Being as Communion*.[36] Our identity

---

[32]Starr, "2 Peter 1:4," p. 85. Stephen Finlan states that divinization is "progress into greater moral excellence." "Second Peter's Notion of Divine Participation," in *Theosis: Deification in Christian Theology*, ed. Stephen Finlan and Vladimir Kharlamov, Princeton Theological Monograph Series, ed. K. C. Hanson (Eugene, Ore.: Pickwick, 2006), p. 46.

[33]Finlan, "Second Peter's Notion," p. 45.

[34]Starr, "2 Peter 1:4," p. 83.

[35]Ibid., pp. 88, 84.

[36]John Zizioulas, *Being as Communion: Studies in Personhood and the Church*, Contemporary Greek Theologians 4 (Crestwood, N.Y.: St. Vladimir's Seminary Press, 1985).

is shaped by our relationships with God and others. We know from experience that we tend to become like our companions. If we live our lives in union with Christ, the Holy Spirit can work Christ's holy character into our lives. Salvation is thus a process of spiritual formation, in the context of relationship, that leads to our eventual glorification along with Christ (Rom 8:29-30).

Exploring the image of participation in Christ might create space for fruitful dialogue between Eastern and Western theologians.[37] For those of us in Western Christian traditions, participation in Christ deserves our attention, if only to balance our traditional emphasis on legal models of salvation. Possible resources might include the writings of the sixteenth-century Dutch Anabaptists, such as Menno Simons and Dirk Phillips, who drew upon participatory images for their understanding of salvation. Similarly, recent studies of Luther, prompted by the work of Finnish scholars, have been retrieving the more participatory dimensions of Luther's theology, including his understanding of union with Christ.[38]

Being in Christ is not transactional but relational. Although it originates in the objective acts of God, and thus is not solely experiential, being in Christ is also a deeply personal relationship that can be experienced as love, joy and peace. The spiritual union between Christ and believers is as real as any physical union. Whatever trials life should bring, being in Christ means that we need not face those trials alone.

While personal, being in Christ is not individualistic. Believers participate in Christ as members of his body, the church. Because they are joined to Christ, believers are joined to one another—whether they like it or not! Taking this truth seriously could transform Protestant ecclesiology. It means that the church is not a collection of individuals who have individual relationships with Christ but interdependent members of a single body who cannot attain health or maturity except in union with one another.

---

[37]See, for example, Thomas N. Finger, "Anabaptism and Orthodoxy: Some Unexpected Similarities?" *Journal of Ecumenical Studies* 31, no. 1-2 (Winter-Spring 1994): 67-91; Veli-Matti Kärkkäinen, *One with God: Salvation as Deification and Justification* (Collegeville, Minn.: Liturgical Press, 2005); Gannon Murphy, "Reformed *Theosis?*" *Theology Today* 65, no. 2 (July 2008): 191-212; and Myk Habets, "Reformed *Theosis*? A Response to Gannon Murphy," *Theology Today* 65, no. 4 (January 2009): 489-98.

[38]For an introduction to the Finnish scholarship on Luther, see Carl E. Braaten and Robert W. Jenson, eds., *Union with Christ: The New Finnish Interpretation of Luther* (Grand Rapids: Eerdmans, 1998).

As with other images of salvation, participation in Christ requires both divine initiative and human response. The Holy Spirit plays a critical role, joining believers to Christ and nurturing their union with him. We must cooperate with the Spirit until Christ is formed in us (Gal 4:19). Salvation is thus a process of spiritual formation empowered by God's grace. For our part, we must practice spiritual disciplines, clothing ourselves with Christ until we grow together into the stature of Christ.

Participation in Christ is inherently transformational. It is not an ontological union but a spiritual union between persons whose personhood is preserved. It pictures salvation as a process of transformation into Christ's image, in which believers are made like God in the way God intended when he created human beings in his own image. When the process is complete, believers will demonstrate God's character, share God's life and reflect God's glory. D. E. H. Whiteley has effectively summarized the significance of this image for Paul: "If St. Paul can be said to hold a theory of the [atonement], it is best described as one of salvation through participation: Christ shared all our experiences, sin alone excepted, including death, in order that we, by virtue of our solidarity with him, might share his life."[39]

FOR FURTHER READING

Best, Ernest. *One Body in Christ*. London: SPCK, 1980.

Dunn, James D. G. *The Theology of Paul the Apostle*. Grand Rapids: Eerdmans, 1998, pp. 390-412.

Finlan, Stephen. "Can We Speak of Theosis in Paul?" pp. 68-80. In *Partakers of the Divine Nature: The History and Development of Deification in the Christian Traditions*. Edited by Michael J. Christensen and Jeffery A. Wittung. Grand Rapids: Baker, 2007.

———. "Second Peter's Notion of Divine Participation," pp. 32-50. In *Theosis: Deification in Christian Theology*. Edited by Stephen Finlan and Vladimir Kharlamov. Princeton Theological Monograph Series. Eugene, Ore.: Pickwick, 2006.

Grossouw, W. *In Christ*. Westminster: Newman, 1952.

Moule, C. F. D. *The Origin of Christology*. Cambridge: Cambridge University Press, 1977, pp. 47-96.

---

[39]D. E. H. Whiteley, *The Theology of St. Paul* (Oxford: Basil Blackwell, 1974), p. 130.

Powers, Daniel G. *Salvation Through Participation: An Examination of the Notion of the Believers' Corporate Unity with Christ in Early Christian Soteriology.* Leuven: Peeters, 2001.

Ramm, Bernard. *Them He Glorified: A Systematic Study of the Doctrine of Glorification.* Grand Rapids: Eerdmans, 1963.

Reid, J. K. S. "The Phrase 'In Christ.'" *Theology Today* 17 (1960): 353-65.

Sanders, E. P. *Paul and Palestinian Judaism: A Comparison of Patterns of Religion.* Minneapolis: Augsburg Fortress, 1977, pp. 447-523.

Smedes, Lewis B. "Being in Christ," pp. 142-54. In *Major Themes in the Reformed Tradition.* Edited by Donald K. McKim. Grand Rapids: Eerdmans, 1992.

Starr, James. "Does 2 Peter 1:4 Speak of Deification?" pp. 81-92. In *Partakers of the Divine Nature: The History and Development of Deification in the Christian Traditions.* Edited by Michael J. Christensen and Jeffery A. Wittung. Grand Rapids: Baker, 2007.

Wedderburn, A. J. M. "Some Observations on Paul's Use of the Phrases 'in Christ' and 'with Christ.'" *Journal for the Study of the New Testament* 25 (1985): 89-91.

12

A PEOPLE
HOLY TO THE LORD

Sanctification, Perfection

IT IS NOT UNCOMMON IN SOME segments of the church for people to deflect praise by saying, "I'm just a sinner saved by grace!" No doubt people do this to express their awareness that they owe their salvation completely to God's mercy rather than to their own merit. However, when Paul refers to Christians, he never calls them sinners. He calls them saints—*hagioi*—holy ones. Even the unruly Corinthians qualify for this title: "To the church of God that is in Corinth, to those who are sanctified in Christ Jesus, called to be saints" (1 Cor 1:2). The New Testament does not reserve the term "saint" for certain Christians of exceptional spiritual attainment but applies it to all of God's people. All Christians are "sanctified in Christ Jesus."

Whether or not they belong to a tradition that emphasizes holiness, all Christians need to know what to expect of the Christian life. So do those who are considering a commitment to Christ. What behavior should we expect of those who claim to be Christian? What growth should we expect for ourselves? Can people really change? Is there hope for Christians who struggle with sin? These questions are addressed by the biblical image of sanctification.

JUSTIFICATION AND SANCTIFICATION

Protestant theology has often subordinated sanctification to justification.

Commonly, sanctification is regarded as the process of becoming holy that follows upon justification, understood as a forensic declaration of righteousness. In sanctification, believers are to become in actuality what they are declared to be by virtue of their legal standing in Christ.[1] In this view, salvation depends solely upon the declaration of justification, not upon actual holiness. Although most theologians argue that growth in holiness should follow justification, the traditional Protestant understanding of justification can provide no reason why it must.[2]

Some Protestants believe that to focus on sanctification is to endanger the truth of justification by implying that something that involves human effort could take believers further than justification by faith alone. For example, Lutheran theologian Gerhard O. Forde, although reluctant to discuss sanctification at all, describes it as "the art of getting used to justification."[3] People who describe themselves as sinners saved by grace are stating a popular version of the Lutheran adage *simul justus et peccator*—at the same time justified and sinner.

Other scholars see two aspects of sanctification—initial sanctification and ongoing sanctification—but they assimilate these to a forensic understanding of justification. In this view, because Christ's righteousness has been imputed to believers in justification, God regards believers as holy even though they are not. This initial sanctification refers to believers' position or status before God because of Christ. Then the ongoing or progressive aspect of sanctification refers to the growth in actual holiness that develops in the lives of believers through the work of the Holy Spirit.[4]

---

[1]See, for example, Millard Erickson, *Christian Theology*, 2nd ed. (Grand Rapids: Baker, 1998), p. 980; and Peter Toon, *Justification and Sanctification*, Foundations for Faith Series, ed. Peter Toon (Westchester, Ill.: Crossway, 1983), p. 42.

[2]Rodney R. Hutton observes, "So long as justification and sanctification are juxtaposed in this manner, there will be little opportunity for resolution of questions related to leading a life holy and acceptable to God." "Innocent or Holy: Justification and Sanctification," *Word & World* 17, no. 3 (Summer 1997): 314.

[3]Gerhard O. Forde, "Lutheran View," in *Christian Spirituality: Five Views of Sanctification*, ed. Donald L. Alexander (Downers Grove, Ill.: InterVarsity Press, 1988), p. 13. The original is italicized.

[4]For example, Stanley J. Grenz expresses the two aspects of sanctification as positional and conditional sanctification. *Theology for the Community of God* (1994; reprint, Grand Rapids: Eerdmans, 2000), pp. 441-43. References are to the 2000 edition. He argues that the punctiliar aspect of sanctification is forensic—a legal declaration of a new status in relationship to God (p. 441). Erickson distinguishes between sanctification as a "formal characteristic" of being set apart and sanctification as "moral goodness or spiritual worth." Although he acknowledges

However, the New Testament does not present justification and sanctification as sequential, nor does it subordinate one to the other. The two terms express two different images of salvation drawn from two different contexts. Justification comes from a forensic context: God vindicates those who have faith in Christ, rather than those who have the law, as the true covenant people of God. Sanctification comes from a cultic context: it establishes the identity of God's people as those who have been set apart to worship and serve him and who therefore have been called to a vocation of holiness. The two images address two different visions of the human predicament. Justification views human beings as covenant breakers who need to be restored to faithful relationship with God. Sanctification regards human beings as defiled by sin and in need of purification. We have already explored the model of justification in chapter nine. In this chapter, we will examine sanctification.

WHAT IS SANCTIFICATION?

In the New Testament, sanctification is not primarily an ethical quality. When Paul calls the Corinthians "those who are sanctified in Christ Jesus, called to be saints" (1 Cor 1:2), he clearly does not mean that they no longer sin. If that were the case, his letters to them would be much shorter! Moreover, Paul does not use sanctification language to refer to a special elite among the Christians in Corinth but to the entire "church of God that is in Corinth." Sanctification must apply in some sense to all Christians regardless of their spiritual maturity or moral character.

Paul's address to the Corinthians illustrates the two dimensions of sanctification. The Corinthians have already been "sanctified in Christ Jesus," but they are also "called to be saints." In the first instance, sanctification is something that has already been done for them in Christ. It is an existing reality accomplished by God. In the second instance, sanctification is something they are to pursue. It is a future reality that depends at least partly on their own efforts. Put another way, this verse expresses sanctification as both an *identity* and a *vocation*.[5] It is both a gift and a

---

that both senses occur in the New Testament, he goes on to contrast sanctification with justification, arguing that justification is an instantaneous legal declaration, while sanctification is a life-long process (pp. 980-82).

[5] John G. Gammie describes holiness as first a presence (God's presence) and then a vocation (for God's people). *Holiness in Israel*, Overtures to Biblical Theology Series (Minneapolis: Fortress,

task. The Corinthians have been set apart to belong to God and to serve him. Because they have been identified with God through Christ, they are called to live lives that reflect the character and purposes of the holy God they serve. If we think of holiness as a vocation, we need not argue that God regards believers as holy (i.e., morally pure) even though they are not. Instead, we can affirm that God regards believers as holy (i.e., consecrated to his service) because they are.

As in the case of justification, sanctification is expressed in the New Testament by words that are all related in Greek but are translated into English by unrelated words. The word *hagiazō* could be translated as to sanctify, to make holy or to consecrate, just as the noun *hagiasmos* could be translated as sanctification, holiness or consecration. Holiness is a quality or state that is required for approaching the divine. The adjective *ha gios* (holy) means belonging to God or dedicated to God's service. In biblical usage, as distinct from classical Greek, *hagios* begins to take on the connotation of purity, in that something that belongs to God must be pure as God is pure.[6]

In the Old Testament, people, places and things can be sanctified— that is, designated as belonging to the sacred rather than to the profane. In Leviticus 10:10, God says to Aaron, "You are to distinguish between the holy and the common, and between the unclean and the clean." Places where God appears, such as the burning bush, are regarded as holy ground, different from ordinary places (Ex 3:5). Some days, such as the Sabbath, are holy because they have been set apart by God for particular purposes (Is 58:13). Furnishings that have been set apart to be used in the Temple cannot be used for any other purpose (Num 18:3). Priests are set apart from other people in order to be dedicated to God's service (Ex 29:1).

Holiness is fundamentally a quality of God. It expresses God's divinity as distinct from the finitude and imperfection of his creatures.[7] "To say that God is holy describes him as the 'Wholly Other' and indicates the numinous power of his being, in the presence of which human beings must perish if

---

1989), p. 195. Joel B. Green links sanctification with vocation in *Salvation*, Understanding Biblical Themes Series (St. Louis: Chalice, 2003), p. 58.

[6]"ἁγιάζω," "ἁγιασμός," "ἅγιος," in *BAGD*, pp. 8-10. H. Seebass argues that unlike *hieros*, which refers to the intrinsically holy or to things consecrated to it, *hagios* has ethical connotations, emphasizing the "duty to worship the holy." "Holy etc.," in *NIDNTT* 2:223.

[7]D. Procksch, "ἅγιος κτλ.," in *TDNT* 1:91; Toon, *Justification and Sanctification*, pp. 37-38.

they are not cleansed." Persons, places and things that have been sanctified or set apart to belong to God are "marks of the transcendent" that represent the presence of God in the world.[8] Since God has chosen Israel as his special possession and dwells with them in covenant relationship, Israel must be "a people holy to the LORD" (Deut 7:6). Because they belong to God, they must worship and serve him only, rejecting all other allegiances. They are "a priestly kingdom and a holy nation" (Ex 19:6), who have been called to live according to God's purposes.[9] Although Israel collectively is a holy people, the members of that people are rarely called saints.

Some shifts in emphasis take place in the New Testament. In the New Testament, the word *hagios* is seldom used for the Father or for Jesus, although Jesus is called the Holy One of God in Mark 1:24 and Luke 4:34 and God's holy servant in Acts 4:27. The great majority of references to God as holy refer to the Holy Spirit. This change reflects the New Testament emphasis on the activity of the Spirit in the new age inaugurated by Christ's death and resurrection. Moreover, holiness is now less a quality of places, things or rites and more a quality of the people of God as they are indwelt by the Spirit and live their lives according to the Spirit.[10] In essence, the cultic context of holiness has become spiritualized. With the coming of Christ, the old barrier between sacred and profane has been removed. God can be worshiped anywhere in spirit and in truth (Jn 4:24). The veil in the temple has been torn in two (Mk 15:38).

SANCTIFICATION AS IDENTITY AND VOCATION

As in the Old Testament, sanctification in the New Testament fundamentally has to do with setting apart the people of God to belong to God and to worship and serve him. But unlike Israel, believers are called *hoi hagioi*,

---

[8]Walter F. Klaiber, "Sanctification in the New Testament," *Asbury Theological Journal* 50, no. 2/51, no. 1 (Fall 1995/Spring 1996): 12.

[9]Rodney Hutton describes two different understandings of sanctification in the Old Testament that resemble my distinction between identity and vocation. In the Deuteronomistic understanding, expressed in verses such as Deuteronomy 7:6, sanctification or holiness is an a priori status that belongs to Israel by virtue of divine election. Israel is God's holy possession—not because of their actions but by God's choice. "They were set apart as holy in spite of what they were like!" By contrast, in the Priestly understanding, expressed in verses such as Leviticus 19:2, sanctification or holiness is "the quality of life to which Israel is called in obedience." The former understanding has a relational context; the latter understanding focuses on the need to avoid defilement in order to remain in the presence of God. "Innocent or Holy," pp. 316-17.

[10]Seebass, "Holy," in *NIDNTT* 2:228.

the saints or holy ones, because they are associated with the Holy Spirit. Holiness here is not primarily moral but is similar to concepts like calling and election. It is thus a "pre-ethical" term. But if believers are being led by the Spirit, they will engage in behavior that reflects the leading of the Spirit.[11]

Peter borrows the language of Exodus to describe the church:

> But you are a chosen race, a royal priesthood, a holy nation, God's own people, in order that you may proclaim the mighty acts of him who called you out of darkness into his marvelous light. Once you were not a people, but now you are God's people; once you had not received mercy, but now you have received mercy. Beloved, I urge you as aliens and exiles to abstain from the desires of the flesh that wage war against the soul. Conduct yourselves honorably among the Gentiles, so that, though they malign you as evildoers, they may see your honorable deeds and glorify God when he comes to judge. (1 Pet 2:9)

Sanctification defines the identity of the church, in that the church has been chosen and set apart to belong to God. Sanctification thus has covenantal associations. The setting apart of the church, like the setting apart of Israel, carries with it an exclusive relationship with God.[12] This identity marks believers as "aliens and exiles" in the world, setting them apart from their contemporaries. But God has called the church to a vocation: to testify to the "mighty acts" of the one who called them. As God's people, believers are to live in a way that honors God before the rest of the world. "Holiness, a state of belonging to God and being dedicated to him, relates directly to the Church's being called to service and sacrifice in the power of the Holy Spirit."[13] One might say that holiness has both centripetal and centrifugal force: it both draws inward and pushes outward. On one hand, the setting-apart and the behavior that goes with it serve to reinforce community boundaries.[14] On the other hand, the integrity of the community

---

[11]Ibid., 2:229.

[12]David Peterson, *Possessed by God: A New Testament Theology of Sanctification and Holiness*, New Studies in Biblical Theology (Grand Rapids: Eerdmans, 1995), pp. 35, 44, 59.

[13]Toon, *Justification and Sanctification*, p. 40.

[14]Robert Hodgson Jr. discusses the social function of holiness in constructing identity and maintaining community boundaries. "Holiness Tradition and Social Description: Intertestamental Judaism and Early Christianity" in *Reaching Beyond: Chapters in the History of Perfectionism*, ed. Stanley M. Burgess (Peabody, Mass.: Hendrickson, 1986), pp. 86-87. Some present-day groups use holiness in a similar fashion, maintaining lists of acceptable actions or (more often)

as it lives out its vocation invites others to join in glorifying God.

Holiness is thus first of all corporate. The church is God's holy people, his treasured possession. The church is also the Bride of Christ, for whom Christ gave himself so that he could "make her holy by cleansing her with the washing of water by the word" (Eph 5:26-27). Cleansing or purification [*katharismos*, verb *katharizō*] is cultic language similar to sanctification. It denotes that someone is qualified to appear before God. The source of sanctification is Christ; the means of sanctification are the gospel and baptism—the former because it presents God's call, and the latter because it enacts the believer's response. Corporate holiness is often expressed in cultic language. For example, the church, composed of both Jews and Gentiles, is a holy temple in which God dwells (Eph 2:21). Because the church is God's holy possession, God will destroy anyone who destroys it (1 Cor 3:16-17).

Besides being corporate, however, holiness is also individual. Paul declares that the bodies of individual believers are temples in which the Holy Spirit dwells (1 Cor 6:19). Like the church, the believer's body belongs to the Lord, so it must be used accordingly. In 2 Timothy 2:20-21, Paul compares the sanctification of believers to the setting apart of utensils in the home: "In a large house there are utensils not only of gold and silver but also of wood and clay, some for special use, some for ordinary. All who cleanse themselves of the things I have mentioned will become special utensils, dedicated and useful to the owner of the house, ready for every good work." The word translated "dedicated" here is *hēgiasmenon* (having been sanctified). The passage illustrates that holiness is not only an identity but also a vocation. Believers are "special utensils," but utensils are designed with a purpose. Sanctification makes believers useful to God by fitting them for good works.

Sanctification is usually a divine action. In various passages it is attributed to the Father (1 Thess 5:23-24), the Son (Eph 5:25-27), and the Spirit (Rom 15:16). New Testament writers agree that the sanctification of believers is based on the work of Christ. Hebrews pictures Christ's death as an act of sacrifice that sanctifies believers definitively: "And it is by God's will that we have been sanctified through the offering of the body of Jesus

---

unacceptable actions in order to maintain social cohesion and identify who is truly a member of the group.

Christ once for all" (Heb 10:10). Jesus is the agent of sanctification because he is the high priest (Heb 2:11, 17) and also because he is the sacrifice whose blood ratifies the new covenant (Heb 10:29; 13:12). In Hebrews, which uses cultic imagery extensively, sanctification is the consecration and purification that is necessary to qualify someone to approach God.

For Paul, sanctification is accomplished by Christ and applied by the Spirit. He declares that Christ "became for us wisdom from God, and righteousness and sanctification and redemption" (1 Cor 1:30). Christ is believers' sanctification in two senses: his work is its source, and believers receive it by being united with him. The parallel with righteousness and redemption suggests that this sanctification takes place at conversion.[15] Similarly, in 1 Corinthians 6, Paul lists various wrongdoers who will not inherit the kingdom of God. He then adds, "And this is what some of you used to be. But you were washed, you were sanctified, you were justified in the name of the Lord Jesus Christ and in the Spirit of our God" (1 Cor 6:10-11). The conjunction of washing (presumably baptism), sanctification, and justification again implies that Paul has conversion in view. Paul tells the Thessalonians that "God chose [them] as the first fruits for salvation through sanctification by the Spirit and through belief in the truth" (2 Thess 2:13). In this passage, sanctification is clearly not a follow-up to justification but an image of salvation in its own right. Sanctification by the Spirit seems to be the divine initiative to which faith is the human response. According to Acts 26:18, Paul quotes Jesus as saying that believers are sanctified by faith in him.

In Acts 15:9, in similar language, Peter declares that God has given the Gentiles the Holy Spirit, "cleansing their hearts by faith." The Holy Spirit cleanses or sanctifies, but human faith is necessary. Like sanctification, cleansing seems to be both punctiliar and ongoing. The vision of the clean and unclean animals, as well as the Gentiles' reception of the Holy Spirit, had demonstrated to Peter that God had cleansed the Gentiles, making them qualified to approach God on the same basis as Jewish believers. Likewise, Hebrews 1:3 states that Jesus "made purification for sins" and

---

[15]According to Gordon D. Fee, sanctification is a figure for conversion, not for "a work of grace *following* conversion." *Paul, the Spirit, and the People of God* (Peabody, Mass.: Hendrickson, 1996), p. 93 (italics in original).

sat down at God's right hand, his work finished. But other New Testament passages picture cleansing as an ongoing need. For example, 1 John 1:9 instructs believers to confess their sins to God so that God can "cleanse [them] from all unrighteousness."

In 1 Peter 1:2, sanctification is part of a trinitarian picture of salvation: Believers "have been chosen and destined by God the Father and sanctified by the Spirit to be obedient to Jesus Christ and to be sprinkled with his blood." As in 2 Thessalonians 2:13, the Father is the one who chooses believers. Then the Spirit consecrates them to be cleansed by Christ's atonement and to follow Christ in obedience.

Vocation is a helpful model for understanding both sanctification and cleansing. At conversion, believers are set apart to belong to God and serve him. In order to serve God, believers must rely on the power and guidance of the Holy Spirit. As they follow the Spirit's leading, they become more and more suited to their vocation. Similarly, while believers are cleansed at their conversion on the basis of the work of Christ so that they can serve God, they must keep going to God for cleansing in order to continue to be useful to him.

The idea of vocation makes sense of the language of calling in the New Testament. Scholars usually assume that calling in the New Testament, especially in Paul, is a technical term for God's invitation to salvation.[16] This is no doubt true. However, people are not called to a salvation with no content. The idea of vocation fleshes out what salvation entails. For example, Paul tells the Corinthians that they are "called to be saints" (1 Cor 1:2). He tells believers that they have been called to a holy life (1 Thess 4:7; 2 Tim 1:9), and he exhorts them to live lives worthy of their calling (1 Thess 2:12; Eph 4:1). Paul's own Damascus Road experience, whether or not it was a conversion, was certainly a call to vocation. According to Acts 26:16, Paul describes it as such. He quotes Jesus as saying, "I have appeared to you for this purpose, to appoint you to serve and testify to the things in which you have seen me and to those in which I will appear to you." In Romans 1:1, he describes himself as one "called to be an apostle, set apart for the gospel of God."

---

[16]See, for example, K. L. Schmidt, "καλέω κτλ.," in *TDNT* 3:489. Schmidt argues that *kaleō* is a technical term for God's invitation to salvation even when salvation is not explicitly mentioned. See also L. Coenen, "Call," in *NIDNTT* 1:275. See also the discussion in chapter ten.

The analogy of vocation explains why sanctification does not originate with human beings but sometimes requires human effort. God sets apart or calls to a vocation, but those who are called or set apart must dedicate themselves to the vocation and live it out in the power of the Spirit. The need for dedication explains the rare instances of "self-consecration" or "self-cleansing" in the New Testament (Jesus in Jn 17:19; believers in 2 Tim 2:20-21). Both for Jesus and for believers, sanctification means distinctiveness from the world, but it does not mean withdrawal from the world. They are set apart so that they can go into the world as witnesses to God: "It is just this distance from the world which is the basis of their existence for the world as messengers of God's reconciling love within the world."[17]

Vocation draws upon two practices in the Old Testament background of sanctification: the calling of prophets and the consecration of priests. Call narratives are quite characteristic of Old Testament prophetic literature. In Jeremiah's call narrative, God announces that he has consecrated Jeremiah to be a prophet to the nations (LXX *hēgiaka*). In Isaiah 6:1-8, the prophet laments his own uncleanness because of his vision of God's holiness. One of the seraphs purifies his speech with a coal taken from the altar so that he can respond to God's call. Like the Old Testament prophets, Christians are set apart and called to testify to God by their words and their lives.

The New Testament also applies priestly language to believers. While the church corporately is a "royal priesthood" (1 Pet 2:9), individual believers are priests also. Peter calls them "a holy priesthood, to offer spiritual sacrifices acceptable to God through Jesus Christ" (1 Pet 2:5). Revelation uses the same conjunction of royalty and priesthood to describe believers (Rev 1:6; 5:10; 20:6). Paul describes his apostleship as his "priestly service of the gospel of God," in which he presents the Gentiles to God as an offering sanctified by the Holy Spirit (Rom 15:16). Although they do not use priestly language to describe it, both James and John instruct believers in their responsibility to intercede for one another in prayer (Jas 5:13-20; 1 Jn 5:16).

The author of Hebrews does not call believers priests, perhaps because he wants to keep the focus on Jesus as high priest, but priestly language is pervasive in the latter part of the book. Believers now have access to God's

---

[17]Klaiber, "Sanctification," pp. 14, 16.

presence as only the high priest once had because Jesus their high priest entered God's the sanctuary and remains there (see Heb 4:14-16; 10:19-25). They can approach God because they have been washed and sprinkled to make them holy (Heb 10:22). Believers have "an altar from which those who officiate in the tent have no right to eat" (Heb 13:10). They can "offer to God an acceptable worship" and present sacrifices of praise and good works (Heb 12:28; 13:15-16).

SANCTIFICATION AS GROWTH IN HOLINESS

Thus the notion of being set apart and consecrated to a special vocation is woven throughout the New Testament. Having been set apart to serve God, believers should reflect the character and priorities of the one who called them, the one to whom they belong: "Therefore, prepare your minds for action; discipline yourselves; set all your hope on the grace that Jesus Christ will bring you when he is revealed. Like obedient children, do not be conformed to the desires that you formerly had in ignorance. Instead, as he who called you is holy, be holy yourselves in all your conduct, for it is written, 'You shall be holy, for I am holy'" (1 Pet 1:13-16, quoting Lev 19:2). Holiness requires discipline and effort, but this effort is a response to God's mercy extended in the gospel and is motivated by the hope inspired by it (1 Pet 1:3).

Living out a vocation of holiness involves both divine initiative and human response. As believers are indwelt by the Holy Spirit, they become a "place of divine presence" that is shaped and filled by God's power.[18] Holiness is God's will for believers (1 Thess 4:3), but it requires their cooperation.[19] They must reject sin and live lives of purity that honor God (1 Thess 4:1-8). Such holiness is not optional. Following the analogy of training for an athletic context, the author of Hebrews exhorts his audience to "pursue peace with everyone, and the holiness without which no one will see the Lord" (Heb 12:14; cf. Heb 12:1-13). Only holy people can dwell in the presence of a holy God (cf. Mt 5:8). The vision of holy living in Hebrews 13 embraces the personal, the interpersonal and the social— welcoming strangers, visiting those in prison, being faithful in marriage,

---

[18]Klaiber, "Sanctification," p. 16.
[19]Sanctification is "is a work of God into which he nevertheless calls for and makes use of the cooperation of the whole Christian community." Toon, *Justification and Sanctification*, p. 40.

rejecting materialism, following leaders, resisting false teaching, enduring persecution with patience, testifying to God and sharing with others.[20] However, despite the human effort involved, God does not intend that believers should somehow generate their own holiness but that they should share his (Heb 12:10).

So how do believers grow in holiness? The New Testament identifies means such as the word of God and prayer (Jn 17:17; 1 Tim 4:5). Believers must also trust God to work through suffering to develop Christlike virtues in them (Heb 12:7-11; cf. Rom 5:3-5). The corporate context of sanctification, discussed above, suggests that believers are meant to support one another in their efforts to cultivate virtue and shun vice (see Eph 4:7-16). Many Christian virtues, such as love, patience and gentleness, must be exercised in relationship to others. The New Testament has no shortage of counsel on holy living. From that wealth of material, I will make three suggestions, which conveniently take a trinitarian shape: in order to grow in holiness, believers must offer themselves to God, imitate Christ, and follow the leading of the Spirit. All three of these insights come from the writings of Paul.

First, believers must offer themselves to God. Romans 6 presents this idea in terms of slavery. Paul exhorts his readers, "No longer present your members to sin as instruments of wickedness, but present yourselves to God as those who have been brought from death to life, and present your members to God as instruments of righteousness. . . . Now that you have been enslaved to God, the advantage you get is sanctification" (Rom 6:13, 22). To grow in holiness, believers must make themselves available to God and serve God rather than sin. While believers have "enslaved" themselves to God at conversion, they must reaffirm that commitment in their actions every day by "presenting" themselves to the right master for that master's service.

In Romans 12:1-2, Paul uses cultic language: "I appeal to you therefore, brothers and sisters, by the mercies of God, to present your bodies as a living sacrifice, holy and acceptable to God, which is your spiritual worship. Do not be conformed to this world, but be transformed by the renewing of your minds, so that you may discern what is the will of God—what is good and acceptable and perfect." In response to their experience of God's grace,

---

[20]On the depiction of holiness in Hebrews 13, see Peterson, *Possessed by God*, p. 76.

believers offer themselves to God to be transformed from the inside out. The body stands for the whole person here. As they submit themselves to God rather than to the world, they find that they are enabled to see God's will more clearly. Both God and the believer have a role in this sanctification. As Morna Hooker observes, "Paul's logic holds divine grace and human response firmly together: without the mercies of God, men are not able to respond to God in true worship; when they experience them, then response to the demand to acknowledge God and to give him glory becomes both imperative and feasible."[21]

Second, besides offering themselves to God, believers must imitate Christ. Paul insists on this: "Be imitators of me, as I am of Christ" (1 Cor 11:1); "Welcome one another, therefore, as Christ has welcomed you" (Rom 15:7); "Let the same mind be in you that was in Christ Jesus" (Phil 2:5). Other writers make the same point: "For to this you have been called, because Christ also suffered for you, leaving you an example, so that you should follow in his steps" (1 Pet 2:21); "Whoever says, 'I abide in him,' ought to walk just as he walked" (1 Jn 2:6).[22] Paul's use of the Christ hymn in Philippians 2:6-11, as model and motivation for the attitude he urges upon believers, is one of the clearest illustrations of the adage that Christ became as we are so that we could become as he is. The attitudes and actions necessary for becoming like Christ are the same attitudes and actions that were necessary for Christ to become like us.[23]

Paul repeatedly refers to the actions of Christ as the paradigm for Christian behavior. Following Christ's example, however, is more than mere imitation; it is identification. Just as Christ identified himself with human beings in the incarnation and atonement, his followers are called to identify with him and allow their lives to be shaped by his. This solidarity is possible because the Spirit of Christ indwells believers and communicates to them the mind of Christ (1 Cor 2:11-16). This identification is so complete that Paul can say, "It is no longer I who live, but it is Christ who lives

---

[21]Morna D. Hooker, "Interchange in Christ and Ethics," *Journal for the Study of the New Testament* 25 (1985): 4.

[22]"Since Christ behaved in a certain way in order to bring salvation to Paul's readers, how can they *not* imitate him in that particular respect? To behave in any *other* way would be to deny the truth of the gospel." Ibid., p. 5.

[23]Ibid., p. 10. The adage is attributed to Irenaeus and expressed in different ways by Athanasius and other church fathers. For a more detailed discussion of the ethical implications of our identification with Christ, see Hooker, "Interchange," pp. 6-11.

in me" (Gal 2:20). In chapter eleven, I discuss more fully what it means for believers to participate in Christ.

Third, in order to be conformed to Christ, believers must follow the leading of the Spirit. As the Spirit of Christ, the Holy Spirit stands in for Jesus in the lives of his followers. Since they cannot literally follow Jesus in discipleship, they follow the leading of the Spirit instead:

> Live [literally, "walk"] by the Spirit, I say, and do not gratify the desires of the flesh. For what the flesh desires is opposed to the Spirit, and what the Spirit desires is opposed to the flesh; for these are opposed to each other, to prevent you from doing what you want. But if you are led by the Spirit, you are not subject to the law. . . . By contrast, the fruit of the Spirit is love, joy, peace, patience, kindness, generosity, faithfulness, gentleness, and self-control. There is no law against such things. And those who belong to Christ Jesus have crucified the flesh with its passions and desires. If we live by the Spirit, let us also be guided by the Spirit. (Gal 5:16-18, 22-25)

According to Gordon Fee, "The first instruction, 'walk by the Spirit,' is the basic command in Paul's ethics." The verb "to walk," often used in Jewish writings to describe a way of life, is Paul's most common expression for ethical conduct (seventeen times).[24] Believers have identified with Jesus in his crucifixion and resurrection—and therefore participate in the victory he achieved over sin and death (cf. Rom 6:1-11). Now alive in the Spirit, they are to "walk by the Spirit" and "be guided by the Spirit." If they do this, the Spirit will produce in them the character qualities that will mark them as belonging to Christ.

The Spirit can develop true holiness in the lives of those who follow Christ: "For the law of the Spirit of life in Christ Jesus has set you free from the law of sin and of death. For God has done what the law, weakened by the flesh, could not do: by sending his own Son, in the likeness of sinful flesh, and to deal with sin, he condemned sin in the flesh, so that the just requirement of the law might be fulfilled in us, who walk not according to the flesh but according to the Spirit" (Rom 8:2-4). The law could not make anyone holy because it was undermined by human sinfulness. But because of the work of Christ, believers have been set free from the law in order to live by the Spirit. Galatians 5 and Romans 8 make clear

---

[24]Gordon D. Fee, *Paul, the Spirit, and the People of God* (Peabody, Mass.: Hendrickson, 1996), p. 107.

that the law is not a means of sanctification.[25] However, if believers follow the leading of the Spirit, they will fulfill the intention of the law—not by law-keeping but by living the transformed life that the law demanded but could not bring about.

Christ is both the standard and the goal of sanctification. Believers live out their vocation of holiness together "until all of us come to the unity of the faith and of the knowledge of the Son of God, to maturity [literally, "to a perfect man"], to the measure of the full stature of Christ" (Eph 4:13). Just as the goal of sanctification is Christ, the context of sanctification is the body of Christ. Believers grow *together* into Christian maturity. Only the church can adequately reflect the holiness of Christ.

PERFECTION

The concept of perfection mentioned in Ephesians 4:13 comes from the same cultic context as sanctification and has a very similar range of meaning. The Greek verb *teleioō* (to perfect) is used in the Septuagint in the sense of consecrating a priest for service.[26] The book of Hebrews uses the word in this sense when it describes Jesus being "made perfect" through obedience and suffering (Heb 5:9; see Heb 2:10). He is becoming fully qualified for his responsibility as our high priest. Similarly, the purification of Jesus' sacrifice makes believers perfect—that is, qualified to appear before God (Heb 10:1). As with sanctification, perfection is both an identity and a vocation. Jesus has made believers perfect forever, in the sense that they are consecrated to worship and serve God (Heb 10:14).[27] But believers also must live out their vocation, so they are exhorted to "go on toward perfection" (Heb 6:1). "Perfection is begun with the new life in Christ, it is sustained and matured in the ongoing ministry of the Spirit, and it is consummated with the final entrance into glory."[28]

When used outside of a cultic context, *teleioō* seems to refer to comple-

---

[25]Contra C. E. B. Cranfield, "Paul's Teaching on Sanctification," *The Reformed Review* 48, no. 3 (Spring 1995): 223.

[26]William L. Lane, *Call to Commitment: Responding to the Message of Hebrews* (Nashville: Nelson, 1985), p. 48.

[27]"By his high-priestly work . . . before God Christ has once and for all 'qualified' those for whom He acts to come directly before God . . . in the heavenly sanctuary as men whose sin is expiated." G. Delling, "τέλος κτλ.," in *TDNT* 8:83.

[28]John R. Walters, *Perfection in New Testament Theology: Ethics and Eschatology in Relational Dynamic*, Mellen Biblical Press Series (Lewiston, N.Y.: Mellen Biblical Press, 1995), p. 264.

tion or maturity. It occurs when Jesus talks about completing his mission (Lk 2:43; Jn 4:34) and when he declares from the cross, "It is finished" (Jn 19:30, using *teleō*). In John 19:28 *teleioō* refers to the fulfillment of Old Testament Scripture in Jesus' death. James argues that faith is brought to completion by works (Jas 2:22). In reference to people, *teleioō* means maturity (1 Cor 2:6; Phil 3:15; Jas 1:4). Paul urges the Corinthians to be adults (*teleioi*) rather than infants in their thinking (1 Cor 14:20; cf. Heb 5:14). He states that the goal of his ministry is to present everyone mature in Christ (Col 1:28). Although God is the one who brings believers to maturity, believers also have the responsibility to purify themselves, removing any hindrances to the maturation process (2 Cor 7:1; Heb 12:1-2; 1 Jn 3:3).

Theologians debate whether entire sanctification or perfection can be experienced in this life. Several passages in 1 John talk about perfection in love or claim that Christians no longer sin (1 Jn 2:3-6; 3:6-10; 4:16-18). However, another verse in the same book declares that if believers claim to have no sin, they are deceiving themselves (1 Jn 1:8). John seems to believe that sinlessness is possible, since, as God's children, believers have God's "seed" in them (1 Jn 3:4-10)—perhaps God's word or the Holy Spirit or the new nature they have by virtue of their birth from above (cf. Jn 3:3). But he seems also to expect that believers will need to confess their sins periodically to receive ongoing cleansing through the blood of Christ (1 Jn 1:5–2:6). In any case, John repeatedly calls his hearers to focus not on perfection but on love. The only effective motivation for holy living is love for God and others, originating in a deep sense of God's love for the believer (1 Jn 4:19).

Paul's blessing to the Thessalonians seems to envision the completion of sanctification as an eschatological event: "May the God of peace himself sanctify you entirely; and may your spirit and soul and body be kept sound and blameless at the coming of our Lord Jesus Christ. The one who calls you is faithful, and he will do this" (1 Thess 5:23-24). Believers can rely on God to complete the work of sanctification he has begun in them by the time Jesus returns (cf. Phil 1:6). Until then, believers would do well to follow the example of Paul himself:

> Not that I have already obtained this or have already reached the goal [literally, "have been perfected," *teteleiōmai*]; but I press on to make it my own, because Christ Jesus has made me his own. Beloved, I do not consider that I have made it my own; but this one thing I do: forgetting what lies behind

and straining forward to what lies ahead, I press on toward the goal for the prize of the heavenly call of God in Christ Jesus. Let those of us then who are mature [*teleioi*] be of the same mind; and if you think differently about anything, this too God will reveal to you. Only let us hold fast to what we have attained. (Phil 3:12-16)

Paul does not yet consider himself perfect (in the sense of finished). So he presses on toward the goal God has set for him, calling those who are perfect (in the sense of mature) to imitate him. He is determined not to lose ground. Sanctification requires perseverance, but it is not focused on achievement. Paul is not pursuing Christlikeness but Christ himself. He wants to know the one who has claimed him (Phil 3:7-8).

CONCLUSION

The people of God have been sanctified in Christ and called to be saints. They are a holy priesthood identified with God and set apart for a vocation of worship and service. They must dedicate themselves to that vocation, pursuing the call of God as the Holy Spirit equips them for their service. Sanctification always comes from God:

- Sanctification is an act of God *for* us, as we are consecrated by the sacrifice of Christ and qualified to come before God in worship and service.

- Sanctification is a call of God *to* us, as we are commanded to demonstrate the character and carry on the ministry of the one to whom we belong.

- Sanctification is a work of God *in* us, as the Holy Spirit progressively conforms us to the image of Christ, our great high priest.

The New Testament picture of sanctification has significant practical implications. For example, it should broaden our understanding of salvation. Viewing salvation not just as a set of blessings but as a vocation might overcome the gap between initial salvation and holy living that is so often visible in our theologies and in our congregations. The idea that worship is our calling as Christians creates a natural foundation for spiritual fomation.[29] It also shifts the balance of responsibility for worship away from the

---

[29]Clarence Tucker Craig argues that "bringing us into nearness to God . . . is the essential meaning of sanctification." "Paradox of Holiness: A New Testament Theology of Sanctification," *Interpretation* 6, no. 2 (April 1952): 161.

pastor and worship team to the whole congregation. Liturgy literally is the work of the people, an activity of the people of God as a whole.

In fact, since believers are both God's royal priesthood and the temple in which God dwells, worship is not just what we do on Sunday morning but how we live our lives. We cannot divide our lives into sacred and secular. Wherever we go is sacred space. Whatever we do is holy service, whether we spend the day in prayer or in bricklaying. Regardless of the jobs we hold, all believers have a sacred vocation.

We must remember that holiness is not a matter of conforming to a narrow list of behaviors but living out of a deep love for God and neighbor, a joyful response to God's love for us. As Christians, we should be known for what (and whom) we love rather than for what we reject. Through our prayer and proclamation, through our integrity and compassion, we testify to the character and purposes of God. This vision of holiness may demand more of us than we are accustomed to. We cannot attain it without depending upon the Spirit of Holiness, who draws us onward in God's inexhaustible grace.

FOR FURTHER READING

Alexander, Donald L., ed. *Christian Spirituality: Five Views of Sanctification.* Downers Grove, Ill.: InterVarsity Press, 1988.

Bloesch, Donald G. *The Christian Life and Salvation.* Colorado Springs: Helmers & Howard, 1991.

Craig, Clarence Tucker. "Paradox of Holiness: A New Testament Theology of Sanctification." *Interpretation* 6, no. 2 (April 1952): 147-61.

Dieter, Melvin, et al. *Five Views on Sanctification.* Counterpoints. Grand Rapids: Zondervan, 1987.

Fee, Gordon D. *Paul, the Spirit, and the People of God.* Peabody, Mass.: Hendrickson, 1996.

Furnish, Victor Paul. *Theology and Ethics in Paul.* Nashville: Abingdon, 1968.

Gammie, John G. *Holiness in Israel.* Overtures to Biblical Theology Series. Minneapolis: Fortress, 1989.

Hooker, Morna D. "Interchange in Christ and Ethics." *Journal for the Study of the New Testament* 25 (1985): 3-17.

Klaiber, Walter. "Sanctification in the New Testament." *Asbury Theological Journal* 50-51, no. 2-1 (1995-1996): 11-21.

Peterson, David. *Possessed by God: A New Testament Theology of Sanctification and*

Holiness. New Studies in Biblical Theology. Grand Rapids: Eerdmans, 1995.

Toon, Peter. *Justification and Sanctification.* Foundations for Faith. Westchester, Ill.: Crossway, 1983.

Walters, John R. *Perfection in New Testament Theology: Ethics and Eschatology in Relational Dynamic.* Mellen Biblical Press Series. Lewiston, N.Y.: Mellen, 1995.

13

CALL TO ENDURANCE

Pilgrimage, Contest, Worship

A LARGE CATHOLIC CHURCH near my own Brethren congregation lets their parking lot be used by commuters who drop off their cars and take a bus to downtown. The sign in their parking lot reads "St. Peter's Park & Ride." Some of us may wish that salvation were that easy. We could get our ticket at conversion and get on the bus. Then, to borrow from the old Greyhound commercials, we could sit back, relax and leave the driving to Jesus.

Unfortunately for our fantasy, the picture of salvation in the New Testament is quite different. Salvation is not just an event but also a process. This final cluster of images, in fact, presents salvation as a difficult journey that requires faithfulness over the long haul. It is a call to endurance, a struggle or contest in which believers must be sustained by worship and prayer. It issues a challenge to Christians today to imitate the faithfulness of their forebears in the faith. It also offers comfort to believers who are undergoing their own time of trial.

PILGRIMAGE AND CONTEST

Salvation as a call to endurance is vividly depicted in Hebrews and Revelation. Both books are written to Christian communities under pressure. Both have an urgent concern for the faithfulness of believers in the midst of temptation and persecution. Both offer prayer and worship as the way to develop clear vision and gain strength to endure. Both call believers to see things from God's perspective and to live in the light of the end.[1]

Both Hebrews and Revelation assume a covenant relationship between God and his people, as evidenced by the covenant formula "I will be their God and they shall be my people" that appears in both books (Heb 8:10; cf. Rev 21:3). Hebrews explores the significance of the transition from the old covenant to the new. Revelation looks forward to the completion of the new covenant when God's promises will be fulfilled.

In Hebrews, salvation is a pilgrimage of faith, a journey toward God's promise that is directed and sustained by God's presence. In Revelation, salvation is a contest (a struggle, in the sense of the Greek word *agōn*) in which believers overcome the world through their faithful testimony unto death in order to receive the prize.[2] In some ways these pictures seem quite different, but they draw on the same foundational narrative—the story of the exodus generation.[3] While Hebrews emphasizes the wilderness wanderings, Revelation uses the language of oppression, struggle, victory and rest. In Hebrews, God's people are on the journey; they have no lasting city. In Revelation, after their final testing, they enter the holy city and receive their inheritance.

In both books, salvation is a call to endurance. Discipleship is costly.

---

[1] I have borrowed the final phrase from Stanley J. Grenz, *Theology for the Community of God* (1994; reprint, Grand Rapids: Eerdmans, 2000), p. 650. References are to the 2000 edition.

[2] Although the word *agōn* is not used in Revelation, the *stephanos*, the wreath given to the victor, does appear (Rev 2:10; 3:11). For a lengthy discussion of wreaths and crowns in the ancient world, see David E. Aune, *Revelation 1–5*, Word Biblical Commentary, ed. David A. Hubbard and Glenn W. Barker (Dallas: Word, 1997), pp. 172-76. Aune notes that the language of overcoming, frequent in Revelation, was used in athletic contests (p. 151). Hebrews uses the language of contest at Hebrews 12:1-4, but the crown of victory is not yet offered to believers. In fact, the author uses Psalm 8 to argue that believers must look to the exalted Christ for a glimpse of the crown of glory that will one day be theirs (Heb 2:7, 9). For another discussion of the crowns in Revelation, see Gregory M. Stevenson, "Conceptual Background to the Golden Crown Imagery in the Apocalypse of John (4:4, 10: 14:14)," *Journal of Biblical Literature* 114, no. 2 (1995): 257-72.

[3] Scholars have pointed out allusions to the exodus in both Hebrews and Revelation. For example, Raymond Brown argues that Hebrews presents salvation in terms of the Exodus narrative. "Pilgrimage in faith: The Christian Life in Hebrews," *Southwestern Journal of Theology* 28 (Fall 1985): 29. For a similar observation on Revelation, see Richard Bauckham, *The Theology of the Book of Revelation*, Theology of the New Testament, ed. James D. G. Dunn (Cambridge: Cambridge University Press, 1993), pp. 70-72. Joel B. Green draws a parallel between the events of the exodus and the oppression of God's people, the plagues, and the divine deliverance recounted in Revelation. The new creation is the new exodus foreseen by Isaiah. In fact, Green believes that "for John, a chief symbol of salvation is the exodus." *Salvation*, Understanding Biblical Themes Series (St. Louis, Mo.: Chalice, 2003), p. 91.

The believers in Hebrews have experienced persecution, but they "have not yet resisted to the point of shedding [their] blood" (Heb 12:4). The author exhorts them to "run with perseverance" the race before them (Heb 12:1). Such perseverance is needed to do God's will and receive what God has promised (Heb 10:36). For believers in Revelation, salvation entails martyrdom. The narrative of Revelation unpacks Jesus' teaching that one must lose one's life to save it (Mk 10:35 and parallels). Receiving eternal life may require the sacrifice of mortal life. As in the Synoptic apocalypses, it is the one who endures to the end who will be saved (Mk 13:13 and parallels).

In both Hebrews and Revelation, faith is eschatological, a trust in God's promise that gives God's people the courage to persevere. In both, worship is both the means of perseverance and the reward for perseverance. Reminders of the temporal and spiritual nearness of God give believers the proper framework in which to understand their present situation. These reminders both encourage and challenge by calling believers back to their covenant commitments. As the people of God live out their faith, they find their inspiration in Jesus, the pioneer (Heb 12:2) and faithful witness (Rev 3:14). Jesus is both the paradigm of perseverance and the one who makes possible the perseverance of his followers.

PILGRIMAGE IN HEBREWS

In Hebrews, the tension of the already/not yet kingdom is very apparent. Believers have had a transforming experience of God's grace, having been "enlightened," having "shared in the Holy Spirit" and having "tasted . . . the powers of the age to come" (Heb 6:4-5). God has rescued them from the old era by giving them a foretaste of the new. God's deliverance has called into existence a new community of salvation.[4] They are living in "these last days" at the "end of the age" (Heb 1:2; 9:26). The "Day [is] approaching" when Christ will return "to save those who are eagerly waiting for him" (Heb 10:25; 9:28).

However, this final deliverance has not yet arrived. In the meantime, the very experience of grace that has created the new community has also made them displaced persons. They have become alienated from all of their former associations. Their newness is a threat to the old order, which

---

[4]The social character of salvation is evident in Hebrews. Nils Alstrup Dahl, "A New and Living Way: The Approach to God According to Heb 10:19-25," *Interpretation* 5 (1951): 402.

is responding with intense pressure on them to renounce their faith. The old era is passing away, and it is hostile to those who no longer live by its rules.[5] The stakes are high: turning back to the old ways would alleviate persecution, but such apostasy would bring a terrible judgment (Heb 6:4-12; 10:26-31). The people of Christ must trust in his promise and endure until he comes.

Hebrews pictures believers as a band of refugees who must follow God to their new home. In his classic study of the motif of "wandering" in Hebrews, Ernst Käsemann describes the necessary relationship between promise and pilgrimage:

> *The Logos grants no final revelation. It calls to a way,* the goal of which it points out by way of promise, and which can only be reached in union with the Logos and its promise. . . . Only obedience that achieves this wandering beneath and together with the Word to the end is evidence that acceptance of the Word has actually occurred. The basic presupposition of our text is that one possesses the εὐαγγέλιον [gospel] on earth only as ἐπαγγελία [promise]. But then it follows *that the form of existence in time appropriate to the recipient of the revelation can only be that of wandering.*[6]

Because God's promise of a permanent home is not yet realized, believers must "wander." More precisely, they must follow the way of Jesus to the goal he has revealed. Contrary to Käsemann, the gospel does not exist *only* as promise; it also has a historical basis in the life, death and resurrection of Christ. Because of the surpassing character of this revelation, believers can have confidence to follow Jesus on pilgrimage toward their promised home.[7]

The author of Hebrews compares believers' experience to that of the exodus generation (Heb 3:7–4:11). That generation also was constituted as

---

[5]As Rudolf Bultmann expresses it, "The eschatological Congregation really no longer belongs to the perishing world. Its members have no home here; their πολίτευμα (citizenship) is in heaven (Phil 3:20), their City is the one that is to come (Heb 13:14). Here, in this world, they are away from home on a pilgrimage. . . . The thing to do, then, is 'to gird up one's loins' for the pilgrimage." *Theology of the New Testament*, trans. Kendrick Grobel (New York: Charles Scribner's Sons, 1951-1955), 1:100.

[6]Ernst Käsemann, *The Wandering People of God: An Investigation of the Epistle to the Hebrews* (Minneapolis: Augsburg, 1984), p. 19.

[7]William G. Johnsson was one of the first to argue that Käsemann's motif of wandering should really be pilgrimage. He turns to the phenomenology of religion to demonstrate that the motif in Hebrews meets all the conditions that define a pilgrimage. "Pilgrimage Motif in the Book of Hebrews," *Journal of Biblical Literature* 97 (June 1978): 239-51.

God's people through a great act of deliverance. They received God's promise of Sabbath rest and followed God toward its fulfillment.[8] On the verge of realizing that promise, they were disobedient and forfeited their inheritance. Although the exodus generation did not enter God's rest, the author of Hebrews believes that the promise is still open. Believers in Christ have become the heirs of that old covenant promise, and of even greater promises under the new covenant, but they must exercise faithfulness and patience in order to reach the goal (Heb 6:12, 17; 8:6).[9]

The author urges his audience not to follow the example of the exodus generation (Heb 4:1-2) but instead to imitate those Old Testament saints who remained faithful to the end even though they never attained the fulfillment of the promise (Heb 11:39). Those saints accepted their alienation from the world, regarding themselves as "strangers and foreigners on the earth" who were "seeking a homeland" (Heb 11:13, 14). Because they had no "lasting city," they sought "the city that is to come" (Heb 13:14; see Heb 11:10, 16). Believers in Christ should likewise follow Jesus "outside the camp and bear the abuse he endured" (Heb 13:13). Just as Jesus endured enmity and death to reach his vindication, believers must persevere through suffering to attain the holiness necessary for theirs (Heb 12:2-3, 7-14).

Those who hope in Christ are on pilgrimage toward the fulfillment of God's promise. Unlike the exodus generation, they travel not to Mt. Sinai but to Mt. Zion: "You have come to Mount Zion and to the city of the living God, the heavenly Jerusalem, and to innumerable angels in festal gathering, and to the assembly of the firstborn who are enrolled in heaven, and to God the judge of all, and to the spirits of the righteous made perfect, and to Jesus, the mediator of a new covenant" (Heb 12:22-24). Although believers have not yet reached this eschatological goal, the verb "have come" (*proselēlythate*) implies that they can have some experience of it in the present. Even now they "are receiving" it (Heb 12:28).

---

[8]The land is presented as a resting place in Deuteronomy 12:9 and Joshua 21:44. H. W. Attridge, *The Epistle to the Hebrews*, Hermeneia (Philadelphia: Fortress, 1989), p. 126.

[9]The word I have translated as "unfaithfulness" in Heb 3:19 (*apistia*) is rendered as "unbelief" by the NRSV, but it can mean either. Similarly, the word I have translated as "faithfulness" in Heb 6:12 (*pistis*) is rendered in the NRSV as "faith," but *pistis* can mean either or both. See R. Bultmann, "πιστεύω κτλ.," in *TDNT* 6:208, and the discussion in earlier chapters of this book. In the context of a call to perseverance, "unfaithfulness" and "faithfulness" seem to be the more appropriate choices.

Believers can endure the eschatological tension because of the encouragement of one another (Heb 10:24-25) and because of their experience of God's presence. They journey in company with the rest of God's people, and God himself goes before them.[10] This is one of the implications of the author's use of *skēnē*—specifically the tabernacle rather than the temple— to describe the heavenly sanctuary. God does not simply call believers to pilgrimage; he goes with them on their journey and sustains them by his presence. Through worship and prayer, believers can have a "foretaste" of the intimacy with God that they will experience in the consummation.[11]

WORSHIP IN HEBREWS

Since the purpose of pilgrimage is to draw near to God, it is appropriate that pilgrims draw strength for the journey from their experiences of worship.[12] Worship aligns their wills with God's and reinforces their commitment to pilgrimage.[13] It nurtures their relationship with the God who guides their journey. Like pilgrimage, worship employs the conceptual categories of nearness and distance. Just as pilgrimage means to move toward a goal, worship means to "approach" or "draw near" to God.

The words used for worship in Hebrews are *proserchomai* (seven times) and *engizō* (twice). Both words mean to approach or draw near. In the Gospels, *proserchomai* is used literally to express physical proximity, as when one person comes to another person. Almost always, others (whether human beings, angels or Satan) come to Jesus (see Mt 4:3, 11; 8:5; 15:1, 12, 30). The word is less common in the Epistles. Most of those instances occur in Hebrews, in which *proserchomai* is a metaphor for approaching

---

[10]Käsemann observes: "Only in union with Christ's companions is there life, faith, and progress on the individual's way of wandering. As soon as a person is no longer fully conscious of membership and begins to be isolated from the people of God, that person must also have left the promise behind and abandoned the goal." *Wandering*, p. 21; see also Attridge, *Hebrews*, p. 128.

[11]David Perkins, "Call to Pilgrimage: The Challenge of Hebrews," *Theological Educator* 32 (Fall 1985): 78 n. 2.

[12]According to David Peterson, "Hebrews presents the most complete and fully integrated theology of worship in the New Testament." *Engaging with God: A Biblical Theology of Worship* (Grand Rapids: Eerdmans, 1992), p. 228.

[13]John Brand, "Sabbath-rest, Worship, and the Epistle to the Hebrews," *Didaskalia* 1 (March 1990): 8; citing an expression used by Derek Kidner in reference to Psalm 95 in *Psalms 73–150*, Tyndale Old Testament Commentary Series (Downers Grove, Ill.: InterVarsity Press, 1975), p. 344.

God in worship (Heb 4:16; 7:25; 10:1, 22; 11:6; 12:18, 22). This metaphorical sense is a natural extension of the literal coming of people to Jesus during his ministry.

The word *engizō* is somewhat less common in the New Testament. When used literally, it means to draw near in either a spatial or a temporal sense: Jesus and his disciples approach Jerusalem (Mk 11:1), and the time of the Passover approaches (Lk 22:1). In Matthew 26:45-46, both "the hour" of Jesus' betrayal and Jesus' betrayer are "at hand." This is the word Jesus uses to announce that the kingdom of God has drawn near in his ministry (Mk 1:15). In Hebrews, *engizō* is used literally in reference to the coming Day of the Lord (Heb 10:25) and metaphorically in reference to drawing near to God in worship (Heb 7:19). James uses the same metaphor: "Draw near to God, and he will draw near to you" (Jas 4:8).

Both *proserchomai* and *engizō* are derived from a cultic context. In the Old Testament, both are used for approaching God in worship, whether in reference to Moses (Ex 24:2; Deut 5:27), to priests (Ex 19:22; Lev 9:7), or to God's people as a whole (Ex 24:2; Lev 9:5). Both words are used in Leviticus 21:21, when God instructs Moses that no one with a blemish may come near to offer sacrifice. Instances of *proserchomai* usually have a concrete object: someone approaches the cloud (Ex 16:9-10), the tent of meeting (Lev 9:5), the altar (Lev 9:8), or the table (Ezek 44:16). Approaching God means approaching the particular location associated with God's presence.

Only those who are qualified may draw near to God. At Sinai, the people are told *not* to approach. God declares, "Moses alone shall come near the Lord; but the others shall not come near, and the people shall not come up with him" (Ex 24:2). Sacred and profane are strictly separated, and crossing that boundary can be dangerous. If an unholy people were to come into the presence of a holy God, they would be destroyed (Ex 19:21). Even the priests must be consecrated before they can safely approach (Ex 19:22). Coming near to the holy without invitation can result in death (2 Sam 6:6-7; Lev 10:1-3; 16:1). Once the tabernacle is established, no one can enter the Holy of Holies except for the high priest on the Day of Atonement to make atonement for the sins of the people (Lev 16:2, 34).

Approaching God does not always refer to formal worship practices, however. For example, God instructs Jeremiah not to approach him to intercede for Israel (Jer 7:16, using *proserchomai*). In his prophetic calling, Jeremiah would not be able to intercede by sacrifice, but only by prayer. Similarly, *engizō* refers not only to the formal cult but also to Israel's relationship with God. Zephaniah predicts that Jerusalem will face judgment because "it has not trusted in the Lord; it has not drawn near to its God" (Zeph 3:2). Through Isaiah, God charges that the Israelites "draw near with their mouths and honor me with their lips, while their hearts are far from me, and their worship of me is a human commandment learned by rote" (Is 29:13).

The prophets insist that true worship requires more than sacrifices. Drawing near to God requires a heart and a life that reflect the will of God. Those who draw near to God in this way will find that God responds in kind. God draws near to his people when they call upon him (Deut 4:7; Jer 23:23; Lam 3:57). Because he understands God's mercy, Isaiah exhorts God's people to "seek the Lord while he may be found, call upon him while he is near" (Is 55:6).

The book of Hebrews draws on this Old Testament background to picture salvation as drawing near to God in worship. The sacrifices under the old covenant cannot perfect "those who approach" (Heb 10:1). But Christ brings a "better hope" through which his followers can approach God (Heb 7:19). He has won access for them into God's presence through his once-for-all sacrifice (Heb 7:27) and through his ongoing intercession: "Consequently he is able for all time to save those who approach God through him, since he always lives to make intercession for them" (Heb 7:25). Now God's people can come to God freely and without fear: "Let us therefore approach the throne of grace with boldness, so that we may receive mercy and find grace to help in time of need" (Heb 4:16).[14] According to William L. Lane, "The high priestly ministry of Jesus has achieved for the people of the new covenant what Israel never enjoyed, namely, *immediate access to God* and the freedom to draw near to him continually."[15]

Because of the perfect mediation of their great high priest (Heb 8:6), believers need no other intermediaries. They have access to God that for-

---

[14]Dahl states that "to the unknown author of the Epistle to the Hebrews, salvation means to have free approach to God and communion with him" ("Living Way," p. 401). Dahl calls worship in Hebrews "hope in action" ("Living Way," p. 409).

[15]William L. Lane, *Call to Commitment: Responding to the Message of Hebrews* (Nashville: Nelson, 1985), p. 77.

merly was granted only to priests. In fact, they function as priests in service to God and to one another. They can "offer to God an acceptable worship" that includes sacrifices of praise and good works (Heb 12:28; 13:15-16). In communion, they share in "an altar from which those who officiate in the tent have no right to eat" (Heb 13:10). Earthly holy places are no longer necessary, because believers can enter the heavenly sanctuary itself, where Christ has gone before them. The author exhorts them to enter God's presence in language that recalls the Day of Atonement ritual:

> Therefore, my friends, since we have confidence to enter the sanctuary by the blood of Jesus, by the new and living way that he opened for us through the curtain (that is, through his flesh), and since we have a great priest over the house of God, let us approach with a true heart in full assurance of faith, with our hearts sprinkled clean from an evil conscience and our bodies washed with pure water. (Heb 10:19-22; cf. Lev 16)

Like the priests of the old covenant, believers have been qualified to approach God. Unlike those priests, however, believers have been qualified "once for all" by the work of their great high priest (Heb 10:10, 14).

Worship makes it possible for believers to see beyond their present suffering to the reality of Christ's triumph: "As it is, we do not yet see everything in subjection to [human beings], but we do see Jesus, who for a little while was made lower than the angels, now crowned with glory and honor because of the suffering of death, so that by the grace of God he might taste death for everyone" (Heb 2:8b-9). Jesus experienced the same hostile world but endured to the end, securing the victory for himself and his followers. His exaltation demonstrates the reliability of God's promises. This vision of the exalted Christ, nourished through worship, enables believers to keep their focus on him rather than on their circumstances: "Let us run with perseverance the race that is set before us, looking to Jesus, the pioneer and perfecter of our faith, who for the sake of the joy that was set before him endured the cross, disregarding its shame, and has taken his seat at the right hand of the throne of God. Consider him who endured such hostility against himself from sinners, so that you may not grow weary or lose heart" (Heb 12:1-3).

Looking to Jesus can enable his followers to persevere because he is not merely their example. He is also their champion or pioneer (*archēgos*) and their forerunner (*prodromos*). These titles for Jesus are unique to Hebrews.

In the Septuagint, the word *archēgos* is used for political or military leaders of Israel.[16] It is applied to Jesus in the passages just cited (Heb 2:10; 12:2). Jesus is the champion of believers because he has won their salvation for them by defeating their enemies.[17] As their pioneer, he can lead them to their promised home.[18] Moreover, as the forerunner of believers (Heb 6:20), Jesus has entered the heavenly sanctuary to ensure their welcome. Because he remains there, believers' hope is not wishful thinking. It is "a sure and steadfast anchor of the soul" that reaches into the very presence of God.[19]

Because all of God's people are qualified to approach God through Christ, any individual believer can enter God's presence at any time. No special holy places are necessary. However, the author of Hebrews puts particular emphasis on corporate worship. He urges his audience to continue their assembling together so that they can encourage one another (Heb 10:25). The pilgrim people of God are a worshiping *community*.[20] The author's declaration that his audience has already come to Mount Zion suggests that corporate worship—the "assembly of the firstborn who are enrolled in heaven"—unites them with all believers living and dead and gives them a foretaste of the heavenly Jerusalem that will be their home for eternity (Heb 12:22-24).[21]

---

[16]J. J. Scott Jr. defines *archēgos* as follows: "Given its full range of meaning, the word designates an individual who opened the way into a new area for others to follow, founded the city in which they dwelt, gave his name to the community, fought its battles and secured the victory, and then remained as the leader-ruler-hero of his people." "*Archēgos* in the Salvation History of the Epistle to the Hebrews," *Journal of the Evangelical Theological Society* 29 (March 1986): 52.

[17]David acted as the champion of Israel when he defeated Goliath. Lane, *Call to Commitment*, pp. 47-48, 51.

[18]Attridge speculates that the author of Hebrews intends in Hebrews 4:8 to make a comparison between Joshua and Jesus as the *archēgos* of the old and new covenants (*Hebrews*, pp. 87, 130).

[19]The image of Christ as high priest and forerunner not only gives a picture of salvation but also "gives the initial steps for discipleship": "In the figure of the high priest the assertion of the sacrificial death 'for us' is connected with that of his going on 'before us' . . . This excludes both a sacrifice theory that leaves the individual completely passive, and the misunderstanding of the high priest as a mere model that we must imitate. . . . [Hebrews] already presupposes a path that God has traveled with his people to Christ. This path continues in the church until the last 'coming' of 'the Day drawing near' and its judge." Eduard Schweizer, *A Theological Introduction to the New Testament* (Nashville: Abingdon, 1991), pp. 106, 107-8.

[20]Susanne Lehne, *The New Covenant in Hebrews*, Journal for the Study of the New Testament Supplement Series (Sheffield, U.K.: JSOT Press, 1990), p. 111; Peterson, *Engaging with God*, p. 250.

[21]William L. Lane argues that the assembly (*ekklēsia*) in Heb 12:23 is a nontechnical term referring to a gathering of God's people "for celebratory worship." *Hebrews 9–13*, Word Biblical Commentary, ed. David A. Hubbard and Glenn W. Barker (Dallas: Word, 1991), pp. 467-69.

Both worship and pilgrimage require faith. Faith makes it possible for people to approach God: "And without faith it is impossible to please God, for whoever would approach him must believe that he exists and that he rewards those who seek him" (Heb 11:6). To have faith is to trust in the character, purposes and promises of God. As many have observed, faith in Hebrews is closely allied to hope: "Now faith is the assurance of things hoped for, the conviction of things not [yet] seen" (Heb 11:1).[22] Faith trusts in God's promises because in Christ it can glimpse the unseen. Because of their faith in God's promise (fulfilled in Christ but yet to be consummated), believers can come boldly into God's presence to receive the grace they need in order to persevere. As William Lane observes,

> Faith is both an openness to the future, which is given expression in obedient trust in the God who has promised, and a present grasp upon truth now invisible but certain because it is grounded in the word of promise. . . . The faith the writer commends to his audience is a confident reliance upon the future, which makes possible responsible action in the present in the light of that confidence. This distinctly eschatological understanding of faith is the corollary of the motif of pilgrimage.[23]

Such faith is not passive but active, expressing itself in obedience. Jesus himself is perfected in obedience: "Although he was a Son, he learned obedience through what he suffered; and having been made perfect, he became the source of eternal salvation for all who obey him" (Heb 5:8-9). Notice that he provides salvation not to "those who believe" but to "those who obey." F. F. Bruce has remarked, "There is something appropriate in the fact that the salvation which was procured by the obedience of the

---

Although this is an eschatological image (as Lane observes), the verb suggests that believers can experience it in some part now.

[22]This description of faith is often interpreted as two different affirmations—hope in God's future blessings and the belief in invisible (perhaps Platonic) heavenly realities. For example, see Attridge, *Hebrews:* "[It] is clear that the first part of the definition relates to the attainment of hoped-for goals, the second to the perception of imperceptible realities" (p. 308). The first affirmation is "eschatological" (p. 310), while the perception of "eternal . . . realities" has "Platonic overtones" (p. 311). See also Bultmann, "πιστεύω κτλ.," in *TDNT* 6:207. I would argue, however, that this description of faith is really a single affirmation of the author's already/not yet eschatological perspective.

[23]Lane, *Hebrews 1-8,* p. cxlix. Grant R. Osborne describes salvation in Hebrews as "the eschatological possession of a forward-looking faith." "Soteriology in the Epistle to the Hebrews," in *Grace Unlimited,* ed. C. H. Pinnock (Minneapolis: Bethany House, 1975), p. 158.

Redeemer should be made available to the obedience of the redeemed."[24]
As the Old Testament prophets insisted, the faith that approaches God in
worship must also be evident in faithful living.

In Hebrews, to believe is to obey (*hypakouō*). The link between faith
and obedience is demonstrated by the stories of chapter 11. Abraham set
out on pilgrimage in obedience to God's call because he believed in God's
promise (Heb 11:8). Other heroes of the faith accomplished great deeds
and endured great trials through their faith. A similar faith will enable the
audience of Hebrews to draw strength from the cloud of witnesses sur-
rounding them and from the One who has gone on before so that they also
may persevere.

While faith or faithfulness (*pistis*) enables believers to approach God,
unbelief or faithlessness (*apistia*) causes them to turn away: "Take care,
brothers and sisters, that none of you may have an evil, unbelieving heart
that turns away [literally, 'withdrawing'] from the living God" (Heb 3:12).
The author warns his audience not to become one of "those who shrink
back and so are lost" (10:39). The picture of apostasy as turning away is
also rooted in the Old Testament (Deut 17:17; 29:18; 30:17). We will return to the idea of apostasy near the end of this chapter.

Thus in Hebrews, believers are "priestly pilgrims."[25] While they follow
Jesus toward their promised home, they are sustained by God's presence
and engaged in God's service. Their ongoing relationship with God
through Christ motivates and empowers them to remain faithful through
their trials.[26] In a sense, worship and pilgrimage are the "already" and "not
yet" dimensions of salvation as experienced by the author and his audience.
As they journey toward their lasting city, they can catch glimpses of it in
their experience of God in worship.

---

[24]F. F. Bruce, *The Epistle to the Hebrews* (Grand Rapids: Eerdmans, 1964), p. 105.

[25]This phrase was coined by Edwin Schick. He observes that the pilgrimage of these priestly
believers "involves a double spatial orientation. There are two movements, one into the Holy
of Holies by the great High Priest, and one outside the camp by his followers." He later
adds, "Going outside to Jesus has been transformed into going to the sanctuary with Christ."
"Priestly Pilgrims: Mission Outside the Camp in Hebrews," *Currents in Theology and Mission*
16 (October 1989): 373, 375. I would argue that the author of Hebrews does not dissolve pilgrimage into worship, however.

[26]Johnsson ties together the ideas of pilgrimage and worship by calling the Christians in Hebrews a "cultic community on the move" ("Pilgrimage Motif," p. 249).

CONTEST IN REVELATION

While Hebrews describes a pilgrimage, Revelation depicts a life-and-death struggle. Believers are engaged in a contest in which both their lives and their eternal destinies are at stake. John's audience is experiencing severe persecution or will experience it soon.[27] The historical referents for the persecutions in Revelation have been a matter of great debate. For our purposes, it does not matter whether we view the events of Revelation as having been fulfilled in the first century or whether we expect that they are still to come. Our concern is with the way the author pictures salvation. His call to endurance is applicable wherever and whenever God's people are under pressure because of their witness.

The seer and his audience share "the persecution and the kingdom and the patient endurance" (Rev 1:9). The opposition to God's people is centered in the secular power, pictured as Babylon, who is drunk on the blood of the saints (Rev 17:6). This secular power is led by a beast and assisted by a religious power (the false prophet) who directs people to worship the secular power and its leader (Rev 13:1-18). In the world of John and his audience, the secular power (the beast from the sea) is the Roman Empire, epitomized as Nero (one of the seven heads), and the religious power (the beast from the land) is the imperial priesthood.[28] God's people are being killed because of their testimony, but the day of their vindication is coming. The wrath of God will be poured out upon the earth in a series of judgments. Babylon will be judged for its history of persecution (Rev 18:1–19:3). Jesus will return to overthrow the kingdoms of the earth and initiate the final judgment.

Although he generally does not use the language of pilgrimage, John does call believers to come out from Babylon so that they will not be included in her judgment (Rev 18:4). Coupled with the plagues visited upon the city, this language clearly alludes to the exodus. In their faithfulness to Christ, believers must depart from one city (Babylon) in order eventually to enter another (the New Jerusalem). They must leave behind the city of the

---

[27]See David E. Aune, "Following the Lamb: Discipleship in the Apocalypse," in *Patterns of Discipleship*, p. 270. Grant Osborne sums up the situation of the audience as "a great deal of daily opposition as well as signs of intensification on the near horizon." *Revelation*, Baker Exegetical Commentary on the New Testament, ed. Moisés Silva (Grand Rapids: Baker, 2002), p. 11.

[28]See Aune, *Revelation 1-5*, p. lxii; Aune *Revelation 6-16*, pp. 660, 779, 780; Bauckham, *Theology*, pp. 35-36, 38.

beast in order to inherit the city of God. In the language of the narrative, however, the refugees do not arrive at the holy city; the holy city comes to them (Rev 21:2). This device underscores that the city is a gift of God.

The eschatological references in Revelation are, if anything, more urgent than in Hebrews, perhaps because the situation it envisions is more dire. John both encourages and challenges his audience by his vision of the nearness of the end. His narrative is bracketed with declarations that the time of the end is near (*engys*: Rev 1:3; 22:10). Jesus is coming "soon" (Rev 3:11; 22:7, 12, 20). The time of harvest has come, and there will be no more delay (Rev 14:15-16; 10:6-7). But Jesus' anticipated coming does not mean that he is absent in the present. He is present in the church as the one who walks among the seven golden lampstands. In the letters to the seven churches, he addresses the concrete situations of John's audience, calling them to preserve the purity of their witness and avoid compromise with the world. He stands at the door of the Laodicean church in entreaty, and he threatens to remove the lampstand of the Ephesian church if they do not repent (Rev 2:5; 3:20). Thus he can come to the church at any time to bring either judgment or deliverance.[29]

As they engage in their contest, believers are called to overcome temptation, suffering and Satan through patient endurance. In fact, *hypomonē* (endurance or perseverance) is one of the key words in the book.[30] Leonhard Goppelt helpfully explains this term as "the endurance of obedient faith."[31] Both particular churches and the church as a whole are called to endurance (Rev 2:2, 3, 19; 13:10; 14:12). Believers must "hold fast" to what they have and remain faithful even unto death (Rev 2:10; 3:11). Jesus promises to preserve those who respond to his call (Rev 3:10).

Just as faith in Hebrews is connected with obedience, faith in Revelation is connected with endurance. Although the verb form of faith (*pisteuō*) does not occur, the adjective faithful (*pistos*) appears several times. In Revelation, the act of believing receives less emphasis than the steadfastness of one's belief. Jesus is the faithful witness (Rev 1:5); as the

---

[29]See David A. deSilva, *An Introduction to the New Testament: Contexts, Methods & Ministry Formation* (Downers Grove, Ill.: InterVarsity Press, 2004), pp. 913-14.

[30]Aune identifies *hypomonē* as part of the *agōn* motif as used by Cynics and Stoics, as well as by Jews and Christians. *Revelation 1-5*, p. 76.

[31]Leonhard Goppelt, *Theology of the New Testament*, ed. Jürgen Roloff, trans. John E. Alsup (Grand Rapids: Eerdmans, 1981-1982), 2:192.

rider on the white horse, his name is "Faithful and True" (Rev 19:11). In Revelation 13:10, believers' faith is explicitly linked to endurance: "Here is a call for the endurance and faith of the saints" (see Rev 2:19). The understanding of faith as faithfulness is even clearer here than in Hebrews.[32] Believers who are "called and chosen and faithful" can share in the victory of the Lamb (Rev 17:14). Somewhat counter-intuitively (from a modern Western perspective), overcoming through faithfulness does not necessarily mean escaping death. In fact, death may be the only means to victory (Rev 2:10). Revelation illustrates why the word "martyr," which originally meant a witness of any sort, came to have the sense of testifying to one's faith through death.[33]

The language of victory—in verb form, to conquer or overcome (*nikaō*)—is common in Revelation. But through his imagery, John redefines the nature of victory.[34] For example, the beast is given power to conquer the saints and subjugate the peoples of the earth (Rev 13:7-8), but this conquest is only a "pseudo-victory." The beast can kill the saints (Rev 11:7), but God can overturn that apparent victory through resurrection (Rev 11:11-12). The slaughter of the faithful is actually the avenue to their glorious triumph (Rev 15:2).[35]

Revelation reverses the value of typical images of power and weakness. The messianic Lion of Judah is actually a slaughtered Lamb. He has conquered through his death. As David Barr observes, "Jesus conquered through suffering and weakness rather than by might. . . . The sufferer is the conquerer, the victim the victor."[36] One of the central paradoxes of the book is that the Lamb who has been slain is also the one who is crowned

---

[32]Bultmann believes that *pistis* should be translated "faithfulness" in Hebrews 13:7 and Revelation 2:13. He argues that *pistis, elpis* (hope), and *hypomonē* (endurance or perseverance) are very closely related in the New Testament, citing Revelation 2:19, 13:10, and 14:12. "πιστεύω κτλ.," in *TDNT* 6:208.

[33]Bauckham observes that "martyr" in Revelation means one's verbal testimony and obedient life. However, the narrative implies that such a witness will bring persecution and death. *Theology*, p. 72.

[34]See the discussion of Christ's victory over the powers in Colin Gunton, "*Christus Victor* Revisited: A Study in Metaphor and the Transformation of Meaning," *The Journal of Theological Studies* n. s. 36 (1985): 142.

[35]Stephen L. Homcy, "'To Him Who Overcomes': A Fresh Look at What 'Victory' Means for the Believer According to the Book of Revelation," *Journal of the Evangelical Theological Society* 38, no. 2 (June 1995): 199.

[36]David L. Barr, "The Apocalypse as a Symbolic Transformation of the World," *Interpretation* 38, no. 1 (January 1984): 41.

king of kings; in fact it is *because of* his redemptive death that he reigns. It is because of the Lamb's redemptive death that he is worthy to open the scroll, and it is as the Lamb that he sits on the heavenly throne (Rev 5:9, 6).

Even the conquest scene of chapter 19 may be an example of the "trans-valuation" of images.[37] The rider on the white horse, whose name is Faithful and True, is Jesus Christ, the Word of God (Rev 19:11, 13). His robe has been dipped in blood before the battle starts, and he is already crowned as King of Kings and Lord of Lords (Rev 19:13, 16).[38] For a climactic apocalyptic battle, the narrative is remarkably restrained.[39] We are told that the beast and false prophet are captured and killed, and their armies are slain by the sword that comes out of the Rider's mouth (Rev 19:20-21). The imagery suggests that Christ's own blood colors his robe, that he has triumphed through his death and has conquered his enemies through his powerful word. Although many interpreters regard this scene as a depiction of Christ's second coming, R. Alastair Campbell argues that it represents a triumphal procession celebrating the defeat of Babylon. In his view, John draws on the imagery of a Roman triumph to satirize Rome's claim to power and divinity. In reality, Christ, not Caesar, is Lord.[40] M. Eugene Boring rightly observes that Revelation's picture of conquest-by-death is either a "blatant case of semantic *chutzpah*" or "as profound . . . a redefinition of the meaning of 'power' as anything in the history of theology."[41]

John's vision of the victorious Christ is the model for the victory of believers. Believers achieve victory by means of their steadfast devotion to Christ, their willingness to maintain their witness even at the cost of their own lives. Like Jesus, who conquers by his word, the sword of his mouth, they conquer through their testimony. But more importantly, they overcome through the blood of the Lamb (Rev 12:11). The Lamb has purchased victory for them

---

[37]The term is from Barr, "Transformation of the World," p. 42.

[38]Pointed out by R. Alastair Campbell, "Triumph and Delay: The Interpretation of Revelation 19:11–20:10," *Evangelical Quarterly* 80, no. 1 (2008): 5.

[39]I. Howard Marshall notes that even when Jesus rides in judgment, he is not shown doing violence. *New Testament Theology: Many Witnesses, One Gospel* (Downers Grove, Ill.: InterVarsity Press, 2004), p. 562. Like Jesus, believers conquer or overcome the world not by doing violence to it but by resisting its temptations and remaining faithful under its persecutions.

[40]Campbell, "Triumph and Delay," pp. 6-8.

[41]M. Eugene Boring, "The Theology of Revelation: 'The Lord Our God the Almighty Reigns,'" *Interpretation* 40, no. 3 (July 1986): 266.

through his own death; they are able to overcome the world because they are with him (Rev 5:5, 9; 17:14). Those who die in the Lord can rest from their labors as they await the consummation (Rev 6:11; 14:13).

Those who overcome receive the prize: "Be faithful until death, and I will give you the crown of life" (Rev 2:10; see Rev 3:11). This "crown of life" probably means the crown or wreath that consists of life.[42] At the end of their contest, those who persevere will receive the victor's prize, eternal life. In the consummation, they will experience the life of the kingdom, as the kingdom of God comes in its fullness (Rev 11:15; 12:10). The victor's crown as the reward for a faithful life is a common metaphor in the Pauline epistles and General Epistles (see 1 Cor 9:25; 2 Tim 4:8; Jas 1:12; 1 Pet 5:4). The *stephanos* worn by believers is like that worn by Christ, who has overcome and is reigning (Rev 14:14). Those who were slain because of their testimony to him will reign with him (Rev 3:21; 20:4). The *stephanos* represents the profound insight that for Christians, as for Christ, victory comes not through destroying one's enemies but through perseverance in suffering. The crown of victory comes by way of the crown of thorns.[43]

Those who overcome are granted the right to enter the land of their inheritance, the new heavens and the new earth. The lasting city, the New Jerusalem, "[comes] down out of heaven from God, prepared as a bride adorned for her husband." Now God will dwell finally and permanently among his people (Rev 21:1-4, 7). This is the eternal Sabbath rest for which the saints of Hebrews longed. Now believers have an everlasting home. Only evildoers are excluded from the city (Rev 22:15)—the reverse of the situation in Hebrews, where Jesus suffered outside the city gate, and the faithful had to follow him outside. At the end of their trials, the faithful can enter the holy city by the gates, because they are citizens here (Rev 22:14).[44] They are home.

---

[42]W. Grundmann, "στέφανος κτλ.," in *TDNT* 7:631.

[43]J. Jeremias draws a parallel between the *agōn* motif in the New Testament and the account of the Jewish martyrs in 4 Maccabees. Their suffering is described in terms of an athletic contest, and their victory comes through martyrdom. "ἀγών κτλ.," in *TDNT* 1:136, 138. Grundmann calls the *stephanos* that crowns the Son of Man in Revelation 14:14 the counterpart of the crown of thorns in the gospels (Mk 15:17; Mt 27:29). The martyr's crown was "the crown of victory . . . which God will give to those who are faithful even to death." "στέφανος κτλ.," in *TDNT* 7:632-33.

[44]Aune states that to "enter in" here is a metaphor for salvation. *Revelation 17–22*, 1174. This language resonates with the language of approach in Hebrews.

WORSHIP IN REVELATION

As in Hebrews, the people of God in Revelation are sustained by their access to God through worship and prayer. Revelation is filled with scenes of worship. John's visions give his audience glimpses into the heavenly sanctuary, where the ark of the covenant is visible (Rev 11:19). The One on the throne and the Lamb are worshiped ceaselessly by the four living creatures, the twenty-four elders and the angels. Their chorus of praise is joined by the rest of creation (Rev 4:8-11; 5:9-14). Unlike Hebrews, which uses the term *skēnē* (tabernacle) even for the heavenly sanctuary—an appropriate dwelling for the God of a pilgrim people—Revelation usually uses the term *naos* (temple) for God's dwelling in heaven.[45] The solidity of the heavenly temple and its ceaseless worship render the earthly worship of the beast thin and pale by comparison. However, in the consummation, *skēnē* does appear, in both noun and verb forms, as God comes to dwell with his people (Rev 21:3).

The language of worship pervades Revelation. John uses the typical words for worship, such as *proskyneō* and *latreuō*, rather than the language of approaching God, perhaps because he is not drawing as strongly on cultic imagery as the author of Hebrews does. Hebrews pictures Christ as the priest who approaches God with the sacrifice that restores the relationship between God and God's people. In Revelation, the sacrifice has been made—the Lamb has been slain—and the High Priest returns to save those who were waiting for him. All that remains is praise.

The worship scenes in Revelation serve as a commentary on events on earth. The events initiated by the seals, trumpets and bowls are interpreted and celebrated by the heavenly chorus. The prayers of the saints provide the incense of the heavenly liturgy (Rev 5:8; 8:3). The voices of the martyrs are heard from under the altar as they cry out to God for vindication. The martyrs are given white robes and told to wait a little longer until the number of the martyrs is complete (Rev 6:9-11).

By alternating between scenes in heaven and scenes on earth, the narrative structure brings home to the audience the truth that God is closer than they might think. John's visions of the heavenly sanctuary bring his audience into the presence of God and allow them to join the chorus of

---

[45]An exception is Revelation 15:5, where the two words seem to be used as synonyms.

praise that celebrates God as creator, redeemer and judge. Through these scenes, John gives his audience the true perspective on their situation.[46] The heavenly visions give them strength to persevere.

For John, the essence of the contest (*agōn*) is a conflict between true and false worship, between the worship of the true God and the worship of Satan and his representatives. Satan's defeat and expulsion from heaven means that the conflict has moved to earth and has intensified (Rev 12:10-12). Rather than worshiping God, much of the world chooses to worship the dragon and the beast (Rev 13:4, 8, 12). God's judgments are coupled with a call to return to the true worship of the creator, but people refuse to repent of their idolatry (Rev 14:7; 9:18-21). Twice the seer himself offers worship to the angelic mediator of his vision, but the angel refuses his worship and redirects it to God (Rev 19:10; 22:8-9). In the end, those who worship the beast will be tormented forever—the antithesis of the rest enjoyed by the worshipers of God (Rev 14:9-11, 13).

Richard Bauckham points out the "polemical significance of worship" in Revelation. Worship of the true God opposes the root of Rome's evil—its worship of human power.[47] One's worship therefore has political consequences: "To worship God is to experience his kingdom; to worship the beast is to war against that kingdom."[48] David Peterson observes that the scenes of worship in heaven, with the elders throwing down their crowns at the feet of the throne, are modeled after ceremonies of the imperial court. They demonstrate that God, not Caesar, is the one who deserves worship and praise. On earth, those who worship the beast are giving to the state the allegiance that belongs to God. But the worship of believers "involves giving proper allegiance to God and the Lamb in every circumstance of life."[49]

As in Hebrews, believers are priests (Rev 1:6), but unlike Hebrews, Christ is pictured not as the high priest but as the object of worship. He is the true witness who overcame the world through his own faithfulness unto death and who now reigns in glory (Rev 1:5-6; 5:5-10). He encourages believers

---

[46]Bauckham, *Theology*, p. 91. Aune points out that both Hebrews and Revelation contrast the story of believers' struggles on earth with scenes of their heavenly triumph. "Following the Lamb," p. 272.

[47]Bauckham, *Theology*, p. 59.

[48]Barr, "Transformation of the World," p. 37.

[49]Peterson, *Engaging with God*, pp. 267, 270-71.

through his example and will come to conquer all their adversaries (Rev 19:11-21). Similarly, John encourages his audience by giving them a glimpse of the cloud of witnesses that have gone before them in the faith, but while Hebrews tells the earthly stories of these witnesses, John shows their pleas coming before the throne of God and recounts their vindication.

Worship is also the chief reward for perseverance. The worship scenes culminate in the marriage supper of the Lamb, at which the bride is dressed in the righteous deeds of the saints (Rev 19:6-9). Those who have overcome, who have been steadfast in their devotion to God and the Lamb, will join the heavenly hosts in their endless worship (Rev 3:12; 7:9-17). They will see the Lord's face, will bear his name, and will worship him at his throne (Rev 22:3-4). The New Jerusalem will need no temple, because the citizens of the city will experience the immediate presence of God and the Lamb (Rev 21:22). Once God dwells among his people, there will be no need for a special place for worship or a special symbol to represent God's presence. Worship will constitute the life of the people of God.

The transformative power of worship depicted in Revelation would have been enacted in the early church, where the book would have been read aloud in the context of a worship service (see Rev 1:3).[50] Through their encounter with the imagery of Revelation, believers would gain not just a new vision of their victory but a new *experience* of it. As David Barr explains, "The hearers are transformed as they comprehend that it is their suffering witness (their *martus*) that brings salvation and judgment to the world, just as the suffering of Jesus was really the overthrow of evil. This is a real experience of the community, not just a glimpse of some future day which is supposed to give them courage to endure present suffering." They are no longer victims but partners with Christ in the advance of God's kingdom.[51]

APOSTASY

Inherent in the idea of salvation as pilgrimage or contest is the possibility that some may fail to reach the goal. In fact, both books are concerned

---

[50]Jerry R. Flora et al., *Adults Approach "The Revelation"* (St. Petersburg, Fla.: Brethren House Ministries, 1985), p. 8. David Barr believes that Revelation should be interpreted within the context of a public worship service, culminating in the Eucharist ("Transformation of the World," p. 46). Whether or not this is accurate, the use of Revelation in worship would help to bring about the transformation its images depict.

[51]Barr, "Transformation of the World," pp. 48-49, 50.

about potential apostasy. While both assure believers that God is near to sustain and save, they do not encourage complacency about final salvation. Believers must hold fast to what they have received, because the faithless will be excluded from the heavenly city (Rev 2:25; 3:11; 20:8). They must exercise faithfulness and patience in order to "realize the full assurance of hope to the very end" (Heb 6:11-12). Like the exodus generation, they can fall through disobedience (Heb 4:11).

Final salvation is conditional upon the exercise of an obedient faith that trusts in God's promise to the very end. The author of Hebrews tells his audience that they are God's household "if we hold firm the confidence and the pride that belong to hope" (Heb 3:6); they have become partners of Christ "if only we hold our first confidence firm to the end" (Heb 3:14). In Revelation, only those who overcome receive the inheritance (Rev 21:7). They will eat from the tree of life and will not be harmed by the second death (Rev 2:7, 11).

The consequences of apostasy are dire. In Revelation, Jesus warns the Ephesian church that failure to repent could mean the end of their existence as a church, and he suggests to believers in Sardis that their names can be blotted out of the book of life (Rev 2:5; 3:5). In Hebrews, believers who turn away from God's covenant in Christ will find that no other avenue of forgiveness remains to them (Heb 10:26-31). Those who renounce their citizenship in God's coming kingdom will find themselves eternally homeless (Heb 6:4-6).[52]

However, while apostasy is possible, it can be avoided. Both books urge believers to see clearly so that they can live faithfully. In both cases, this clarity comes from the vision of Jesus attained through worship (Heb 12:2; Rev 1:13-16). Jesus, the champion, forerunner and faithful witness, is both the model and the mediator of saving faithfulness. The exalted

---

[52]The people in Hebrews 6:4-6 have had experiences of the kingdom that are available only to believers. See Lane, *Hebrews 1–8*, pp. 141; and Attridge, *Hebrews*, pp. 169-70. The argument is sometimes made that the word "tasted" means here that these people have sampled the gifts of salvation without fully experiencing them. However, the author's use of *geuomai* in Hebrews 2:9 refers to a definitive experience: "but we do see Jesus, who for a little while was made lower than the angels, now crowned with glory and honor because of the suffering of death, so that by the grace of God he might taste death [*geusētai thanatou*] for everyone." See the discussion in Scot McKnight, "The Warning Passages of Hebrews: A Formal Analysis and Theological Conclusions," *Trinity Journal*, n.s., 13 (1992): 46-48. As Attridge notes, those who reject God's provision in Christ, which is the prerequisite to repentance, "simply, and virtually by definition, cannot repent." *Hebrews*, p. 169.

Christ will provide everything necessary, as long as believers keep their eyes on him.

CONCLUSION

Hebrews and Revelation are vivid examples of the power of images to re-envision reality.[53] By inviting their audiences to reframe their view of reality through worship, these books give comfort and encouragement to believers who are trying to find meaning in their trials. The true power of Revelation lies not in apocalyptic predictions of the end of the world but in transforming the present world of its hearers so that their lives and their sufferings have eternal meaning.[54] The same could be said for Hebrews.

The image of salvation as a call to endurance challenges Protestant—especially evangelical—soteriology in several ways. For instance, it directly confronts the evangelical over-emphasis on the initial conversion event as the determiner of salvation. In Hebrews and Revelation, there are no simple formulas or quick fixes. Instead, salvation is a process that requires steadfastness and patience. Its goal is eschatological: believers work out their salvation on the basis of their trust in God's future. Faith is faithfulness, a steadfast clinging to God's promise, anchored in the faithfulness of Christ.

However, while believers can look forward to vindication, they have no excuse for triumphalism. Like their redeemer, they win through to final salvation not by power but by suffering. Grasping this perspective would enable Christians to engage more authentically with those on the margins of society or in their own congregations who are struggling. Furthermore, as the balance of Christianity shifts to the Two-Thirds World, any credible understanding of salvation must enable people to give meaning to suffering.

Hebrews and Revelation remind us that the church is not the world. As the old hymn reminds us, this world (or more accurately, this age) is not our home. The images of pilgrimage and contest provide a good corrective for a Protestant theology that is often too much at home in the world and too comfortable playing by the world's rules. These images should teach us to beware of complacency or compromise. Yet this picture of salvation does not call us out of the world, but into the midst of it, with all its troubles. In our engagement with the world, we witness to the new covenant

---

[53]See the discussion in the Introduction.
[54]Barr, "Transformation of the World," pp. 39-40.

that God has established through Christ, with the judgment and the hope that it brings. Seeing ourselves as displaced persons could give us a fresh perspective on the plight of the homeless, the refugee, the illegal immigrant. We might more effectively address the agents of alienation and reach out to their victims.

As was the case with the imagery of the kingdom of God, the imagery of pilgrimage and contest shows that salvation means following Jesus. To follow him is to maintain an exclusive allegiance that supersedes and determines all other loyalties, whether personal, social or political. To follow him also means to become like him, a transformation that happens only through the journey of discipleship. Finally, to follow him means to see him for who he truly is. We discover this through worship, which reminds us of our calling both from and to God and gives us the true perspective on our lives.

Thus the call to endurance is also a call to worship. Worship is "an act of rehearsal" for the coming kingdom. The vision of worship in Revelation should remind us of the goal, when people from all nations and languages will join together to worship God and the Lamb. Keeping that goal before our eyes might transform our worship in the present.[55] Based on the worship of Revelation, David Peterson issues a challenge to the contemporary church: "Do our hymns and acclamations help us to rejoice in God's gracious and powerful rule, acknowledge its blessings and look forward to its consummation in the new creation? Do they challenge us to take a firm stand against every manifestation of Satan's power and to bear faithful witness to the truth of the gospel in our society?"[56] If our worship has been transformed by the vision of Christ, it will have the power to shape and strengthen us for the struggle that remains.

The images of pilgrimage, contest and worship again remind us that salvation is a covenant relationship, both with God and with others. Salvation, one might say, is a team effort. We engage in the contest of life in company with the rest of God's covenant people, under the direction and in the power of our covenant God. The cloud of witnesses, both past and present, call us to faithful endurance as we press on together, in company with the One who calls us, to the fulfillment of all God's promises.

---

[55]Justo L. González, *For the Healing of the Nations: The Book of Revelation in an Age of Cultural Conflict* (Maryknoll, N.Y.: Orbis, 1999), pp. 104, 109.
[56]Peterson, *Engaging with God*, p. 278.

FOR FURTHER READING

Aune, David E. "Following the Lamb: Discipleship in the Apocalypse," pp. 269-84. In *Patterns of Discipleship in the New Testament*. Edited by Richard N. Longenecker. McMaster New Testament Studies Series. Grand Rapids: Eerdmans, 1996.

————. *Revelation*. 3 vols. Word Biblical Commentary. Nashville: Thomas Nelson, 1997-1998.

Barr, David L. "The Apocalypse as a Symbolic Transformation of the World." *Interpretation* 38, no. 1 (January 1984): 39-50.

Bauckham, Richard. *The Theology of the Book of Revelation*. Theology of the New Testament. Edited by James D. G. Dunn. Cambridge: Cambridge University Press, 1993.

Boring, M. Eugene. "The Theology of Revelation: 'The Lord Our God the Almighty Reigns.'" *Interpretation* 40, no. 3 (July 1986): 257-69.

Brown, Raymond E. "Pilgrimage in Faith: The Christian Life in Hebrews." *Southwestern Journal of Theology* 28 (Fall 1985): 28-35.

Campbell, R. Alastair. "Triumph and Delay: The Interpretation of Revelation 19:11–20:10." *Evangelical Quarterly* 80, no. 1 (2008): 3-12.

González, Justo L. *For the Healing of the Nations: The Book of Revelation in an Age of Cultural Conflict*. Maryknoll, N.Y.: Orbis, 1999.

Homcy, Stephen L. "'To Him Who Overcomes': A Fresh Look at What 'Victory' Means for the Believer According to the Book of Revelation." *Journal of the Evangelical Theological Society* 38, no. 2 (June 1995): 193-201.

Johnsson, William G. "The Pilgrimage Motif in the Book of Hebrews." *Journal of Biblical Literature* 97, no. 2 (1978): 239-51.

Käsemann, Ernst. *The Wandering People of God: An Investigation of the Epistle to the Hebrews*. Minneapolis: Augsburg, 1984.

Lane, William L. *Call to Commitment: Responding to the Message of Hebrews*. Nashville: Thomas Nelson, 1985.

————. *Hebrews*. 2 vols. Word Biblical Commentary. Edited by David A. Hubbard and Glenn W. Barker. Dallas: Word, 1991.

————. "Standing Before the Moral Claim of God: Discipleship in Hebrews," pp. 203-24. In *Patterns of Discipleship in the New Testament*. Edited by Richard N. Longenecker. McMaster New Testament Studies Series. Grand Rapids: Eerdmans, 1996.

McKnight, Scot. "The Warning Passages of Hebrews: A Formal Analysis and Theological Conclusions." *Trinity Journal*, n.s., 13 (1992): 21-59.

Osborne, Grant R. "Soteriology in the Epistle to the Hebrews," pp. 144-89. In

Grace Unlimited. Edited by Clark H. Pinnock. Minneapolis: Bethany House, 1975.

Perkins, David. "Call to Pilgrimage: The Challenge of Hebrews." *Theological Educator* 32 (Fall 1985): 69-81.

Peterson, David. *Engaging with God: A Biblical Theology of Worship.* Downers Grove, Ill.: InterVarsity Press, 2002.

CONCLUSION

SALVATION IN THE NEW TESTAMENT is a vision of God's work for us and in us, through Christ and by the Holy Spirit, a vision that is composed of interdependent and mutually interpreting images. We might think of this vision as a multifaceted diamond or a three-dimensional picture created by the merging of many two-dimensional slices taken from different angles. To use a musical metaphor, it is a polyphonic composition whose individual lines have their own integrity but flow together to create a complex but coherent whole.[1] What, then, do we find when we examine the resulting whole?

Despite their rich diversity, the New Testament images of salvation tell a single story—the story of God's love for his broken creation, his desire for covenant relationship, and his patient shaping of a people who would reflect his love to one another and to the world. In the story's climax, the Creator enters his creation in the person of Jesus of Nazareth, identifying with his creatures in both life and death, and then, through resurrection, opening the way to life eternal. In Jesus Christ, through the power of his indwelling Spirit, God's people now are called to carry on God's redemptive mission. Remembering God's past faithfulness, they live and work in anticipation of the conclusion of the story, to be told when Jesus returns.

These images reflect a number of common themes. All of them assume a dire predicament that requires divine intervention. Although different images may emphasize one of the trinitarian persons more than the others, all of the images are consistent with a model in which salvation is initiated

---

[1]For the musical metaphor, see Michael Slusser, "Primitive Christian Soteriological Themes," *Theological Studies* 44 (1983): 555-69.

by the Father, accomplished by the Son, and actualized by the Spirit. While divine grace always has priority, human beings must respond to God's offered grace with faith, expressed as belief, trust and faithfulness.

Beyond these familiar themes, the New Testament vision of salvation has several important features that might challenge our theologies. I will highlight seven of these.

Salvation is not first of all about us, but about God—specifically, about what God has done in Christ for the redemption of the world. It is not merely a means for individuals to solve their problems or go to heaven but a cosmic plan to reorder all of reality around Jesus Christ (Eph 1:10). The starting point for soteriology is not human need but divine grace. It is only because of what God has done for us in Christ that we can clearly see the hopeless situation we were in because of sin. A fully biblical understanding of salvation is therefore Christocentric rather than anthropocentric. In the New Testament perspective, we do not invite Jesus into our lives; he invites us into his.

Salvation is based upon the whole career of Christ, not just his death. Each image of salvation emphasizes some parts of his career more than others. But this survey has shown that the work of Christ is not restricted to the cross. It includes his incarnation; his ministry of teaching, healing and exorcism; his relationships; his death; his resurrection; his exaltation and intercession; and his coming again to redeem and judge. This holistic view of the work of Christ leads us to a more holistic understanding of salvation. Just as salvation requires the entirety of Christ's existence, it embraces the entirety of ours.

Salvation requires our allegiance. Although believing the right things about Jesus is important, it is not enough. When Jesus invites us into his life, we must enter that life on his terms. He expects exclusive allegiance. No one can live in the kingdom who is not a subject of the king. It is only as the Lord that Jesus saves.[2] "The LORD redeems the life of his servants; none of those who take refuge in him will be condemned" (Ps 34:22). This requirement of allegiance has implications for evangelism and the Christian life.

---

[2]The position advocated by some evangelicals in the 1990s that one can be saved by believing in Jesus as savior without submitting to Jesus as Lord is an example of straining out gnats and swallowing camels. While it is important to defend the centrality of faith in conversion, we must not do so at the expense of the nature of salvation itself.

Salvation is fundamentally covenantal. Our allegiance takes the form of a covenant relationship—a relationship of trust and faithfulness between God and God's people, established by Christ and empowered by the Spirit. Although this relationship is initiated by God's grace and can never be earned, it does involve obligations on both God's part and ours. This means that obedience is an integral part of the process of salvation. Like any relationship, salvation requires investment by both parties in order to grow. It is not a no-fault insurance policy. With repeated unfaithfulness, there is no guarantee that the relationship will continue. Unlike other relationships, however, one party is guaranteed to be eternally faithful.

Salvation is inescapably social. Although personal, salvation is not individualistic. Persons are not saved in isolation but into the people of God, the body of Christ. This new community is to be a living image of salvation in witness and service to the world. Like the triune God they reflect, human beings are relational. To be fully what God intends, they must be not autonomous individuals but persons-in-relationship.[3] Our language of salvation should reflect this reality. Instead of mentioning the church (if at all) as an afterthought, our presentations of the gospel must make the church an integral part of the invitation to salvation.[4] Perhaps it is time for Protestants to rediscover the insight of the church fathers that there is no salvation outside the church. The community of faith is usually the medium of salvation, if not the means. People enter the community through conversion and thereafter experience salvation as members of the redeemed community.

Salvation is transformational, not transactional. God's purpose in salvation is to enable a broken creation to become a true reflection of its creator. Salvation is not a "Get Out of Jail Free" card. It involves a radical reorientation of one's life that initiates a process of growth into the image of

---

[3]Stanley J. Grenz, *Theology for the Community of God* (1994; reprint, Grand Rapids: Eerdmans, 2000), p. 76. References are to the 2000 edition.

[4]"Steps to Peace With God" by the Billy Graham Evangelistic Association does not mention the church. <www.billygraham.org/SH_StepsToPeace.asp>. Campus Crusade's "Four Spiritual Laws" includes the suggestion to join a church at the end, after information on assurance of salvation and ways to grow in the Christian life. <http://4laws.com/laws/text/>. By contrast, James Choung has developed an evangelistic diagram that has a more corporate and holistic emphasis, using the phrases "designed for good," "damaged by evil," "restored for better," and "sent together to heal." See his book, *True Story: A Christianity Worth Believing In* (Downers Grove, Ill.: InterVarsity Press, 2008).

Christ. Instead of front-loading salvation, as Protestants have tended to do since the Reformation, we must focus more attention on the growth and completion of salvation. How many people who "come to Christ" grow to maturity in Christ? What can we do as stewards of the rest of creation to assist God in his redemptive purposes? A fully biblical understanding of salvation will consider not only what we have been saved *from* but what we have been saved *for.*

Salvation is eschatological. Although it can be experienced partially in the present, salvation urges us forward to the completion of God's purposes in the consummation. To understand our true identity, we should look not backward but forward to this goal. An awareness of the judgment and glory to come should motivate us to make the best use of the time we have now. As an outpost of the coming kingdom, the church should proclaim and model the new life that is possible in God's new creation. In a postmodern context that is increasingly skeptical of truth claims, our life together and our engagement in the world may be the proclamation that matters most.

As faithful stewards of the revelation we have been given, we must allow the breadth of the biblical witness to inform—and sometimes correct—our theology and our practice. These images can help us see God and ourselves with fresh eyes. Taking these images seriously, with all their implications, would transform our lives and revitalize our mission as the church. God's invitation to salvation addresses all of us, whatever our culture, gender, ethnicity, language or nation. Only a fully biblical understanding of salvation will equip us to reach every person with the good news of God's redeeming love.

Author Index

Subject Index

abiding in Christ, 78, 93-100, 248, 281
abundant life, 22, 47, 85, 100, 123, 141, 259
adikia, 205
adoption, 20, 57, 112, 175, 177-79, 180n. 27,
  185-87, 192, 193, 224, 238
agōn, 289, 304n. 43, 306
agorazō, 147
aiōnios, 87-89
akoloutheō, 76
alētheia, 205
allegiance, 32, 46, 66, 76, 79, 83, 139, 141, 186,
  273, 306, 310, 314-15
already and not yet, 54, 71, 82, 89, 91, 104,
  112n. 28, 116, 118, 131, 135n. 34, 155, 158,
  159, 172, 187, 194, 290, 292, 296
ametamelēta, 231
Anabaptism, 24, 36, 40, 266
anagennaō, 104
analogy, 15-18, 70, 151, 216, 240-42, 278, 279
anōthen, 104-5
antilytron, 147, 149
anti-Semitism, 62, 198n. 10, 244
aparneomai, 76
aphesis, 163
aphiēmi, 163, 168
apistia, 140, 205, 292n. 9, 299
apolyō, 153, 154, 161, 163, 168
apolytrōsis, 147
apostasy, 123, 291, 299, 307, 308
approaching God, 59, 272, 276, 279, 293-99,
  304n. 44, 305
archai, 154
archēgos, 296, 297
Arminianism, 219, 226
arrabōn, 55
atonement, 20, 21, 39n. 27, 129-31, 150n. 19,
  151, 154, 171, 180, 184, 204, 205, 209, 211,
  251, 267, 277, 281, 294, 296
bāhar, 220
baptism, 66, 83, 106-9, 113, 116, 136, 137, 139,
  165, 190, 212, 231, 256, 257, 275, 276
basileia tou theou, 67
basileuō, 67
being in Christ. *See* participation in God or
  Christ
belonging
  to a master, Christ, or God, 54, 56, 62,
    110, 114, 134, 147, 152, 160, 222, 223,
    229, 251, 260n. 23, 272-75, 277, 279,
    282, 285, 306
  to a group, 32, 48, 74, 116, 260n. 23, 291n.
    5. *See also* community; membership

běrit, 45, 49
biblical hermeneutics, 27
biblical theology, 27-30, 31n. 9, 32, 33n. 12,
  33n. 13, 39
bios, 86
body of Christ, 109, 113, 142, 190, 149, 189,
  249, 257, 258, 262, 263, 266, 283, 315
born again. *See* new birth
calling, 61, 72-82, 94, 115, 118, 128, 129, 131,
  135, 138, 139, 141, 142, 167, 184, 186, 188,
  192, 193, 201, 202, 214, 221-23, 226,
  228-32, 234-36, 238, 240, 244, 245, 255,
  258, 261, 263, 265, 269, 271-75, 277-79, 281,
  284, 285, 288-93, 295, 299-302, 306, 309,
  310, 313
Calvinism, 219, 226, 246
character (of God or the believer), 67, 80, 105,
  106, 110n. 24, 115, 117, 198n. 7, 204, 211,
  231, 233, 244, 261, 263-67, 271, 272, 279,
  282, 285, 286, 298
charizomai, 163, 169
cheap grace, 13
cheirographon, 164
chosen. *See* election
Christlikeness, 103, 134, 136n. 35, 161, 224,
  226, 252, 261, 265, 267, 280, 282, 285
Christus Victor, 17, 19, 25, 38, 154, 171, 302
church, 13, 16, 17, 20-22, 24, 25, 27, 28, 30,
  33, 35-39, 41, 43, 55, 62-64, 67, 72, 77,
  80-83, 97, 99, 100, 106, 112, 114, 116, 117,
  123, 135, 138, 139, 142, 143, 150, 151, 153,
  154, 162, 166, 169, 171-73, 176, 180, 184,
  188-90, 193, 194, 196, 200, 209, 210, 215-17,
  222, 227, 228, 230, 232, 233, 236, 242-45,
  256-58, 263-66, 269, 271, 274, 275, 278,
  281, 283, 288, 297, 301, 307-10, 315, 316
citizenship, 14, 23, 32, 66, 70, 79, 80, 83, 135,
  173, 189, 291n. 5, 304, 307, 308
cleansing, 51, 52, 59, 96, 107, 108, 126, 128,
  129, 131, 152, 164, 166, 212, 232, 242, 248,
  271, 273, 275-78, 283, 284
communion, 95, 97, 100, 257, 258, 265, 295n.
  14, 296
community, 19, 20, 35, 36, 40, 43, 47-49, 62,
  69, 74, 75, 77, 79, 80, 93, 95, 96, 100, 109,
  111, 113, 114, 116, 117, 119, 123, 127, 128,
  139, 142, 162, 170, 172n. 67, 173, 177, 184,
  190, 192, 199, 244, 245, 259-63, 274, 279n.
  19, 288, 290, 297, 299n. 26, 307, 315. *See also*
  belonging; membership
confession
  of Christ, 72, 83, 139, 223

Scripture Index